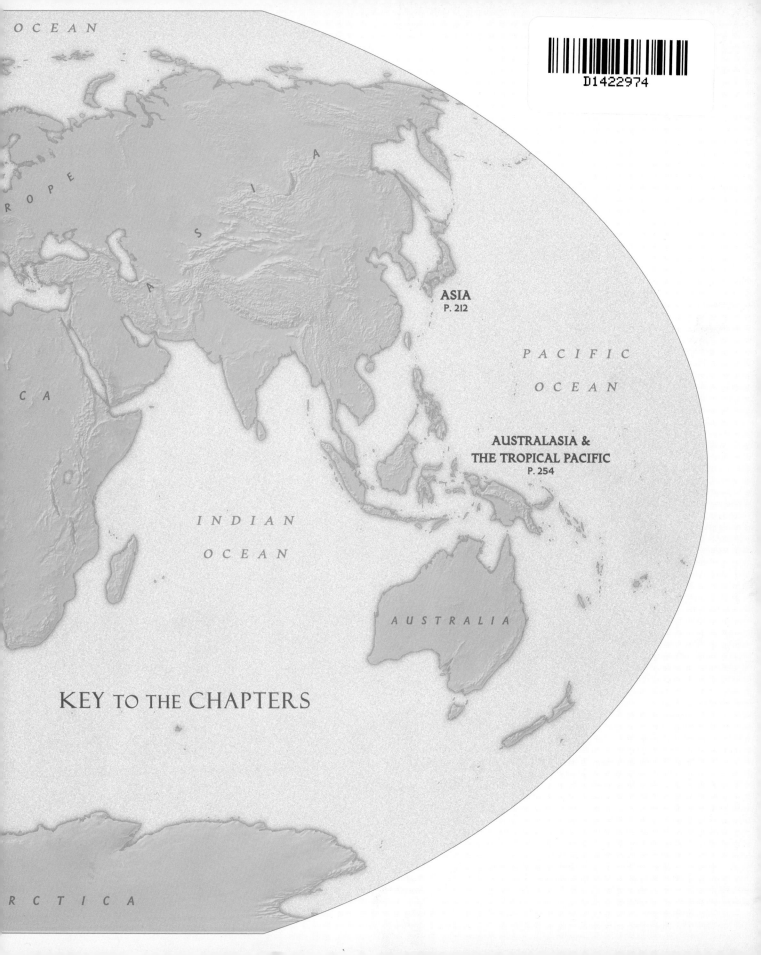

OCEAN

ROPE

CA

A S I A

ASIA
P. 212

PACIFIC

OCEAN

AUSTRALASIA &
THE TROPICAL PACIFIC
P. 254

INDIAN

OCEAN

AUSTRALIA

KEY TO THE CHAPTERS

RCTICA

GLOBAL BIRDING

Traveling the World in Search of Birds

LES BELETSKY

WITH BIRDING NARRATIVES BY DAVID L. PEARSON

NATIONAL GEOGRAPHIC

WASHINGTON, D.C.

CONTENTS

PAGE 1: Blue Bird-of-paradise *Paradisaea rudolphi* Tari Valley, Papua New Guinea
PAGE 2-3: Black-browed Albatross *Thalassarche melanophris* South Georgia Island
OPPOSITE: Rainbow Bee-eater *Merops ornatus* Queensland, Australia

CHAPTER 1

BIRDING FROM A GLOBAL PERSPECTIVE

Perhaps the main reason that most people travel internationally to birdwatch is not to see exotic or strange birds but to see more species.

BIRDING FROM A GLOBAL PERSPECTIVE

LONG AGO, SOMEONE PUT AN INEXPENSIVE PAIR OF BINOCULARS IN YOUR hands and pointed to some birds. You started watching, got hooked. You learned the easy jays, thrushes, and woodpeckers, the troublesome flycatchers and sparrows, even some of the difficult shorebirds. A couple of your birding buddies say your middle name must be "wood-warbler," and on a good day now you can distinguish a soaring Broad-winged Hawk from a Red-shouldered Hawk from a half mile away. You're definitely getting pretty good. You recently invested in great binoculars and a half-decent spotting scope. But you've been birding now for a number of years, in various parts of the United States, and you're starting to notice that you see much the same birds every year. Sure, there are a few (well, to be fair, more than a few) North American birds you'd still like to find for the first time, but wouldn't it be a major thrill to be set down in the middle of another continent, in a place with completely different birdlife, a place where *every single bird you see is a new species?* This is the exciting province of global birding, the subject explored in this book.

Novelty is a key to rewarding birdwatching. Simply seeing new species, rather than the same ones you see regularly around your neighborhood and your frequent birding sites, is a wonderful, invigorating experience. We all look forward to seeing new birds, and many of us clearly remember (and some of the more organized among us write down) when and where we first saw this new species or that new species. My first sighting of a Snowy Owl, for instance, which occurred in Washington State a few years ago, will stay with me forever. If you're like most birders, you've taken your binoculars along

PREVIOUS PAGES: **Malagasy Kingfisher** This small kingfisher is endemic to Madagascar and the Comoro Islands—here seen sitting in the mist below one of Montagne d'Ambre National Park's famous waterfalls. *Madagascar*

OPPOSITE: **Keoladeo National Park** Formerly known as Bharatpur Bird Sanctuary, this park is located in northern India. It is well known for its rich and varied birdlife, especially waterfowl and wading birds. *India*

Tufted Coquette The ten tiny, but dazzling hummingbirds known as coquettes (all in the genus *Lophornis*) occur from Mexico south to Bolivia. The Tufted Coquette is resident on the island of Trinidad and in northern South America. *Trinidad and Tobago*

on business or pleasure trips to different parts of the country, and birded in various states. So you've seen more than just your local birds, but still, the types of birds you see, the various native families, are much the same no matter where you go in the continental United States or Canada. You doubtless sometimes wish you could see completely different kinds of birds, or the more diverse segments of families that have only a few representatives here but are incredibly more numerous in other regions.

Take, for example, hummingbirds. There are eight species with widespread breeding ranges in the United States, but more than three hundred others are found from Mexico to Argentina. Variety is often the spice of a birdwatcher's life, and global birding provides maximum opportunities to see novel birds, many of surprising beauty or with exotic behaviors. So if you're a relative beginner, let's explore some of the basics of bird diversity and distribution . . . and determine why birding beyond North America can be such an exciting prospect.

NORTH AMERICAN BIRDS FROM A GLOBAL PERSPECTIVE

Perhaps the main reason that most people travel internationally to birdwatch is not to see exotic, spectacular, or strange birds but to gain opportunities to see more species. A hefty segment of the birder population keeps lists of the birds spotted in the wild—a life list—and to a portion of those birders, lengthening their lists is an important goal, one often pursued with zealous enthusiasm. But for North American birders, even those who travel throughout Canada and the United States, it becomes increasingly difficult to experience new species. The reason is that only about 700 bird species regularly occur in North America north of Mexico, a fairly small proportion of the world's bird diversity.

How many bird species are there worldwide? The absolute number is difficult to pinpoint, but most authorities now place the total at about 10,000. So let's say that about 700 of the world's approximately 10,000 birds regularly occur in the United States and Canada. With a little reflection, we can see that this number seems inappropriately small. After all, the United States and Canada take up about 13 percent of Earth's land surface, but 700 is only 7 percent of 10,000. If bird species were distributed evenly over the world's land area, we could expect about 1,300 domestic species. Clearly, therefore, the world's birds are not uniformly distributed. Rather, there are uneven patterns to bird distribution, with some regions of the globe getting a larger share, other regions getting less. (Chapter 2 explores the reasons for this uneven distribution.) The United States and Canada, so economically blessed, so fortunate in their freedoms, so amply supplied with diverse natural resources, could be considered avifaunally challenged. As a consequence, if we remain in the region delineated by the Rio Grande in the south, the Pacific Ocean in the west, the Atlantic in the east, and the Arctic Circle in the north, and discount the few Siberian and Mexican species that occasionally find their way to North America as vagrants, we're never going to see more than about 700 species.

The most spectacular birds are found outside of North America, and most are permanent, nonmigratory residents there. Sure, North America harbors some striking species, such as loons, spoonbills, some beautiful hawks, a handful of hummingbirds, woodpeckers perhaps, and some songbirds such as jays, bluebirds, and an abundance of beautiful wood-warblers. The study and enjoyment of these and other North American birds can fill a lifetime. But where are our larger, colorful, visually arresting birds—our parrots, our toucans, our motmots and turacos? Where are our birds with amazing, frilly plumes, such as birds-of-paradise and lyrebirds? Where are our large flightless birds—our ostriches, emus, and cassowaries? For the most part, we don't have any. So let me just say, if you like our bluebirds, wait until you see Brazil's stunning violet-blue Hyacinth Macaw; if you enjoy our Belted Kingfisher, wait until you see Thailand's huge Great Hornbill and Costa Rica's colorful Keel-billed Toucan; and if you like meadowlarks and Yellow-headed Blackbirds, wait until you see Australia's velvety yellow and black Regent Bowerbird.

Golden-winged Warbler
One of the most beautiful wood-warblers, the Golden-winged breeds in the eastern United States and spends the winter months in southern Central America and northern South America. *United States*

If you watch Discovery Channel or National Geographic shows, or peruse science magazines or newspaper science sections, you'll often see fascinating documentaries or articles about bird behavior. Some amazing things are shown or discussed in these presentations—for instance, jaw-dropping breeding behaviors of incredible complexity or seeming difficulty. Take the way many penguins breed in their frozen world, amid huge colonies of their peers, hunched over their single large egg or chick for weeks at a time. Or those male bowerbirds that build large courting structures of plant materials and decorate them, and then show them to females to convince them to mate. Or the mound-builders, chicken-like birds that scrape together huge mounds of dirt and vegetation, bury their eggs in the mounds, and then allow the heat of the rotting vegetation to incubate the eggs. Or the hornbills with their unique nesting behavior, during which the female of the pair is encased within a tree cavity and fed by her mate while she incubates eggs and feeds her young. The closest you would find any of these birds is Ecuador's Galápagos Islands, where the world's northernmost penguin species occurs; for the bowerbirds and mound-builders, you would need to take a 13-hour plane ride toward the Australian region; and for hornbills, Africa would be your nearest destination. The point is, as the global media increasingly draw attention to dramatically interesting birds, growing numbers of us who are highly intrigued by birds fervently desire to travel abroad to see these exciting birds ourselves and satisfy our curiosities about them.

Another reason birders travel internationally concerns avian scarcity and abundance. Most North American birds are common—perhaps difficult at times to spot, but usually present in good numbers. North America, in fact, boasts many of the most abundant bird species, some of which gather periodically into huge flocks, creating compelling avian spectacles. For example, individual winter roosts of "blackbirds"—Red-winged Blackbirds,

FIELD GUIDE & SITE GUIDE BOOKS

■ *A Birder's Guide to Metropolitan Areas (2001)*
P.E. Lehman
American Birding Association

■ *Birdfinder: A Birder's Guide to Planning North American Trips (1995)*
J.A. Cooper
American Birding Association

■ *Birding in the American West (2000)*
K.J. Zimmer
Cornell University Press

■ *National Geographic Field Guide to the Birds of North America, 5th ed. (2006)*
J.L. Dunn and J. Alderfer, editors
National Geographic Society

■ *National Geographic Guide to Birding Hotspots of the United States (2006)*
M. White and P.E. Lehman
National Geographic Society

■ *The Sibley Guide to Birds (2000)*
D. Sibley
Alfred A. Knopf

■ *Smithsonian Field Guide to the Birds of North America (2008)*
T. Floyd
HarperCollins

Common Grackles, Brown-headed Cowbirds—in the southeastern United States sometimes encompass more than ten million individuals. There's nothing wrong with common birds, of course. But many birders, consciously or not, rate birds according to their relative abundances in nature, assigning greater value to spotting and watching rare species. Why this is so is not exactly clear, but it expresses a very common human preference for rare items, to possess things (even bird sightings) that most others do not. In this view, seeing an American Robin or a Red-winged Blackbird, with their enormous populations, holds scant interest; seeing a California Condor or a Whooping Crane, or any other species in which the total world population is, say, a thousand individuals or fewer, is fabulous and memorable.

Sometimes these considerations cause birders to behave in ways that the uninitiated find strange. For instance, no one goes out of his or her way to see an American Crow; they are abundant. But to see a Mariana Crow—a close relative of the American Crow that exists in extremely small numbers only on some tiny oceanic islands, and looks more or less like many other crows—some birders make special, very expensive trips to the remote mid-Pacific. Birdwatchers who seek rare birds quickly exhaust such opportunities in North America and look for them in other regions. Unfortunately, owing to increasing development, habitat alteration, and deforestation, an ever growing number of bird species are becoming rare.

Some species, of course, move beyond simple rarity to become threatened, their continued existence uncertain. Owing mainly to the actions of people, many birds and other animal species are endangered and approaching extinction. Because of the increasing emphasis on the importance of the natural environment by schools, and the media's continuing exposure of environmental issues, many people have an enhanced appreciation of the natural world and an increased awareness of global environmental problems. They also have the very human desire to want to see wild animals before they are gone. So a percentage of travelers who seek out birds in other countries do so because these species are threatened or endangered, and perhaps the objects of conservation or media attention. Sometimes, visiting sites to see particular birds is an effort

Whooping Crane Adult (right) with two juveniles. Birders from around the world come to the Texas Gulf Coast to see these endangered birds during the winter months. During the summer they nest in remote freshwater marshes in Canada's Wood Buffalo National Park. *United States*

OPPOSITE: **Keel-billed Toucan** Just about everyone knows what a toucan looks like, but the Neotropical toucan family (Ramphastidae) is made up of 40 species: 19 toucanets, 4 mountain-toucans, 10 aracaris, and 7 toucans. The Keel-billed Toucan is resident from Mexico to Venezuela. *Panama*

to help the birds, because a percentage of the money spent on a tour or for admission to a nature reserve goes for conservation of the threatened species. This is one of the greatest benefits of "ecotourism"—using the visits of international nature travelers as a reason and a financial resource for the preservation of threatened species and habitats.

A good example is provided by some of the larger parrot species in Amazonian Peru. Many of these parrots are threatened by deforestation and because they are in demand by the illicit trade in exotic pets. But these parrots have been found to gather in large groups, often on riverbanks, to eat clay-containing soils. (Why they engage in this behavior is a subject of research; it may be that chemicals in the clay counteract dangerous toxins ingested from the parrots' seed diet and perhaps protect the birds' gastrointestinal tract from damage.) The spectacle of giant red, blue, and green macaws and other parrot species in large groups, milling around a riverbank, has been publi-cized widely. Now thousands of people each year journey from North America and Europe to see these traditional "clay lick" sites, for instance, in and around Peru's Manú National Park. Now the local communities there have a good incentive to protect the forest and its parrot inhabitants, because many local people make their livings from this nature tourism as guides, drivers, hotel employees, and in other jobs. Some of the money that birders spend in the area is channeled into parrot research and other con-servation projects.

About 50 bird species in the United States are considered "globally threatened," and about 25 of those are classified as endangered at this time. Canada has very few globally threatened species, and they overlap with those classified in the United States. Someone with a desire to view many rare birds would have to travel to other countries: Brazil and Indonesia, for instance, each have more than 110 globally threatened bird species, and Colombia, Peru, Ecuador, China, the Philippines, India, and New Zealand each have more than 60 (see table 5, p. 46). The reason these places have so many threatened birds is that, in various ways, their natural environments, especially the birds' habitats, have been severely damaged by people.

Many Europeans plan trips to the United States and Canada to see the birds there and experience the incredible scenery and national parks of the region. From the perspective of the foreign birder visiting North America for the first time, the experience can be exhilarating. After all, birds such as the Bald Eagle, Wild Turkey, Great Horned Owl, and Pileated Woodpecker are impressive. There are entire, diverse bird families represented in the United States and Canada that are lacking in Europe. European birders visiting here for the first time, for instance, find the flycatchers, vireos, wood-warblers, and blackbirds, among others, quite exotic and interesting.

Well-known birding hot spots such as Cape May, New Jersey (for shorebirds and a great variety of migrants); southern Florida and the Everglades (waterbirds); the Texas coast (spring migration); southeastern Arizona (desert birds; hummingbirds); and Monterey Bay, California (seabirds), to name just a few, are located throughout North America. These locations, many of them easily reached, harbor a great variety of North American species that are particularly interesting to travelers from abroad.

If you are traveling to North America from your home abroad, there are numerous field guides and site guides to assist you, and information on where and when to visit is readily obtained. For a start, see the sidebar listings in this section.

VISITING OTHER COUNTRIES TO WATCH THEIR BIRDS

Birders use many kinds of information when making international travel decisions. Important factors are the novel bird groups that can be seen in a given country or region, the total number of species there, and the number of endemic species (those that occur nowhere else). In some cases, particular species are a main attraction—because they are endemic, rare, difficult to see, or ecologically or culturally

Kakapo "Night parrot" in the Maori language, this is the world's only flightless nocturnal parrot. As of February 2010 only 123 individuals were known to exist. *New Zealand*

OPPOSITE: **Red-and-green Macaw** Clay licks—exposed clay banks with a high sodium content—are parrot magnets, like this one in Manú National Park. *Peru*

significant (for instance, the Resplendent Quetzal in Central America, famously described as the most spectacular bird in the New World; Brazil's endangered Hyacinth Macaw, one of the world's largest parrots; or Australia's rare Golden-shouldered Parrot). Of course, after all of the avian factors are weighed, they must be balanced against such prosaic concerns as distance from home, accessibility of various destinations, trip costs, and safety considerations. But given that you've considered such factors and selected a country or region of the world to visit for birding, how is it actually done? Not all birders making international trips have the same degree of comfort with foreign languages, differing customs, and unknown levels of safety. Some travelers prefer entirely independent itineraries; others prefer structured trips. Novice birders and those wanting help locating birds in habitats with which they are unfamiliar may want to travel with a birding guide; others will prefer to explore and birdwatch on their own.

There are advantages and disadvantages to every way that birders in other countries choose to travel and birdwatch.

For adventurous people, those wishing to explore and proceed at their own pace, and for the budget-oriented, going on your own is often the preferred method of travel. You can simply explore anywhere you want, randomly or around traditional tourist areas and national parks, or you can purchase and follow the suggestions of a "site guide," a book that lists, maps, and gives directions to particularly good birding spots. (See sidebar lists in each sub-region.) The main disadvantage of independent bird travel is that in unfamiliar habitats and dealing with novel types of birds, you're going to miss some species that, if you were with a local expert, you would be more likely to see. Most guides know the vocalizations of their local birds and will detect and locate some species by their songs and calls, and some guides will play recordings to attract particular species.

A way around this problem is to hire a local bird guide when arriving at a destination—for a day at a particular national park, for instance, or on multi-day trips within a given country or region. Guides can be found by word of mouth. For example, check at national park or wildlife refuge offices, or at local travel agencies. Another useful resource is local birding or conservation organizations. (See sidebar lists in each sub-region.) Some site guide books also offer suggestions for locating local birding guides. In many regions, such birding guides are a real bargain, and employing them helps support the local economy. Your experiences with guides will vary, but even if they are not experts at identifying every species, they will often know good spots to see birds. Local guides, however, are often very good, and almost every time I've engaged a local bird guide I know I've seen more species than if I had birded alone. A bird guide or, for that matter, any local person birding with you, can also be an asset in explaining your activities when you are tramping through unfamiliar territory and stumble across local residents, workers, and property owners.

One way to enhance your trip is to stay for at least brief periods at "eco-lodges" or "birding lodges"—hotels or resorts that cater to tourists interested in nature activities such as birding. Depending on the lodge, there may be naturalist guides on the staff that lead local tours, or the operators may be able to put you in touch with guides. There may be nature trails on the property or nearby where you can birdwatch. Some lodges are located in spectacular settings—rustically built in the middle of a rain forest, for example, or at the edge of a national park. Birding lodges are hotels that specialize in providing accommodations and services to birders. Typically, eco-lodges and birding lodges are not the least expensive accommodations available in an area, and sometimes they are quite costly, but many traveling birders find them excellent places to stay. The information, guiding, and comradeship of other birders gained may be worth the extra expense. Professional nature and birding tours (see below) often have their clients stay at such lodges. Most eco-lodges have websites; a worldwide list of selected lodges is currently (2010) available at www.birdingpal.org/lodging.htm. The American Bird Conservancy's new website (www.conservationbirding.org/index.html) features birding routes and eco-lodges in the Americas that contribute to bird conservation.

Hyacinth Macaw This is the largest flying parrot species in the world. It is native to semi-open wooded areas in central and eastern South America, and is locally common in Brazil's Pantanal region. *Brazil*

If you are not comfortable being on your own in a foreign country, driving, taking buses, and in other activities, or if you want to visit a place that could be somewhat dangerous because of local wildlife or other unknowns, making your trip with a tour company will be the best choice.

GENERAL TOURS AND NATURE TOURS

If you have ambitions for your international trip other than seeing novel birds (such as sightseeing and cultural activities), you can simply take a "general tourism" tour and birdwatch as you go. Most others on your tour will confine their sightseeing to landscapes and cultural attractions; you will also look at birds. However, there will be no nature or bird expert on the tour, and you will be on your own when it comes to finding and identifying birds.

Nature tours are specialized tours for people, including birders, interested chiefly in visiting natural areas to see and experience local habitats and wildlife. Advantages of such trips are many: The tour company has done pre-trip research for you and knows good places to take you for wild scenery, typical habitats, and potential for wildlife sightings. Usually national parks and other natural areas well known for wildlife are on tour itineraries. All transportation, accommodations, and meals are usually provided. Most important, at least one naturalist guide accompanies the tour, to identify species and explain habitats, ecology, and conservation concerns. In other words, all the uncertainties of independent travel are removed, and you have professionals to guide you.

Tours are easily booked from the United States and Canada, but some travelers prefer to take trips with smaller, local tour companies that they discover at their destinations. Whether you are in San José, Costa Rica, and want a tour of national parks; in Cuiaba, southern Brazil, and want a tour of the Pantanal wildlife area; in Bangkok, and want to visit natural attractions; in Nairobi, and want to join a five-day safari; or in Broome, northwestern Australia, and want a tour of the remote Kimberley region; or in almost any other popular birding destination, there are myriad local tour companies, often with colorful brochures at transportation hubs, hotels, and tourist information kiosks. Such local tours are usually less expensive than all-inclusive tours booked from home and sometimes can be arranged at the last minute.

Falkland Islands This group is birding Carcass Island in the Falklands—home to nesting Magellanic and Gentoo Penguins. By necessity, almost all visits to Antarctica or the subantarctic islands are ship-based, organized tours. *Falkland Islands*

On any nature tour, the quality of guides is a paramount issue—good, knowledgeable guides often make for successful, enjoyable trips. Some tours will have a single guide, someone who accompanies you throughout a trip and takes care of everything (except perhaps driving), including logistics, leading walks and hikes, giving talks, identifying flora and fauna, and answering questions. Other companies will provide more leaders: perhaps two guides, one from the United States and one local. Many tour companies separate the logistics and guide functions, having one tour leader handle all logistics and then having a naturalist guide to give informational lectures and lead clients on nature walks. More expensive nature tours often have better guides; at the extreme, some very expensive tours, such as those offered through famous natural history museums, are accompanied by expert naturalists—often well-known biologists who study the flora and fauna of the destination region.

Indian Roller The roller family (Coraciidae) is a group of 12 species related to bee-eaters and kingfishers. Fortunately for birders, these brilliant birds inhabit open country and are easily seen. The Indian Roller has a large range extending from Arabia to Malaysia. *India*

Disadvantages of nature tours are the ones that attach to any group tour. In return for having the tour company plan your trip and take care of all your travel needs, you surrender the abilities to go where you want and apportion your time as you wish. You must follow the tour schedule. Also, for the duration of the tour, you are going to be in close proximity to other travelers—say 8 to 20 other people with whom you are going to spend anywhere from one to three weeks. If one or more of those people turn out to be obnoxious in any way—well, I don't need to elaborate. Finally, nature tours, especially those with great guides, can be expensive. However, prices vary tremendously. For instance, if you're a college student willing to lug your own belongings, sleep in tents, and be transported in the back of trucks instead of air-conditioned minibuses, you might find a low-priced tour. But most mid-range tours to the tropics, for instance, will have you in air-conditioned buses and nice hotels, and will be fairly expensive ($100 to $200 per day per person, plus airfare).

For birders, a general nature tour can be disappointing because the emphasis is not on birds (or, at least, not always). General nature tours may point out, and even feature, large, gaudy, and glamorous birds such as cranes, herons, flamingos, parrots, hornbills, and toucans, but may ignore, and have little information about, less conspicuous birds. You may, for example, take a safari in Kenya that visits two or three national parks, expecting to see birds as well as mammals, and then discover that the leader points out lions, giraffes, and crocodiles but that he and others on the tour have little interest in stopping to look at birds, especially small songbirds.

If you are interested in a tour featuring nature and birds but also want good exposure to local culture, there are several ways to go. First, some nature tours include a day or two of visiting cultural attractions and/or have "free" days for you to explore towns on your own. Also, many tour companies offer tour "extensions" before or after your main trip that allow you, for added expense, to visit famous cultural areas. For example, many tours to Ecuador and the Galápagos Islands offer an extension for clients to visit Peru's Incan ruins at Machu Picchu. And, of course, you can always explore on your own either before or after a tour.

The way to take an organized tour, making sure that the main emphasis is on birds, is to take a specialized birding tour. The current popularity of birding in the United States and the United Kingdom is sufficient to support a number of tour companies that cater expressly to birders. These tours are usually pricey, but enthusiastic birders with good financial resources like them because they include expert bird guides, aim to maximize the number of species spotted, and the ambiance is birds, birds, birds. Accommodations are often very good to luxurious and, when available, eco-lodges and birding lodges are preferred stopover sites (but because the emphasis is on birding, don't be surprised if some hotels are reached after dark and vacated before dawn the next day). The guides employed by these tour companies are generally expert birders with extensive experience in the destination countries. Sometimes, to maximize bird-finding, there are

King Penguin A city of penguins—the huge breeding colony of King Penguins at St. Andrews Bay numbers about 150,000 birds. The brown birds—"oakum boys"—are nearly full grown juveniles that have yet to go to sea and are still being fed by their parents. *South Georgia Island*

both company bird guides and local bird guides along on a trip. Premium bird tours sometimes have as a guide, for example, an author or contributing bird artist associated with a field guide (birding celebrities!). Itineraries are carefully selected to maximize the potential number of species. For instance, on a trip to Thailand, the tour will be sure to visit all the main habitat types—evergreen forest, mixed deciduous forest, limestone forest, pine forest, marshes, mangroves—so that you have the chance to see the species characteristic of each habitat. Sometimes the strong motivation to see certain species can lend an almost "production-line" feeling to proceedings: Your guide will tell you that you'll stop in location A to "pick up" species X and Y and then you'll move on to location B to look for species Z. In other words, guides try to leave little to chance; they visit sites where certain species, often endemics, are usually spotted. Just as on many bird walks or birding trips that you may have taken at home, the tradition on such tours is to meet in the evening, perhaps while relaxing over drinks, and total up and discuss the species seen that day.

PLAN OF THIS BOOK

This book presents all the ornithological information you need to plan a birding trip outside North America. It will tell you where the most diverse, beautiful, and interesting birds are, and how to see them. It will also tell you where in the world

experienced birders like to travel, and why. If you are considering an international birding trip, this information will help you decide which regions you would like to visit. If your trip is already planned, this information will tell you about the kinds of birds you might encounter.

The next chapter delves into bird distribution and biogeography, essential information for bird seekers with a global agenda. Following that, the main section of the book—arranged continent by continent—consists primarily of regional accounts that describe the characteristic birdlife. The beginning of each chapter consists of a brief introduction to the world region covered by the chapter, followed by general comments on birding in the region. Next, ten or so significant families of birds found in the region are briefly discussed. "Significant families" are those that have many species in the region, those for which the region is widely known, and some that are endemic or almost endemic to the region.

The remainder of each chapter is divided into sections that more specifically detail birds and birding in each sub-region. For example, Chapter 8 covers Australasia and the tropical Pacific, and is divided into four sub-regions: (1) Australia, (2) New Zealand, (3) New Guinea, and (4) Hawaii and the tropical Pacific. The information for each sub-region is presented in four parts: an introduction with general comments; geography and habitats; birdlife; and a section that lists significant bird families of the sub-region and some of the species global birders often seek there. Such lists, by no means exhaustive, are bound to be subjective; another compiler, with a different birding aesthetic, would undoubtedly compile somewhat different lists. Still, there are certain species or families that, for various reasons, many birders make a special effort to see—primarily because the birds in question are endemic, rare, celebrated for cultural reasons or, quite frequently, especially beautiful.

To give you a better feel for the adventures that await you overseas, David L. Pearson, a world-class birder and a biology teacher and researcher, has written 36 narrative sidebars. Each narrative—there are usually two in each sub-region—details a search for a particular species or birding at a special location. Additional sidebars within each sub-region present information about birding books (field guides and site guides) and birding organizations to help you organize and prepare for a trip.

A NOTE ON BIRD CLASSIFICATION AND TERMINOLOGY

The book assumes that readers are somewhat familiar with animal classification, in which animals are placed in distinct groups based on their evolutionary relationships. These groups begin at the most general level and progress to the most specific level in what is termed a taxonomic hierarchy. For example, the Peregrine Falcon is classified as belonging to **class** Aves, the birds; **order** Falconiformes, the birds of prey; **family** Falconidae, encompassing all the falcons, which are one type of bird of prey; **genus** *Falco*, containing one subgroup of the falcons; and **species** *Falco peregrinus,* which is the scientific name (always italicized) for the bird commonly known as the Peregrine Falcon.

Further, the reader should be aware of the main classification division among birds between *passerines* and *nonpasserines*. The passerine birds (order Passeriformes) are the perching birds, with feet specialized to grasp and to perch on tree branches. These are the more recently evolved birds, the most "advanced," and they include all the small land birds with which we are most familiar—such as flycatchers, vireos, chickadees, robins, jays, crows, swallows, wrens, warblers, blackbirds, finches, and sparrows. The passerine order is the most diverse of the 27 bird orders, including more than half of all bird species and about half of the bird families. A major subgroup within the passerines (containing about 4,600 species) is called the *oscines,* or *songbirds,* which have a distinctive, advanced syrinx, the sound-producing organ in their respiratory passages. Other bird groups within the passerine order, such as the cotingas, manakins, and New World flycatchers, are often referred to as *suboscines*. The remainder of the globe's birds—seabirds and shorebirds, ducks and geese, hawks and owls, parrots and woodpeckers, and a host of others—makes up the non-passerines, divided among the other 26 orders of birds.

Bugun Liocichla New birds are still being discovered. This small babbler was first sighted in 1995 and formally described as a new species in 2006. Although it may occur in other locations, the only known population consists of 14 birds in northeast India (Eaglenest Wildlife Sanctuary, Arunachal Pradesh). *India*

Avian taxonomy is not a static science. New evidence of evolutionary relationships can change how a single species is classified or where a whole family should be placed in the higher-level sequence. New species of birds continue to be discovered; even bird families are created (or deleted) to reflect the most up-to-date research. Because of this flux, it is helpful for global birders (and bird book authors) to have a single baseline reference to defer to. This book's taxonomic reference is the sixth edition of *The Clements Checklist of Birds of the World* (Cornell University Press, 2007), which divides the globe's birds into 27 orders, 203 families, and 9,930 species. When families of birds or specific species are listed in this book they follow the taxonomic sequence found in the sixth edition of Clements. For interested readers, online updates to the Clements Checklist and a downloadable, updated world checklist can be found at a website maintained by the Cornell Lab of Ornithology (www.birds.cornell.edu/clementschecklist/corrections). The latest annual update in December 2009 lists 221 families and 9,995 species.

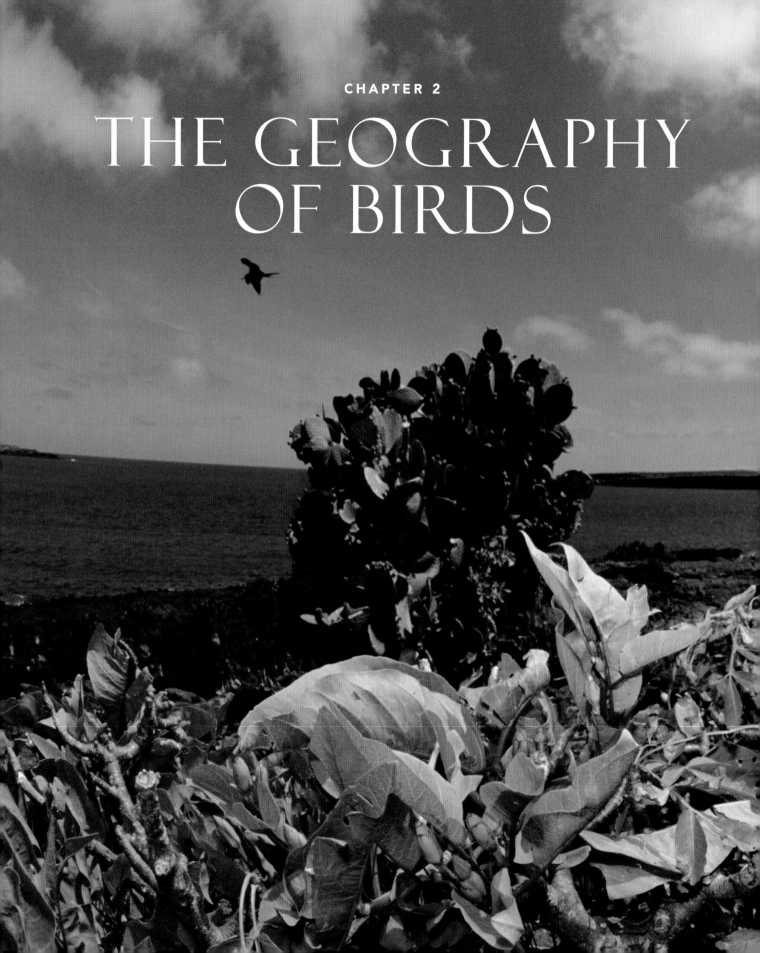

CHAPTER 2

THE GEOGRAPHY
OF BIRDS

THE GEOGRAPHY OF BIRDS

TO SAMPLE THE VAST DIVERSITY OF THE WORLD'S BIRDS, BIRDERS OFTEN take leave of their home countries and travel to other regions of the globe. But even with fast international air travel, the world is still a pretty big place. Where do birders most want to go, and which birds do they wish most to see? Bird species are not distributed uniformly or randomly over the Earth's surface. Rather, there are uneven patterns in avian distribution—and it is these patterns that knowledgeable birders contemplate when deciding where they want to travel. There are a few things to consider: (1) general patterns of animal distribution; (2) why some species have very limited distributions (endemism); and (3) the globe's various faunal regions, their characteristic faunas, and their relative species richness (that is, their numbers of species).

When we talk about the distributions of animal (or plant) groups and species, we are discussing *biogeography,* which, just as it sounds, is a field of study that combines biology and geography. Its aim is to explain the geographic distribution of living things. By invoking fossil evidence and the knowledge of where various kinds of animals first developed, and combining that information with knowledge of continental drift over evolutionary time, the climatic histories of the continents, and the ecological relationships of organisms, biogeography provides logical explanations for the animal distribution patterns we see on Earth. A few brief examples:

Naturalists were long puzzled by the current distribution of the larger flightless birds—one or a few species on each of the southern continents—tinamous (which can fly modestly) and rheas in South America, the Ostrich in Africa, the Emu and

PREVIOUS PAGES: **Great Frigatebird** The view in the background is of Darwin Bay, Genovesa Island. Charles Darwin's short visit to the Galápagos archipelago in 1835 was an important experience that later influenced his thinking on evolution. The endemic birds of the islands, especially the diversity of closely related mockingbird and finch species, offer an unambiguous example of species evolution. *Galápagos Islands, Ecuador*

OPPOSITE: **Ostrich** The flightless Ostrich is fairly common and widely distributed in Africa; birds in southern Africa (shown) have grayish necks and legs, which in northern birds are colored pinkish. *Botswana*

cassowaries in Australia and New Guinea, and kiwis in New Zealand. Now, our recently acquired knowledge of continental drift offers some answers. Most likely, these birds represent the few surviving descendants of an ancient group that occurred in Gondwana (or Gondwanaland)—the Southern Hemisphere supercontinent that began to break apart between 180 and 100 million years ago. Gondwana's pieces gradually drifted away from one another, forming the separate continents we see today. Fossil remains in New Zealand (the moas) and Madagascar (elephant birds) support the idea that these large flightless birds were once more common and widespread.

The ranges of some other birds have diminished. For example, the todies, a small group of tiny, dazzling forest birds, are now restricted to the West Indies—but a tody fossil found in Wyoming, tens of millions of years old, shows that the todies were once much more widespread. Present-day todies are a "relict" group—one that is narrowly distributed now, but that was once widespread. Likewise, fossils of a bird found in Colorado, now identified as a mousebird, indicate that the mousebird group, now confined to Africa, was once more widespread.

Bird distributions sometimes change much more quickly than on time scales of millions of years, and biogeography provides explanations for these kinds of changes as well. For example, it is thought that many of North America's wood-warblers have advanced thousands of miles northward, as far as Canada's boreal forests, during the past 20,000 years. This is since North America's last glacial period, when the northern portion of the continent was covered with a thick ice sheet. Even now, North

Monteverde Cloud Forest Reserve Lush vegetation is typical of tropical regions. The great diversity of plant life fosters the great diversity of birdlife. *Costa Rica*

American birders see this type of process in action as Red-bellied Woodpeckers, Carolina Wrens, Great-tailed Grackles, and other species are being recorded farther and farther north.

A few terms will be important to the discussion below. *Biodiversity* means the different types of animals, plants and other life forms found within a region. *Species richness* is the number of species that occurs in an area, which is the simplest measure of biodiversity. *Avifauna* is the sum of the species of birds living in a given geographic area (such as Africa) or ecological zone (such as rain forest).

THE TROPICS: WHERE THE BIRDS ARE

There are several significant patterns in the geographic distribution of animal species, but the principal one, recognized for almost two centuries, can be called the *global diversity gradient*. The pattern is that many groups of animals, such as insects, lizards, and birds, show a trend in diversity related to latitude. The higher latitudes (the North Pole and the South Pole are at 90° latitude and the Equator is at zero degrees latitude) have relatively few species, and toward the Equator, the number of species increases. Thus, tropical Ecuador—on the Equator—has about 1,500 bird species, twice as many as the entire United States, which is more than 30 times larger than Ecuador but is situated at higher latitudes.

Green Broadbill The stunning green plumage of the male actually provides excellent camouflage in the evergreen rain forests it inhabits. This bird has come out into the open to bathe, but is easily overlooked when it perches quietly inside the forest canopy. *Thailand*

The pattern is conspicuous and continuous. For instance, in the tiny but tropical Central American country of Costa Rica, there are about 600 breeding bird species. Moving northward, about 400 breeding species occur in tropical southern Mexico; 200 occur in temperate northern Mexico; 180 occur in the temperate Pacific Northwest, and about 100 occur in parts of northern Canada and Alaska. The pattern even holds for such animals as ants (222 species in Brazil and 7 in Alaska) and freshwater fish (about 2,500 in the Amazon River region, 500 in Central America, 170 in the Great Lakes).

The cause of this trend in species richness is not completely known. There are a variety of possible explanations, and it is likely that some combination of them accounts for the pattern. Most basically, sunlight energy increases, photosynthetic rates are higher, and, thus, more food is available as latitudes become lower toward the Equator. Because animal and plant life is supported by the energy of the sun,

Three-wattled Bellbird This member of the cotinga family (Cotingidae) is endemic to Central America. The vocalizing male (left) is displaying to the female perched beside him. His bell-like *bonk* call is thought to be among the loudest birdcalls in the world. *Costa Rica*

where there is more sun energy (as in the tropics), there will be more species. Also, more solar energy in the tropics (together with other factors such as increased moisture and higher temperatures) leads to more plant "productivity," which means more plants, larger plants, and more lush habitats, such as forests. Because animals "live on" plants—both physically and with respect to their food—more plant material and more types of plant communities in a region mean more animals can live there.

Although this argument makes great intuitive sense, it is not always the case that more "productive" habitats contain more species, so other factors may also affect the global diversity gradient. For one thing, history matters: Older animal communities, where the native animal groups have had more time to evolve, diversify, and create new species, will have accumulated more species. Tropical animal communities are "older" in the sense that tropical animals have had a longer period of time for evolution to occur in a relatively stable, favorable climate. This is because the tropics are thought to have had a relatively constant, favorable environment for tens of millions of years—at least as compared to many temperate regions, which have had repeated bouts of major climatic changes (such as ice ages and associated glacial coverage) that tend to lead to species extinctions. For instance, many people know that a range of large mammal species of North America became extinct around the time of the Pleistocene glaciation, including mastodons and mammoths, but large birds became extinct also. These apparently included many eagles, vultures, and the teratorn, which may have been the largest flying bird ever. (Note that there are various theories about the factors that may have caused Pleistocene mass extinctions.)

Regardless of the underlying causes of the global diversity gradient, the contemporary manifestation is great species richness in the tropics and relatively impoverished faunas in temperate regions and Arctic regions. For a traveling birder's purposes, this means that *visiting the tropics will almost always yield opportunities to see more new species than visiting temperate or Arctic regions.*

Tropical birds, on average, tend to be brighter and more colorful than their temperate zone counterparts and more visually alluring to most birders. I don't know that anyone has made a quantitative study of the subject, but there is no doubt that many of the world's most colorful birds and the ones with the most ostentatious appearances are denizens of the tropics.

A case can also be made that many of birddom's most interesting behaviors are found among tropical birds. In many cases, it is probably the richness of tropical environments that led to the evolution of such behaviors. A great example is found among the often very colorful cotingas, members of a diverse Neotropical passerine family of about 70 species that includes the typical cotingas, pihas, bellbirds, cocks-of-the-rock, umbrellabirds, and fruitcrows. Although some breed monogamously, some are "lekking" species that breed promiscuously. Lekking males establish display sites on tree branches or on ground courts, and several of these display sites near each other constitute a "lek." Females visit leks, attracted by the males' vocalizations and dancing display antics, compare the males displaying, and choose one or more to mate with. Afterward, the females go off by themselves to nest and raise their young. At their leks, males of some species may spend up to 80 percent to 90 percent of daylight hours displaying and trying to attract females. It is apparently the birds' fruit-eating that allows this kind of breeding system. This is because fruit in the tropics is very abundant and easy to find and so the male birds don't have to devote most of their day to foraging. Thus, the free time that fruit-eating affords permits both the prolonged display time in these breeding systems as well as the requisite ability

Four-colored Bushshrike
One of the most beautiful woodland birds on the African continent, but devilishly hard to get a good look at. This bushshrike is a shy and retiring species that inhabits dense, shrubby riparian woodland; male is shown.
South Africa

Swallow-tailed Gull Endemic mainly to the Galápagos—it occurs on most of the islands. This is the world's only nocturnal gull and its large eyes are an adaptation to its nighttime feeding behavior. *Galápagos Islands, Ecuador*

of females to feed young themselves. It is generally thought that the abundance of fruit, in fact, probably permitted the evolution of non-monogamous breeding in many tropical birds. Non-monogamous breeding in temperate-zone birds developed for other reasons. For instance, some species are thought to be polygynous because, when breeding habitats vary dramatically in quality, a female bird can breed better as the second or third mate on a male's high-quality territory than she could as a sole mate on another male's low-quality territory.

ISLAND BIOGEOGRAPHY

Another major pattern of species richness concerns islands. Many of the world's islands are good birding destinations because, beyond being fun to visit, many island species don't occur in mainland areas, and some island birds are interesting for other reasons (such as being flightless). But not all islands are great birding destinations, especially with respect to numbers of species present. The general rules are that the size of an island's avifauna decreases (1) as island size decreases, and (2) as distance from the nearest mainland increases. In other words, the smaller and more remote the island, the fewer bird species found there. The reasons for these trends in island biodiversity are relatively straightforward. To begin, we need to consider how organisms first arrive on islands.

If a "new" island appeared today just off the coast of California, it may have broken off from the mainland because of tectonic or seismic activity in the Earth's crust. In this case, the island might retain most of the animal species that occur on the nearby mainland. In contrast, the island may have arisen from the sea floor not far from the mainland, perhaps via volcanic activity, and would at first be barren of life. In the latter case, many animal species from the mainland, especially birds, which can fly and easily travel to the nearby new island, might soon colonize it. But not all species of birds or other types of animals on the mainland will cross to the new island. This is one reason why even nearshore islands tend to have fewer species than the nearest mainland areas. (Another reason is that an island's smaller size limits potential habitat types and resource availability.)

What about remote islands such as those that arose volcanically from the sea floor in mid-ocean? As an example, consider the Hawaiian Islands, volcanic cones in the mid-Pacific that are about as isolated as islands can be—located more than 2,000 miles from North America and about 3,500 miles from Japan. Islands such as Hawaii are too far away from mainland areas for mainland species to colonize easily. A large expanse of ocean is probably nature's most effective barrier to the spread of plant and animal species. Only a few types of organisms have the ability to cross oceans and, by chance, only a few species of each type will do so.

How do these species cross oceans? (1) They keep dry and fly. Birds and bats might arrive utilizing their own wing power. Some colonizers, such as snakes or mammals, could swim to previously uncolonized islands, but only over short distances. This would not apply to the Hawaiian Islands, which have no near sources of colonizing immigrants. (2) They arrive passively by drifting or rafting ashore. Tiny plant seeds and tiny spiders and insects may drift in on the wind. Seeds and fruit that can survive immersion in salt water can drift long distances through the ocean. Coconuts, for instance, appear to be adapted for long-term drifting, and this is why coconut palms line ocean beaches in many regions of the world. (3) They come by "boat"—rafting in on bits of floating vegetation or on trees washed off mainland areas during storms.

South Island Wren One of only three members of the New Zealand Wren family (Acanthisittidae), all of which are endemic to New Zealand. The other two species in the family are Rifleman and Bush Wren; the latter is probably extinct. The South Island Wren (also known as Rock Wren) occurs in the high mountains of South Island. *New Zealand*

Eggs or adults of many kinds of animals may reach remote islands this way—spiders, insects, even small rodents. Finally, because seabirds and ducks cover vast distances in their ocean-crossing feeding and migratory flights, some organisms could travel over thousands of miles of open ocean in mud on birds' feet (plant seeds or insect, fish, and amphibian eggs) or even in bird intestines (plant seeds). Many native plants of Hawaii may have, in fact, first arrived in the islands as seeds in bird intestines.

Hawaii's native animal life conforms closely to these principles. The islands are thought to have no native amphibians or reptiles. The frogs and lizards that occur there now were brought by people—early settlers from other Pacific islands during the past 10 or 15 centuries or more recent travelers in wooden boats, steel-hulled ships, and Boeing jets. The only native land mammal in Hawaii is a bat. As for birds, Hawaii's complement consists largely of seabirds and waterbirds. The relatively few native landbird species there are thought to have all evolved from a few ancestor species that long ago arrived in the islands by chance, perhaps diverted by storms during over-ocean migrations. Today, of course, many new species of plants and animals occur in Hawaii and reach other remote oceanic islands with people's intentional or unintentional help—that is, they are *introduced*. Introduced organisms are often called "aliens" or "invaders" to separate them from native species, which evolved on the islands or reached them naturally on their own. Among Hawaii's current landbirds, only a relative few, such as the Hawaiian honeycreepers, some thrushes, and a monarch flycatcher, are native.

So the methods by which birds and other animals colonize islands explain the relationship between distance from mainland and number of species present: the greater the distance, the fewer species manage to colonize. But, what about the relationship between island size and number of species? A large island may have almost all the various kinds of habitats that a mainland region has: low, middle, and high elevation zones, beach, scrub, forests, grasslands, wetlands, etc., and each habitat can support a characteristic avifauna. Smaller islands tend to have fewer species, such as

Chabert Vanga The 15 species of vangas (family Vangidae) are mainly endemic to Madagascar; one also occurs on the nearby Comoro Islands. The small family shows an incredible diversity of shapes, sizes, and colors. This Chabert Vanga is sitting on its neatly woven nest. *Madagascar*

birds, because smaller islands have fewer habitat types and in turn fewer "niches" that bird species can occupy. For instance, some coastal islands are composed primarily of rocks along the water and forested interiors. At the extreme, mid-ocean atolls— barely rising from the ocean's surface—often consist simply of coral beach, some grasses and shrubby vegetation, and coconut palms.

The lesson here for a traveling birder searching for high species richness is that, if you're given a choice of islands to visit, remember: *The larger the island and the closer to the mainland, the more species you can expect there.* But, you say, you know some knowledgeable birders who take trips to or talk enthusiastically about small, mid-ocean islands. Why should birders want to visit tiny, remote islands if, almost by definition, they have very limited avifaunas? This brings us to another facet of bird distribution, and one of the most important to global birding: endemic species.

ENDEMICS: SOME BIRDS OCCUR IN VERY LIMITED AREAS

Much of international birding revolves around a single seven-letter word—endemic— a word not normally used by most people and almost never used with the meaning it has in the spheres of zoology and birding. The most widely used meaning of "endemic" is "prevalent in a particular place." It often refers to diseases—as in "yellow fever is endemic to central Africa." But a second definition, subtly different from the first, is the one that concerns us here: "peculiar to a particular place." An endemic species, or group of species, is one that occurs in a certain area and nowhere else. And, simply put, it is upon this word, this definition, and the biology and ecology it represents, that much of global birding is based.

When informed birders travel, it is for locally endemic species that they usually search most diligently. When in Australia, you look for Emus because you're not going to see them in the wild anywhere else. The Hawaiian honeycreepers— a renowned group of small, mostly threatened and endangered species with oddly shaped bills—are endemic to the Hawaiian Islands. Darwin's finches, 14 species of small, drab songbirds with various bill types, are endemic to the Galápagos Islands (with one of the species occurring on Costa Rica's far-offshore Cocos Island). Todies, a tiny group of diminutive birds related to kingfishers, are endemic to a few islands in the West Indies. The Hyacinth Macaw, a large, endangered parrot, is endemic to a few bits of Brazil and neighboring parts of Paraguay and Bolivia. For birders traveling internationally in search of numerous, novel, and/or infrequently spotted bird species, a knowledge of endemism—its causes and implications—is essential. So let's explore endemism, explain why some bird groups or species are endemic to very small regions, and discuss where to see the most endemic species.

TABLE 1

BIRD DIVERSITY: NUMBER OF SPECIES

1,793	Peru
1,757	Colombia
1,719	Brazil
1,534	Ecuador
1,528	Indonesia
1,347	Bolivia
1,346	Venezuela
1,269	China
1,185	India
1,133	Dem. Rep. of the Congo
1,104	Kenya
1,075	Mexico
1,054	Tanzania
1,023	Uganda
1,005	Argentina
1,002	Myanmar
962	Sudan
945	Thailand
923	Angola
918	Panama
899	Cameroon
889	Nigeria
868	Nepal
852	Costa Rica
840	Ethiopia
825	South Africa
787	Vietnam
776	Australia
766	Zambia
760	Papua New Guinea

Many species occur in more than one country. The information in this table is based on *The Clements Checklist of Birds of the World,* 6th edition (Cornell University Press).

The word "endemic" has no meaning until the size or type of place referred to is specified. For example, a given species of sparrow may be endemic to the Western Hemisphere, to a single continent such as South America, to a mountainous region of Peru, or to a speck of an island off Peru's coast. (As far as anyone knows, all species, all organisms of our world, are endemic to Earth.) Therefore, a modifier is often used with the word "endemic" to clarify the meaning of the writer or speaker. There are hemispheric endemics, continental endemics, regional endemics, country endemics, state endemics, and island endemics.

The term "near-endemic" is used to indicate a species or group that occurs in a particular place and perhaps one or a few other areas nearby. For instance, the threatened Palm Cockatoo, a two-foot-long, blackish, crested species, occurs over the northeastern tip of Australia but also in nearby New Guinea. It can be termed

TABLE 2 Countries with the Most Endemic Bird Areas (EBAs)			
COUNTRY	EBAS	EBAS ENTIRELY WITHIN COUNTRY'S BORDERS	RESTRICTED-RANGE SPECIES
INDONESIA	23	17	403
MEXICO	18	14	83
PERU	16	6	211
BRAZIL	15	9	164
COLOMBIA	14	4	192
PAPUA NEW GUINEA	12	8	167
CHINA	12	8	56
ECUADOR	9	1	160
AUSTRALIA	8	8	78
ARGENTINA	8	4	49
PHILIPPINES	7	7	126
VENEZUELA	7	3	110
INDIA	7	2	74
TANZANIA	6	1	53
MADAGASCAR	5	5	49
CHILE	5	2	26
BOLIVIA	5	1	61
SOUTH AFRICA	5	1	25

Endemic Bird Areas are defined by BirdLife International as geographic areas that contain the complete breeding ranges of two or more restricted-range species, which may or may not be restricted to a particular country (see text). The information in this table is based on *Endemic Bird Areas of the World* (BirdLife International).

an Australian near-endemic (and a New Guinea near-endemic); it is endemic to the "Australasian" region (which includes Australia, New Zealand, New Guinea, and some of the Pacific islands). The Hyacinth Macaw, referred to above, is a Brazilian near-endemic. (The term "specialty," often used in birding, usually refers to a species that is not necessarily endemic to a given place, but has a restricted range, and so is of particular interest to birders when visiting a given location where it occurs.)

While the term "endemic" has great utility for birders, it's not very useful when invoked to describe species with huge distributions; most often, when birders use the term, they are referring to species with smaller, restricted distributions. A European birder arriving in the United States or Canada for the first time might have American Crow on his or her list of new species to see, and it is certainly true that this crow is restricted to North America and so is endemic to the continent. But calling the American Crow an "endemic," though technically correct, loses something in the usage. Similarly, asking that European birder, "How many Western Hemisphere endemics did you see on your trip?" or "How many North American endemics did you spot?", while also technically OK and answerable, is not so useful or interesting, because a very large number of species are being referred to and many of them have huge distributions.

To get a better idea of how birders use the term, consider New Zealand, which consists of two large islands (North Island and South Island) and many smaller islands. More than 200 bird species occur in and around New Zealand, most being seabirds, shorebirds, or waterbirds. About 60 of these species are endemic to New Zealand. So when birders from around the world visit, they routinely ask each other, "So, which of the endemics have you seen?"—referring to the 60 species. Or they might ask, "Which of the land endemics have you seen?"—referring to the 14 passerines that occur there and a few other landbirds, such as kiwi and the few endemic parrots. Or they might even ask, "Which of the passerine endemics have you seen?" New Zealand's Chatham Islands, a group of islands 500 miles east of the main islands, are home to seven species of birds endemic to these islands (and also, of

Golden Bowerbird This male is bringing flowers to decorate his bower in hope of attracting females to mate with. The Golden Bowerbird is endemic to tropical rain forests of Queensland in northeastern Australia. *Australia*

course, to New Zealand)—and so, after a trip there, a birder might tell others stories that begin with "First, let me tell you which of the Chatham endemics I saw."

Not only species are endemic—many genera and even entire families are endemic to particular regions of the world. For instance, the New World blackbird family, with about 27 genera and 100 species, is endemic to the New World; the leafbird family, with only one genus and eight species, is endemic to Asia; and the cotinga family, with 30 genera and 71 species, and the manakin family, with 17 genera, 57 species, are both endemic to South and Central America.

Soon after you start using the term "endemic" to describe birds you see or want to see, almost inevitably you will stumble upon one of biogeography's fundamental questions: Why are some species endemic to small areas while others are spread over huge regions such as full continents, or even most of the world? Barn Swallows, European Starlings, House Sparrows, Peregrine Falcons, and Ospreys, for instance, are five of the most widespread birds, each occurring on multiple continents. Another way of asking this is: What determines a species' present distribution? History is the answer. When a species' distribution is confined to a certain or small area, the reason is that (1) there are one or more barriers to further spread (an ocean, a mountain range, and/or a thousand miles of tropical rain forest), (2) the species evolved only recently and

Secretary-bird An extraordinary long-legged raptor endemic to sub-Saharan Africa. This "eagle on crane legs" stalks grasslands for prey such as snakes and lizards, which are often killed by foot stamping. If disturbed it usually prefers to run rather than fly away. *South Africa*

has not yet had time to spread, or (3) the species evolved long ago, spread long ago, and now has become extinct over much of its prior range.

A history of isolation also matters: the longer a group of animals and plants are isolated from their close relatives, the more time they have to evolve by themselves and to change into new, different, and unique groups. The best examples are on islands. Some islands once were attached to mainland areas, but continental drift and/or changing sea levels led to their isolation in the middle of the ocean; other islands arose wholly new via volcanic activity beneath the seas. For instance, the island of Madagascar was once attached to Africa and India. The organisms stranded on its shores when it became an island have had probably 150 million years in isolation to develop into the highly endemic fauna and flora we see today. It's thought that about 80 percent of the island's plants and animals are endemic—half the bird species, about 800 butterflies, 8,000 flowering plants, and essentially all the mammals and reptiles. Other islands where high concentrations of endemic animals abound include Indonesia, where about 15 percent of the world's bird species occur, a quarter of them endemic; New Guinea, where about half the birds are endemic; and the Philippines, where half the mammals are endemic.

Peruvian Plantcutter
A Peruvian endemic known only from scattered locations on the northwest coastal plain. It is a member of the cotinga family (Cotingidae) and endangered—the world population may be as few as 1,000 individuals. Female is shown. *Peru*

Knowledge of endemism is important for two practical reasons, one conservation oriented and one recreational. First, species that are endemic to small areas often bear a special environmental vulnerability. Basically, when and if their numbers fall, these species or groups face a greater chance of extinction than others because there are no other populations in distant places that might survive. Good examples are species that are endemic to islands. If a species of bird occurs only on a single island, all of its eggs are "in one basket," so to speak: If a calamity happens—a powerful hurricane, a volcanic eruption—the entire species could become extinct. This type of extinction of birds has apparently happened often on islands, as humans colonized. People caused habitat destruction and brought animal predators that the native birds had no fear of or experience with. It is estimated that about 108 bird species have become extinct in the last 400 years, 97 of them island endemics. The problem persists: About 900 of the 9,930 living bird species are island endemics, and so are continually vulnerable.

Similarly, about 75 percent of mammals driven to extinction recently were island dwellers. Knowledge of the existence and distribution of endemic species is therefore crucial for conservation of biodiversity. If biodiversity is to be preserved, then identifying areas with with large numbers of unique, or endemic, species (centers of endemism), and targeting those areas for conservation attention, is a potentially profitable strategy. In other words, we don't have to make much of an effort to conserve species that are distributed worldwide or hemisphere-wide: their broad ranges often provide protection against quick extinction. But endemics, with their restricted distributions, are inherently vulnerable and deserving of immediate attention.

A recent concept in conservation biology has been the idea of "hot spots"—relatively small areas of the world supporting very high numbers of endemic species. These areas should receive priority conservation attention. For instance, it's estimated that fully 20 percent of the Earth's endemic plants occur over just half a percent of the world's land area. Preserve that half a percent and save 20 percent of endemic plants. For birds, the message is equally clear. About 75 percent of the bird species considered globally threatened occur over just 5 percent of the world's land surface.

From a recreational wildlife-viewing standpoint, if there is a specific type of wildlife you'd like to see, you must first know to which area it is endemic, then travel there: Madagascar for vangas and lemurs. Africa or Asia for hornbills and elephants. Asia for leafbirds and tigers. Australia for Emus and koalas. New Zealand for kiwis and Yellow-eyed Penguins. If you wanted to visit a region where you might encounter large varieties of strange, exotic wildlife, a region with a high degree of endemism would be just the ticket—such as some of the hot spots mentioned above.

To birders only beginning to travel internationally, endemics are of particular interest because, almost by definition, they will be species that a birder has not seen before. Moreover, endemics have a propensity to be very interesting birds. They are intriguing sometimes for their extremely limited distributions, but also for their forms and behaviors. Island endemics, for instance, because of their evolutionary development in isolation from many other birds and from mammal predators, often have compelling adaptations that draw our attention—such as New Zealand's flightless kiwis, the flightless rails characteristic of some Pacific islands, and Hawaii's beautiful, long-billed honeycreepers.

Juan Fernandez Firecrown
A critically endangered hummingbird endemic to Robinson Crusoe Island, one of the three Juan Fernandez Islands located off the Chilean coast. *Robinson Crusoe Island, Chile*

So, endemics are the species that birders typically seek most eagerly on their international trips. Logically then, *to optimize the number of novel species seen on a birding trip, seek out regions with high numbers of endemics*. Where do the most endemics occur?

Very helpful to jet-setting birders in quantifying regional endemism is the recent classification of selected parts of the world's land masses into regions of varying size called Endemic Bird Areas (EBAs). A conservation organization, Birdlife International, made these classifications in the early 1990s as, essentially, avian hot spot indicators: EBAs with high concentrations of endemics would serve as regional indicators of high biodiversity in general, and so these would indicate areas where conservation attention should be high. EBAs (calculated using a special definition of endemic: a species with a limited range) are geographic areas that contain the complete breeding ranges of two or more restricted-range bird species (but not necessarily the complete ranges of all restricted-range species in the EBA).

Tui The Tui (from its Maori name) is one of the largest members of the diverse honeyeater family. It is endemic to New Zealand and the overall population is healthy. In fact, it is one of the most common (and vocal) birds in urban Wellington, and a bird well known to most New Zealanders. *New Zealand*

	NEARCTIC	NEOTROPICAL	PALEARCTIC	AFROTROPICAL	ORIENTAL	AUSTRALASIAN
TABLE 3 *Bird Diversity by Zoogeographic Regions and Continents*						
BREEDING SPECIES	850	3,500	1,300	1,900	2,100	1,600
	NORTH AMERICA	SOUTH AMERICA	EUROPE	AFRICA	ASIA	AUSTRALIA
BREEDING SPECIES	670	3,100	500	2,000	2,400	600
FAMILIES	78	92	69	103	108	88
ENDEMIC FAMILIES	0	9	0	17	5	7
ENDEMIC BIRD AREAS (EBAS)	2	47	1	38	49	7

Numbers are based on a worldwide avifauna consisting of approximately 9,900 species and 203 families. Some species and families occur in more than one region and numbers are approximate. North America in this table includes only Canada and the United States. The information in this table is based on: *The Clements Checklist of Birds of the World*, 6th edition (Cornell University Press); *Birds of the World Database* (CD, Lynx Edicions); *Endemic Bird Areas of the World* (BirdLife International); and *BirdArea* (CD, Santa Barbara Software).

Birdlife International considers a species to have a restricted range if the bird occurs over no more than 19,300 square miles (an area the size of West Virginia). About 2,560 bird species (26 percent of all bird species) meet this definition of restricted range, and about 220 EBAs each support from 2 to 80 species (most with 2 to 10 species). About half of all the EBAs are islands. For an example of a set of EBAs, let's look at South America's Chile. One of Chile's five EBAs is "Central Chile," where the following eight restricted-range species occur: Chilean Tinamou, Chestnut-throated Huet-huet, Moustached Turca, White-throated Tapaculo, Ochre-flanked Tapaculo, Crag Chilia, Dusky-tailed Canastero, and Chilean Mockingbird. Another Chilean EBA is the Juan Fernandez Islands, where three restricted-range species live: Juan Fernandez Firecrown, Juan Fernandez Tit-tyrant, and Masafuera Rayadito.

A final note on endemism, concerning the philosophy of traveling birders: The degree of endemism attached to a particular bird group or species often determines the "value" birders assign to seeing various birds. Species with more limited distributions, those endemic to tiny areas (and so "highly" endemic), are often the ones birders most want to see. Rare or threatened birds that are also endemic to small regions are perhaps the most ardently pursued.

By this point you are probably almost out the door, binoculars in hand, your purchase of airline tickets and field guides awaiting only the next piece of information: just where *are* the most endemic species, the most diverse EBAs? To answer this, we

OPPOSITE: **Eurasian Spoonbill** Of the six species of spoonbills in the world, this is the most widespread. These birds likely bred in Europe and migrated to this part of western Africa for the winter. *Western Sahara, Morocco*

should first consider geography and how biologically oriented people, such as biologists and hard-core birders, divide the world into sections.

ZOOGEOGRAPHIC ZONES: MAJOR WILDLIFE AREAS OF THE WORLD

Various methods can be used to describe the particular regions in which bird groups and species occur. We can divide terrestrial parts of the Earth into discrete hemispheres or continents and then say, for instance, which bird groups occur on each continent (example: toucans are a South American group). *Old World* vs. *New World*, a historical division, also has some utility (example: the blackbird family, including blackbirds, grackles, orioles, meadowlarks and others, is a New World group). Old World refers to the regions of the globe that Europeans knew of before Columbus's voyages: Europe, Asia, Africa. New World refers to the Western Hemisphere: North and South America. The main climatic regions of the Earth—*tropical, temperate,* and *Arctic*—are frequently used to describe bird distributions (example: parrots are a pantropical group). The tropics, always warm, are the regions of the world that fall within the belt from 23.5° N latitude (the Tropic of Cancer) to 23.5° S latitude (the Tropic of Capricorn; see map opposite). The world's temperate zones, with more seasonal climates, extend from 23.5° N and S latitude to the Arctic and Antarctic Circles, at 66.5° N and S. Arctic regions, more or less always cold, extend from 66.5° N and S to the poles. Occasionally the terms *boreal* and *austral* are used, the former referring to northern, primarily north temperate, regions; the latter referring to southern, especially south temperate, regions.

Ever since the 1800s, however, when biologists began traveling regularly among the continents and noticing great similarities in wildlife within broad regions of the world, but major differences among regions, there has been a scheme to divide the Earth into six "zoogeographic" (or faunal) zones, or "realms" (see map opposite). These divisions, initially proposed (for birds) by Philip Sclater in 1858, and followed and generalized for all land animals by Alfred Russel Wallace in 1876, were based on the distributions of bird families known at that time. That these divisions are still in common use today to describe animal distributions testifies to the abilities and knowledge of the 19th-century naturalists who drew them. Unless you took a school course in biogeography, it is unlikely you have ever dealt with these divisions—but now, as birders interested in international exploration, you will often stumble across them in field guides, bird reference books, and conversations with other birders.

The first two of the six zoogeographic zones are located north of the tropics: the Nearctic (NEE-arctic; mainly North America including Greenland) and the Palearctic

---

TABLE 4

BIRD DIVERSITY: NUMBER OF ENDEMIC SPECIES

375	Indonesia
313	Australia
202	Brazil
192	Philippines
113	Peru
98	Madagascar
90	Mexico
76	Papua New Guinea
68	Solomon Islands
67	Colombia
59	New Zealand
50	China
45	Venezuela
40	India
35	Ecuador/Galápagos
28	Jamaica
25	Fiji
25	São Tomé & Príncipe
24	Sri Lanka
22	Tanzania
21	Cuba
20	Bolivia
18	Cormoro Islands
17	Ethiopia
16	Argentina
15	South Africa
15	Taiwan
13	Dem. Rep. of the Congo
13	Micronesia
12	Palau

The information in this table is based on *The Clements Checklist of Birds of the World,* 6th edition (Cornell University Press).

(PAY-lee-arctic; Eurasia and northern Africa). Three of the other zones are largely tropical: the Neotropical (Central America, South America, and the West Indies), the Afrotropical (also called Ethiopian; sub-Saharan Africa and Madagascar), and the Oriental (also called Indomalayan; all of southern Asia from India east to southeastern China and Southeast Asia). The sixth zone, the Australian (also called Australasian; encompassing Australia, New Zealand, and New Guinea), has both tropical and south temperate components. These six zones contain most of the world's terrestrial wildlife.

Antarctica is not included, but the seventh continent, of course, has few terrestrial vertebrate animals. In this book, Antarctica information is found at the end of the chapter on South America, its closest neighbor and the jumping-off point of most visits.

Other problem places with respect to regional classification are the remote Pacific islands. They have few unique groups of birds or other animals that would set them apart in a separate zone, and they have small numbers of groups from several of the continental faunas. For convenience, many birding references include the Pacific islands in the Australasian zone.

Each of the six zoogeographic zones contains a characteristic set of bird families. This is not to say that every family is restricted to a particular zone; in fact, most occur in more than one zone. But each zone has families that are either endemic to it

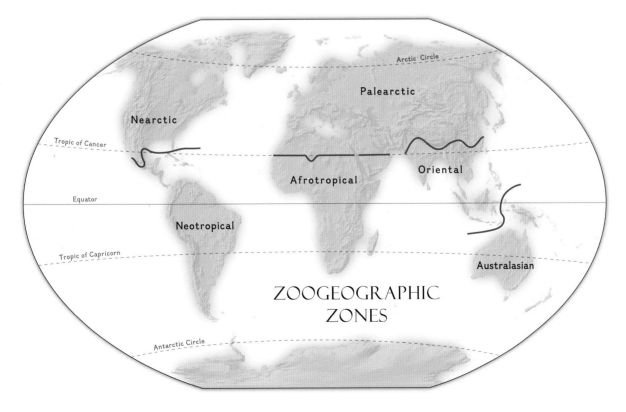

ZOOGEOGRAPHIC
ZONES

St. Lucia Parrot Endemic to the island of St. Lucia. Conservation and education programs have helped to save this large *Amazona* parrot from almost certain extinction. The wild population dropped to about 100 birds during the late 1970s but now numbers about 500. *St. Lucia*

TABLE 5
COUNTRIES WITH THE MOST GLOBALLY THREATENED SPECIES

122	Brazil
115	Indonesia
93	Peru
86	Colombia
85	China
76	India
69	Ecuador
69	New Zealand
67	Philippines
54	Mexico
51	Russia
49	Argentina
49	Australia
44	Thailand
42	Malaysia
41	Myanmar
40	Japan
40	Tanzania
39	Vietnam
36	Papua New Guinea
35	Madagascar
35	South Africa
32	French Polynesia
32	Nepal
31	Dem. Rep. of the Congo
30	Republic of Korea
29	Bolivia
28	Bangladesh
27	Kenya
27	Pakistan
27	Paraguay

About 1,220 species of the world's 9,900 birds are considered globally threatened. Some threatened bird species occur in more than one country. The information in this table is based on the 2008 IUCN Red List of Threatened Species (www.iucnredlist.org).

or reach their greatest species diversity there. For example, among nonpasserines the Neotropical zone is known for rheas, tinamous, screamers, guans and chachalacas, trumpeters, potoos, hummingbirds, trogons, motmots, and toucans; among passerines, for ovenbirds and woodcreepers, antbirds, cotingas, manakins, tyrant flycatchers, tanagers, and blackbirds.

Table 3 shows the relative sizes of the avifaunas in the various zoogeographic zones and continents. The Neotropical and Oriental zones, which include mostly tropical lands, contain the most diversity. The breakdown by continents shows a similar pattern, and South America and Asia have the most Endemic Bird Areas. Tables 1, 2, 4, and 5 show the countries with the greatest number of species, the most EBAs, the most endemic species, and the most globally threatened species.

(Note: The exact numbers presented in the tables are not very important because the total number of species on a continent or in a country varies depending on the method of counting and the source consulted. For example, sources may or may not include seabirds, which often have large oceanic distributions, in their counts. Some avifauna totals include only birds that breed within a given region, while others include all birds in the region, including nonbreeding migrants. Species numbers also change when various new systems of classification come into vogue. Therefore, it is more important to consider the relative differences between the values in the tables than the absolute numbers.)

If you've read this far, and studied the accompanying tables, you now have a pretty good idea where birders want most to travel. To some degree, the selection of an international destination depends on your particular interests—whether you perhaps most want to see seabirds, or flightless landbirds, or very rare birds, or large parrots, etc. But, in general, the best places to go are those with the highest avian species richness and the greatest degrees of endemism. In these locations you will see the most species and prob-ably the most interesting birds. The tropics—in South and Central America, Africa, and Asia—have by far the most bird species, the most bird families, and the most endem-ics. The tropics also include 77 percent of the EBAs. South America has more than 90 families, about 3,100 species, and seven countries each with more than 1,000 species. Relatively close to the United States and Canada, this southern continent would clearly be a desirable destina-tion for many North American birders initiating interna-tional birding explorations.

Silver-eared Mesia Unlike many of the species referred to in this chapter, which have restricted ranges, this one is found through-out Asia. It is one of the 274 members of the bab-bler family (Timaliidae). *Singapore*

Using their knowledge of biogeography, some birders head for regions of the world where they can see mixtures of bird types. Some examples: Panama, at the southern end of Central America and connected to South America via Colombia, has Central Ameri-can birds but also some species that are more widespread in South America. Mexico, straddling the border region between the tropics and north temperate zone, and with many habitat types—especially tropical rain forests in the south and temperate forests and deserts in the north—boasts great species diversity, with elements of both the Neotropical and Nearctic avifaunas. Thailand has a rich Oriental avifauna, but also, in its northern reaches, includes some Palearctic birds that are at the southern extremes of their ranges.

Visiting regions of the world with great bird diversity and high numbers of endemic species are thrilling prospects for most birders. Journeying to tropical Asia or Africa, for instance, for chances to see some of the numerous and amazing birds there, can be among the high points of a lifetime's birding. But excellent international birding experiences are often found much closer to home, as Chapter 3 will show.

CHAPTER 3

MEXICO, CENTRAL AMERICA & THE WEST INDIES

ATLANTIC

OCEAN

United States

Gulf of
Mexico

Brownsville

Hotspot for Endemic Species
Sierra de Bahoruco
page 88

Baja California

Sierra Madre Occidental

Durango

Tropic of Cancer

Mazatlán

Tamaulipas

Nearby Neotropical Birding
Río Corona
page 71

Cuba

Greater
Antilles

Haiti

W E S T

Puerto
Rico
(U.S.)

I N D I E S

Tufted Jay
Mazatlán–
Durango Highway
page 72

M
e
x
i
c
o

Oaxaca

Jamaica

Dominican
Republic

Lesser Antilles

Puerto Rican Parrot
Luquillo Mountains
page 87

Dwarf Jay
Mountains above Oaxaca
page 80

Belize

Honduras

Caribbean

Sea

Lesser Antilles

Guatemala

Nicaragua

Trinidad
and Tobago

El Salvador

PACIFIC

Costa
Rica

Panama

Resplendent Quetzal
Cerro de la Muerte
page 79

OCEAN

Equator

Atlantic
Ocean

miles

| 0 | 250 | 500 | 750 | 1000 |

| 0 | 500 | 1000 | 1500 |

kilometers

BIRDING IN

MEXICO, CENTRAL AMERICA & THE WEST INDIES

W HEN AMERICAN AND CANADIAN BIRDERS CONSIDER LEAVING their countries to bird elsewhere, Mexico, Central America, and the West Indies—the islands of the Caribbean Sea—are often the places they think about first. The logic at work here is simple yet powerful: These are usually the closest international sites, traveling to them and through them is often relatively inexpensive and safe, and, not incidentally, they harbor some of the world's most striking birds. For instance, the region is a parrot paradise, with a cohort of more than 50 species. These include such standouts as the huge red, blue and yellow Scarlet Macaw and the green and blue Military Macaw (both birds in Mexico and Central America) and the smaller Cuban Parrot (in the West Indies). Toucans are broadly distributed in the tropical reaches of Mexico and Central America, including such easily spotted beauties as the Keel-billed Toucan, which has a spectacular, multi-colored bill that often lands this bird on the covers of this area's travel books. Motmots, handsome kingfisher relatives that often sport curious tennis-racquet-like tail-tips, also inhabit the region. Finally, like tiny Caribbean sprites, several of this region's larger islands are inhabited by brightly colored small birds known as todies, representing a family unique to this part of the world.

Furthermore, visiting these nearby regions allows birders to begin delving more deeply into several families that are only lightly represented in the United States and Canada but are much more diverse in the Neotropics. Among these: hummingbirds, with 14 species in the United States and Canada but more than 100 species in Mexico, Central America, and the Caribbean; trogons, with a single regularly occurring

PREVIOUS PAGES: **Palenque** The jungle habitat surrounding this archaeological site of the classic Maya period offers superb birding for such species as Slaty-tailed Trogon, Keel-billed Toucan, Blue crowned Motmot, and a host of others. *Mexico*

species in the United States Southwest but 17 in Mexico, Central America, and the Caribbean; and tanagers, with 4 regular species in the United States and Canada but more than 80 in Mexico, Central America, and the Caribbean. Also, a trip to these regions allows birders to begin exploring some of the large and exotic bird families that are chiefly South American in distribution but that reach their northernmost extensions in parts of Mexico and in Central America, including groups such as ovenbirds, woodcreepers, antbirds, cotingas, and manakins.

NORTHERN MEXICO

Northern Mexico, of course, lies just south of the United States and many Americans are familiar with such Mexican border cities as Tijuana, Nogales, Ciudad Juarez, and Matamoros. South of the border zone, Mexico's heavily developed Pacific beach-resort areas of Mázatlan, Puerto Vallarta, and Acapulco, as well as portions of the Baja California Peninsula, attract hundreds of thousands of sun-seeking Americans and Canadians each year. But northern Mexico also possess a wealth of easily accessed birding sites. Some of the main ones are the cape ("Cabo") region of Baja California, especially around the heavily touristed towns of San José del Cabo and La Paz, where Baja endemics such as Xantus's Hummingbird, Gray Thrasher, and Belding's

Sonoran Desert This large desert famous for its saguaro cacti extends from northern Mexico into the southwestern United States. Most of the desert birds found here occur on both sides of the border, but many are easier to locate on the Mexican side. *Mexico*

Yellowthroat are to be found; the area around Mázatlan, in Sinaloa state, where the coastal habitats of beaches, lagoons, and mangroves yield frequent sightings of pelicans, boobies, and frigatebirds, and the pine and pine-oak woodlands above the city contain such striking Mexican endemics as Thick-billed Parrot, Eared Quetzal, and Tufted Jay; the small fishing town of San Blas, located just south of Sinaloa, in the state of Nayarit, where birders look for Bare-throated Tiger-Heron and Rufous-necked Wood-Rail in coastal swamps and mangroves, and Mexican Parrotlet, Cinnamon Hummingbird, Mexican Woodnymph, Russet-crowned Motmot,

Gray Silky-flycatcher One of only four species in the silky-flycatcher family (Ptilogonatidae), not a tyrant flycatcher. The Gray Silky, as it is often called, inhabits pine-oak and evergreen forests from northern Mexico to Guatemala. *Mexico*

Black-throated Magpie-Jay, San Blas Jay, and Golden Vireo in the dry inland thorn forests. Even the chaotic and densely populated Mexico City area can be a birding destination: the UNAM Botanical Garden, on the campus of Mexico's largest university and near the center of the city, is a great place to see a variety of local birds, as are a host of nearby national parks, such as the scenic Popocatépetl National Park, 50 miles southeast of the city.

SOUTHERN MEXICO AND CENTRAL AMERICA

Southern Mexico and Central America are probably best known to travelers for their holiday beach resorts at, for instance, Cancún and Cozumel in Mexico and Ambergris Cay in Belize; for the region's famed Maya ruin sites, including Chichén Itzá and Tikal; for the popular ecotourism destination of Costa Rica; and for the trans-isthmus canal that divides Panama. But American birders know this region as a nearby area where they can gain easy access to a large and exciting avifauna that includes almost the full spectrum of Neotropical bird families. Among the important birding sites visited frequently in this region are southern Mexico's Yucatán Peninsula, where birders often target the area's many archaeological parks. Here, usually in forested or parklike settings, ancient stone structures may be subjects of some interest, but binoculars are always handy to spot the birds that live among the ruins, including such beauties as Ocellated Turkey, Turquoise-browed Motmot, Yucatan Jay, Gray-throated Chat, and Rose-throated Tanager (most of which are endemic to the area). Also in southern Mexico, the large states of Oaxaca and Chiapas attract birders. Oaxaca, a mecca for

tourists visiting its charming capital, Oaxaca City, has several good archaeological sites that double as birding habitat, including the stunning mountaintop-plateau site of Monte Albán. And Chiapas boasts Palenque National Park, where extensive ruins, some excavated and partially restored, some still covered with jungle, are set among towering trees of dense lowland tropical forest. Central American countries that are preferred birder destinations include Belize and northern Guatemala, which, although divided politically from Mexico, can be considered to be physically part of the Yucatán Peninsula, and, to the south, Costa Rica and Panama.

WEST INDIES

Most visitors to the Caribbean go for sun, sand, and surf, but increasingly people leave the beach for part of their stay to explore the islands' incredible natural attractions: stunning mountain scenery, wonderful hiking trails, and glimpses of birds—many of them now rare and endangered—that occur nowhere else. For these types of natural attractions, favored islands or island groups include the Bahamas, Cuba, Jamaica, Dominican Republic, Puerto Rico, Dominica, and Matinique. Among knowledgeable birders, the West Indies are perhaps

known best for the endemic tody and Palmchat families, for hosting the world's four species of lizard-cuckoos (cuckoos that specialize on eating small lizards), and for having an abundance of species with very restricted distributions, many endemic to single islands or island groups. For example, the Cuban Blackbird occurs only in Cuba, the Jamaican Blackbird is restricted to Jamaica, the Martinique Oriole is found only on Martinique, and the Montserrat Oriole is unique to Montserrat.

A final word on the areas treated in this chapter—northern and southern Mexico, Central America, and the West Indies: they have in common that they are excellent destinations for family holidays, places where the non-birders in a family can enjoy ocean beaches and resorts, nightlife, shopping and, often, world renowned cultural-heritage sites, while the birders feast on spotting the great variety of birds.

Fiery-billed Aracari This member of the toucan family (Ramphastidae) is restricted to the Pacific slope of Costa Rica and western Panama. *Costa Rica*

OPPOSITE: **Monteverde Cloud Forest Reserve** Walls of dense vegetation make spotting forest birds a challenge and you'll hear more birds than you see. Species diversity is very high though, so walking the same trail on a different day or time of day often yields new species. *Costa Rica*

BIRDING IN THE AREA

Birding in Mexico, Central America, and the West Indies has been popular since the 1970s. Now, over most of this area, it is generally safe and is enjoyed year-round by thousands. Lately, drug-related violence in northern Mexico has captured headlines and probably made many Americans fearful of visiting this area, particularly the border region. But Baja California and central and southern Mexico are still heavily traveled, and only a very tiny percentage of tourists ever have bad experiences or become crime victims. Theft is a problem in some areas, for example, from cars at some traditional tourist attractions. But, with the same degree of caution that one would exercise in almost any major city or in unfamiliar surroundings, most of Mexico can be visited on one's own, without a guide. Local people are generally friendly, rental

Scarlet-rumped Cacique Caciques are rather large, mostly black members of the American oriole and blackbird family (Icteridae). The Scarlet-rumped inhabits lowland forests from Nicaragua to Peru, and builds a beautifully woven, pendant nest. *Panama*

cars are widely available, many of the roads are excellent and roadside scenery is often very appealing. Driving can be quite adventurous in places like Chiapas, where roads sometimes cling to the sides of mountains, rise above the clouds, and have no shoulders or guard rails, and where, amid the many hair-pin turns, accompanying traffic

often includes very slow-moving and also very fast-moving trucks and buses. In many regions of Mexico, and in some other places, such as the Dominican Republic, police seeking bribes from drivers can be a minor problem. Another annoyance, particularly in Mexico: roadside police and military checkpoints. In Chiapas, due to political problems, and anywhere in Mexico near the Guatemala or Belize borders, drivers must expect frequent stops for such checkpoints; documents may need to be produced and bags are sometimes searched for drugs.

Scarlet Ibis Few colors rival the intense red of these birds in flight. On the island of Trinidad they favor coastal mangrove swamps and are easily seen at the Caroni Swamp. Their range extends to northern South America. *Trinidad and Tobago*

The small countries of Central America vary dramatically in the comfort levels they offer to independent birders. Friendly Costa Rica can certainly be navigated on one's own, especially if one has at least a smattering of Spanish. And portions of Belize and Panama can be explored with a self-drive vehicle. But guided tours or, at least, accompanying local guides, would be good choices for most birders wanting to visit Guatemala, Honduras, El Salvador, or Nicaragua, and wander outside of standard tourist centers.

Birding in the West Indies is generally safe and easy, the greatest dangers being, first and foremost, the tropical sun, and then the usual, if usually minor, irritants of mosquitos, sand flies, chiggers, centipedes, and scorpions. The islands differ extensively in size and ease of getting around. On larger islands with cities and on many smaller, heavily touristed islands, car rentals are readily available. One annoyance with island hopping is that some islands here adhere to driving on the right side of the road, while others utilize the left—so an ability to adapt quickly is necessary. On some islands, where cars are not easily rented, and in Cuba, it will be useful to engage a local guide, perhaps with car and driver. As of this writing, most United States citizens still face legal difficulties traveling to Cuba. ■

BIRDS OF THE REGION SIGNIFICANT GROUPS

NEW WORLD QUAIL | POTOOS | HUMMINGBIRDS | TROGONS | TODIES | MOTMOTS | WRENS | MOCKINGBIRDS AND THRASHERS
GNATCATCHERS | VIREOS | OTHER SIGNIFICANT FAMILIES

Most of the significant families detailed here are shared with the neighboring United States. These include the New World quail, hummingbirds, trogons, wrens, mockingbirds and thrashers, gnatcatchers, vireos, and New World sparrows. Two of the remaining families are among the most interesting: the motmots, noteworthy in that there are more species in diminutive Central America than in the much larger South America, and the todies, whose five species are endemic to the West Indies.

■ New World Quail

New World quail are chicken-like birds of the Americas, included in order Galliformes with similar birds such as pheasants, partridges, grouse, and turkeys. The family, Odontophoridae, has 31 species, variously called quail, tree-quail, wood-quail, wood-partridges and bobwhites, and 20 of these occur within the coverage region of this chapter. Many are drably colored—various shades of brown and gray with black and white spots and streaks, colors and patterns that serve them well as camouflage in their on-the-ground lifestyles. But some—such as the Montezuma Quail and the Black-throated Bobwhite—have exquisitely marked faces and heads that are often topped with conspicuous crests. It is probably for these often perky crests, along with their reputations as important game birds, that this group is best known.

New World quail occur in diverse habitats, from forest and forest edge to savanna and open agricultural lands. Most species are gregarious, traveling in small family groups of up to 30 individuals; but some occasionally congregate in groups of a thousand or more. These are wary, elusive animals that blend well into their surroundings and, typically, a birder's first clue that they are in the area is their sudden, loud launch from almost underfoot. They are then so quick to find new cover that, more often than not, they disappear before binoculars can be focused on them—very frustrating birds indeed!

OPPOSITE: **Maroon-fronted Parrot** This species is endemic to northeastern Mexico; the world population has been estimated at only 2,000 birds. It frequents pine forests and nests colonially in cliff crevices. In the spring it often feeds on flowering agaves, as seen here. *Mexico*

Scaled Quail A desert-dwelling species common in northern Mexico and most U.S. borderlands. Seen in pairs or small groups (coveys) that run for cover when alarmed. *Mexico*

■ Potoos

Potoos are nocturnal, forest-dwelling birds that are distributed from Mexico south into Argentina, with three of the seven members of the family, Nyctibi-idae, occurring in the region treated in this chapter. These are medium-size birds (8 to 23 inches long), brown or gray-brown with black and white markings or mottling. In their usual upright posture, they are somewhat owl-like, and contributing to this impression is their large head, huge eyes, wide but short bill, and short legs. During the day, potoos such as the Northern Potoo (from Mexico, Central America, and the West Indies) and Common Potoo (from Central and South America) sit in trees, and with their camouflage coloring and their bills pointed into the air, they look remarkably like dead branches. At night, they hunt for large insects, small birds, liz-ards, and occasionally small mammals. Not often seen, potoos are known mainly by their mournful

vocalizations and, in fact identifying them to spe-cies is most usefully accomplished via their sounds. When potoos are seen by birders during daylight hours, it is typically only by chance that someone spots one sleeping in a tree—and then a positive identification is usually only made after several min-utes of going back and forth as to whether the object being studied through binoculars is definitely a bird or, indeed, an old, broken-off tree branch.

Common Potoo A potoo and chick day-roost in typical cryptic postures. Like owls, they call mostly at night, with a deep, stran-gled call, unnerving when first experienced. Common Potoos occur from Nicaragua to southern South America. *Costa Rica*

Hummingbirds

Most North Americans are familiar with hummingbirds. They are the smallest birds, easily one of the most recognizable, and undoubtedly among the most beautiful. They are capable of very rapid, acrobatic flight, more so than any other kind of bird, and the bones of their wings are modified to allow for perfect, stationary hovering flight and also for the unique ability to fly backward. Limited to the New World, the hummingbird family, Trochilidae, contains about 340 species. More than 120 of these occur within Mexico, Central America, and the Caribbean. The variety of forms encompassed by the family, not to mention the brilliant iridescence of most of its members, is indicated in the names attached to some of the different subgroups: in addition to ones called hummingbirds, there are emeralds, sapphires, sunangels, sunbeams, comets, metaltails, fairies, woodstars, woodnymphs, pufflegs, sabrewings, thorntails, thornbills, and lancebills. These small birds are usually gorgeously clad in iridescent metallic greens, reds, violets, and blues. Not all hummingbirds are vividly outfitted; one group, called hermits, is known for their relatively dull plumages. All hummingbirds get most of their nourishment from consuming flower nectar. They have long, thin bills and specialized tongues to lick nectar from long, thin flower tubes, which they do while hovering. Hummingbirds occupy a broad array of habitat types, from exposed high mountainsides at 13,000 feet to sea level tropical forests and mangrove swamps.

Birders often find hummingbirds in wild habitats but there's no denying that the sugar-water feeders many people place outside residences, hotels, and guesthouses are also prime spotting venues. Often, many species congregate at the same feeder, although not always amicably. It can be quite wondrous to sit quietly on a hotel's shady veranda in a place such as Monteverde, Costa Rica, and watch the area's myriad hummingbirds buzz about a feeding station. Especially striking are the species with very long bills or extremely elongated tails—the two species of streamertails endemic to Jamaica being good examples of the latter condition.

Snowcap The male is unmistakable with purple body and white crown. This small hummingbird is resident from eastern Honduras to Panama—and on many birders' wish lists. *Costa Rica*

Trogons

The colorful trogons are generally regarded by wildlife enthusiasts to be among the globe's most glamorous feathered animals and, among birders, to be among their favorite birds to see. The trogon family, Trogonidae, is distributed through tropical and subtropical regions of the Neotropics, Africa, and southern Asia. It consists of 40 species of medium-size (9 to 16 inches long) forest-dwellers with compact bodies, short necks, and chicken-like bills; 17 occur in the region covered here. The trogon plumage pattern is fairly uniform: Males have glittering green, blue, or violet heads and chests, with contrasting bright red, yellow, or orange underparts, while females are duller,

In spite of trogons' highly distinctive calls (for instance, trogon *cow-cow-cow* calls are one of the characteristic sounds of many New World tropical forests) and brilliant plumages, they can be difficult to locate and even to see clearly when spotted perched on a tree branch. This is because, like green parrots, partly green trogons easily meld into dark green overhead foliage. Trogon behavior is not much help because these birds usually perch for long periods with little moving or vocalizing. Trogons, therefore, are most often seen when flying. This often occurs in sudden bursts as they flip off the branches on which a moment before they sat motionless, and sally out in short undulating flights to snatch insects, their main food. Quetzals eat mainly fruit.

■ Todies

Todies are a small group of diminutive, active birds recognized mainly, it must be said, by globetrotting

Cuban Trogon This beautiful species with uniquely shaped tail feathers is a Cuban endemic and also the national bird. It is found in wet and dry forests at all altitudes. *Cuba*

usually with brown or gray heads. A striking physical characteristic of trogons is the tail, which is long and squared-off and usually has horizontal black and white stripes on the underside. One trogon stands out from the flock: the regal-looking Resplendent Quetzal. Famously described as "the most spectacular bird in the New World," this quetzal generally resembles other trogons, except that the male's emerald green head is topped by a ridged crest of green feathers and, truly ostentatiously, long green plumes extend up to two feet past the end of the male's typical trogon tail. It is the object of many conservation efforts in Central America and birders visiting the region often make strenuous efforts not to miss it.

Cuban Tody Although this species is endemic to Cuba, it is widely distributed there. Its nest consists of a short tunnel that it digs into an earthen embankment. *Cuba*

birdwatchers. Endemic to the West Indies, these tiny birds are appreciated for their bright colors, relatively confiding nature, and insect-catching ways. The five tody species (Cuba, Jamaica, and Puerto Rico each support a single species; Hispaniola has two) compose family Todidae, which is included in order Coraciiformes with the kingfishers and motmots. All todies look much alike—in fact, during most of the 19th century they were all thought to be single species (known as the Jamaican Tody). They are emerald green above, with ruby red throats and whitish underparts tinged with yellow or pink. All have relatively large heads, plump bodies, and short, stubby tails. Some individual todies are as small as 3.5 inches in length; the largest, Hispaniola's Broad-billed Tody, ranges up to 4.5 inches.

Todies are voracious insect-eaters. Like hummingbirds, their tiny size means they have fast metabolisms, and so must feed frequently to obtain enough energy; some have been known to eat up to 40 percent of their body weight in a day. Typically a tody sits quietly on a twig with its head cocked upward, alertly scanning the leaves above for insect prey. Most of the todies are widely distributed and common throughout their ranges. Spotting todies is usually not difficult and most birders who look for them in appropriate wooded habitats are successful. Given the presence of at least a small bit of screening vegetation, these small animals often let people approach them fairly closely.

◼ Motmots

Motmots, despite their funny name, are among the New World's most alluring birds, with bodies of blended shades of green and cinnamon, crisp black masks, and, in some, head patches of brilliant blue or turquoise. For lovers of wild birds, seeing some of the motmots, perhaps with sunlight glinting off their

bright turquoise-bejeweled crowns, can be a paramount experience. In addition to their beauty, motmots are known for their far-carrying, hooting calls (the *BOO-boop, BOO-boop* calls of the Blue-crowned Motmot probably gave the group its name), which are characteristic sounds of many Neotropical forests,

Blue-crowned Motmot The huge range of this species comes close to the Texas border with Mexico and extends to northern Argentina. About 20 subspecies have been described, and future taxonomic work may result in the "splitting" of this single species into four or five separate species. *Costa Rica*

and for their unusual-shaped tails. The motmot family, Momotidae, with ten species, is included in order Coraciiformes with the kingfishers and bee-eaters. Its distribution ranges from Mexico to northern Argentina and is unusual in that more of its members (eight species) occur in tiny Central America than in relatively huge South America (five species; some species occur in both regions). These small to medium-size birds (6.5 to 19 inches long) have fairly long, broad bills, down-curved at the end and serrated at the edges, the better to hold their animal prey. The most peculiar motmot feature, however, is the tail. It has two especially long central feathers that each have a section of barbless vane, below which each feather terminates with a racquet-like tip.

Motmots are mainly residents of forests and woodlands, but also occur in other, more open, habitats, such as orchards, tree-lined plantations, and suburban parks. In fact, typically one of the best and easiest places to see motmots, especially the gorgeous Turquoise-browed Motmot, is in and around the many park-like archaeological ruin sites that dot southern Mexico and Central America—even the heavily visited ones such as Chichén Itzá near Cancún. Motmots are predators on insects, spiders, small frogs, lizards, and snakes, which they snatch in the air, from leaves, and from the ground. They also eat small fruits, which they collect from trees while hovering. An unusual feature of motmot behavior is that usually they are active well into the twilight, going to sleep later than most other birds.

Wrens

Wrens are mostly small brownish songbirds with an active, snappish manner and characteristically upraised tails. They are recognized for a variety of traits: their vocal abilities (long, complex songs and duetting), breeding habits (for example, some are polygamous), capacity to live in association with people (the common House Wren, ranging from Canada to southern Chile, tends to forage around and nest in human-crafted structures), and geographic distribution. The 80 wren species, composing family Troglodytidae, are confined to the Western Hemisphere—all, that

Band-backed Wren Related to the Cactus Wren (of the U.S. Southwest and northern Mexico), this large, conspicuous wren ranges from eastern Mexico to northern Ecuador. *Costa Rica*

is, except the familiar Winter Wren, which, in addition to its wide range in North America, occurs over a broad swath from northern Africa through Eurasia. All in the family are generally called wrens except one marsh-inhabiting South and Central American species, previously believed to be part of the mockingbird family, called the Black-capped Donacobius. Forty-seven members of the wren family occur in this chapter's coverage area.

Many wrens are secretive and spotting them often depends on searching their habitats. The ones that live in dense habitats, such as rain forests, thickets, and marshes, can be very difficult to locate even after long periods of watching, but some that live in open areas, such as desert scrubs and grasslands, are easier to view.

Mockingbirds and Thrashers

Mockingbirds and thrashers are handsome, long-tailed songbirds best known for the striking ability some of them possess to imitate the calls and songs of other birds, and even sounds of other types of animals. The precise reason for the vocal mimicry is not known, but it probably relates to mate attraction: males with longer, more complex, and more varied songs may be more attractive to females. Some in the group are continuous singers, producing not the usual brief two- or three-second-long songs we associate with many common songbirds, but long strings of vocalizations—incredible, virtuoso singing performances. This family, Mimidae, distributed from southern Canada to southern South America, consists of 35 species of mockingbirds, thrashers, catbirds (named for their cat-like mewing vocalizations) and tremblers (named for their habit of drooping their wings and trembling); most are tropical and 24 species occur in the region covered in this chapter.

With their frequent, loud vocalizations and long tails, and in the open habitats they prefer, mockingbirds are often conspicuous—especially when singing

Gray Trembler Endemic to St. Lucia and Martinique, this bird is fairly common at all elevations. The closely related Brown Trembler occurs on more islands of the Lesser Antilles. *St. Lucia*

from, as many do, high song perches that stick out among other, lower, vegetation. They occur in scrub areas as well as forest edges and some forests; they are also common garden and park birds. Mockingbirds, catbirds, and many thrashers are mainly birds of the ground, shrubs, and low trees. They skulk about when not singing, foraging for insects and other small invertebrates, also taking some fruit and berries. The two trembler species, restricted to the West Indies, are more arboreal, using their long bills to toss and tear vegetation, looking for insects. Seeing some species in the mockingbird family can be easy, but others are quite good at hiding from observers; some of the thrashers, for instance, have reputations of being able to disappear quickly on their territories, apparently by running away.

Gnatcatchers

Gnatcatchers are small, slender songbirds that are typically spotted flitting about tree foliage. The 15 species, family Polioptilidae, include 3 called gnatwrens. All 15 are confined to the New World, where they range from extreme southern Canada to northern Argentina, and 9 are distributed within the region covered in this chapter. In the past, the gnatcatchers were usually included in the large family Sylviidae, the Old World warblers, but recent studies suggest they are not closely related to that group. Gnatcatchers and gnatwrens are known among birders as active, agile little birds that often constantly wave or twitch their tails, which are usually held at an upright angle.

Four to five inches long, gnatcatchers are mainly bluish gray, with long, narrow, black and white tails and, usually, some black on their heads. Gnatwrens, as indicated by their name, are more wren-like in appearance, being predominantly brown. All in the family have longish, slender bills, longer in gnatwrens. These

Long-billed Gnatwren This member of the gnatcatcher family occurs from southeastern Mexico to Brazil. Active and restless, gnatwrens frequent vine tangles and undergrowth. *Panama*

birds, chiefly arboreal, move quickly about forests, forest edges, woodlands, mangroves, and even some semi-open scrub areas. Most usually stay fairly high in trees, but gnatwrens prefer undergrowth regions of forests and woodlands. Some of the gnatcatchers are fairly easy to spot, but others, especially the ones that live in the dense undergrowth of tropical rain forests can, understandably, be difficult to see.

◾ Vireos

Vireos are mainly small, drably colored birds of New World forests and woodlands that flit about tree canopies looking for insects to eat. They are known for their persistent singing; in some areas, during early afternoon, for instance, vireos are often the only birds heard. Also, like other groups of small songbirds that contain multiple species that are confusingly similar in appearance and habits, vireos are notorious for presenting stiff challenges to birdwatchers trying

to identify them to species. The family, Vireonidae, has about 52 species broadly distributed through the New World; included, with distributions limited to Mexico through South America, are about 15 species known as greenlets, 4 shrike-vireos, and 2 peppershrikes One, the Red-eyed Vireo, has one of the widest nesting ranges of any bird species in the Western Hemisphere, from northern Canada southward to parts of Argentina. Thirty-six vireo species occur in the covered region.

Between four and seven inches long, vireos have short necks and stout legs. They can be separated into groups by their bills: typical vireos have medium-size bills slightly hooked at the tip; greenlets have pointed bills; shrike-vireos have stout bills with hooked tips; and peppershrikes have heavy bills flattened sideways with a large hook at the tip. Most vireos are plainly colored in green, olive, or gray-brown above, and yellow, grayish white, or buff below, and many have head stripes or eye-rings. Greenlets, small, warbler-like,

Green Shrike-Vireo This colorful vireo resembles a small tanager more than the drab vireos that are familiar to North American birders. It typically stays in the rain forest canopy, where it is difficult to spot. *Panama*

and sometimes difficult to identify to species even for experts, are mainly olive above, yellowish or grayish below. The shrike-vireos and peppershrikes, chiefly limited to tropical areas and the largest members of the family, are somewhat more colorful, usually with head patches of chestnut or blue. Vireos occur in forests, forest edges, woodlands, and, especially in the greenlets, in scrublands. They eat principally insects taken from tree leaves and branches, and occasional small fruits. They move over branches and twigs more slowly than similar birds such as wood-warblers. As for spotting vireos: Their diminutiveness, drab colors, and, for many, high-canopy-living, often lead to difficulties.

■ Other Significant Families

Several other bird families with significant presences in Mexico, Central America, and the West Indies also deserve mention. The first, a spectacular and well-known group needing no elaboration here, is the parrots, family Psittacidae, with more than 50 species in the covered region. Three other families with large numbers of representatives in the covered region don't require much explanation because American and Canadian birders are already intimately familiar with them—the wood-warblers, the tanagers, and the sparrows.

Of the 118 species of wood-warblers, also called New World warblers (family Parulidae), about 85 can be seen in Mexico, Central America, and/or the West Indies. While some of them are full-time residents of these areas, many are migrants that breed in North America north of the Rio Grande and winter in more southerly climes. For instance, about 50 warbler species are regularly or at least occasionally seen in the West Indies, most of them migrants just passing through the region.

Only six tanagers occur north of Mexico, and all but one of them have recently been placed in the family of cardinals and buntings—technically the United States is left with one tanager and Canada has none! The tanagers (family Thraupidae) are a much more numerous and diverse group in the Neotropics. Of the 226 species found in the world, about 57 occur in Mexico and Central America, with an additional 9 species endemic to the West Indies. Most of these species are called tanagers or have tanager in their hyphenated names, such as bush-tanager, thrush-tanager, or ant-tanager, but the tanager family also includes species called conebills, honeycreepers, and dacnises, among others.

Red-breasted Chat Formerly considered a wood-warbler but recently reclassified with cardinals and buntings, this beautiful species inhabits the thorn forests of western Mexico. *Mexico*

As for the sparrows, family Emberizidae, about 90 of the 330 species of the world are found in Mexico, Central America, and/or the West Indies. This group, in addition to more familiar-sounding ones like sparrows, towhees, and juncos, includes others such as seedeaters, seed-finches, grassquits, grass-finches, bullfinches, brush-finches, and flowerpiercers. Mexico is especially rich in sparrow diversity with 15 endemic species.

The composition of the northern Mexico avifauna starts changing right around the United States/Mexico border.

NORTHERN MEXICO
& BAJA REGION

I'T'S SAFE TO SAY THAT MEXICO IS PROBABLY *NOT* THE FIRST PLACE THAT LEAPS TO mind when you think of traveling internationally for birding or other wildlife watching. It's a huge country (one of the world's 15 largest) with a big population growing at a fast pace. There is widespread poverty and governmental neglect and corruption. There are also major environmental threats, chiefly destruction of natural habitats, and the country has had, until recently, a poor conservation record. But there are also some excellent reasons to place Mexico high on your list of birding priorities. The most significant, not generally recognized, is that Mexico actually possesses astounding biodiversity. It's home to fully 10 percent of the world's non-fish vertebrate animals (7 percent of amphibian species, 12 percent of reptiles, 11 percent of birds, 10 percent of mammals) and about 12 percent of all plant species. A main reason for Mexico's mega-diversity may be that the country straddles two major climate regions—the north temperate zone it shares with the United States and Canada, and the tropics it shares with Central America and northern South America—and so has animal groups common to both. In terms of zoogeographic regions, Mexico encompasses portions of both the Nearctic and Neotropical regions, and so has animals characteristic of both of these. Moreover, due to its varied topography, multitude of habitat types, and some highly isolated habitats that act as "biological islands," Mexico is a center of biological endemism—meaning that much of its biodiversity, including a good number of bird species, occurs nowhere else. Another positive aspect of birding Mexico is that it is fairly inexpensive to get there, especially when compared with trying to reach some other international birding destinations; traveling within the country, likewise, can be quite a bargain.

OPPOSITE: **Blue-footed (right) and Brown Boobies** The Gulf of California, also known as the Sea of Cortez, is rich with sea life and seabirds such as these two species of boobies. *Mexico*

Boat-billed Heron This Neotropical heron has plumage similar to the Black-crowned Night-Heron, but a look at its head reveals some major differences. The massive bill allows it to deal with large prey and its oversize eyes give it excellent night vision. Boat-bills live in mangrove swamps and freshwater lowlands from Mexico south to Peru, Brazil, and northeastern Argentina. *Mexico*

LOCAL BIRDING & CONSERVATION ORGANIZATIONS

■ **PRONATURA MEXICO**
(www.pronatura.org.mx)
an organization working to protect Mexico's fauna, flora, and ecosystems since 1981

■ **SOCIEDAD AUDUBON DE MEXICO**
(www.audubonmex.org)
Mexico's sole Audubon society, situated in San Miguel de Allende, a town in the mountains of central Mexico

■ **CIPAMEX**
(Society for the Study and Conservation of Birds in Mexico; www.ibiologia .unam.mx/cipamex/index .htm)
an organization that seeks to further the study and conservation of Mexican birds and their habitats

GEOGRAPHY AND HABITATS

Mexico is bordered on the north by the United States and on the south by Guatemala and Belize. This section focuses on the birds of northern Mexico and Baja California, with northern Mexico defined as mainland Mexico from the United States border south to the northern border of the state of Oaxaca and the center of the state of Veracruz. About 800 miles in length, Baja California is one of the longest peninsulas in the world and has about 2,000 miles of coastline. Most of Baja is dry, rough desert. There are high mountains in the north (Sierra de Juarez and Sierra de San Pedro Mártir), which rise as high as 10,150 feet, and also at the southern tip of the peninsula (Sierra Victoria rises to 6,600 feet).

The rest of northern Mexico can be divided into four regions: The northwestern region, in the rain shadows of various mountain ranges, is mostly desert, part of the Sonoran Desert that extends from across the border in the United States. In the northeastern region there is a coastal plain that runs between the Gulf of Mexico and one of the central mountain ranges, the Sierra Madre Oriental. The northern part of these lowlands is driest near the border with Texas but becomes steadily moister and greener farther south. Habitats here range from desert scrub in the north to deciduous woodland in the middle of the region, to tropical forests in the south. The central region of northern Mexico consists of the Central Highlands, a huge area of higher elevation terrain, including high mountains and a huge, dry, central plateau that includes part of the Chihuahuan Desert. The main mountain range here, running roughly north to south, is the Sierra Madre Occidental, essentially a continuation of the Rocky Mountains. Main habitats of the Central Highlands include desert, grassland, ranchland, and, in higher areas, oak and pine-oak woodland. A fourth region, the southwest, is smaller than the other three and lies between some southern mountain ranges and the Pacific Ocean. Here there is a dry, rocky coastline, dry deciduous forests along the coastal plain, pine-oak forests at mid-elevations, and cloud forests at higher altitudes.

BIRDLIFE

About 1,054 bird species occur regularly in Mexico, with 772 breeding there and the remainder spending only winters or passing through on their migrations. Approximately 88 percent of the total, or about 923 species, are found in northern Mexico, as defined above, and Baja. Of course, many "Mexican" species also occur in the United States, some breeding in both countries and some breeding to the north of the border and wintering to its south. A significant feature of the northern Mexico avifauna is that, relative to that in the United States and Canada, its composition starts changing

BIRDING THE RÍO CORONA

The Río Corona, located just over 100 miles south of Brownsville, Texas, in the Mexican state of Tamaulipas is where many lowland Neotropical birds reach the northern extent of their ranges. The evergreen forests that line this coastal plain river drainage are an easy two-hour drive south from the U.S. border. Much of this forest habitat is gone now, but it still exists in patches along this river and along some other nearby coastal rivers, and you can find birds here that never or perhaps only a few times have made their way into Texas. These include: Thicket Tinamou, Crane Hawk, Roadside Hawk, Yellow-headed Parrot, Blue-crowned Motmot, Lineated Woodpecker, Spot-breasted Wren, Blue Bunting, and Crimson-collared Grosbeak.

An interesting facet of bird biogeography here is that, in the last few decades, some species of birds native to tropical habitats along the Río Corona have extended their breeding distributions northward into or beyond the borders of south Texas, including Green Parakeet, Red-crowned Parrot, Tropical Kingbird, Clay-colored Robin, and Yellow-green Vireo. At the same time, several species from farther south in coastal Mexico, such as Olivaceous Woodcreeper, Mangrove Swallow, and Scrub Euphonia, have moved into the Río Corona area to breed. Although the introduction of captive birds may explain the sudden appearance in Texas of some of these species such as the parrots, the recent arrival of so many other tropical nesting species at a time when available habitat in south Texas is declining leads to an alternative explanation for these expansions of range: that they are in line with what would be expected from regional climatic warming and associated ecological changes. —D.P.

Blue Bunting This bunting is a relative of the familiar North American Indigo Bunting. This is a male; the female is a plain bird with warm brown plumage. *Mexico*

right around the United States/Mexico border. In this area, some temperate-zone species reach the southern extent of their distributions and some tropical species, at the northernmost extent of their ranges, start to appear. Members of this latter group, some of whose ranges extend slightly into the United States, include Laughing Falcon, Plain Chachalaca, Squirrel Cuckoo, Tropical Kingbird, Masked Tityra, Rose-throated Becard, and Tropical Parula. Then, several hundred miles farther south, for instance, in the San Blas area on Mexico's Pacific coast, between Mázatlan and Puerto Vallarta, representatives of some of the mainly Neotropical families begin making appearances, including some tinamous, motmots, and woodcreepers. Thus, a North American birder intent on experiencing some bird types more characteristic of Central or South America, but unwilling to travel far, can actually achieve his or her objective in central Mexico.

Other significant groups of northern Mexico, consequential by dint of the large numbers of species present relative to the total numbers of species in their respective families, include hummingbirds, with about 40 species occurring in northern Mexico; silky-flycatchers, with 2 species; wrens, with 23 species; mockingbirds and

Tufted Jay With a tiny range, this jay is listed as near threatened, but the inaccessibility of the canyons it inhabits has helped to protect it. *Mexico*

BIRDING THE MÁZATLAN-DURANGO HIGHWAY

Because Mázatlan is a popular tourist site on the Pacific coast of northwestern Mexico, it is relatively easy and inexpensive to travel and stay there. And if some of your family members are not interested in birding, then this city, filled with resorts, restaurants and plenty of family-friendly tourist activities, is especially perfect. During one late December vacation, my wife and I left the rest of our extended family on the beach, and spent the day birding the spectacular highway that climbs from the coastal thorn scrub near the town of Villa Union, just north of Mázatlan, high into the pine-oak woodlands of the Sierra Madre Occidental.

Lilac-crowned Parrot, Citroline Trogon, and Flammulated Flycatcher were on the lower reaches of the road. The real avian treasures were higher up in the pines near Barranca Rancho Libre. Huge flocks of White-naped Swifts circled overhead. Mixed-species flocks containing Gray-crowned Woodpecker, Spotted Wren, and Red-headed Tanager, and the highly endemic Tufted Jay moved around us. And we were very lucky to have flocks of Thick-billed Parrots streak across the canopy and occasionally land to feed on pinecones. All these birds were seen from roadside pulloffs and small side roads or paths that intersected the main highway. All in all, a great day's birding.

We noticed that there were a few small mountain hotels and restaurants along this road. By overnighting here, you could stay fairly close to Barranca Rancho Libre and skip the long mountain drive up and then back to Mázatlan. A couple of days spent exploring the avian-rich pine forests and enjoying the mountain scenery would yield many more species. —D.P.

Xantus's Hummingbird This attractive species is endemic to southern Baja California, where it is fairly common. It is a lowland species found in native arid scrublands, open woodland, and gardens. *Mexico*

FIELD GUIDE & SITE GUIDE BOOKS

■ *A Bird-Finding Guide to Mexico* (1999)
S.N.G. Howell
Cornell University Press

■ *A Guide to the Birds of Mexico and Northern Central America* (1995)
S.N.G. Howell and S. Webb
Oxford University Press

■ *A Field Guide to Mexican Birds* (1999)
R.T. Peterson and E.L. Chalif
Houghton Mifflin Harcourt

■ *Birds of Mexico and Central America* (2006)
B. van Perlo
Princeton University Press

■ *Where to Watch Birds in Central America, Mexico, and the Caribbean* (2002)
N. Wheatley and D. Brewer
Princeton University Press

thrashers, with 12 species; gnatcatchers, with 6 species; vireos, with 21 species; and sparrows, with about 60 species. Among northern Mexico's major habitats, its deserts and other scrub areas are perhaps most renowned. These arid zones, usually vegetated mainly with thorny bushes, cacti and small trees, support a characteristic avifauna that includes many widespread species of quail, hummingbirds, woodpeckers, thrashers, gnatcatchers, jays, and sparrows.

Although Mexican endemics found in northern Mexico occur in various localities, there are several concentrations. In the Central Highlands, such endemics as Long-tailed Wood-Partridge, Strickland's Woodpecker, Gray-barred Wren, Russet Nightingale-Thrush, Red Warbler, Black-polled Yellowthroat, and Striped and Sierra Madre Sparrows can be found. Another hot spot of endemism is southwestern Mexico, which harbors hummingbirds such as Mexican Hermit, Mexican Woodnymph, Short-crested Coquette, Blue-capped Hummingbird, and White-tailed Hummingbird, as well as White-throated Jay and Blue Seedeater. In addition, 19 species are restricted to Mexican islands, for instance, the Revillagigedo Islands, located in the Pacific Ocean 400 miles off western Mexico. Here there are several endemics, particularly on the largest island of Socorro, where live the Socorro Parakeet and Socorro Wren.

Significant Species
of Northern Mexico & Baja
83 FAMILIES FOUND IN THIS REGION

■ **CHACHALACAS, GUANS, AND CURASSOWS** (Cracidae), **5 species**

Rufous-bellied Chachalaca* *Ortalis wagleri*
striking species endemic to northwestern Mexico

■ **PARROTS** (Psittacidae), **13 species**

Military Macaw *Ara militaris*
huge green and blue parrot that is decreasing in the
wild due to deforestation and capture for the pet trade;
very loud and vocal, often heard before it is seen

Thick-billed Parrot* *Rhynchopsitta pachyrhyncha*
large uncommon parrot endemic to pine forests of
northwestern Mexico

Mexican Parrotlet* *Forpus cayanopygius*
tiny green and turquoise parrot often seen in small
flocks; endemic of northwestern Mexico

Red-crowned Parrot* *Amazona viridigenalis*
green parrot with reddish patches; endemic to
northeastern Mexico

■ **OWLS** (Strigidae), **22 species**

Cape Pygmy-Owl* *Glaucidium hoskinsii*
small owl endemic to the mountains of Baja California's
Cape Region

■ **HUMMINGBIRDS** (Trochilidae), **42 species**

Xantus's Hummingbird* *Hylocharis xantusii*
endemic to scrub areas of Baja California

Mexican Woodnymph* *Thalurania ridgwayi*
green hummingbird endemic to a small region
of western Mexico

Golden-crowned Emerald* *Chlorostilbon auriceps*
fork-tailed hummingbird endemic to western Mexico

Bumblebee Hummingbird* *Atthis heloisa*
tiny hummingbird endemic to highlands
of central Mexico

■ **TROGONS** (Trogonidae), **6 species**

Eared Quetzal* *Euptilotis neoxenus*
endemic to northwestern Mexico's pine forests; occasionally seen in the mountains of southeastern Arizona

Mountain Trogon *Trogon mexicanus*
trogon found in montane forests from northwestern
Mexico to Central America

■ **TYRANT FLYCATCHERS** (Tyrannidae), **47 species**

Tufted Flycatcher *Mitrephanes phaeocercus*
small cinnamon-colored flycatcher endemic to highland
regions from northern Mexico to Central America

Flammulated Flycatcher* *Deltarhynchus flammulatus*
endemic to arid thorn forests of western Mexico

■ **WRENS** (Troglodytidae), **24 species**

Spotted Wren* *Campylorhynchus gularis*
common wren endemic to northern and central Mexico

Happy Wren* *Thryothorus felix*
small wren endemic to western Mexico

■ **MOCKINGBIRDS AND THRASHERS** (Mimidae), **13 species**

Gray Thrasher* *Toxostoma cinereum*
skulking species endemic to arid areas of
Baja California

Blue Mockingbird *Melanotis caerulescens*
all slaty blue with black mask; endemic to Mexican
woodlands, pine forests, and scrub areas

■ **THRUSHES** (Turdidae), **21 species**

Brown-backed Solitaire *Myadestes occidentalis*
endemic to highland forests from northern Mexico
to northern Central America

Russet Nightingale-Thrush *Catharus occidentalis*
Mexican endemic of oak and pine-oak forests

Aztec Thrush *Ridgwayia pinicola*
black and white thrush endemic to mountain regions
of northern Mexico south to Oaxaca

■ **JAYS AND CROWS** (Corvidae), **20 species**

Black-throated Magpie-Jay* *Calocitta colliei*
long-tailed, crested jay endemic to northwestern
Mexico

San Blas Jay* *Cyanocorax sanblasianus*
striking black and blue jay endemic to western Mexico

Tufted Jay* *Cyanocorax dickeyi*
black, blue, and white jay with a bushy crest;
endemic to a small region of northwestern Mexico

Sinaloa Crow* *Corvus sinaloae*
small, glossy crow endemic to northwestern Mexico

■ **VIREOS** (Vireonidae), **21 species**

Golden Vireo *Vireo hypochryseus*
bright yellow and olive-green vireo; endemic to
western Mexico

■ **WOOD-WARBLERS** (Parulidae), **57 species**

Altamira Yellowthroat* *Geothlypis flavovelata*
endemic to a small region of northeastern Mexico

Belding's Yellowthroat* *Geothlypis beldingi*
endemic to the southern portion of Baja California

Black-polled Yellowthroat* *Geothlypis speciosa*
endemic to lakes and marshes over a small region
of central Mexico

Red Warbler *Ergaticus ruber*
small red bird endemic to highland areas of
western and central Mexico

Red-breasted Chat *Granatellus venustus*
endemic to western Mexico

■ **TANAGERS** (Thraupidae), **17 species**

Red-headed Tanager *Piranga erythrocephala*
endemic to western Mexico; the male is olive
and yellow with a red head

Rosy Thrush-Tanager* *Rhodinocichla rosea*
gray and pinkish bird that skulks through thorn
forests and arid woodlands in western Mexico

■ **NEW WORLD SPARROWS** (Emberizidae), **57 species**

Sierra Madre Sparrow* *Xenospiza baileyi*
small sparrow endemic to mountainous areas of
northwestern and central Mexico

Green-striped Brush-Finch* *Buarremon virenticeps*
greenish olive bird endemic to western and
central Mexico

■ **GROSBEAKS AND BUNTINGS** (Cardinalidae), **16 species**

Crimson-collared Grosbeak* *Rhodothraupis celaeno*
endemic to northeastern Mexico; the male is black
and pinkish red

Hooded Grosbeak *Coccothraustes abeillei*
handsome bird endemic to the highlands of
Mexico and Guatemala

Orange-breasted Bunting *Passerina leclancherii*
beautiful species with blue, green, and yellow plumage;
endemic to southwestern Mexico

■ **NEW WORLD BLACKBIRDS** (Icteridae), **24 species**

Yellow-winged Cacique *Cacicus melanicterus*
black-crested, black and yellow bird of western
and southern Mexico

*Restricted to Northern Mexico and Baja

Orange-breasted Bunting This common but beautiful west Mexican endemic is found in arid and semi-arid thorn forests, clearings, and even along roadsides. *Mexico*

Some Other Species Global Birders Often Seek

Blue-footed Booby *Sula nebouxii*
common booby of the Pacific coast, occurs from Mexico
to Peru

Bare-throated Tiger-Heron *Tigrisoma mexicanum*
large heron with a densely striped back and bare throat;
occurs from Mexico to Colombia

Elegant Quail* *Callipepla douglasii*
crested quail of brushy woodlands and fields; endemic
to northwestern Mexico

Boat-billed Heron *Cochlearius cochlearius*
striking heron with a huge bill; found from Mexico
to Argentina

Rufous-necked Wood-Rail *Aramides axillaris*
skulking mangrove-loving bird that occurs from Mexico
to Ecuador

Collared Plover *Charadrius collaris*
broadly distributed from Mexico to Argentina

Lesser Roadrunner *Geococcyx velox*
smaller than the Greater Roadrunner; endemic to
Mexico and Central America

White-naped Swift* *Streptoprocne semicollaris*
Mexico's only endemic swift; restricted to the
western region

Russet-crowned Motmot *Momotus mexicanus*
motmot with a reddish brown crown; limited to western
Mexico and Guatemala

White-striped Woodcreeper *Lepidocolaptes leucogaster,*
endemic to mountain woodlands of western Mexico

Sinaloa Martin *Progne sinaloae*
large swallow that breeds in northwestern Mexico

Gray Silky-flycatcher *Ptilogonys cinereus*
mainly gray and yellow bird endemic to mountain
forests of Mexico and Guatemala

Given the relatively small area represented by this region, the number of bird species found here is impressive.

Tropic of Cancer

Mexico

Caribbean Sea

CENTRAL AMERICA

Pacific Ocean

CENTRAL AMERICA
& SOUTHERN MEXICO

MANY BIRDERS FIRST CONFRONT NEOTROPICAL BIRDS IN THE CENTRAL American region. The diversity of types and species that one discovers upon exiting a jet in the southern reaches of Mexico or in one of the seven small countries that constitute Central America is, of course, quite exciting. But the quick appearance of so many different kinds of birds with which one is unfamiliar can be also a bit overwhelming. Taking a long walk along a rain forest trail in, say, Costa Rica's Caribbean region can yield sightings of, for instance, tinamous, guans, curassows, parrots, trogons, motmots, toucans, woodcreepers, antbirds, manakins, and cotingas—to name just a few kinds that most American birders will find highly novel. So one's initial exposure to this area can be challenging—but challenging in a way that most birders love.

The region discussed here ranges from the Mexican states of Oaxaca and Chiapas in the north to Panama in the south, and includes a host of popular and hugely rewarding birding sites. Most, but not all, of them are relatively inexpensive to reach and easy to explore. These include, but are certainly not limited to: in Oaxaca, the dry thorn-scrub areas and arid oak forests north and south of Oaxaca City, including the archaeological sites of Monte Albán, Mitla, Yagul, Lambityeco, and Dainzú; in Chiapas, the lowland Palenque National Park, the higher elevation San Cristóbal area, the Lagunas de Montebello National Park, and the El Triunfo Biosphere Reserve; in the Yucatán Peninsula (comprised of the Mexican states of Campeche, Yucatán, and Quintana Roo), mainly the readily reached Maya ruin sites such as Chicanná, Ek Balam, Chichén Itzá, Uxmal, Kabáh, and Cobá; in Belize, a number of sites including Lamanai, one of the country's most accessible ancient Maya sites, the Crooked Tree

OPPOSITE: **Monteverde Cloud Forest Reserve** This suspension bridge allows for eye-level views of birds and other wildlife. Monteverde is justifiably famous for its diverse birdlife—over 400 species, including the Resplendent Quetzal—and an incredible number of orchids. *Costa Rica*

Red-capped Manakin This photograph shows a male (right) displaying to a female in a sequence known as "moon walking." Most manakins—there are 57 species in this widespread Neotropical family—engage in spectacular lekking courtship displays. *Panama*

Wildlife Sanctuary, the Cockscomb Basin Wildlife (Jaguar) Sanctuary, and Ambergris Caye, a large offshore island; in northern Guatemala, the wonderful Tikal Maya ruins and national park; in Costa Rica, myriad areas including highland volcanic and cloud forest national parks not far from the country's capital, San José, Caribbean lowland areas such as Tortuguero National Park and the La Selva Biological Station, Pacific lowlands including Carara Biological Reserve and Manuel Antonio National Park, and the famous ecotourism site of Monteverde, an area of mid-elevation cloud forests in the north-central portion of the country; and in Panama, the treetop views from the Canopy Tower Ecolodge at Soberanía National Park near Panama City and the remote Cana Station in Darién National Park.

GEOGRAPHY AND HABITATS

Oaxaca and Chiapas are large southern Mexican states that border the Pacific Ocean. Both have some lowland portions, in their southern reaches that border the Pacific and in their north, bordering the states of Veracruz and Tabasco, but more than two-thirds of their combined area is ruggedly mountainous. These two states are among the most diverse in Mexico with respect to habitats, but from a birder's standpoint, it is their forests, especially those found at higher elevations, that are perhaps most important. Many endemic birds occur in the mountainside oak and pine forests here. Chiapas also contains an extensive region of tropical rain forest, part of the largest stand of virgin rain forest found north of the Amazon region. The Yucatán Peninsula is basically a large, flat, thumb-shaped limestone rock that projects northward from

Mexico's southern tip into the Caribbean Sea. The northern third of the peninsula, where Cancún and the city of Mérida are located, is quite flat and relatively dry, and much of the rest of it is hilly and scrubby, and wetter. Parts of the southern portion of the peninsula are heavily covered by tropical deciduous forest, especially in the area of the Calakmul Biosphere Reserve, which is contiguous with the forests of northern Guatemala. Central America itself—by our definition consisting of Guatemala, Belize, Honduras, El Salvador, Nicaragua, Costa Rica, and Panama—has a mountainous spine running more or less through its longitudinal center, with extensive highlands, above 6,000 feet in elevation, particularly in Guatemala and Costa Rica. Major habitat types in Central America include broadleaf rain forest, deciduous forest, coniferous forest at higher altitudes, and coastal mangrove forest.

BIRDLIFE

Southern Mexico and Central America are treated together in this section of the book because their birdlife is in many ways similar, with most of the same families represented in the two regions. The diversity is not as great as that found in nearby

BIRDING CERRO DE LA MUERTE, COSTA RICA AND SPOTTING THE RESPLENDENT QUETZAL

The Pan-American Highway in central Costa Rica runs along the Cordillera de Talamanca (the Talamanca Mountain Range), and it provides access to high-elevation alder forest and alpine habitats as well as to several of Costa Rica's endemic or near-endemic bird species, such as Fiery-throated Hummingbird, Timberline Wren, Silvery-throated Jay, Flame-throated Warbler, Wrenthrush, Peg-billed Finch, and Volcano Junco.

On my first stay at a basic hotel along the highway near the crest of a mountain named for death—Cerro de La Muerte (literally, "death hill")—all these range-restricted bird species were, from my point of view, only icing on the cake.

My paramount goal in coming here was to have an opportunity to experience one of the high points of global birding: spotting the Resplendent Quetzal in the wild. I could not care less that it wasn't a Costa Rican endemic. For me there was no other bird worth looking at that day. I could find no fruiting trees where it might be feeding, and I didn't know of any nest sites. So I started walking down the paved highway, and after several hours I reached some big stands of alder. As I stared down the empty road, about to give in to my hunger pangs and return to the hotel, a huge green blob of feathers with a long streamer tail that undulated in waves darted across my field of vision at canopy height. I rushed the hundred yards or so down the road to where it had crossed, and there it sat, out in the open, on a large branch next to the road—my first and forever my most memorable male Resplendent Quetzal. —D.P.

Resplendent Quetzal Gaudiest of the trogon family (Trogonidae) and Guatemala's national bird, the male's streamers are elongated upper tail coverts, not tail feathers. *Costa Rica*

South America but, given the relatively small area represented, the number of species found here is impressive. For example, the Yucatán Peninsula boasts about 470 species, and the numbers in each of Central America's small countries can appear somewhat staggering—very small Belize has about 550 species; Costa Rica, about 840; tiny El Salvador, about 500; Guatemala, about 690; Honduras, about 690; Nicaragua, about 650, and Panama, about 900. This high diversity certainly attracts birders wishing to add appreciably to their life lists. There is now a thriving industry of domestic and international bird tour operators and eco-lodges here (especially in Belize, Costa Rica, and Panama) that seek to expose birders to maximum numbers of species. Intensive two- or three-week birding trips that visit varied habitats in, say, Costa Rica, can result in the spotting of more than 300 species and, for truly determined birders willing to give up a lot of sleep, more than 400.

The high avian species numbers in southern Mexico and Central America are related to the fact that most of the Neotropical bird families are represented (Central America lacks only a few Neotropical families restricted to South America, such as rheas, screamers, and trumpeters), as are a few mainly Nearctic families that reach the

Dwarf Jay Three other small jays in the genus *Cyanolyca* live in Mexico: Azure-hooded, Black-throated, and White-throated. All prefer humid montane forests, yet their ranges barely overlap. *Mexico*

SPOTTING THE DWARF JAY

Endemic to a small portion of the high altitude and humid pine-oak forests of southern Mexico, the Dwarf Jay is a reasonably reliable sighting only in the mountains above the city of Oaxaca. After having failed to see this species two days in a row, I rose at dawn to see a heavy blanket of fog settling in on the forested peaks where it occurs. Desperation overcame logic, and I decided to drive back up the mountain to find a bird elusive even in good weather. When I arrived at the gravel road that led along the mountain crest through the best habitat, the clouds were skimming the tops of the tall pine trees, but it was not raining and the fog was not obscuring my vision in the lower parts of the trees. I quickly found Amethyst-throated Hummingbird, Mountain Trogon, Strong-billed Woodcreeper, Tufted Flycatcher, Red Warbler, Collared Towhee, and Rufous-capped Brush-Finch,

but once again, no sign of the Dwarf Jay. Then, off in the distance, I heard the loud babbling of a mixed flock of Gray-barred Wrens and Steller's Jays. Dwarf Jays are very quiet but often travel with these other, noisier, species. I walked quickly down the road toward the cacophony of the flock, and there, among the other species, were six silent Dwarf Jays actively but surreptitiously feeding in the upper levels of the pine trees.

Why do they follow or associate with these other species? Mixed-species feeding flocks are a common phenomenon in both temperate and tropical forests. The two best guesses to explain this behavior are food is more easily found when a whole group searches for it and, with more eyes looking around, predators have a more difficult time getting near the flock to grab an individual bird. —D.P.

Great Curassow The cracids (family Cracidae) include 50 species of guans, chachalacas, and curassows restricted to the Neotropics. This male Great Curassow was photographed at the El Cielo Biosphere Reserve, an excellent birding area in the state of Tamaulipas. *Mexico*

FIELD GUIDE & SITE GUIDE BOOKS

◼ *A Bird-finding Guide to Costa Rica* (2009)
B. Lawson
Cornell University Press

◼ *A Bird-finding Guide to Panama* (2008)
G.R. Angehr, D. Engleman, and L. Engleman.
Comstock

◼ *Birds of Belize* (2004)
H.L. Jones
University of Texas Press

◼ *The Birds of Costa Rica: A Field Guide* (2007)
R. Garrigues and R. Dean.
Cornell University Press

◼ *A Field Guide to the Birds of Costa Rica* (1989)
F.G. Stiles and A.F. Skutch
Cornell University Press

◼ *A Guide to the Birds of Mexico and Northern Central America* (1995)
S.N.G. Howell and S. Webb
Oxford University Press

◼ *A Guide to the Birds of Panama* (1989)
R.S. Ridgely and J.A. Gwynne, Jr.
Princeton University Press

southern extent of their distribution here (including turkeys and silky-flycatchers). About 90 bird families occur in the area. Among the significant ones, in terms of species numbers, are the herons and egrets, hawks, falcons, parrots, hummingbirds, trogons, motmots, woodcreepers, and tanagers. Some other groups stand out, and provide great birding pleasure, simply because they are somewhat more diverse here than they are in North America. The kingfishers come to mind: Many American birders spend most of their birding lives seeing only the one kingfisher that ranges over most of the United States, the Belted Kingfisher. But being initially exposed to the four or five other kingfishers that occur in Central America can be a great, somehow liberating, experience. The birdlife of the region covered here slowly changes from its northernmost to southernmost extent. In Oaxaca and Chiapas, many of the bird families characteristic of the United States and Canada are still represented, but these are increasingly eliminated as one moves southward into Central America. And at the southern end of Central America, a few mainly South American groups—barbets, tapaculos—penetrate northward, but only as far as Panama and Costa Rica. Birds endemic to southern Mexico and Central America are concentrated in a few areas. In the Mexican portion of this region they occur in good numbers especially in the southern highlands of Oaxaca and Chiapas (more than 40 endemics in the pine-oak forests here, for example) and on the Yucatán Peninusula, which has more than 20 endemics. Cozumel Island, just off Cancún, has a number of endemics including the unimaginatively named Cozumel Emerald, Cozumel Vireo, Cozumel Wren, and Cozumel Thrasher. Of the Central American nations, only two have substantial numbers of endemics: Costa Rica has six and Panama, ten.

Significant Species
of Central America & Southern Mexico

90 FAMILIES FOUND IN THIS REGION

◼ TINAMOUS (Tinamidae), 6 species

Great Tinamou *Tinamus major*
Central America's largest tinamou

Slaty-breasted Tinamou* *Crypturellus boucardi*
endemic to southern Mexico and Central America

◼ GUANS, CHACHALACAS, AND CURASSOWS (Cracidae), 8 species

Horned Guan* *Oreophasis derbianus*
endemic to cloud forests of Chiapas and Guatemala;
endangered

Great Curassow *Crax rubra*
large, crested bird; difficult to see

◼ TURKEYS (Meleagrididae), 1 species

Ocellated Turkey* *Meleagris ocellata*
one of the globe's two turkeys; endemic to the Yucatán
Peninsula region

◼ PARROTS (Psittacidae), 30 species

Scarlet Macaw *Ara macao*
red, blue and yellow, one of the world's most striking
parrots

Red-fronted Parrotlet* *Touit costaricensis*
very small, colorful parrot endemic to Costa Rica
and Panama

Yellow-headed Parrot *Amazona oratrix*
medium-size green parrot with yellow head;
endangered

◼ HUMMINGBIRDS (Trochilidae), 101 species

Violet Sabrewing* *Campylopterus hemileucurus*
larger, purplish hummingbird with downcurved bill;
found in southern Mexico and Central America

Fiery-throated Hummingbird* *Panterpe insignis*
small hummer with a difficult-to-see reddish throat;
found only in the mountains of Costa Rica and Panama,
where it is common

Mexican Sheartail* *Doricha eliza*
tiny hummer, male with deeply forked tail; southern
Mexican endemic

Volcano Hummingbird* *Selasphorus flammula*
endemic to the high mountains of Costa Rica and
Chiriqui, Panama

◼ TROGONS AND QUETZALS (Trogonidae), 15 species

Violaceous Trogon *Trogon violaceus*
typical, yellow-bellied trogon

Resplendent Quetzal *Pharomachrus mocinno*
most spectacular trogon, the adult male has a metallic green
tail with streamers longer than his body

◼ MOTMOTS (Momotidae), 8 species

Tody Motmot *Hylomanes momotula*
small and chunky, the littlest motmot

Turquoise-browed Motmot* *Eumomota superciliosa*
most striking motmot; endemic to southern Mexico
and Central America

◼ TOUCANS (Ramphastidae), 6 species

Fiery-billed Aracari* *Pteroglossus frantzii*
medium-size toucan with red upper bill; endemic to
Costa Rica and Panama

Keel-billed Toucan *Ramphastos sulfuratus*
large toucan with an amazingly colorful bill

◼ SAPAYOA (Sapayaoidae), single-species family, 1 species

Broad-billed Sapayoa *Sapayoa aenigma*
fairly rare, olive-colored bird of Panama and northern
South America

◼ OVENBIRDS AND WOODCREEPERS (Furnariidae), 40 species

Beautiful Treerunner* *Margarornis bellulus*
mostly brown bird endemic to small region of Panama

Brown-billed Scythebill *Campylorhamphus pusillus*
woodcreeper with a long, strongly down-curved bill

◼ TYPICAL ANTBIRDS (Thamnophilidae), 30 species

Black-hooded Antshrike* *Thamnophilus bridgesi*
small blackish bird with white speckling; endemic to
Costa Rica and Panama

Immaculate Antbird *Mymeciza immaculata*
small dark bird with blue skin around its eye

◼ COTINGAS (Cotingidae), 10 species

Snowy Cotinga* *Carpodectes nitidus*
male is a striking all-white bird with a black bill;
endemic to Central America

Three-wattled Bellbird* *Procnias tricarunculatus*
male is brown with a white head and has three worm-like hanging wattles; endemic to Central America

Bare-necked Umbrellabird* *Cephalopterus glabricollis*
large black bird with a distinctive crest; endemic to Costa Rica and Panama

■ MANAKINS (Pipridae), **12 species**

Long-tailed Manakin* *Chiroxiphia linearis*
small and showy, the male with long tail streamers

Orange-collared Manakin* *Manacus aurantiacus,*
small, with a broad orange collar; endemic to Costa Rica and Panama

■ TYRANT FLYCATCHERS (Tyrannidae), **about 115 species**

Golden-crowned Spadebill *Platyrinchus coronatus*
tiny, with a greenish back and golden crown

Fork-tailed Flycatcher *Tyrannus savana*
very long-tailed flycatcher; broadly distributed

■ SILKY-FLYCATCHERS (Ptilogonatidae), **3 species**

Long-tailed Silky-flycatcher* *Ptilogonys caudatus*
gray and yellow, crested; endemic to Costa Rica and Panama

■ WRENS (Troglodytidae), **about 40 species**

Boucard's Wren *Campylorhynchus jocusus*
large streaked wren endemic to southwestern Mexico, mainly Oaxaca

Timberline Wren* *Thryorchilus browni*
small wren endemic to mountains of Costa Rica and Panama

■ MOCKINGBIRDS AND THRASHERS (Mimidae), **9 species**

Black Catbird* *Melanoptila glabrirostris*
all-black; endemic to Yucatán Peninsula region

Blue-and-white Mockingbird* *Melanotis hypoleucus*
bluish above, white below; endemic to Chiapas and northern Central America

Ocellated Thrasher *Toxostoma ocellatum*
spotted breast; endemic to central and southern Mexico

■ THRUSHES (Turdidae), **26 species**

Slate-colored Solitaire *Myadestes unicolor*
cloud forests of southern Mexico and northern Central America

■ CROWS, JAYS, AND MAGPIES (Corvidae), **15 species**

Dwarf Jay* *Cyanolyca nana*
blue species with pale blue throat; endemic to pine-oak forests of Oaxaca region

White-throated Magpie-Jay *Calocitta formosa*
gorgeous blue-and-white, long-tailed jay

■ VIREOS (Vireonidae), **24 species**

Chestnut-sided Shrike-Vireo *Vireolanius melitophrys*
large, very handsome vireo of mountain areas

■ NEW WORLD WARBLERS (Parulidae), **about 70 species**

Flame-throated Warbler* *Parula guttutalis*
gray, white, and red; endemic to Costa Rica and Panama

Wrenthrush* *Zeledonia coronata*
short-tailed, dark; endemic to Costa Rica and Panama

■ TANAGERS AND RELATIVES (Thraupidae), **about 60 species**

Spangle-cheeked Tanager* *Tangara dowii*
colorful tanager of mountain forests; endemic to Costa Rica and Panama

Viridian Dacnis *Dacnis viguieri*
striking tanager, male is bluish green and black; endemic to Panama and Colombia

■ SPARROWS, BUNTINGS, AND RELATIVES (Emberizidae), **about 60 species**

Peg-billed Finch* *Acanthidops bairdii*
uncommon finch of higher altitudes; endemic to Costa Rica and Panama

Volcano Junco* *Junco vulcani*
grayish olive sparrow of higher elevations; endemic to Costa Rica and Panama

Some Other Species Global Birders Often Seek

Bare-throated Tiger-Heron *Tigrisoma mexicanum*
mid-size, heavily barred heron

King Vulture *Sarcoramphus papa*
uncommon whitish vulture

Black Hawk-Eagle *Spizaetus tyrannus*
raptor with bushy crest and black and white barred legs

Sungrebe *Heliornis fulica*
small, grebe-like; from south Mexico to South America.

Sunbittern *Eurypyga helias*
chicken-size bird found in rivers, streams, and swamps; occurs from Guatemala to South America.

Black-crowned Antpitta *Pittasoma michleri*
small, striking ground bird; from Costa Rica to Colombia

Bananaquit *Coereba flaveola*
widely distributed; sole species of family Coerebidae

Restricted to Central America and Southern Mexico

For birders attempting to see at least one species representing each of the globe's 200 or so bird families, a trip to the West Indies is required.

THE WEST INDIES

TWO MAIN KINDS OF BIRDERS VISIT THE WEST INDIES. THE FIRST, EASILY THE MORE numerous, is comprised of people, many of them casual birders, whose primary mission to the islands is a relaxing vacation. They bring along their binoculars to spot birds that are readily viewable in hotel gardens, at recreational seashores, and in easily reached parks and nature reserves. The second type consists of serious birders, many of whom have already traveled to such high avian diversity locations as South America and Asia, where they sought to add many hundreds, if not thousands, of species to their life lists. Now, in the Caribbean, by island-hopping and covering a lot of ground, they seek not huge species numbers but, instead, glimpses of the many regional and island endemics. The degree of endemism here is fairly high, with many birds restricted to single islands or single archipelagos. So, the main attraction to birders of the West Indies is the potential there to see many birds that have highly restricted ranges. The chance to view such species triggers behavior that in many quarters would be considered odd: that of paying good money to fly or boat to an isolated island for the sheer chance of seeing a few birds that live there and nowhere else. There's a definite element of challenge involved: Many of the region's island endemics are becoming increasingly rare, so locating and getting a good look at them is often no easy task. Aside from its good numbers of restricted-range species, the West Indian avifauna is also distinctive in that it encompasses a few bird groups found nowhere else.

GEOGRAPHY AND HABITATS

Travel destination islands in the West Indies range from the very large, such as Cuba and Hispaniola, to the very small, like Antigua and Dominica. The region is often

OPPOSITE: **Little Tobago Island** The island topography of the Caribbean is varied—from low-lying keys (or cays) to volcanic islands with high mountains. At 10,164 feet, Pico Duarte in the Dominican Republic is the highest peak in the region. *Trinidad and Tobago*

Ruby-topaz Hummingbird
This gem-like, short-billed hummingbird is common on the island of Trinidad and occurs on other islands off the coast of Venezuela. It also has an extensive South American range. The female lacks the red crown and orange gorget. *Trinidad and Tobago*

separated into four parts. The first is the Greater Antilles, which encompasses the four large islands of Cuba, Jamaica, Hispaniola (containing Haiti and the Dominican Republic) and Puerto Rico, as well as the much smaller Cayman Islands south of Cuba, and the Virgin Islands (such as St. Thomas and St. Croix) east of Puerto Rico. Second is the Bahamas group and the Turks and Caicos Islands, which lay just north of the Greater Antilles and are situated somewhat more in the Atlantic Ocean than in the Caribbean. The third is the Lesser Antilles, comprising a semicircle of small islands that runs in a roughly north-to-south axis starting from a point east of Puerto Rico and the Virgin Islands (at the island of Anguilla) and terminating near the Caribbean coast of Venezuela (at the island of Grenada). Also often considered to belong to the Lesser Antilles are Aruba, Curaçao, and Bonaire, which are located just off the coast of Venezuela. Likewise, Trinidad and Tobago, also off Venezuela, are sometimes grouped into the Lesser Antilles. The fourth part of the West Indies is the islands of the southwestern Caribbean, which lay east of Nicaragua and include Swan Island, Providencia, and San Andrés. Most of the West Indies are in the tropics, but the northern islands of the Bahamas project into the subtropics.

Major habitat types in the region include densely vegetated rain forest that, at high elevations, is often covered by low clouds and so is called cloud forest. The very highest rain forests on wetter mountains have stunted vegetation and are called elfin or dwarf forests. Dry forests, usually more open than rain forests, are found in regions where rainfall over the year is less. Savanna habitat is now found on most islands, some of it caused by people who altered the natural habitats for agriculture and other development. Dry regions of islands are often covered with thorny woodlands with low trees or open cactus scrub. Mangroves are widespread in coastal areas. Other West Indian habitats include beaches, rocky coasts, ponds, marshes, freshwater swamps, lagoons, and streams.

BIRDLIFE

About 450 bird species occur in the West Indies, some authorities citing more, some less, depending on how many seabirds of the surrounding waters, and how many species that are seen only irregularly, are included in the total. About 160 occur only in the Caribbean, with 108 of them being endemic to particular islands or archipelagos and the rest being more broadly distributed in the region. The West Indies are considered part of the Neotropical animal realm but the birdlife here includes elements of the Nearctic as well—especially the small Neotropical migrants such as

SPOTTING THE PUERTO RICAN PARROT

The Puerto Rican Parrot is the only native parrot species on the island of Puerto Rico. It was listed as an endangered species in 1967. As of March 2006 there were a total of about 200 parrots, counting both captive and wild individuals. The wild population is now found only at the Caribbean National Forest in the Luquillo Mountains and is declining. Recent surveys show there are now fewer than 30 wild birds.

In 1990 my wife and I decided to look for as many endemic species on Puerto Rico as we could find. After a week of driving from one end of the island to the other, the only one of the endemics we were still missing was the parrot. We had driven up to the parking area of the Luquillo Mountains to await their usual flyover in the morning, and again at midday and in the evening, all to no avail. Finally on the day before our flight home to Arizona, we remained at the parking area so late into the early evening that we could barely see. But then, in the brief dusk of the tropics, we first heard and then saw two Puerto Rican Parrots come screeching by and then disappear into the distance about 20 seconds later. We considered the sighting a great success.

Unfortunately, despite valiant efforts of captive breeding and reintroduction into the wild, the habitat for this rare parrot may be so reduced that it can no longer adequately support the species. Sad to say, but future global birders may not have the same chance we did to spot this beautiful bird. —D.P.

Puerto Rican Parrot Many native parrots of the West Indies are in decline, while on many islands, the introduced species are thriving. *Captive, Puerto Rico*

wood-warblers, some of which breed in the United States and Canada but winter in the Caribbean or stop off there on their way farther south. Some species are very abundant and distributed essentially throughout the region—the Common Ground-Dove, Gray Kingbird, and Bananaquit being prime examples. Others are rare and endemic to single small islands. Some of these latter birds are now critically endangered, including the region's three largest parrots—Dominica's Imperial Parrot, St. Lucia's St. Lucia Parrot, and St. Vincent's St. Vincent Parrot.

For those rare birders attempting to see at least one species representing each of the globe's 200 or so bird families, a trip to the West Indies is required. Two families are endemic. The first is Todidae, containing the five tody species. The other is Dulidae, containing only the Palmchat, which is an arboreal, medium-size brown and streaked songbird that is related to waxwings. This species is endemic to Hispaniola and is the national bird of the Dominican Republic.

Landbird families that are particularly well represented in the West Indies include parrots, hummingbirds, thrushes, and New World sparrows. As mentioned at the beginning of this chapter, the world's four species of lizard-cuckoos are confined to

White-winged Warbler This heavy-billed wood-warbler, endemic to Hispaniola, is found in the Dominican Republic's Cordillera Central and Sierra de Bahoruco but rarely in Haiti. *Dominican Republic*

BIRDING THE SIERRA DE BAHORUCO, DOMINICAN REPUBLIC

My favorite birding site in all of the Caribbean is in the mountains of the Dominican Republic up against the Haitian border. At 28 species, there are more endemic birds on Hispaniola than any other island in the West Indies, including the Palmchat, a bird in a family (Dulidae) all by itself, and two species of todies, members of the Caribbean family (Todidae). Of these endemics, all but two can be reliably found on the Sierra de Bahoruco. In this beautiful and wild mountain range, endemic bird species occupy habitats ranging from the deciduous scrub, palm, and mesquite habitats in the arid lowlands up through the moist broadleaf and pine forests at 5,000 feet, where fog and clouds often move in by afternoon.

We rented an all-wheel-drive vehicle and before dawn drove to the town of Puerto Escondido at the north base of the mountains. The steep road up quickly changed from gravel to sand and finally to little more than a rocky streambed. I feared for the vehicle's health, but every birding stop along the way was exciting. In March the bushes, shrubs, and tree foliage were full of wintering North American warblers and thrushes in full breeding plumage and ready to fly northward. At dawn we were above a remote Dominican Republic/Haiti border guard station when the high-altitude resident species began to appear: White-fronted Quail-Dove, Hispaniolan Trogon, Rufous-throated Solitaire, Golden Swallow, Red-legged Thrush, La Selle Thrush, White-winged Warbler, Black-crowned Palm-Tanager, and Antillean Euphonia. In the highest pine forests were nesting Pine Warblers and the Hispaniolan Crossbill. It took three separate days to locate all the endemics possible, and our last endemic find was the rare Bay-breasted Cuckoo. —D.P.

Jamaica This birding group, lead by the late Robert Sutton (second from right), is taking in the avian sights at the east end of Jamaica. The island is home to 28 endemic bird species. Robert Sutton and his wife Ann have written extensively about Jamaica's unique birdlife and championed its conservation. *Jamaica*

the West Indies, part of this region's complement of ten cuckoos. Other groups of particular interest in the region are the only two species of tremblers, members of the mockingbird/thrasher family that are restricted to the Lesser Antilles, and the only four species of spindalis (formerly called striped-headed tanagers), which occur in the Greater Antilles, the Bahamas, and, in the case of one species, also in Cozumel. The region also boasts a multitude of tropical seabirds, with such striking ones as boobies, frigatebirds, tropicbirds, and a number of tern species.

Due to their relatively large number of species, their endemics, and/or for their relatively easy accessibility, birders tend to visit the following islands: In the Greater Antilles they go to Cuba (with about 350 species, 24 of them endemic to the island and many others endemic to the West Indies), Jamaica (265 species, 28 endemic), Dominican Republic (245 species, 28 endemic), Puerto Rico (250 species, 13 endemic) and the Cayman Islands (180 species, 0 endemic). In the Lesser Antilles they gravitate to Guadeloupe (190 species, 1 endemic), Dominica (170 species, 2 endemic), Martinique (187 species, 1 endemic) and St. Lucia (160 species, 3 endemic), and many also visit the Bahamas (320 species, 2 endemic).

FIELD GUIDE & SITE GUIDE BOOKS

■ *A Field Guide to the Birds of the West Indies* (1993)
J. Bond
Houghton Mifflin Harcourt

■ *Birds of Cuba* (2000)
O.H. Garrido and
A. Kirkconnell.
Christopher Helm

■ *Birds of the Dominican Republic and Haiti* (2006)
S. Latta et al.
Princeton University Press

■ *A Guide to the Birds of Puerto Rico and the Virgin Islands* (1989)
H.J. Raffaele
Princeton University Press

■ *Birds of the West Indies* (2003)
H.J. Raffaele et al.
Princeton University Press

■ *Where to Watch Birds in Central America, Mexico, and the Caribbean* (2002)
N. Wheatley and D. Brewer.
Princeton University Press

Significant Species of the West Indies

ABOUT 70 FAMILIES FOUND IN THIS REGION

■ **PIGEONS AND DOVES** (Columbidae), **20 species**

Blue-headed Quail-Dove* *Starnoenas cyanocephala*
rare light-blue-headed dove; endemic to Cuba

Plain Pigeon* *Patagioenas inornata*
plain-looking gray-brown pigeon; endemic to
the Greater Antilles

Ring-tailed Pigeon* *Patagioenas caribaea*
large pigeon with a black-banded tail; endemic
to Jamaica

■ **PARROTS** (Psittacidae), **22 species**

Cuban Parakeet* *Aratinga euops*
green parrot often with scattered red head feathers;
endemic to Cuba

Black-billed Parrot* *Amazona agilis*
green parrot with a blackish bill; endemic to Jamaica

Hispaniolan Parrot* *Amazona ventralis*
maroon-bellied parrot endemic to Hispaniola and
nearby islands

Imperial Parrot* *Amazona imperialis*
region's largest parrot; endangered and endemic to
the island of Dominica

■ **CUCKOOS** (Cuculidae), **10 species**

Great Lizard-Cuckoo* *Coccyzus merlini*
largest species of lizard-cuckoo; endemic to Cuba
and the Bahamas

Puerto Rican Lizard-Cuckoo* *Coccyzus vieilloti*
large cuckoo endemic to Puerto Rico

Bay-breasted Cuckoo* *Coccyzus rufigularis*
shy cuckoo endemic to Hispaniola, but nearly extirpated
from Haiti

■ **HUMMINGBIRDS** (Trochilidae), **17 species**

Red-billed Streamertail* *Trochilus polytmus*
endemic to Jamaica, where this striking, long-tailed
hummer is common

Blue-headed Hummingbird* *Cyanophaia bicolor*
endemic to Dominica and Martinique; the male is
a striking violet-blue and green

Bahama Woodstar* *Calliphlox evelynae*
colorful hummingbird endemic to the Bahamas

Bee Hummingbird* *Mellisuga helenae*
smallest living bird, about the size of a large bee
and weighing less that 0.1 ounce; endemic to Cuba

■ **TODIES*** (Todidae), **5 species**

Narrow-billed Tody* *Todus angustirostris*
endemic to Hispaniola, where it is threatened in Haiti
but still common in the Dominican Republic

Jamaican Tody* *Todus todus*
occurs only on Jamaica; like other todies, nests in a burrow
excavated in a steep bank or rotten tree trunk

■ **WOODPECKERS** (Picidae), **12 species**

Antillean Piculet* *Nesoctites micromegas*
endemic to Hispaniola, the Caribbean's smallest woodpecker; found from sea level to montane pine forest

Fernadina's Flicker* *Colaptes fernandinae*
restricted to Cuba, where it is the largest woodpecker

Jamaican Woodpecker* *Melanerpes radiolatus*
common Jamaican endemic

■ **TYRANT FLYCATCHERS** (Tyrannidae), **23 species**

Giant Kingbird* *Tyrannus cubensis*
large flycatcher endemic to Cuba

Sad Flycatcher* *Myiarchus barbirostris*
very small flycatcher endemic to Jamaica

Jamaican Becard* *Pachyramphus niger*
all-black species restricted to Jamaica

■ **PALMCHAT*** (Dulidae), **1 species**

Palmchat* *Dulus dominicus*
conspicuous bird from Hispaniola, brown above, streaked
below, about eight inches long

■ **MOCKINGBIRDS AND THRASHERS** (Mimidae), **9 species**

Bahama Mockingbird* *Mimus gundlachii*
brown and white mockingbird, from the Bahamas and
Jamaica and occasionally seen in the Florida Keys

White-breasted Thrasher* *Ramphocinclus brachyurus*
occurs only on St. Lucia and Martinique

Brown Trembler* *Cinclocerthia ruficauda*
confined to the Lesser Antilles; typically "trembles"
a bit as it forages on the ground

■ **THRUSHES** (Turdidae), **13 species**

Forest Thrush* *Cichlherminia lherminieri*
uncommon and shy bird restricted to the Lesser Antilles

Cuban Solitaire* *Myadestes elisabeth*
plain-looking bird common in Cuba

Red-legged Thrush* *Turdus plumbeus*
found mainly in the Bahamas and Greater Antilles

La Selle Thrush* *Turdus swalesi*
endangered thrush from Hispaniola

■ **VIREOS** (Vireonidae), **12 species**

Thick-billed Vireo* *Vireo crassirostris*
occurs in a few areas of the West Indies, but especially
in the Bahamas

Puerto Rican Vireo* *Vireo latimeri*
Puerto Rican endemic found in all kinds of forest

■ **WOOD-WARBLERS** (Parulidae), **about 50 species, including
many migrants from North America.**

Plumbeous Warbler* *Dendroica plumbea*
gray and white warbler found on Guadeloupe
and Dominica

Arrow-headed Warbler* *Dendroica pharetra*
streaky black and white warbler limited to Jamaica

Elfin-woods Warbler* *Dendroica angelae*
uncommon Puerto Rican endemic discovered in 1971

Some Other Species Global Birders Often Seek

West Indian Whistling-Duck* *Dendrocygna arborea*
endangered duck species mainly occurring in the
Bahamas and Greater Antilles

Gundlach's Hawk* *Accipiter gundlachi*
rare hawk of Cuba's forests

Zapata Rail* *Cyanolimnas cerverai*
very secretive rail endemic to Cuba's Zapata Swamp

Northern Potoo *Nyctibius jamaicensis*
nocturnal bird found on Jamaica and Hispaniola

Hispaniolan Trogon* *Priotelus roseigaster*
endemic to Hispaniola's mountain forests

Golden Swallow* *Tachycineta euchrysea*
iridescent bluish-green swallow found only in Jamaica
and Hispaniola

Zapata Wren* *Ferminia cerverai*
famous Cuban singer; endemic to Cuba's Zapata Swamp

Cuban Palm Crow* *Corvus minutus*
large Cuban crow, one of five crow species endemic to
the West Indies

Bananaquit *Coereba flaveola*
very common small songbird of the West Indies and
Central and South America, and the sole member of
its family, Coerebidae

Hispaniolan Crossbill* *Loxia megaplaga*
crossbill endemic to the mountains of Hispaniola

Antillean Euphonia* *Euphonia musica*
beautiful little yellow and bluish or greenish bird from
Hispaniola, Puerto Rico, and the Lesser Antilles

Hispaniolan Spindalis* *Spindalis dominicensis*
stikingly marked tanager limited to Hispaniola

Zapata Sparrow* *Torreornis inexpectata*
olive-gray and yellow sparrow found only over small
parts of Cuba

Greater Antillean Bullfinch* *Loxigilla violacea*
small blackish bird with red markings, found in the
Bahamas, Hispaniola, and Jamaica

Yellow-shouldered Blackbird* *Agelaius xanthomus*
blackbird with yellow shoulder patches from Puerto Rico

St. Lucia Oriole* *Icterus laudabilis*
black and orange-yellow oriole restricted to St. Lucia
in the Lesser Antilles

Restricted to the West Indies

Palmchat Endemic to the island of Hispaniola, the Palmchat
is the sole member of the family Dulidae. It occurs so broadly
that it has been designated the national bird of the Dominican
Republic. These noisy, gregarious birds are conspicuous and
widespread throughout the island, nesting especially in the
crowns of palm trees. *Dominican Republic*

CHAPTER 4

SOUTH AMERICA
& ANTARCTICA

C a r i b b e a n   S e a

A T L A N T I C

O C E A N

Mangrove Finch
Isabela Island
page 126

Giant Antpitta
town of Nanegalito
page 118

Venezuela

Colombia

Guyana

Suriname

French Guiana
(France)

Equator

Nanegalito

Ecuador

*Galápagos
Islands*

Charles Mockingbird
Champion and Gardener Islands
page 125

A N D E S

Brazil

Peru

White-cheeked Cotinga
Santa Eulalia Valley, high above Lima
page 117

Lima

Bolivia

Paraguay

Tropic of Capricorn

Rufous-throated Dipper
mountains above Tucumán
page 133

Tucumán

Pelligrini

Uruguay

Yellow Cardinal
near the town of Pelligrini
page 134

P A C I F I C

O C E A N

A
r
g
e
n
t
i
n
a

C
h
i
l
e

A
N
D
E
S

*Falkland
Islands*

miles
0   500   1000

0   500   1000

kilometers

*South Georgia
Island*

King Penguin Breeding Colo
South Georgia Island
page 142

*ANTARCTIC
PENINSULA*

Penguins and Leopard Seals
Antarctic Peninsula
page 141

Antarctic Circle

Some of the Earth's most unusual and beautiful birds call this region home, and many are endemic here.

BIRDING IN

SOUTH AMERICA & ANTARCTICA

T HE GREATEST CONCENTRATION OF BIRD SPECIES OCCURS IN SOUTH America. The numbers, for a birder, are rather astounding. About a third of all bird species (more than 3,100 of 9,930) are to be found here, and there are a good number of countries, some of them fairly small, that each sport more than a thousand species. Amazingly, several—Colombia, Peru, Ecuador, Brazil—have more than 1,500! Remember, the entire United States and Canada combined have less than half this many.

The reasons for South America's embarrassment of avian riches have to do with its largely tropical setting, addressed in Chapter 2, and its great variety of habitats, each with its own characteristic avifauna. The vast expanse of Amazon rain forest, which covers about a third of the continent, probably contains more bird species on and above a given plot of ground (up to 300 species per square kilometer!) than any of the globe's other habitat types. This certainly contributes significantly to South America's great bird diversity. But, surprisingly to many birders, it is not just the lush lowland forests that have lots of birds. The Andes Mountains, which stretch more than 4,000 miles from north to south in the western portion of the continent, also contribute substantially. There, high-elevation habitats are separated from each other in places by deep valleys, and many of the highland spots (essentially "biological islands") have developed their own unique set of species. Along with many mid-elevation species that differ on the Andes' eastern and western slopes, these add greatly to South America's overall species totals.

PREVIOUS PAGES: **Serra dos Orgaos National Park** This park, located about a one-hour drive from the city of Rio de Janeiro, was created in 1939 to protect the watershed and native forest. The rock formation in the center is known as Dedo de Deus (God's Finger). *Brazil*

Whatever the explanation for the high bird diversity, it is not unusual for a persistent journeyman birder on a two- to three-week trip to see between 400 and 500 species. This suggests that for any and all global birders wishing to expand their life lists significantly, South America will be written into their travel plans probably sooner than later. For a birder, the "bird continent," as it has been called, is not to be missed.

Of course, it is not just species numbers that powerfully attract birders to South America—it is also the birds themselves. Some of the Earth's most unusual and beautiful birds call this region home, and many are endemic here. To mention a few of the curious endemic families one can experience on a trip to this region: The rheas (family Rheidae) are two species of flightless Ostrich-like birds, one of which—bizarrely—is typically found above 11,000 feet in the Andes. The screamers (Anhimidae) are three species of large, long-legged marsh birds related to the ducks that possess very loud calls. The Hoatzin (Opisthocomidae), a large, crested bird related to cranes, lives in small groups in trees near water, and eats only leaves; most observers conclude that it must resemble the flying reptiles that mingled with the terrestrial dinosaurs. The gnateaters (Conopophagidae) consist of eight species of small, short-tailed, understory forest birds that, even to this day, remain poorly known. Nonendemic groups with spectacular members here include the parrots (many beautiful species culminating with the huge, endangered, cobalt blue Hyacinth Macaw), trogons, and toucans. Especially spectacular are the cotingas. These include such standouts as the western Amazon's turquoise blue Plum-throated Cotinga, the northern Andes' crested, bright orange Andean Cock-of-the-rock, and northern South America's Bearded Bellbird, which somewhat creepily has a chin full of hanging, stringy wattles.

Ivory-billed Aracari The aracaris are medium-size members of the toucan family with yellow underparts often crossed with bands of red and black. Nine species of aracari occur in northern South America. *Ecuador*

NORTHERN SOUTH AMERICA

Northern South America (defined here as essentially the northern half of the continent) claims the first four spots on the list of the world's most bird-diverse countries (see table 1, p. 35): Peru, Colombia, Brazil, and Ecuador. Birdwatching locations over this vast area are, of course, many and varied. There are now hosts of commercial and nonprofit nature, ecotourism, and birding operations designed to assist North Americans and others in reaching remote and not-so-remote natural areas and observing wildlife, particularly birds. Among the most renowned is Peru's Manú National Park. This vast wilderness reserve (more than 3.7 million acres) contains tremendous biodiversity and is famed among birders for the list of more than 1,000 bird species spotted within its boundaries. The explanation for this huge total is that the park encloses three main ecological zones: Andes highlands, middle elevations of the Andes' eastern slope, and portions of the Amazon lowlands. Each has a largely different and diverse avifauna. Reaching prime birding spots at Manú requires above-average time and effort, often one- or two-day motorized boat trips to remote eco-lodges. Gung-ho "listers" and the more adventurous will always savor such trips, but northern South America also offers great birding for those with less time and ambition. A great example is the easily reached Bellavista Cloud Forest Reserve located in Ecuador's Mindo region, just a two-hour drive from the country's capital, Quito. Here, amid the splendid waterfalls and trails mainly in the area's cloud forests, more than 400 birds have been observed. Local eco-lodges provide accommodation, guides, and delightful hummingbird feeders that attract up to 20 species that you can ogle close-up. When I visited, wondrous birds such as Toucan Barbet and Plate-billed Mountain-Toucan were easy to see; indeed, a small group of these large, colorful toucans swept past me at eye level, landing low in trees only a few yards away—a truly thrilling experience.

GALÁPAGOS ISLANDS

Ecuador's Galápagos Islands, a set of small islands located on the Equator about 600 miles west of the mainland, need little introduction. They gained fame as the site of Charles Darwin's wildlife observations and collecting that contributed to his formulating the theory of evolution by natural selection. Now a popular destination for ecotourists, the Galápagos are also a magnet for birders wishing to see not only the celebrated finches that propelled Darwin in his thinking ("Darwin's Finches") but also such unusual endemics as the Galapagos Penguin, the world's northernmost penguin, and the aptly named Flightless Cormorant.

SOUTHERN SOUTH AMERICA

For this book's purposes, southern South America refers to the continent's "southern cone" region, which is occupied mainly by Argentina and Chile but also by Uruguay,

Paraguay, and parts of southern Brazil and southern Bolivia. There are wonderful birding sites here, which are typically visited less heavily than the more celebrated birding destinations in the northern half of the continent. In southwestern Brazil (and spilling over into adjacent portions of Bolivia and Paraguay) lies the Pantanal, one of the world's largest freshwater wetland areas. It must be considered one of the Western Hemisphere's prime locations for wildlife viewing. During the dry season, water in flooded areas recedes, leaving large patches of grassy savanna, and water-associated wildlife retreats and concentrates in remaining marshes, lakes, and waterways. Both of those processes greatly facilitate wildlife-watching. Another special place is northern Argentina's Iguazu National Park, a UNESCO World Heritage site where, amid shady subtropical forest and broad, raging waterfalls (Iguazu Falls), more than 400 bird species live. This is a park where you can have, as I did, such avian adventures as watching a Toco Toucan, the largest of the toucans, probe leaf clusters of a tree with its humongous orange bill, extract from the leaves a large black tarantula, smack the spider a few times, and then swallow it. One birding caution for this region: If you have trouble differentiating many of North America's relatively few

Torres del Paine National Park The steep granite spires of this park in southern Chile draw photographers and rock climbers from around the world. Birders can look for 15 bird of prey species, including Andean Condor, and see other sought-after species such as Chilean Flamingo, Lesser Rhea, and Magellanic Woodpecker. *Chile*

flycatchers (as most of us do), be forewarned that of Argentina's approximately 1,000 bird species, more than 12 percent are flycatchers.

ANTARCTICA

Antarctica, the most forbidding and environmentally extreme continent, is nonetheless a definite destination for some intrepid, well-off wildlife-watchers, especially birders. But bird sightings there are very specialized, mainly limited to penguins and such other seabirds as albatrosses and petrels. Of course, some birders and other nature lovers look forward their entire lives to the moment they can experience for themselves the look and feel of an Antarctic breeding colony of Emperor Penguins—an experience unavailable anywhere else. Tours of coastal portions of the Antarctic mainland or to offshore islands are conducted generally on specially strengthened cruise ships or on large, powerful ships called icebreakers (often former Soviet Arctic research vessels converted for this profitable "second calling"). Tours generally depart from the southern tip of South America or from New Zealand, but before you start packing, you should know that the total cost of such two-weeks-plus trips can approach the size of the down payment on a small house.

Andean Cock-of-the-rock
This fabulous species, a member of the cotinga family, is highly sought after by visiting birders. It is found at mid-elevations in the Andes from Colombia to Bolivia. A closely related species, the Guianan Cock-of-the-rock, lives in humid forests from eastern Colombia to northern Brazil. *Peru*

TRAVELING IN THE REGION

Birdwatching in northern South America means traveling to places like Venezuela, Peru, or Brazil and probably moving through Amazonian rain forest or other tropical forest habitat. You can rent cars, take buses, and even trains by yourself, especially if you speak at least elementary Spanish (or, for Brazil, Portuguese). But for most birders, joining an organized tour, either one run by an international birding or nature tour company or one organized in destination countries, is going to be the safer, more comfortable way. If you dislike being with a group, need no assistance with bird identification, and disdain organized tours, consider contacting a local tour company and arranging for a car and driver. In many areas of South America, you will find the cost of such services on par with those of rental cars. It is less hassle than dealing with rental companies and is much more relaxing to have a local person familiar with the region

doing the driving. For the adventurous, independent-minded birder, Argentina and Chile can certainly be visited on one's own, without guides and tour groups.

Before departing main tourist areas in South America, it is smart to make reservations at eco-lodges or hotels at or near the parks or reserves you are going to explore, so you have definite destinations and secure overnight accommodations. Many eco-lodges offer packages that include room, board, and guides, as well as transportation to the lodge. They may pick you up at the nearest airport and transport you first by road in a bus and then by river in a motorized dugout canoe. Visits to the Amazon region often involve river boat trips, with the boat acting as the eco-lodge, providing room, board, and guides. Journeying to the Galápagos, likewise, generally centers on all-inclusive boat trips.

Birding by local people in many areas of South America is becoming more common. This stems in part from exposure to the frequent visits of global birders over the past 40 years, who are working on their life lists and wandering far and wide with their binoculars. But also at work is the increase in college education in South America. Students are taking biology, ornithology, and conservation courses, and some go on to graduate study in the biological sciences. It is not unusual to discover local college students with great interest in birds and birding who spend time as nature guides at South American ecotourism operations and eco-lodges.

Most countries of South America are safe for North American birders to visit. The big exception is Colombia, where a decades-long guerilla war, narcotics-related violence, and rising street crime, not to mention frequent kidnappings, conspire to make birding a potentially dangerous enterprise. Few birders take a chance, even though the pull of visiting the country with the globe's second longest bird list is powerful. Venezuela, adjacent to Colombia, also has a four-digit bird list and is a good alternative for many, even though its government is now stridently anti-U.S., and violent crime and kidnappings have been on the upswing. Remnants of the Shining Path guerrilla group still bedevil Peru occasionally, but the outbreaks of violence are typically far from usual tourism and birding centers. Even usually friendly Ecuador can be dangerous near its border with Colombia, and Argentina goes through periods of anti-U.S. feeling. However, excepting Colombia, most international birding experts would agree that you can bird most regions of South America while staying safe and having a great time.

Antarctica is in a class by itself as a birding location. The costs, logistics, and legal and safety considerations involved in visiting the region dictate that everyone join an organized tour. ■

OPPOSITE: **Chinstrap Penguin** This medium-size species and the similar-size Adelie Penguin are the most common penguins breeding on the Antarctic Peninsula. Chipstraps breed in large colonies and favor rough, boulder-strewn locations. *Antarctic Peninsula*

BIRDS OF
THE REGION SIGNIFICANT GROUPS

TINAMOUS | PENGUINS | SCREAMERS | TRUMPETERS | JACAMARS | PUFFBIRDS | OVENBIRDS AND WOODCREEPERS | ANTBIRDS | TAPACULOS | COTINGAS | MANAKINS | OTHER SIGNIFICANT FAMILIES

The significant South American families described here can be grouped into three kinds. The first is larger birds seen mainly on the ground, including the tinamous, screamers, and trumpeters. The second group is composed of two families of distinctive, arboreal insect-eaters that belong to the same nonpasserine order—the jacamars and puffbirds. The final group consists of several families of perching birds, some generally more dully plumaged, and two, the cotingas and manakins, that are often riotously bright and colorful.

▨ Tinamous

Tinamous are secretive chicken-like birds occasionally stumbled across as they walk along or cross roads or forest trails. They occur from central Mexico south to southern Argentina and Chile and are best known for their songs—loud, pure-tone, melodious whistles. These vocalizations are some of the most characteristic sounds of Neotropical forests and are often heard on the soundtracks of movies with rain forest settings. There are about 45 tinamou species, and the family Tinamidae is thought to be ancient and probably most closely related to more primitive birds like the rheas and Ostrich. These birds are 6 to 18 inches long, chunky bodied, with fairly long necks, small heads, and slender bills. They have short legs and tails. Males and females look alike.

Compared to most other bird families, our knowledge of tinamous is relatively scant, probably because studying them is difficult. Some inhabit very remote areas, such as the Amazon forests or the high Andes, and their habitats are usually densely vegetated and often marshy. They are also stealthy and superbly camouflaged, appearing in understated browns, grays, and olives and often marked with dark spots or bars.

Tinamous inhabit a variety of environments including grasslands and thickets, but most commonly they are forest denizens. Except during breeding, they lead a solitary existence. They are among the most

OPPOSITE: **Andean Condor** Ranging the length of the continent, this magnificent vulture is an icon of South America. It is a mountain bird in the north, but from Peru southward can also be seen at sea level. Adults and near-adults (right) have extensive white on the upper wings and a white neck ruff. *Peru*

Spotted Nothura The Spotted Nothura is one of the most common tinamous, inhabiting rather open, lowland areas from Brazil to Argentina, where it is often hunted. *Brazil*

terrestrial of birds, foraging, breeding, and usually sleeping on the ground. Very poor flyers, they take flight only when alarmed by predators or surprised, and then only for short distances. Their main form of locomotion is running along the ground. Tinamous' diet consists chiefly of fruit and seeds, but they also take insects such as caterpillars, beetles, ants, and occasionally small vertebrates such as mice. Some South American species dig to feed on roots and termites. Tinamous avoid being eaten themselves primarily by staying still, easily blending with surrounding vegetation, and walking slowly and cautiously. Outside of protected areas, tinamous are still hunted extensively for food. Although seeing tinamous in the wild is difficult, they respond to playback of their vocalizations by approaching loudspeakers, and some birders spot tinamous using this technique.

■ Penguins

Penguins (family Spheniscidae) are iconic birds of the Southern Hemisphere oceans. Although they are instantly recognizable on land, their stocky, streamlined bodies and flightlessness are evolutionary adaptations to their highly specialized life underwater.

Powerfully propelled by their modified wings that resemble flippers, they are supreme divers. The largest species, the Emperor Penguin, about three feet tall, is known to have reached depths of almost 1,500 feet and stayed underwater for up to 11 minutes in pursuit of prey (fish and marine invertebrates); smaller species regularly descend to depths of over 150 feet. Penguins come to land (or ice) only to breed, but this is a protracted affair that goes on for many months with the male and female swapping nest duty. One tends the egg or newly hatched chick while the other is at sea feeding; the chick is fed on regurgitated food from the returning parent.

Rockhopper Penguin The Rockhopper is aptly named; notice its strong legs and feet with sharp claws that enable it to scramble up steep rock faces to reach its breeding colonies. This is the smallest of the six species known as crested penguins. *Falkland Islands*

Penguins are most abundant in Antarctica and around subantarctic islands, where they exploit the rich feeding conditions of the cold waters, but the 17 species have a wide distribution that also reaches from Australia to southern Africa and South America. The northernmost species, the Galapagos Penguin, occurs on the Equator. During the austral summer, a stop at South Georgia Island to observe the massive King Penguin breeding colony of over 300,000 birds is an unforgettable birding spectacle. Penguin identification at sea can be challenging, but on land, where most birders observe them, penguins' species-specific markings usually render them easily recognizable. Even though their plumage is mostly monochromatic, the patterns of the face and the colors of the bill, and in some species, a bright yellow crest, differentiate them.

■ Screamers

Screamers are very large, stocky birds that look like plump blackish geese on the ground, but can resemble eagles when flying. The three species belong to the uniquely South American family Anhimidae, which is closely related to the duck family. They range in length from 30 to 37 inches, weigh up to 11 pounds, and have smallish chicken-like heads with crests.

The Northern Screamer is limited to northern Colombia and Venezuela, but the Horned and Southern Screamers have broad South American distributions. Screamers are essentially waterbirds, but they spend much of their time out of lakes and marshes, feeding in other open habitats such as meadows and flooded savanna. They graze mainly on aquatic vegetation, consuming roots, leaves, flowers, and seeds. Surprisingly for large waterbirds, they often perch in treetops to give their very loud calls, which may be repeated for long periods. Screamers are strong fliers and frequently soar to great heights. Because of their

Horned Screamer The "horn" referred to in its name is a modified feather that grows from its forehead; also note the long, sharp spur at the bend of the wing, a feature of all three species of screamer. *Peru*

large size and occupation of generally open habitats, two of the screamers are fairly easy to locate. In fact, they are sometimes seen feeding among grazing domestic animals, in, for example, southern Brazil. Only the Northern Screamer is difficult to spot, given its limited range in Colombia and Venezuela in an area that relatively few birders visit, and its general rarity.

■ Trumpeters

Trumpeters are chicken-size terrestrial birds that inhabit dense tropical forests. The family Psophiidae is related to cranes and has three species, which are

Gray-winged Trumpeter Of the three species of trumpeter, the Gray-winged has the most northerly range. The typical hunched posture of all the trumpeters gives them a distinctive silhouette. *Peru*

flights into trees to escape danger and to roost at night. Trumpeters are almost always in groups of several to 15 individuals. Where they are hunted, they are very shy and are rarely seen in their rain forest habitats. However, they still maintain healthy populations in regions of undisturbed forest. In some regions trumpeters are kept as pets by local people, and are often spotted running around villages, bullying domestic chickens and sometimes acting like guard dogs.

■ Jacamars

Jacamars are slender birds with very long, fine bills used to catch insects in flight. Their plumage varies among species from fairly drab to brightly colored and iridescent. Most are sufficiently brilliant, with glittering green and blue backs and heads, that the group is considered one of the flashiest in the Neotropics. Their overall appearance—shimmering plumage, long, delicate bills, and often seemingly excited

Rufous-tailed Jacamar Of the 18 species of jacamars (family Galbulidae), the Rufous-tailed has the most extensive range, occurring from Mexico to northern Argentina. It is a common bird in many lowland areas. *Brazil*

restricted to northern and central South America. They are 18 to 20 inches long and have a generally humpbacked appearance. They also have short bills, fairly long necks, and longish legs. The sexes look alike. True to their name, trumpeters have in their vocal repertoires loud deep calls that sometimes sound like a trumpet.

Trumpeters feed by walking along the forest floor, looking for fallen fruits and scratching with their feet to stir up insects. Their flying is generally limited to

demeanor—causes many first-time observers to wonder if they might be oversize hummingbirds. But the 18 jacamar species in the family Galbulidae are not even close relatives of hummingbirds, being most closely related to puffbirds (see below). Jacamars, which occur from southern Mexico to southern Brazil, range from 5.5 to 13 inches long. Male and female usually differ slightly in color pattern.

Typically forest-dwellers, many jacamars are frequently seen along small forest streams and at clearings. They perch on tree limbs, alertly snapping their heads back and forth, scanning for meals. Spotting a flying insect, they dart out suddenly to grab it in mid-air with the tip of the sharp bill. They often return to the same perch, beat the insect against the perch a few times, and then swallow it. After a jacamar grabs an insect such as a large butterfly, the long bill may aid in tightly grasping the insect's body while it attempts to escape and in holding wasps and other stinging insects at safe distances from vulnerable anatomy. Other common diet items are beetles, bees, and dragonflies. Birders often have no problem spotting jacamars because these birds tend to perch in open areas in forest-edge habitats. Although they often sit for periods without moving much (except for their heads), they also make frequent aerial feeding sallies that attract attention.

■ Puffbirds

Puffbirds, like their close relatives the jacamars, are arboreal birds of Neotropical forests that make a living catching insects. There the resemblance ends, because puffbirds differ from jacamars in general form, brightness of coloration, main feeding method, and even in general demeanor. Jacamars are slender with long, fine, mostly straight bills; puffbirds are stocky with thick, heavy, hooked bills. Jacamars are often colorful and glossy; puffbirds are covered in subdued browns, grays,

black, and white. Jacamars snatch insects from the air; puffbirds take a lot of their prey off leaves, branches, and from the ground. Jacamars have alert, convivial personalities; puffbirds are seemingly dull, often sitting quietly and still on tree branches for long periods, sometimes even allowing people to approach very closely before fleeing. The sedate dullness of these birds led many early observers to consider them stupid. They are not dumb, of course; their slow ways are related to

White-whiskered Puffbird The puffbird's heavy bill allows it to subdue rather large prey items, such as this frog. As far as is known, puffbirds are tunnel nesters, excavating a nest hole in an earthen bank or termite mound. *Ecuador*

their foraging methods. The 35 species in the puffbird family Bucconidae are distributed from southern Mexico to northern Argentina, with most occurring in the Amazon region. Many are fairly small, but they range from 5 to 11.5 inches in length. They have distinctively large heads and loose plumage that, when fluffed out, produces a chubby, puffy appearance.

Most puffbirds hunt by perching quietly on tree limbs, waiting patiently to spot a large insect, spider, or small frog, lizard, or snake on a nearby tree trunk or on the ground. The puffbird swoops from its perch and seizes the luckless prey in its bill. The bird then returns to a perch, beats the prey on the perch to stun it, and finally swallows it. Some puffbirds will also dart out suddenly to snatch flying insects in midair. Some species are quite social, occurring in groups of up to ten, which are often discovered perched together in a row on a branch or utility wire. Not all are quiet: Black-fronted Nunbirds, for example, often sit together in family groups on a branch high in a tree and sing their loud, raucous songs for minutes at a time. Like jacamars, many puffbirds spend much of their time perched in the open in forest-edge habitats such as streamsides, roadsides, and forest clearings and, therefore, are often readily spotted by birders.

■ Ovenbirds and Woodcreepers

Ovenbirds are a paradoxical Neotropical group. They are quite numerous, and diverse in many ways, but with a few significant exceptions, they are largely unknown in the regions in which they occur. They are mainly insect-eating brown birds that live and forage on or near the ground. Adding to their inconspicuousness are their drab, often cryptic plumages, their unobtrusive, usually stealthy behavior, and their typically unmelodic, undistinguished vocalizations. Although nondescript, ovenbirds are widely recognized by naturalists for their ecological diversity, for instance, their varied foraging behavior, their occupation of essentially all terrestrial habitats of South America, and especially their nests. These nests, which vary in architecture and construction

Montane Woodcreeper This species is fairly common in humid montane forest at mid-elevation in the Andes from Colombia to Bolivia, but it will take a close look to separate it from other very similar-looking woodcreepers. *Ecuador*

materials, can be quite impressive, particularly the mud/clay and straw Dutch-oven-like nests that provide the group's common name. Because of its large "oven" nests, often placed on structures such as fence posts and utility poles, the plain-looking Rufous Hornero is very familiar to local people over a broad swath of South America.

Ranging from four to ten inches long, most ovenbirds have short, rounded wings, long tails, and strong legs and feet. The sexes within a species look alike. The ovenbird family Furnariidae has about 240 species, distributed from southern Mexico to southern South America. Ovenbirds occur in all land habitats from sea level to high mountain elevations and from wet forests to dry deserts. The majority, however, are tropical forest residents. They all consume insects, mainly taking their prey from the undersides of leaves and branches. The fairly uniform coloring of ovenbirds—various shades of brown, reddish brown, and gray, some with streaks or spots—and typically skulking behavior render the group a frustrating one for birdwatchers. These birds are hard to observe and are sometimes difficult to tell apart.

Also in the family Furnariidae are about 55 species known as woodcreepers. These mainly small brown birds pursue a mostly arboreal existence. They are common birds of forests but also of forest edges, woodlands and some other semi-open areas. Although woodpecker-like in some ways, woodcreepers are typically inconspicuous and go about their lives little noticed and unappreciated by most people. Like woodpeckers, they seek insects and spiders by climbing quickly over tree trunks and branches, clinging to vertical and angled surfaces with powerful feet with sharp, curved claws, and with their stiff tail feathers acting as props. But unlike woodpeckers, woodcreepers have drab plumages and retiring personalities, and most inhabit dark interiors of forests—all traits fostering inconspicuousness. Further, whereas woodpeckers are noisy, pecking at and hammering trees, woodcreepers are relatively quiet, singing simple, often soft, songs. They also lack the tree-drilling and drumming behaviors of woodpeckers.

Woodcreepers occur from central Mexico south to central Argentina. Fairly uniform in size, shape, and coloring, most woodcreepers are slender birds, 5 to 14 inches long. The sexes look alike, with plumages mostly of various shades of brown, chestnut, or tan. Most have some spotting, streaking, or banding, particularly on the head, back, and underparts. Bills vary extensively, from short and slender to long and robust; some are strongly downcurved. Birdwatchers,

probably the largest group who regularly notice them, regard woodcreepers as problematic, because in the low light levels of their typical forest habitats, they can be difficult to identify to species. When discernible, bill size and shape, and the color, body size, and type of plumage streaking are used as distinguishing traits.

■ Antbirds

Antbirds are rather drably attired inhabitants of the lower levels of Neotropical forests. They are recognized mainly for an intriguing feeding specialization: Many regularly follow army ant swarms, snatching small creatures that leave their hiding places to avoid the predatory ants. The antbirds are now often divided into two groups: a large family, Thamnophilidae, encompassing about 210 species of "typical" antbirds that tend to perch and forage in low vegetation, and a smaller family, Formicariidae, of about 60 species of predominantly ground-dwelling antbirds known as antpittas and antthrushes.

Like several other Neotropical families, such as the ovenbirds, antbirds are clearly ecologically very significant—species diverse, widespread, ubiquitous in

Chestnut-backed Antbird Antbirds can be tough, tough to see and then tough to identify. The bare blue skin surrounding the eye of this species narrows the identification choices, but some other antbirds have a similar feature. *Ecuador*

some major habitats, abundant—yet they are usually entirely unknown among the great majority of people who live where they occur. The reasons are that antbirds are clad predominantly in inconspicuous browns and grays and, save for a few exceptions, are secretive and live amid dense forest vegetation. Consequently, they are often difficult to observe for any length of time; in fact, most are typically heard but almost never seen. This and the fact that many species look much alike render the group an especially difficult one for birders. Much effort is sometimes expended to catch even brief glimpses of these birds.

Antbirds are distributed from southern Mexico to central Argentina. They range in length from 3 to 13.5 inches. Generally, smaller ones are called antwrens and antvireos, mid-size ones are called antbirds, and larger species are called antshrikes, antthrushes, and antpittas. Some species have bushy crests, bright red eyes, or patches of bright bare skin around the eye. Confined generally to thick vegetation in forest areas, antbirds mainly eat insects, although some of the larger species also take fruit or small lizards, snakes, and frogs. Whereas some forage in mixed-species flocks that follow army ants, others forage on the ground or on foliage. They rummage through leaf litter, tossing dead leaves aside with their bills as they search for insects, or search the undersides of leaves and branches. Some stay on the shady forest floor, but many inhabit the lower to middle levels of forests; and a few are canopy birds.

■ Tapaculos

Tapaculos are mostly dark-colored ground birds of the Neotropics that occur from Costa Rica to the southern tip of South America. Many are inhabitants of the Andes region. Members of the family Rhinocryptidae (with 58 species, including birds called

Ocellated Tapaculo This is one of the easier tapaculos to identify with its distinctive pattern of white dots (thus it name, ocellated) over most of its body and its large size. The problem is, this species is very secretive and thus rarely seen. *Ecuador*

huet-huets, gallitos, bristlefronts, and crescent-chests) tend to be obscure, having drab plumages, shy habits, and unmelodic vocalizations. They are noted for their diverse representation in southern South America, for many species' quite small geographic ranges, and for the way they often hold their tails upright.

Ranging from four to nine inches long, tapaculos tend to have shortish, heavy bills, short tails (but there are exceptions), and long legs with strong feet used for scratching at soil and moving leaf litter. They are clad in shades of brown and gray plus, sometimes, black and white; some are mainly blackish. In most, the sexes look alike, but in some, they differ conspicuously. Tapaculos predominantly inhabit forests and woodlands, but a few species occur in more open habitats such as scrub areas and tussock grasslands. They tend to be secretive and are usually observable for only short periods, so their habits are poorly known and they can be difficult for birders to locate and identify. They run and sometimes walk or hop along the ground, utilizing their weak flight abilities infrequently and then only briefly. Meals consist of insects, spiders, and occasional centipedes, snails, berries, and seeds. Most find food either by scratching the ground with their feet to expose hidden prey, or by taking it from the ground or from low vegetation. Most species are numerous, but many have very limited distributions.

■ Cotingas

Mainly due to their flashy colors but also for their array of shapes and ecologies, cotingas are always placed among the Neotropics' glamour birds. The

Green-and-black Fruiteater This sedate member of the cotinga family often perches quietly for long periods, making it difficult to see. The fruit it subsists on is often plucked while hovering. *Ecuador*

group encompasses tiny, warbler-size birds and large, crow-size birds; fruit-and-insect eaters but also some that eat only fruit; species in which the sexes look alike, but many in which males are spectacularly attired in bright spectral colors and females are plain; and, without doubt, some of the strangest-looking birds of the New World. The family Cotingidae contains about 70 species and occurs from southern Mexico south to northern Argentina.

The diversity of the cotingas is reflected in their names. In addition to cotingas, there are bellbirds, cocks-of-the-rock, purpletufts, umbrellabirds, fruiteaters, fruitcrows, mourners, pihas, plantcutters, and the Capuchinbird and Sharpbill. Perhaps the only generalizations that apply to all are that they have short legs and short, wide bills, the better to swallow fruits. Males of many species are quite ornate, with patches of gaudy plumage in unusual colors. For instance, some of the typical cotingas are lustrous blue and deep purple, and some are all white; others are wholly black, or green and yellow, or largely red or orange. Among the most unusual-looking cotingas are the bellbirds, some of which have worm-like wattles hanging from their heads, and the umbrellabirds, which have umbrella-shaped black crests.

Cotingas live primarily in tropical and subtropical forests, usually staying high in the canopy. They are fruit specialists, taking fruits from trees, often while hovering. Some, such as the pihas and fruitcrows, supplement their fruit diet with insects taken from treetop foliage, and a few catch flying insects. Some cotingas are often seen solitarily, but others apparently live in pairs or small groups. Some, such as umbrellabirds, bellbirds, cocks-of-the-rock, and pihas, are lekking breeders in which males individually stake out display trees and repeatedly perform vocal and visual displays to attract mates. Females then enter display areas (leks), assess the jumping and calling males, and choose ones with which to mate. Many cotingas are birds of the rain forest's high canopy, thus making it hard for birders to get good views of them. Some, such as the cocks-of-the rock, are most easily found at their leks, where the males' displays, often on tree branches only several yards off the ground, attract attention.

◼ Manakins

Manakins are a Neotropical group of small, stocky birds with short bills and tails, big eyes, brightly colored plumages and some of the most elaborate

Wire-tailed Manakin Most male manakins (like this one) are dazzling and easy to identify. On the other hand, the females of many species are very plain and similar—featuring subtle combinations of olive and light yellow plumage—and if seen alone are often unidentifiable. *Ecuador*

courtship displays practiced by birds. Some male manakins are outstandingly beautiful, predominantly glossy black but with brilliant patches of bright orange-red, yellow, or blue on their heads, or with deep blue on their undersides or backs. The exotic appearance of male manakins is enhanced on some species by long, streamer-like tails. Females, in contrast, are duller and less ornate. To accompany courtship displays, the wing feathers of some species, when moved in certain ways, make whirring or snapping sounds. Manakins, family Pipridae, occur only from southern Mexico to central South America. There are about 57 species, and they range in length from 3.5 to 6 inches excluding tail streamers.

Manakins are very active birds, chiefly of lowland forests, although some range up into cloud forests. Most are tropical, but some inhabit subtropical regions. Residents of the forest understory, they eat mainly small fruits, which they pluck from bushes and trees while in flight, and they also take insects from foliage. Males, singly or in pairs or small groups, during the breeding season stake out display sites on tree branches, in bushes, or on cleared patches of the forest floor. Then they spend considerable time giving lively displays, trying to attract females. An area that contains several of these performance sites is called a lek. At the lek, male manakins "dance," performing rapid acrobatic movements, sometimes making short up-and-down flights, sometimes rapid slides, twists, and turn-arounds, sometimes hanging upside down on a tree branch while turning rapidly from side to side and making snapping sounds with their wings. Females, attracted to leks by the sounds of male displays and by their memories of traditional lek locations, examine the energetically performing males and then choose the ones with which they want to mate.

Some manakins have very small ranges in South America. This, combined with the fact that many of these birds inhabit dark forest understories, means that some species are difficult to locate and see. Also, several species are greenish without any bright color patches, making them even more difficult to spot. Many birders finally see manakins at their leks, where the birds, often in groups, spend a lot of their time.

■ Other Significant Families

The bird diversity of South America and Antarctica is so great that at least 17 more families can be considered significant: **Rheas** (Rheidae), two species of gray-brown Ostrich-like birds restricted to central and southern South America; **Albatrosses** (Diomedeidae), large, heavy seabirds wandering primarily over the Southern Hemisphere oceans, with ten species occurring around South America and Antarctica; **Flamingos** (Phoenicopteridae), with four of the world's six species represented here, three of them endemic to the continent and two restricted to the Andes; **New World Vultures** (Cathartidae), with six of the group's seven species found in South America, including the Andean Condor; **Hoatzin** (Opisthocomidae), a single-species family endemic to South America; **Sunbittern** (Eurypygidae), a single-species family; a large streamside bird that ranges from southern Mexico to Bolivia; **Seriemas** (Cariamidae), two species of tall, long-legged birds of open habitats that rarely fly, endemic to South America; **Magellanic Plover** (Pluvianellidae), a pale gray plover with short legs that is different enough from other plovers to be placed in its own family, endemic to southern South America; **Seedsnipes** (Thinocoridae), four species of short-billed and short-legged shorebirds that look like crosses between pigeons and quails, restricted to western and

Paradise Tanager The diversity of tanagers in South America is extraordinary. The Paradise Tanager—a widespread and common bird—is one of the flashiest. Mixed-species feeding flocks at fruiting trees are prime birding spots and may contain six or more species of tanagers as well as other species. *Ecuador*

southern South America; **Sheathbills** (Chionididae), two species of pigeonlike, scavenging white shorebirds, found mainly in association with penguins; **Parrots** (Psittacidae), with South America possessing about 130 species; **Oilbird** (Steatornithidae), a single-species family and a truly unusual species, related to nightjars, with a bat-like existence; **Broad-billed Sapayoa** (Sapayoaidae), single-species family; a small, inconspicuous, greenish bird of Panama and northern South America; **Gnateaters** (Conopophagidae), eight species of small, stocky, short-tailed birds of forests and woodlands, endemic to northern South America; **Tyrant Flycatchers** (Tyrannidae), with more than 85 percent of this family's 435 species (the globe's most diverse bird family) represented in South America; **Tanagers** (Thraupidae), with almost 200 species in South America; **New World Blackbirds** (Icteridae), with more than 60 species in South America.

A frequent experience is that you will be walking along a trail, seeing few birds, and then suddenly a mixed-species foraging flock with up to 20 or more species swooshes into view.

Atlantic
Ocean

Equator

SOUTH
AMERICA

Tropic of Capricorn

NORTHERN SOUTH AMERICA

T HE NORTHERN HALF OF SOUTH AMERICA ENCOMPASSES NOT ONLY THE CONTI-nent's vast Amazon region and the northern Andes Mountains, but other biodi-verse zones such as Venezuela's Caribbean coast and the tree and scrub savanna—the *cerrado*—of Brazil's northeast and central-east. This half-continent is home to more of the world's bird species than any other comparably size piece of land. Thus, although northern South America might be a little farther from North America, both in distance and perhaps culturally than is Central America, going the extra dis-tance and investing in higher airfares can be hugely worthwhile. After all, to a birder with adequate resources, what could be more important than gaining access to the world's largest avifauna? While entree to many birding sites may not be quite as easy and straightforward as in many parts of Costa Rica or Belize or southern Mexico, wonderful birding destinations can be reached and enjoyed with small effort.

Ecuador is a prime example. At the continent's western extreme, wedged between the Amazon Basin to its east and the Pacific to its west, it is friendly to North Americans and sufficiently safe for all kinds of travel and exploration. It possesses a broad range of eco-zones and habitats. There are mid-elevation cloud forests in the Mindo area. The *páramo,* a wet, grassy, high-elevation habitat, is accessible at Papallacta Pass, along a main highway through the Andes east from Quito. Alpine lakes and extensive páramo are featured at El Cajas National Park, near the highland city of Cuenca. Lowland rain forest is plentiful in Ecuador's portion of the Amazon region, called El Oriente. Dry deciduous forests are found in the coastal lowlands just west of the nation's largest city, Guayaquil. And scrub forest habitats occur in Ecuador's south coastal region, known ecologically as *tumbesia.* Ecuador has its own field guide, offers a range of prices for

OPPOSITE: **Chapada dos Guimarães National Park** This park is located in the Brazilian state of Mato Grosso near the state capital of Cuiaba. It is a region of steep cliffs and waterfalls at the edge of the highland plateau (or *planalto*) that rises above the surrounding savanna. *Brazil*

Plate-billed Mountain-Toucan There are four species of beautiful mountain-toucans, and all are endemic to the Andes of northern South America. They tend not to perch in the open, but their far-carrying calls often make their presence known and lead to sightings. *Ecuador*

LOCAL BIRDING & CONSERVATION ORGANIZATIONS

■ **BRAZILIAN ORNITHO-LOGICAL SOCIETY** (www.ararajuba.org.br) promotes the study and conservation of Brazil's birds

■ **FUNDACIÓN PROAVES** (www.proaves.org) involved with the study and conservation of Colombia's biodiversity, especially birds; operates nature reserves

■ **FUNDACIÓN JOCOTOCO** (www.fjocotoco.org) established to protect the habitat of globally threatened species of birds in the Andes of Ecuador

■ **NEOTROPICAL BIRD CLUB** (www.neotropicalbirdclub .org) fosters interest in Neotropical birds and promotes conservation in the region

■ **PERU VERDE** (www.peruverde.org) dedicated to conserving Peru's wildlife and wildlands; operates a travel agency (www.inkanatura .com) to funnel birders and other ecotourists into its own eco-lodges

travel and accommodations, is a frequent destination for many nature and birding tour companies, and has a plethora of in-country tour operators that can put trips together with or without accompanying birding guides. Add the fact that more than 1,500 bird species are found within the country's borders, and you can see how Ecuador has become one of the birding world's most desired destinations.

Peru, just south of Ecuador, is much larger but is somewhat similar in that it offers a huge terrestrial avifauna and a range of major eco-zones to visit, from Pacific coastal desert lowlands, to cloud forests on the Andes' slopes, to grassy puna habitat in the high Andes, to the Peruvian Amazon region in the east. In addition to land birds, Peru hosts millions of seabirds off its Pacific shores, a consequence of the cool Humboldt Current, which supports abundant marine life. Peru, of course, also offers the wonderful tourist attractions of the Machu Picchu Incan ruins tucked high in the Andes and Lake Titicaca. The lake, by the way, is home to many species of waterfowl, three species of flamingos, and the flightless and endemic Short-winged Grebe. Other common birding areas in northern South America include Amazonian Brazil, with access points like Belém and Manaus in the north and Alta Florista in the south; Venezuela, especially forested areas in the coastal mountains west of Caracas and the savanna and grasslands of west-central Venezuela (the plains, or "llanos"); and Bolivia, with various sites around the cities of Cochabamba, Santa Cruz, and La Paz.

GEOGRAPHY AND HABITATS

Northern South America extends from the Caribbean coasts of Colombia and Venezuela south to the latitude of extreme southern Peru or central Bolivia, and from the Atlantic to the Pacific Ocean. The dominating physical feature of this region is the Greater Amazon Basin. This region of rivers and rain forests covers about 2.3 million square miles and includes parts of nine countries: from the Atlantic west to the base of the Andes in Bolivia, Peru, Ecuador, and Colombia, and from Venezuela, Guyana, Suriname, and French Guiana south into central Brazil. The Brazilian portion alone contains more than half the Amazon region's area. The Amazon forests make up

SPOTTING THE WHITE-CHEEKED COTINGA

Not only is the White-cheeked Cotinga endemic to the west Andean slopes of central Peru, but within its small range it is spottily distributed in only a few patches of high-altitude polylepis forest. To actually see this bird, you have to do more than simply visit within its range. You have to be at just the right altitude at the right season, and you have to be there at the right time of day before the bird performs it typical daily downslope and then upslope movements. After five unsuccessful attempts at supposedly the best place in the world to find this cotinga, Oyon in the Santa Eulalia Valley high above Lima, I decided to camp out at a large grove of polylepis trees near Oyon and spend as much time as it took to see a White-cheeked Cotinga.

At 11,000 feet in the Andes, the nights are very cold and the ground seems extra rocky. At dawn following my first night camped there, I sat on a ridge and looked down on the forest. Giant Conebill and Stripe-headed Antpitta made early appearances. Then finally, at 7:30 a.m., first one then three other White-cheeked Cotingas made their way downslope toward me. They casually ate fruits and berries as they flew from bush to bush, and within a few minutes they had moved down the mountainside and out of sight. The same thing happens in reverse in the late afternoon, but more quickly, as these cotingas return to higher elevation roosting sites. Birding sometimes includes more than knowing a site or having good identification skills; it means being lucky, having patience, and persevering. —D.P.

White-cheeked Cotinga If you can find one, the bold white cheek patch, dark cap, and streaked underparts make this species easy to identify. The male and female are identical in plumage. *Peru*

nearly one-third of the tropical lowland rain forests of the world—the globe's largest surviving tract of continuous forest. One note about visiting the Amazon region: Dry trails in remote areas are often few and far between. Therefore, much of the visitation and birding occurs on boats, which ply the region's waterways from the Amazon proper to its major tributaries such as the Río Napo, Río Solimões, Río Negro, and Río Tapajós, and even to smaller rivers.

The other major geographical feature of northern South America is the Andes, which in this region extend from Venezuela in the north to southern Peru in the south. Through much of this length, the highest parts of the range are a pair of parallel, north-south ridges separated by a lower, narrow plateau at 7,000 to 13,000 feet elevation. At high altitudes on the Andes' slopes, temperatures are low and moisture is scarce, but there are still some forests here. Above this level, up to the permanent snowline at about 18,000 feet, there are only low grassy areas—tundra-like zones that support their own specialized avifauna. Other important habitats in northern South America include patches of tropical dry forest on the Pacific coast and Brazil's inland arid scrubs and coastal moist forests on the Atlantic side.

Giant Antpitta As described in the text, this individual was lured in with food to pose for its portrait. The Giant Antpitta stands about 9.5 inches tall. *Ecuador*

SPOTTING THE GIANT ANTPITTA

Two Ecuadorian brothers, Angel and Wilson Rodrigo Paz, live near the Andean town of Nanegalito. The Paz brothers once planned to clear their plot of cloud forest for agriculture but then discovered that the antpitta birds they hunted loved earthworms. They wondered whether these elusive birds could attract tourists to their land so they set up an ecotourism operation. The brothers now earn much more than they would have earned with their original plan to cut down the forest.

Meanwhile, there is also payoff for dedicated birdwatchers. Antpittas are almost always extremely hard to see. They are shy ground-dwellers and tend to rely on camouflage and extreme wariness to escape their many predators. They are best known by their haunting calls and low whistles, but these tend to be ventriloquial and almost impossible to locate. The Giant Antpitta, with a limited range restricted to Colombia and Ecuador, is especially sneaky, and until the efforts by the Paz brothers, they had been seen only by the luckiest and most persistent birders. Usually they move silently on the ground, perhaps showing partial glimpses of themselves before disappearing into the undergrowth of the forest floor. They can seemingly hide where no bird should be able to hide.

After a short walk full of cloud forest birds, the Paz brothers sat me down on the edge of a path in the cloud forest and started rattling a can of worms and calling "Maria!" A Giant Antpitta came trotting, then two Yellow-breasted Antpittas approached, then finally a reticent Moustached Antpitta. This is an amazing experience. The business acumen of these two Ecuadorians has served as an example of grassroots forest conservation in which everyone wins. —D.P.

BIRDLIFE

Northern South America as defined here sports the great majority of South American birds, many more than 2,000 species. It also possesses the greatest species diversity of most bird groups mentioned in this chapter's introduction and discussion of significant bird families. More than 35 Endemic Bird Areas are situated in the region. Some of the better known and more species-rich endemic hot spots include the Chocó forests on the Pacific slope of the Andes in western Colombia and Ecuador; the Tumbesian forests and scrub areas of coastal western Ecuador and northwestern Peru; the *tepuis* (or table mountains), forests, savanna, and scrubs of southern Venezuela and northern Brazil; and the forests and scrubs of the Peruvian Andes.

Some birders who enter tropical rain forests for the first time, especially those of the Amazon region with its reputation for great bird diversity, naturally expect to be quickly confronted by fabulous birds walking, hopping, perching, swooping, and vocalizing everywhere. But a surprise to many during their first penetration of Amazon forest trails or waterways is that hordes of birds are not immediately seen or heard. During large portions of the day the forest is mainly quiet, with few birds noticeably active. Birds are often present, but many are inconspicuous—small brownish birds near to the ground, and green, brown, or gray birds in the high canopy.

A frequent experience is that you will be walking along a trail, seeing few birds, and then suddenly a mixed-species foraging flock with up to 20 or more species swooshes into view. Birds fill the trees around you at all levels, some hopping along the ground, some moving through the brush, some clinging to tree trunks, others in the canopy—more birds than you can easily count or identify. Then, just as suddenly, the flock is gone, having moved on in its meandering path through the forest. Tropical birds often participate in these mixed-species flocks, spending nonbreeding periods traveling around a large territory or semi-nomadically in the company of many other species. Some of these flocks contain primarily insect-eating birds, others primarily seedeaters, and still others typically follow swarms of army ants, feasting on the insects and other small animals that bolt from cover at the approach of the predatory ants. Many birds participate in mixed-species foraging flocks, including motmots, woodcreepers, antbirds, fruitcrows, gnatcatchers, vireos, tanagers, honeycreepers, orioles, caciques, and oropendolas.

Tanagers stand out in northern South America. These small passerines are often amazingly colored, such as the unmistakable Paradise Tanager, with its black body, green head, blue throat and chest, red lower back, and yellow rump. Tanagers are probably among the New World tropics' most visible birds because of their habit of associating in mixed-species tanager flocks that gather in the open to feed in fruit trees. You will often find a mixed flock of tanagers settling into a tree full of ripe fruit to enjoy a meal.

FIELD GUIDE & SITE GUIDE BOOKS

■ *The Birds of Ecuador, Vol. 2: Field Guide* (2001)
R.S. Ridgely and P.J. Greenfield
Cornell University Press

■ *Birds of Northern South America: An Identification Guide, vol. 2* (2007)
R. Restall, C. Rodner, and M. Lentino
Yale University Press

■ *Birds of Peru, rev. ed.* (2010)
T.S. Schulenberg, D.F. Stotz, D.F. Lane, J.P. O'Neill, and T.P. Parker III
Princeton University Press

■ *Birds of Venezuela, 2nd ed.* (2003)
S.L. Hilty
Princeton University Press

■ *A Field Guide to the Birds of Brazil* (2009)
B. van Perlo
Oxford University Press

■ *A Guide to the Birds of Colombia* (1986)
S.L. Hilty and W.L. Brown
Princeton University Press

■ *A Guide to Birdwatching in Ecuador and the Galápagos Islands* (1996)
R.S.R. Williams, B.J. Best, and T. Heijnen
Biosphere Publications

■ *Where to Watch Birds in South America* (2000)
N. Wheatley
Princeton University Press

Significant Species
of Northern South America

ABOUT 90 FAMILIES FOUND IN THIS REGION

■ **TINAMOUS** (Tinamidae), **41 species**

Red-winged Tinamou *Rhynchotus rufescens*
broadly distributed species of grasslands and woodlands

Curve-billed Tinamou* *Nothoprocta curvirostris*
high-elevation Andean species of Ecuador and Peru

■ **SCREAMERS** (Anhimidae), **3 species**

Horned Screamer* *Anhima cornuta*
large, stocky bird of marshy areas with a long head feather, or "horn"

■ **GUANS, CHACHALACAS, AND CURASSOWS** (Cracidae), **40 species**

Yellow-knobbed Curassow* *Crax daubentoni*
large, black and white, crested curassow with a large yellow knob on the male's bill

Blue-throated Piping-Guan *Pipile cumanensis*
large black bird with white crest, blue wattle, and red legs

■ **TRUMPETERS*** (Psophiidae), **3 species**

Gray-winged Trumpeter* *Psophia crepitans*
long-legged, chicken-size bird of forest areas

■ **PARROTS** (Psittacidae), **about 125 species**

Scarlet-shouldered Parrotlet* *Touit huetii*
tiny parrot that occurs in several isolated patches over northern South America

Red-fronted Macaw* *Ara rubrogenys*
large parrot restricted to mountain valleys of Bolivia

■ **POTOOS** (Nyctibiidae), **6 species**

Andean Potoo* *Nyctibius maculosus*
restricted to the northern Andes

■ **HUMMINGBIRDS** (Trochilidae), **about 240 species**

Sword-billed Hummingbird* *Ensifera ensifera*
extremely long-billed hummingbird of the Andes

Crimson Topaz* *Topaza pella*
multicolored, long-tailed hummingbird of Venezuela, Suriname and northern Brazil

Marvelous Spatuletail* *Loddigesia mirabilis*
Peruvian hummingbird; male has extremely long tail streamers with racket-shaped tips

■ **TROGONS** (Trogonidae), **14 species**

Masked Trogon* *Trogon personatus*
trogon mainly of mountainous forest regions

Golden-headed Quetzal *Pharomachrus auriceps*
trogon of the Andes Mountains

■ **JACAMARS** (Galbulidae), **18 species**

Coppery-chested Jacamar* *Galbula pastazae*
jacamar of middle elevations in Ecuador and Colombia

■ **PUFFBIRDS** (Bucconidae), **34 species**

Two-banded Puffbird* *Hypnelus bicinctus*
puffbird of savanna and other open habitats

Swallow-wing* *Chelidoptera tenebrosa*
small, distinctive puffbird with an unusual fluttering flight

■ **BARBETS** (Capitonidae), **15 species**

Scarlet-hooded Barbet* *Eubucco tucinkae*
green and red barbet; endemic to a small region where Peru, Brazil, and Boliva meet

Toucan Barbet* *Semnornis ramphastinus*
boldly marked, large-billed barbet of the northern Andes

■ **TOUCANS** (Ramphastidae), **34 species**

Plate-billed Mountain-Toucan* *Andigena laminirostris*
large, colorful, blue-chested toucan of the Andes west slope

Red-necked Aracari* *Pteroglossus bitorquatus*
rain forest species of central and southern Brazil and parts of Bolivia

■ **OVENBIRDS AND WOODCREEPERS** (Furnariidae), **about 220 species**

Lesser Hornero* *Furnarius minor*
found along large rivers in the Amazon region

Short-billed Leaftosser * *Sclerurus rufigularis*
small, brown, terrestrial insect-eater with a broad Amazon region distribution

Zimmer's Woodcreeper* *Dendroplex kienerii*
found in various wooded habitats along major Amazonian rivers

■ **TYPICAL ANTBIRDS** (Thamnophilidae), **about 200 species**

Black-and-white Antbird* *Myrmochanes hemileucus*
occurs in the forest understory on Amazon region river islands

Black-bellied Antwren* *Formicivora melanogaster*
very small antbird, chiefly of northeastern and southern Brazil and Bolivia

■ **ANTTHRUSHES AND ANTPITTAS** (Formicariidae), **about 60 species**

Rufous-breasted Antthrush *Formicarius rufipectus*
chestnut, rufous, and black species ranging from Costa Rica south along the Andes to Peru

Moustached Antpitta* *Grallaria alleni*
endangered species from high elevations in Colombia and northern Ecuador

■ **GNATEATERS*** (Conopophagidae), **8 species**

Chestnut-belted Gnateater* *Conopophaga aurita*
small, stub-tailed bird of the forest floor, broadly distributed

■ **TAPACULOS** (Rhinocryptidae), **about 45 species**

Trilling Tapaculo* *Scytalopus parvirostris*
found in wet forests of Andean Peru and Bolivia

■ **COTINGAS** (Cotingadae), **about 60 species**

Sharpbill *Oxyruncus cristatus*
olive-green cotinga; different enough from other cotingas that it is sometimes placed in its own single-species family

Pompadour Cotinga* *Xipholena punicea*
bird of wet forest canopies; male purplish, female gray

Long-wattled Umbrellabird* *Cephalopterus penduliger*
rare and restricted to small parts of Colombia and Ecuador; male has an incredibly long black wattle hanging from its lower throat

Guianan Cock-of-the-rock* *Rupicola rupicola*
an incredible bird; male bright orange with a semicircular crest

■ **MANAKINS** (Pirpidae), **about 50 species**

Blue-rumped Manakin* *Lepidothrix isidorei*
found in wet forests of the northern Andean foothills; male black with white cap and blue rump

Orange-crested Manakin* *Heterocercus aurantiivertex*
found in small areas of Ecuador and Peru, usually near rivers and streams

■ **TYRANT FLYCATCHERS** (Tyrannidae), **about 330 species**

Ecuadorian Tyrannulet* *Phylloscartes gualaquizae*
very small flycatcher from wet forests of the Andean foothills of Ecuador and northern Peru

Ochraceous-breasted Flycatcher* *Myiophobus ochraceiventris*
flycatcher with a yellowish-to-orange crown patch, from highland northern Andean forests

■ **TANAGERS AND ALLIES** (Thraupidae), **about 170 species**

Bicolored Conebill* *Conirostrum bicolor*
occurs in mangroves in coastal northern South America as well as some inland areas

Buff-breasted Mountain-Tanager* *Dubusia taeniata*
blue above, yellow below, this tanager is found in highland forests of the northern Andes

Paradise Tanager* *Tangara chilensis*
multicolored species that occurs over a broad swath of the region

■ **NEW WORLD BLACKBIRDS** (Icteridae), **about 58 species**

Mountain Cacique* *Cacicus chrysonotus*
black and yellow; occurs in middle- to high-elevation wet forests of the northern Andes

Green Oropendola* *Psarocolius viridis*
widely distributed oropendola of South American rain forests

Some Other Species Global Birders Often Seek

Greater Rhea *Rhea americana*
larger of the two rheas; occurs in woodlands, savannas, and grasslands

Short-winged Grebe* *Rollandia microptera*
flightless grebe; occurs mainly in Lake Titicaca

Zigzag Heron* *Zebrilus undulatus*
small, little-known species endemic to this region

Sungrebe *Heliornis fulica*
small, grebe-like, in the small finfoot family (Heliornithidae); occurs from southern Mexico to South America

Sunbittern *Eurypyga helias*
chicken-size bird (single-species family Eurypygidae) found in rivers, streams, and swamps

Harpy Eagle *Harpia harpyja*
huge raptor of lowland forests

Hoatzin* *Opisthocomus hoazin*
large, crested, ancient-looking bird; only member of single-species family Opisthocomidae

Oilbird *Steatornis caripensis*
flies at night, appears like a giant moth; only member of single-species family Steatornithidae

Ladder-tailed Nightjar* *Hydropsalis climacocerca*
long-tailed nightjar broadly distributed in the Amazon region

Broad-billed Sapayoa *Sapayoa aenigma*
small greenish bird; only member of single-species family Sapayaoidae

*Restricted to Northern South America

Which Galápagos birds do traveling birders want to see? The short answer: all of them.

THE GALÁPAGOS ISLANDS

Galápagos Islands

Isla Pinta

Equator · Isla Marchena

Isla San Salvador

Isla Fernandina · Isla Santa Cruz

Isla Isabela · Isla San Cristóbal

Pacific Ocean · Isla Santa María

T HE GALÁPAGOS ISLANDS ARE SPECIAL FOR A NUMBER OF REASONS, BUT FORE-most is their indigenous wildife. The land vertebrates found here, mainly reptiles and birds, are not very diverse in terms of numbers of species, but this is more than compensated by their amazing forms, curious behaviors, and high degree of endemism. Indeed, for those interested in nature and wildlife, a trip to these remote islands is often a life goal, placed on a list together with an East African safari and a visit to the Amazon rain forest.

The Galápagos are justifiably famous for reptiles such as the Galápagos tortoise, marine iguana, and Galápagos land iguana, but the birds are more numerous, more beautiful, and usually more obvious. Quite strikingly, they are also very confiding. As soon as you step ashore on one of these fascinating islands, you begin to notice that the wildlife is surprisingly tame. The marine iguanas perched on the rocks near your landing site don't flinch or run as you step among them, the Galápagos sea lions lolling on the beach hardly shift their sunning routines as you walk by their noses, and the large breeding birds barely look at you as you wander past their nests only feet away. The wildlife on these remote islands evolved in the absence of large terrestrial predators; therefore, they apparently don't "know" what to make of us humans. But it is clear they have no reflexive fear of our close approach. Much of the time they appear to ignore us. This tameness makes it almost certain that each visitor takes home lasting memories of incredible wildlife encounters, particularly with birds. My Galápagos experiences encompass some of my most treasured birding moments. These include wading ashore on one island, sitting on a downed beachside log to put on my shoes, and then noticing right behind the log not four feet from

OPPOSITE: **Galapagos Hawk**
A Galápagos tortoise makes a convenient perch for a hawk scanning for a meal. Both the tortoise and the hawk are endemic to this unique island archipelago. *Isabela Island, Galápagos Islands, Ecuador*

Flightless Cormorant The only cormorant in the Galápagos island chain, and found only on Fernandina and Isabela Islands. The stubby wings are useless for flight. This pair (the smaller female on the right) is at its nest site. *Fernandina Island, Galápagos Islands, Ecuador*

LOCAL BIRDING & CONSERVATION ORGANIZATIONS

■ **CHARLES DARWIN FOUNDATION FOR THE GALÁPAGOS ISLANDS** (www.darwinfoundation.org) founded in 1959, works to conserve the ecosystems, including wildlife and habitats, of the Galápagos; operates the Charles Darwin Research Center, located on Santa Cruz Island

me, a pair of absolutely gorgeous gulls, Swallow-tailed Gulls, standing silently and unconcernedly around their nest. Galapagos Mockingbirds brazenly approached me during my island walks to beg quite vocally for water from my plastic bottle. I wandered along a trail right through a breeding colony of Waved Albatrosses, as the large seabirds—somewhat eerily—barely reacted to my presence.

All of the islands together, 13 major and several smaller, compose Ecuador's Galápagos Province and Galápagos Islands National Park. The entire zone, except for a few settled areas, is strictly protected. The great majority of international visitors get there by air from mainland Ecuador, either from Quito or Guayaquil. Upon arrival, most are immediately transferred to boats of various sizes that usually spend 5 to 14 days cruising among the islands. Many of the boats have only 10 to 20 passengers. Guides on each boat lead their groups on daily walking tours around the islands. By late afternoon everyone is back on board; no one is allowed to stay overnight on an island. These inclusive boat trips range from quite deluxe and, hence, expensive, to budget priced. There's a boat for every wallet size. The large nature tour and bird tour companies also offer tours to the Galápagos, often on big boats with more people and more guides and often itineraries that include visits to greater numbers of islands.

GEOGRAPHY AND HABITATS

The Galápagos Islands are in the Pacific, on the Equator, about 600 miles directly west of Ecuador's coast. These volcanic islands vary considerably in size. The 13 main ones range from Isabela, the largest at 1,800 square miles, to Genovesa, at 5.4 square miles. The islands have volcanic cones that rise high above the Pacific. Isabela's highest peak tops out at about 5,600 feet above sea level. Galápagos rainfall is highly seasonal, with most precipitation falling usually from January to April. The best time to visit is generally October through February, from the end of the dry season to the start of the wet. Native birds are breeding at this time, and migrant shorebirds are present.

Galápagos habitats vary considerably with altitude. Often there are tidal lagoons and mangroves along the coasts. Up to about 600 feet in elevation there typically exists a zone of dry tolerant shrubs and yellowish tree cacti. Proceeding upward, there is a forest zone dominated by large trees known as scalesia trees, which are endemic to the Galápagos, then a zone of low scrubs, and then at the highest elevations a "pampas" zone with ferns, grasslands and distinctive trees adapted to foggy conditions.

SPOTTING THE CHARLES MOCKINGBIRD

The second rarest landbird in the Galápagos is probably the Charles Mockingbird. This species used to occur commonly on the large island of Floreana, but now its population of about 150 individuals is restricted to the two tiny satellite islands that lie off the coast of Floreana: Champion and Gardner. This bird feeds on the ground, hopping through the undergrowth on powerful legs and using its beak as a probe or for breaking into potential food items. This mockingbird moves in groups of four to ten related individuals, several of which may help in raising the dominant pair's young. Introduced rats and feral cats appear to be the reason for this species' elimination on Floreana Island.

Because of the mockingbird's threatened status, no one is allowed to land on Champion and Gardner islands or even to anchor offshore. These islands are steep-sided and covered with thick thorn scrub and opuntia cactus. Trying to look onto the island to see a bird from a moving ship that is bouncing beyond the surf is difficult to impossible. Only if the ship is small enough to approach shore fairly closely, and the observers are lucky, can they see a mockingbird or two jump onto the top of a cactus and sing. This is what we did, and in a half hour we saw seven individuals, or about 5 percent of the world's total population.

If you seek a similar experience, make sure your captain is experienced and resolute because, in addition to a little luck, it was obvious to all involved that the captain's skills in boat handling had a lot to do with our seeing these mockingbirds. Successful birders quickly learn to give credit where credit is due. —D.P.

Charles Mockingbird Four species of mockingbirds are present in the Galápagos, all are endemic. *Floreana Island, Galápagos Islands, Ecuador*

BIRDLIFE

Which Galápagos birds do traveling birders want to see? The short answer: all of them. Luckily, excluding migrants that can also be viewed elsewhere in the world, there aren't that many species here. A complete checklist for the islands would have about 60 names, about half seabirds and other water-associated birds and half landbirds. Keys to seeing as many species as possible include making sure to spend enough time there, at least six to seven days, and visiting as many of the major islands and as many of the islands' distinct habitats as possible. The duration of your stay is important because the longer the boat trip undertaken, the more islands that are visited. Visiting multiple islands is essential because different species occur on different islands. For instance, the Waved Albatross breeds only on Española Island, the Flightless Cormorant occurs only on Isabela and Fernandina, and the rare Mangrove Finch is found solely in Isabela's mangrove swamps.

Aside from such charismatic, singular endemics as the Galapagos Penguin, Flightless Cormorant, and Galapagos Hawk, the birds most visitors are especially curious about and most want to see are undoubtedly the Darwin's finches, also

Mangrove Finch Except for the Mangrove Finch, all the other Darwin's finches survive in good numbers. There are a total of 14 species, but not all scientists agree about how they should be categorized. *Isabela Island, Galápagos Islands, Ecuador*

SPOTTING THE MANGROVE FINCH

The Mangrove Finch, one of the Darwin's or Galápagos finches, is one of the rarest birds in the world. There are now only two known breeding populations with a combined total of fewer than 100 adults. Both populations are found on the northwestern coast of the island of Isabela at sites known as Playa Tortuga Negra and Caleta Black. The population formerly on Fernandina Island is extinct. This species is extremely specialized. It feeds mainly on insects and occasionally uses twigs or cactus spines to pry out insect grubs from tunnels in wood. The Mangrove Finch lives only in mangrove stands that are separated from the sea by sandy beaches.

On a recent tour I led to the Galápagos, I pleaded with our ship's captain for a special stop at Playa Tortuga Negra, so I could look for the last Galápagos finch still missing from my life list. I was begrudgingly allowed one hour to get from the ship to the mangroves

behind the beach, find the bird, and then return to the ship. I asked for volunteers among the passengers to help me, and six of them agreed. With no waste of motion or effort, we clambered into the Zodiac inflatable boat, endured a near wipeout landing in heavy surf, ran up the long sandy banks, entered the quiet mangrove stand and waited. I "squeaked" once by kissing the back of my fingers, and out of the canopy flew a Mangrove Finch to investigate, landing only 25 feet away. We watched this bird in all of its magnificent dirty tan plumage for about ten minutes. Then we ran for the beach, loaded the Zodiac, and roared back to the ship with only two minutes to spare. Sometimes in global birding you take advantage of whatever opportunities come, even though this helter-skelter approach now seems somewhat unbecoming in the case of this rare and endangered finch. —D.P.

Ecotourists Most visitors to the Galápagos book a ship-based tour in order to visit a variety of islands. Small inflatable boats ferry passengers ashore and also serve as convenient observation platforms. *Galápagos Islands, Ecuador*

called Galápagos finches. There are 14 species, all except one confined to the Galápagos. (The exception occurs only on Cocos Island, a Costa Rican possession 400 miles away.) These birds are rather plain in color, mostly blackish or brownish, some having light underparts. But bill shapes and sizes vary considerably among the species, from the small, thin, insect-catching bill of the Warbler Finch to the massive, seed-crunching bill of the Large Cactus-Finch. It was this aspect of the finches that Darwin concentrated on after he returned home to England and began examining his collected specimens in detail. These bill differences associated with different species living on different but nearby islands became some of the evidence Darwin marshaled to support his ideas about how species changed and new species developed. Adding to the excitement of seeing birds that played a significant role in Darwin's thinking is the fact that two of these species, the Woodpecker Finch and Mangrove Finch, are known to use tools in their feeding behavior. They hold cactus spines or small twigs with their bills and insert them into tree holes to help extract insects. Other must-sees for birders are breeding colonies of albatrosses, boobies, and frigatebirds that you can walk through. And if you've never seen albatrosses and boobies perform their "dancing" courtship displays, or frigatebird males inflating their huge red throat sacs and calling at passing females, then you're in for great treats.

FIELD GUIDE & SITE GUIDE BOOKS

■ *Birds, Mammals and Reptiles of the Galápagos Islands, 2nd ed.* (2006)
A. Swash and R. Still
Yale University Press

■ *Ecuador and the Galápagos Islands: Travellers' Wildlife Guide* (2004)
D.L. Pearson and L. D. Beletsky
Interlink Books

■ *A Guide to the Birds of the Galápagos Islands* (1996)
I. Castro and A. Phillips
Princeton University Press

■ *Wildlife of the Galápagos* (2002)
J. Fitter, D. Fitter, and D. Hosking
Princeton University Press

Significant Species
of the Galápagos Islands
32 FAMILIES FOUND IN THIS REGION

■ PENGUINS (Spheniscidae), **1 species**

Galapagos Penguin* *Spheniscus mendiculus*
world's northernmost penguin

■ ALBATROSSES (Diomedeidae), **1 species**

Waved Albatross *Phoebastria irrorata*
breeds, for the most part, only in the Galápagos

■ PETRELS AND SHEARWATERS (Procellariidae), **2 species**

Galapagos Petrel* *Pterodroma phaeopygia*
endemic petrel closely related to the Hawaiian
Petrel

■ STORM-PETRELS (Hydrobatidae), **3 species**

White-vented Storm-Petrel *Oceanites gracilis*
small storm-petrel limited to the Galápagos and
Pacific coast of South America

Wedge-rumped Storm-Petrel *Oceanodroma tethys*
restricted to the Galápagos and Pacific coast of
South America

Small Ground-Finch This Darwin Finch is found on many of the
islands and has the most varied diet. Here it is seen feeding on
cactus fruit. *San Cristóbal Island, Galápagos Islands, Ecuador*

■ TROPICBIRDS (Phaethontidae), **1 species**

Red-billed Tropicbird *Phaethon aethereus*
broadly distributed large seabird with very long
tail streamers

■ BOOBIES (Sulidae), **3 species**

Nazca Booby *Sula granti*
common booby in the Galápagos, formerly considered
the same species as Masked Booby

Blue-footed Booby *Sula nebouxi*
common in the Galápagos, they "dance," showing their
blue feet to their mates

■ CORMORANTS (Phalacrocoracidae), **1 species**

Flightless Cormorant* *Phalacrocorax harrisi*
the islands' only cormorant; has stubby wings

■ FRIGATEBIRDS (Fregatidae), **2 species**

Great Frigatebird *Fregata minor*
widely distributed, males inflate large red throat sac
in courtship display

■ FLAMINGOS (Phoenicopteridae), **1 species**

American Flamingo *Phoenicopterus ruber*
occurs in saltwater lagoons on some of the islands

■ HAWKS, EAGLES, AND KITES (Accipitridae), **2 species**

Galapagos Hawk* *Buteo galapagoensis*
large brown hawk present on many of the islands

■ RAILS (Rallidae), **3 species**

Galapagos Rail* *Laterallus spilonotus*
very small, the islands' only endemic rail

Paint-billed Crake *Neocrex erythrops*
small dark rail that also occurs in South America

■ GULLS (Laridae), **4 species**

Lava Gull* *Larus fuliginosus*
all-gray gull with a darker head

Swallow-tailed Gull* *Creagrus furcatus*
handsome night-feeding gull with a dark head during
breeding and a red fleshy eye ring

■ **PIGEONS AND DOVES** (Columbiadae), **1 species**

Galapagos Dove* *Zenaida galapagoensis*
small reddish brown pigeon, the only member of its
family in the islands

■ **TYRANT FLYCATCHERS** (Tyrannidae), **2 species**

Galapagos Flycatcher* *Myiarchus magnirostris*
small brownish gray and yellow flycatcher; present on
many of the islands

■ **MOCKINGBIRDS** (Mimidae), **4 species**

Galapagos Mockingbird* *Nesomimus parvulus*
grayish or brownish above, white below; present on
most of the main islands

Hood Mockingbird* *Nesomimus macdonaldi*
slightly larger than the Galapagos Mockingbird; found
only on Española (Hood) Island

■ **FINCHES** (Fringillidae), **13 species**

Small Ground-Finch* *Geospiza fuliginosa*
small dark finch, occurs on most of the islands

Large Cactus-Finch* *Geospiza conirostris*
large-billed finch found on only a few of the islands

Mangrove Finch* *Camarhynchus heliobates*
small, lighter colored than most of the other finches;
found now only on Isabela Island

Large Tree-Finch* *Camarhynchus psittacula*
dark above, light below; found on many of the islands

Woodpecker Finch* *Camarhynchus pallidus*
grayish olive above, lighter below; uses sticks to
"fish" for its insect food

Warbler Finch* *Certhidea olivacea*
smallest of the Galápagos finches, with a small,
sharp bill

Restricted to the Galápagos Islands

Waved Albatross These seabirds are endemic to Española Island; they breed from March to January. Pairs engage in elaborate and ritualized courtship dances. After the pose shown here, the bill is snapped shut with a loud clap. *Española Island, Galápagos, Ecuador*

More than 1,500 bird species occur in southern South America, with Chile and Argentina alone having a combined total of about 1,100 species.

SOUTHERN SOUTH AMERICA

SOUTHERN SOUTH AMERICA IS A TREASURE TROVE OF WONDERFUL DESTINATIONS for nature observation, from Brazil's Pantanal wetlands in the north to Argentina's Tierra del Fuego National Park in the south—and, not incidentally, for many fantastic birds. Perhaps foremost among these are three huge, charismatic species. One is the Andean Condor, monarch of the region's high mountain zones and one of the largest flying birds, with a ten-foot wingspan. The other two are rheas, flightless birds that weigh in at up to 55 pounds. (The condor and the rheas can also be seen in parts of northern South America, but their population strongholds are in the south.) A few species of penguins are common in the southern reaches of Chile and Argentina and there are places, for instance, at Punta Tombo on Argentina's central eastern coast, where you can easily walk among breeding colonies of Magellanic Penguins. Parrots in the region include the stunning blue Hyacinth Macaw, an endangered species more than three feet in length that is the world's largest parrot, and the Burrowing Parrot, a noisy, gregarious, yellow-bellied species that nests in cliffside burrows. For those seeking truly unusual birds, southern South America is the main residence of the globe's two species of seriemas, large, long-legged birds of open habitats, and of the endemic Magellanic Plover, a small gray plover that is different enough in form and behavior from other plovers that it is considered the sole member of its family.

A nice plus for this region is a contrast with northern South America: In the north, the Amazonian rivers and rain forests and the Andean mountainside cloud forests are a bit forbidding and cause most visitors to utilize guides and organized tours; but southern South America has many great birding destinations that can be explored independently. Chiefly in Chile and Argentina, a pair of birders with even

OPPOSITE: **Andean Flamingo** This species along with its close relative the Puna (or James's) Flamingo lives around shallow, high-elevation saline lakes in southern Peru, northern Chile, and parts of Argentina. From a distance they can be difficult to separate from each other, but the Andean has yellow legs and is larger. Like all flamingos, they feed on microorganisms they filter from the water. *Chile*

Black-faced Ibis This striking ibis is commonly seen foraging in fields and pastures in southern Argentina and Chile. The subspecies *branickii*, sometimes regarded as a separate species (Andean Ibis), lacks the black throat wattle and lives at high elevations in Ecuador, Peru, and Bolivia. *Argentina*

LOCAL BIRDING & CONSERVATION ORGANIZATIONS

■ **ASOCIACIÓN ORNI-TOLÓGICA DEL PLATA** (www.avesargentinas.org.ar) Argentine bird conservation, education, and observation society headquartered in Buenos Aires

■ **AVESCHILE (LA UNIÓN DE ORNITÓLOGOS DE CHILE)** (www.unorch.cl) works to protect Chile's birds and natural environments; headquartered in Santiago

■ **BRAZILIAN ORNITHO-LOGICAL SOCIETY** (www.ararajuba.org.br) promotes the study and conservation of Brazil's birds

■ **FUNDACIÓN PUMALIN AND THE CONSERVATION LAND TRUST** (www.parquepumalin.cl) works to buy and preserve natural lands in Chile and Argentina

a modicum of adventurous spirit, with a rental vehicle and a map, can fairly easily reach myriad national parks and other birding areas on their own.

GEOGRAPHY AND HABITATS

The area under consideration here is the southern half of the South American continent, extending from the tropics of northern Chile, southern Brazil, and extreme northern Argentina south to the tip of the continent at subantarctic Tierra del Fuego and Cape Horn. The outstanding wildlife site in southern Brazil is the Pantanal, which lies against Paraguay and Bolivia. It is relatively small when compared to the huge Amazon region, but is nonetheless quite a large zone. Access is mainly via the area's sole main road, the Transpanteneira Highway, from Cuiabá to the Pantanal's north or Campo Grande to the south. Major habitats are palm savanna, parkland and riverside forest. Visitors here usually stay at ranches called *fazendas,* some with modern tourist facilities, along the Transpanteneira, and most birding also occurs along this bumpy, frazzling road. Best time to visit the Pantanal is usually during its dry season, April–October.

Chile and Argentina are especially pleasurable to visit because of their abundance of open, appealing habitats and beautiful scenery, including the vast pampas of northeastern Argentina and the subalpine and alpine zones of Chile's southern

Andes region. Chile, a long, narrow country along South America's Pacific coast, has the incredibly dry Atacama Desert in its northern reaches as well as high Andean grasslands, deciduous forests in its midsection, and evergreen forests and Patagonian grasslands in the south. Argentina, at more than one million square miles in area, is one of the largest countries. Regions of primary interest to birders include the mountainous northwest, the subtropical open forests, savanna, and scrub habitats of the Gran Chaco region in the north, the grassland plains, or pampas, south and west of Buenos Aires, and the cool grassland steppe and lakes of Patagonia in the south. Many of the south temperate birds breed during the southern spring/summer, so that is often the best time for birders to visit.

BIRDLIFE

More than 1,500 bird species occur in southern South America, with Chile and Argentina alone having a combined total of about 1,100 species. A prominent feature of the birdlife in this region, at least to North Americans, is that most species tend to breed during North America's winter months. Of course, this is because the

SPOTTING THE RUFOUS-THROATED DIPPER

On my first trip to northwestern Argentina in 1972, I was bound and determined to see the Rufous-throated Dipper, a species endemic to the eastern chain of the Andes Mountains in extreme northern Argentina. Like other dippers, it dwells only on wet boulders and rocks along rushing mountain streams.

We rented a tiny Citroën vehicle in the city of Tucumán and drove up into the nearby mountains toward Tafi del Valle. Only 15 minutes from the stream site where a pair of these dippers was supposedly hanging out, our rental car died near a monument to El Indio (an Incan messenger). In this time before cell phones or, indeed, any other phones in this area, one of us had to watch the car and the other had to hitchhike back to Tucumán. Four hours later a tow truck appeared from the rental car company and took the car away, but there was no room for me in the truck. I then had to hitchhike down to the city, arriving well after dark and, needless to say, with no Rufous-throated Dipper on my life list.

Finally in 2008 I had a chance to return to northwestern Argentina. In a new and dependable van I arrived at a bridge over the river three miles beyond the still standing El Indio statue, and there a pair of dippers sat for me on a wet boulder for five minutes. The pressure was off, the sighting seemed so easy—and only 36 years delayed. —D.P.

Rufous-throated Dipper The curious dipper family (Cinclidae) is made up of only five species. They all live a similar aquatic lifestyle. *Argentina*

seasons are reversed in the Southern Hemisphere, with spring starting in September and summer in December. In another major reversal, many birds that breed in the south temperate regions of Chile and Argentina migrate northward for their non-breeding periods, often to the tropical Amazon region. Research into these "austral migrants" is still in its early stages, so the identities of all the species that make these seasonal movements are not yet known. Also, as in other mountainous regions, many Andean birds make altitudinal movements with the changing seasons, moving to lower elevations for the colder nonbreeding months. Some North American breeders that migrate to the Neotropics make it as far south as southern South America, including some shorebirds, flycatchers, swallows, and the Bobolink.

In addition to such charismatic groups as rheas and parrots, southern South America is known for its tinamous (about 20 species), grebes (6 species), herons, egrets, and bitterns (about 15 species), ibises (7 species), flamingos (3 species), ducks, geese, and swans (endemics including Black-necked Swan, Upland Goose, and Flightless Steamerduck), woodpeckers (about 30 species), ovenbirds and wood-creepers (about 80 species), tapaculos (about 18 species), flycatchers (more than 145

Yellow Cardinal This is a male; the female has more subdued plumage coloration with mostly gray underparts and a white border around the black throat patch. *Location unknown*

SPOTTING THE YELLOW CARDINAL

Once common and widespread in southern South America, the beautiful song of the attractive Yellow Cardinal has been its downfall. Trapping for the cage bird industry has helped reduce this species to endangered status. It now occurs sparsely over a small portion of its former range in northeastern Argentina and part of Uruguay.

To look for the Yellow Cardinal, we traveled to the isolated portion of Argentina that lies between the Parana River and the Uruguay River, an area of extensive swampland mixed with dry thorn scrub near the town of Pelligrini. We knew that this area could still hold a small population of these birds, but didn't know where to look . . . exactly. After some inquiries, we spoke with a local guide who told us that he had seen a pair of cardinals the week before on the grounds of a nearby ranch

house, and that maybe they were still in the neighborhood.

Early the next morning, we eagerly drove to this area and walked around the ranch's outbuildings and into the nearby thorn forest. With no sighting, and as the temperature and humidity soared, we decided that five hours of searching was all we could abide. We reluctantly gave up the search and returned to our vehicle parked near the ranch house. To our surprise, four birds were sitting on the car's roof rack and taking turns coming down to the side mirror to attack their images. As we approached this noisy scene, it became evident that we had parked the vehicle right on the territorial boundary of two pairs of Yellow Cardinals. They kept up their aggressive behavior toward the vehicle for an hour, and we were elated to have such close and lasting views of this extremely rare species. —D.P.

Upland Goose This goose (male is shown) occurs from central Argentina and Chile to Tierra del Fuego; a larger subspecies lives on the Falkland Islands. *Argentina*

FIELD GUIDE & SITE GUIDE BOOKS

■ *Birds of Argentina & Uruguay (2004)*
D. Yzurieta and T. Narosky
Vazquez Mazzini

■ *Birds of Argentina and the South-west Atlantic (2010)*
M. Pearman
Christopher Helm Publishers

■ *Birds of Chile (2003)*
A. Jaramillo
Princeton University Press

■ *Birds of Patagonia, Tierra del Fuego & Antarctic Peninsula, the Falkland Islands & South Georgia (2003)*
E. Couve and C. Vidal
Fantástico Sur, Chile

■ *Birds of South America: Non-Passerines: Rheas to Woodpeckers (2006)*
F. Erize and M. Rumboll
Princeton University Press

■ *Birds of Southern South America and Antarctica (1998)*
M.R. de la Pena and M. Rumboll
Princeton University Press

■ *Brazil: Amazon and Pantanal: Travellers' Wildlife Guide (2005)*
D.L. Pearson and L.D. Beletsky
Interlink Books

species), tanagers (more than 40 species), sparrows and seedeaters (more than 60 species), and American blackbirds (about 25 species). The last group sports a variety of cowbirds, oropendolas, caciques, blackbirds, meadowlarks, and orioles, among others. There are, in fact, three different meadowlark species in southern South America and two blackbird species formally known as marshbirds. Another avian feature of southern South America is the region's abundance of seabirds, particularly off Chile's coast. Here, the nutrient-rich, cold-flowing Humboldt Current moves northward, supporting a diverse and abundant marine life that includes six species of albatrosses and many other tube-nosed seabirds, as well as Peruvian Booby, Guanay Cormorant, and Red-legged Cormorant.

Some of the more common birding locations in Chile are the high-elevation Andean habitats not far from Santiago as well as the dry coastal ranges and desert lowlands situated between Santiago and the Pacific Ocean. In southern Chile, the beech forests, grassy meadows, lakes, and mountains of Torres del Paine National Park have more than 100 species, including Andean Condor and Lesser Rhea. Popular, easily reached birding areas in Argentina include the grassy marshlands around Buenos Aires, Iguazu National Park (mentioned above), and spots around Ushuaia, Argentina's southernmost city, located at the southern end of Tierra del Fuego. In southern Brazil, the Pantanal's huge populations of waterbirds are a prime attraction. These include Horned and Southern Screamers, nine species of ducks, more than ten species of herons, and storks such as the Maguari Stork, Jabiru, and Wood Stork.

Significant Species of Southern South America

ABOUT 80 FAMILIES FOUND IN THIS REGION

■ **RHEAS*** (Rheidae), **2 species**

Lesser Rhea* *Rhea pennata*
large and flightless; occurs mainly in Argentina and Chile, including in high-elevation puna habitat

■ **TINAMOUS** (Tinamidae), **20 species**

Chilean Tinamou* *Nothoprocta perdicaria*
small tinamou of grassy areas; endemic to Chile

Brushland Tinamou* *Nothoprocta cinerascens*
tinamou of scrubland and open woods, mainly in Argentina

■ **PENGUINS** (Spheniscidae), **7 species**

Humboldt Penguin *Spheniscus humboldti*
medium-size, less common penguin with a limited breeding range off western South America

Magellanic Penguin* *Spheniscus magellanicus*
common penguin of waters off southern Chile and southern Argentina

■ **SCREAMERS** (Anhimidae), **2 species**

Southern Screamer *Chauna torquata*
large gray bird of marshes and lake edges, with red feet

■ **DUCKS, GEESE, AND SWANS** (Anatidae), **35 species**

Spectacled Duck* *Anas specularis*
wetlands bird of forested areas of southern Argentina and Chile

Flightless Steamerduck* *Tachyeres pteneres*
large, bulky, gray duck found along southern Chile's rocky coasts

Torrent Duck *Merganetta armata*
found in fast-flowing rivers and streams of the Andes

■ **SERIEMAS** (Cariamidae), **2 species**

Red-legged Seriema *Cariama cristata*
large, long-legged, crested bird of open woodland, scrub and savanna habitats

■ **PARROTS** (Psittacidae), **31 species**

Hyacinth Macaw *Anodorhynchus hyacinthinus*
spectacular and endangered; large blue parrot often seen in the Pantanal

Burrowing Parrot* *Cyanoliseus patagonus*
olive-colored parrot with red belly and blue wing patches

Austral Parakeet* *Enicognathus ferrugineus*
dull green parrot of south temperate forests and woodlands

■ **OVENBIRDS AND WOODCREEPERS** (Furnariidae), **about 115 species**

Crag Chilia* *Chilia melanura*
ovenbird of mountain scrub zones; endemic to a small part of Chile

Chilean Seaside Cinclodes* *Cinclodes nigrofumosus*
dark bird of rocky marine beaches; endemic to northern and central Chile

Thorn-tailed Rayadito* *Aphrastura spinicauda*
small, very active ovenbird mainly of southern temperate forests

Rufous Hornero *Furnarius rufus*
famous for its oven-like nests; the national bird of Argentina

White-throated Woodcreeper *Xiphocolaptes albicollis*
large woodcreeper of eastern Brazil and northeastern Argentina

■ **TYPICAL ANTBIRDS** (Thamnophilidae), **about 45 species**

White-bearded Antshrike* *Biatas nigropectus*
restricted to small areas of southeastern Brazil and northeastern Argentina, occurs mainly in thick bamboo forests

Mato Grosso Antbird* *Cercomacra melanaria*
small bird of forest thickets; male black, female gray

■ **TAPACULOS** (Rhinocryptidae), **about 20 species**

Moustached Turca* *Pteroptochos megapodius*
gray-brown bird of dry, rocky slopes; endemic to Chile

Crested Gallito* *Rhinocrypta lanceolata*
gray-brown and chestnut ground bird with a conspicuous crest

Spotted Bamboowren* *Psilorhamphus guttatus*
small brown and gray bird usually inhabiting stands of bamboo

■ **COTINGAS** (Cotingidae), **8 species**

Rufous-tailed Plantcutter* *Phytotoma rara*
bird of mostly open habitats, from central Chile
southwards; eats grasses and leaves

Hooded Berryeater* *Carpornis cucullata*
striking fruit-eater with black head and yellow chest,
endemic to southeastern Brazil

Black-and-gold Cotinga* *Tijuca atra*
male black with yellow wing patch, female greenish;
endemic to a tiny region of southeastern Brazil

■ **TYRANT FLYCATCHERS** (Tyrannidae), **about 140 species**

Russet-winged Spadebill* *Platyrinchus leucoryphus*
very small olive-brown bird of wet forest undergrowth

Chocolate-vented Tyrant* *Neoxolmis rufiventris*
mainly terrestrial flycatcher that breeds in southern
Argentina

Salinas Monjita* *Xolmis salinarum*
brown and white flycatcher endemic to a small portion
of northwestern Argentina

■ **BUNTINGS, SPARROWS, AND ALLIES** (Emberizidae),
about 85 species

Red-backed Sierra-Finch* *Phrygilus dorsalis*
stocky gray and rufous finch of high mountain areas

Patagonian Yellow-Finch* *Sicalis lebruni*
gray and yellowish finch of grassy plains of southern
Patagonia

Some Other Species Global Birders Often Seek

Peruvian Diving-Petrel *Pelecanoides garnotii*
one of the world's four diving-petrel species

Guanay Cormorant *Phalacrocorax bougainvillii*
black and white cormorant of South America

Maguari Stork *Ciconia maguari*
black and white, endemic to South America

Chilean Flamingo *Phoenicopterus chilensis*
flamingo of the Andes and pampas

Andean Condor *Vultur gryphus*
huge vulture with a wingspan of up to 10.5 feet

White-throated Caracara* *Phalcoboenus albogularis*
bird of forests and open mountain areas; endemic to
southern portions of Chile and Argentina

Chaco Chachalaca* *Ortalis canicollis*
found in the chaco region of Bolivia, Paraguay,
and northern Argentina

American Painted-snipe* *Rostratula semicollaris*
dark brown, black and white, with a longish, downcurved bill; one of three painted-snipes (family Rostratu-
lidae) and the only one in the Western Hemisphere

Andean Avocet *Recurvirostra andina*
black and white, high-altitude avocet of the Andes

Diademed Sandpiper-Plover *Phegornis mitchellii*
plover of the high Andes

Magellanic Plover* *Pluvianellus socialis*
breeds around high-elevation lakes and ponds of
extreme southern Chile and Argentina; the only
member of single-species family Pluvianellidae

Rufous-bellied Seedsnipe *Attagis gayi*
ptarmigan-like bird of the Andean alpine zone; one
of four seedsnipes (family Thinocoridae)

Snowy Sheathbill *Chionis albus*
white, pigeonlike bird with fleshy wattles at the base
of the bill; one of two sheathbills (family Chionidae)

Snowy-crowned Tern* *Sterna trudeaui*
little-known tern, restricted to southern South America

Chaco Owl* *Strix chacoensis*
dark brown owl heavily barred and spotted with white

Plovercrest* *Stephanoxis lalandi*
hummingbird endemic to southeastern Brazil and northeastern Argentina; male with a long green crest

Three-toed Jacamar* *Jacamaralcyon tridactyla*
endemic to southeastern Brazil

Spot-backed Puffbird *Nystalus maculatus*
puffbird of woodlands and savanna

Saffron Toucanet *Baillonius bailloni*
rain forest species, mainly olive and yellow

Chilean Flicker* *Colaptes pitius*
gray-capped flicker, endemic to Chile and extreme
southwestern Argentina

Rufous Gnateater *Conopophaga lineata*
forest and woodland species, small, stocky,
and short-tailed

Helmeted Manakin *Antilophia galeata*
mainly confined to woodlands of central and southern
Brazil; the male is black with red crest, cap, and back

Rufous-throated Dipper* *Cinclus schulzi*
occurs only around mountain streams over a small
region of southern Boliva and northwestern Argentina

Chilean Mockingbird* *Mimus thenca*
brown mockingbird endemic to central Chile

Pampas Meadowlark* *Stunella defilippii*
uncommon bird of the pampas, now mainly in northeastern Argentina; male dark above with red underparts

*Restricted to Southern South America

Probably all persons with a deep interest in natural history and wildlife, and adequate means and adequate health, should make a trip to Antarctica once in their lives.

SOUTH AMERICA
Atlantic Ocean
Pacific Ocean
Falkland Islands
South Georgia Island
Antarctic Circle
ANTARCTICA

ANTARCTICA

ANTARCTICA IS THE SOLE CONTINENT LACKING A COMMERCIAL AIRPORT AND A tourist hotel (not to mention a McDonald's, a Starbucks and a Coca-Cola distributor). Therefore, essentially all birders who manage to visit the "white continent" do so by boat. These natural history cruises, which are possible solely during the relatively benign Antarctic summer, began in the 1950s, when only the very well-off could take such expensive and exclusive trips. But with the strong growth of the adventure cruise industry during the 1980s and 1990s, prices declined somewhat and the numbers of Antarctic trips made per year increased markedly. By the mid-1990s, some 7,000 to 9,000 people cruised to Antarctica each year, and more do so now. Although many of these two- to four-week wildlife-viewing cruises are very expensive, there are often "budget" deals to be had for less-desirable cabins on ships that sail at less-than-optimal dates. Generally, more expensive cruises (1) have fewer passengers (50 to 100 instead of 200); (2) more onboard guides, naturalists and lecturers; (3) spend more time on or near the Antarctic Peninsula (usually the main destination of such trips); (4) try to have passengers out "on the ice," exploring and watching wildlife more times per day and for more hours overall; and (5) sometimes arrange visits to Antarctic scientific research stations.

Antarctic trips depart from either southern South America (usually from Ushuaia, Argentina, "the southernmost city in the world") or, much less frequently, from New Zealand. There are several reasons for preferring South American departures: Antarctica lies only about 600 miles from the southern tip of South America, but about 1,200 miles from New Zealand; traversing these southern oceans can be a rough experience; and the climate in parts of the Antarctic Peninsula, which is close

OPPOSITE: Chinstrap Penguin Fantastic blue icebergs are a visual highlight of any Antarctic trip. This one is graced by the presence of Chipstrap Penguins, whose sharp claws allow them to scramble up the icy slopes. *Weddell Sea, Antarctica*

Long-tailed Meadowlark About ten passerine species breed on the Falklands. This colorful species (male is shown) is a common and widely distributed resident in the archipelago. It is closely related to the two meadowlark species found in North America. *Falkland Islands*

to South America, is a bit milder than that of the rest of the continent (such as the Ross Sea region, where cruises from New Zealand typically land passengers). The ships from South America cross the Drake Passage, the body of water between Tierra del Fuego and Antarctica, sometimes stopping at various islands (such as the South Shetland Islands and Elephant Island) on their way to the Antarctic Peninsula, which juts out toward Cape Horn. The Antarctic Peninsula is the target destination of these cruises both because passengers want to step onto an actual part of the Antarctic continent and because perhaps the greatest bird species objective of most travelers, the Emperor Penguin, is found there. Note that not all Antarctic cruises visit the Antarctic Peninsula; some travel only to subantarctic and Antarctic islands. Subantaractic islands (often defined as those positioned between 50° S and 60° S latitude) include the Falkland Islands and South Georgia Island east of southern Argentina, and some of New Zealand's remote small islands situated between that country's main islands and Antarctica. Larger subantarctic islands support many seabirds such as penguins, petrels, storm-petrels, and cormorants, but also a variety of other birdlife: ducks and geese, raptors, shorebirds, gulls, and even a few small passerine (perching) birds.

Probably all persons with a deep interest in natural history and wildlife, and adequate means and adequate health, should make a trip to Antarctica once in their lives. Aside from hazards associated with any adventure cruise to a remote area (your ship striking an iceberg or running aground on rocks, and being far from major medical help), these trips are generally safe. This continent itself is apolitical: It is considered by all to be an international territory, although some countries have tried to stake claims, and it

LOCAL BIRDING & CONSERVATION ORGANIZATIONS

■ **ANTARCTIC AND SOUTHERN OCEAN COALITION** (www.asoc.org) promotes Antarctic conservation

■ **ANTARCTICAN SOCIETY** (www.antarctican.org) organization for people who have visited or are interested in the continent

is governed by international treaties and conventions. Tourism supposedly is the only commercial industry presently allowed on or immediately around the entire continent.

GEOGRAPHY AND HABITATS

Antarctica is mainly covered with a permanent cap of ice that extends over about 5.4 million square miles, an area larger than Europe or Australia. This icecap, which covers flatlands, mountains, valleys, and even freshwater lakes, averages a mile thick but is more than double that over some regions. Only small bits of bare land occur on the continent, mostly in the form of high mountain peaks that pierce the snow-cap and some windswept coastal areas. Despite all the frozen water, Antarctica is extremely dry, with less than five inches of precipitation falling annually (as snow) over most of its surface—an amount comparable to that found in hot deserts such as the American Southwest's Mojave. During the austral summer (winter in North America), when birders typically visit, the sun never sets but temperatures rarely top the freezing point. Aside from bacteria and other microorganisms, and algae, there's precious little year-round life on the continent. There are a few invertebrate animals

BIRDING THE ANTARCTIC PENINSULA

A long finger-like projection jutting far northward, the Antarctic Peninsula produces the warmest temperatures and highest bird diversity of any location on the "white continent." Of all the islands and inlets along this jagged peninsula, one of the most beautiful and bird-filled is Paradise Bay. It is also one of only two places that most cruise ships are allowed to stop and land passengers on the continent itself. Here, stalking leopard seals wait for Gentoo Penguins to dive from the protection of their iceberg havens. Both wintering Arctic Terns and nesting Antarctic Terns hover over the water, plunging into its surface whenever small fish come close. And South Polar Skuas, Kelp Gulls, and hundreds of Cape Petrels wheel in immense flocks, driven by the constant wind. Often cloudy, it is only when the sun peeks through that the reason for this place being named Paradise Bay becomes obvious. The bay is surrounded by sharp, steep, black massifs and tall glaciers. Dazzling white icebergs of myriad shapes and sizes float everywhere and these, and the clear ocean water, provide striking backdrops for birds sitting on snowy crests, flying directly above the water, or swimming in large flocks under the water in pursuit of krill. Tame minke whales also come near shore here and the gulls and terns that usually attend them also move in closely, eagerly awaiting fish and krill left over from the whales' feeding. —D.P.

Leopard seal with Chinstrap Penguin These predatory seals patrol where penguins enter the water. The penguins are well aware of the danger and often try to outwait the waiting seals. *Antarctic Peninsula*

that can withstand long periods of very low temperatures, some lichen, fungi, and mosses, and a couple of species of flowering plants. All of these organisms are more likely to be found on the Antarctic Peninsula, which has a slightly milder and wetter climate than the rest of the continent.

The Falkland Islands and South Georgia are two subantarctic island groups in the South Atlantic visited regularly by birders. Both are British territories. The Falklands consist of two main islands and many smaller ones located about 300 miles east of southernmost Argentina. Perhaps the only permanent settlement of any size on any subantarctic island occurs here—about 3,000 people live in the Falklands. There is scheduled air service here and tourist accommodations, rental vehicles, and boat charters are available. Much of the land of the main islands is taken up with farmland, grazing pastures, grassland, shrubland, and peat bogs. Extensive penguin and cormorant breeding colonies, as well as colonies of seals and sea lions, occur on the main islands but especially on the smaller, surrounding islands. South Georgia, located almost a thousand miles farther east from the Falklands, and a bit more southerly in latitude, is a far more isolated and bleak place. There is a large main

King Penguin Standing about three feet tall and weighing up to 35 pounds, the King is a large penguin—only the Emperor Penguin is larger. *South Georgia Island*

BIRDING SOUTH GEORGIA ISLAND

For a jaw-dropping birding experience, South Georgia Island, located east of Tierra del Fuego in the subantarctic zone, is unrivaled. Salisbury Plain is one of the only relatively flat areas on the protected north coast of the island. Here, sandwiched between two huge glaciers, melted runoff produces an extensive gravel beach that is ideal for nesting King Penguins. More than 200,000 of these tall black and white birds gather in the breeding season, honking, courting, mating and feeding their tall brown chicks that are called "oakum boys" (because their color resembles old ships' ropes). Adding to the rich array of sights and sounds here are predatory Brown Skuas searching boldly for unattended eggs, Snowy Sheathbills collecting tidbits of offal left behind by predators, and Antarctic Giant Petrels exhibiting red heads and necks bloodied from feasts on dead fur seals.

On the nearby, rat-free, satellite island, Prion Island, individuals from a colony of huge Wandering Albatrosses engage in elegant courting displays or sit quietly on their nests situated among hilltop bunch grasses, where the wind is always blowing. Each pair's tall mud nest is located next to a large flat area that serves as the pair's take-off runway.

The long narrow wings of these birds are better adapted for around-the-world soaring over windy oceans than for taking off from dry land—thus the need for take-off runways. On South Georgia one can also find the globe's most southerly passerine (perching) bird, the endemic South Georgia Pipit, as well as a carnivorous subspecies of the Yellow-billed Pintail (*georgica*) that can often be observed exploiting a unique food source—dead seal carcasses it finds along the shore. —D.P.

Antarctic Peninsula Even in the austral summer months when birders and tour ships can visit, the Antarctic Peninsula presents a wintery visage. The flying bird is a giant petrel—there are two species—but this one is too far away to identify precisely. *Antarctic Peninsula*

FIELD GUIDE & SITE GUIDE BOOKS

■ *Antarctica: A Guide to the Wildlife, 5th ed.* (2008)
T. Soper
Bradt Travel Guides

■ *Birds and Mammals of the Antarctic, Subantarctic and Falkland Islands* (2004)
F.S. Todd
Sunbelt Publications

■ *Birds of Southern South America and Antarctica* (1988)
M.R. de la Pena and M. Rumboll
Princeton University Press

■ *The Complete Guide to Antarctic Wildlife: Birds and Marine Mammals of the Antarctic Continent and the Southern Ocean, 2nd ed.* (2008)
H. Shirihai
Princeton University Press

island and a chain of much smaller islands. The climate is usually inhospitable, and the terrain is rugged and mountainous, with many glacier-covered areas and snow and ice at higher elevations. However, the soils are rich enough to support plant life such as tussock grasses, ferns, mosses, and a few flowering plants.

BIRDLIFE

Only seabirds occur on or close to the Antarctic continent, and these include penguins, albatrosses, petrels, storm-petrels, cormorants, gulls, terns, and skuas. Some breed there and breeding can last for much of the year. For instance, Emperor Penguins begin their breeding in March and often don't finish until December. Others, however, like many of the albatrosses, breed elsewhere (often on subantarctic islands), but fly into the airspace above Antarctic waters on their wanderings in search of good food sources.

The subantarctic islands of South Georgia and the Falklands have many seabirds also—and are celebrated for these among the many birders who visit there. But due to their somewhat milder climates and areas of ice-free terrain, these islands have larger, more diverse avifaunas than Antarctica. The Falklands, especially, with a climate moderate enough to sustain sheep ranching, support 60-plus breeding birds including two grebes, about 15 members of the duck and goose family, a few raptors, and about 10 perching bird species. In the latter group are a swallow, a pipit, an endemic wren, a thrush, a finch, a meadowlark, and, of course, the House Sparrow. About 30 species have been recorded breeding on South Georgia Island.

Significant Species
of Antarctica
9 FAMILIES FOUND IN THIS REGION

■ **PENGUINS** (Spheniscidae), **5 species**

Emperor Penguin* *Aptenodytes forsteri*
largest penguin and often a main goal of a birder's trip to Antarctica; breeds only in Antarctica

Gentoo Penguin *Pygoscelis papua*
medium-size penguin with a bright red-orange bill

Adelie Penguin* *Pygoscelis adeliae*
along with the Emperor, this smaller penguin is confined to Antarctica, breeding only in ice-free areas

Chinstrap Penguin *Pygoscelis antarcticus*
common species of the Antarctic Peninsula and Antarctic and subantarctic waters

■ **ALBATROSSES** (Diomedeidae), **4 species**

Wandering Albatross *Diomedea exulans*
largest albatross, with the longest avian wingspan (up to 11.5 feet)

Gray-headed Albatross *Thalassarche chrysostoma*
small, mostly black and white, found in southern oceans everywhere but mainly in subantarctic regions

Black-browed Albatross *Thalassarche melanophris*
small albatross occurring throughout Antarctic and subantarctic waters

Light-mantled Albatross *Phoebetria palpebrata*
medium-size, gray-bodied albatross that occurs in Antarctic and subantarctic waters

■ **PETRELS AND SHEARWATERS** (Procellariidae), **6 species**

Antarctic Giant Petrel *Macronectes giganteus*
very large petrel of southern oceans worldwide

Southern Fulmar *Fulmarus glacialoides*
medium-size petrel that breeds in Antarctica and on subantarctic islands

Antarctic Petrel *Thalassoica antarctica*
nests on Antarctic islands, patrols southern oceans

Cape Petrel *Daption capense*
distinctive black and white petrel, often in flocks

Snow Petrel *Pagodroma nivea*
pure white petrel that nests on the Antarctic Peninsula (among other places) and is restricted to ice-packed Antarctic waters; often a seabird Antarctic birders very much want to see

■ **STORM-PETRELS** (Hydrobatidae), **2 species**

Wilson's Storm-Petrel *Oceanites oceanicus*
spends summer months in Antarctic waters

Black-bellied Storm-Petrel *Fregetta tropica*
wide-ranging oceanic species

■ **SHEATHBILLS** (Chionidae), **1 species**

Snowy Sheathbill *Chionis albus*
white, pigeon-like bird with fleshy wattles at the base of the bill; scavenges food especially around penguin colonies

■ **SKUAS** (Stercorariidae), **2 species**

South Polar Skua *Stercorarius maccormicki*
predatory gull-like bird that nests coastally in Antarctica

Brown Skua *Stercorarius antarcticus*
common around the Antarctic Peninsula

Some Other Species Global Birders Often Seek

Antarctic Shag *Phalacrocorax bransfieldensis*
breeds on the Antarctic Peninula

Kelp Gull *Larus dominicanus*
occurs in many parts of Southern Hemisphere oceans and also on Antarctic Peninsula

Antarctic Tern *Sterna vittata*
found widely in the southern oceans and occurs on the Antarctic Peninsula

Some Significant Species of South Atlantic Subantarctic Islands

King Penguin *Aptenodytes patagonicus*
second-largest penguin; breeds in South Georgia, the Falklands, and some other subantarctic islands

Imperial Shag *Phalacrocorax atriceps*
black and white cormorant of southern South America with a separate subspecies in the Falklands

Ruddy-headed Goose *Chloephaga rubidiceps*
heavily barred goose of the Falklands and southern South America

Falklands Steamerduck *Tachyeres brachypterus*
large, flightless, goose-like duck endemic to the Falklands

Yellow-billed Pintail *Anas georgica*
South American species also occurring on South Georgia and the Falklands

Striated Caracara *Phalcoboenus australis*
one of two caracaras in the Falklands; overall blackish brown with white striations on neck and chest

Blackish Cinclodes *Cinclodes antarcticus*
dark, mid-size ovenbird in the Falklands and also the Tierra del Fuego region

South Georgia Pipit *Anthus antarcticus*
endemic to South Geogia Island; found in tussock grasslands and along shorelines and streams

Cobb's Wren *Troglodytes cobbi*
small, plain, brownish wren, similar to the House Wren; endemic to the Falklands

Austral Thrush *Turdus falckandii*
large, dark thrush with yellowish bill, legs, and eye ring; resident in the Falklands and also Chile and Argentina

Long-tailed Meadowlark *Sturnella loyca*
occurs in the Falklands and southern Chile and Argentina; male blackish above, bright red below

Restricted to Antarctica

Grytviken This outpost on the north side of South Georgia Island was once a whaling station. Now it is visited by ecotourists who explore the ruins and observe the reestablished wildlife, including abundant penguins, albatrosses, and seals. *South Georgia Island*

CHAPTER 5

EUROPE & THE MIDDLE EAST

miles
0   500
0   750
kilometers

ATLANTIC

OCEAN

Iceland

Arctic Circle

Norway

Sweden

Finland

North
Sea

United
Kingdom

Ireland

York

Nesting Seabirds
Flamborough Head
page 165

Denmark

Estonia

Latvia

Lithuania

Russia

Belarus

Baltic Sea

Netherlands

Belgium

Germany

Poland

Luxembourg

Czech Rep.

Ukraine

France

Liech.

Switz.

Austria

Slovakia

Hungary

Moldova

Slovenia

Croatia

Romania

Andorra

Monaco

San
Marino

Italy

Bosnia &
Herzegovina

Serbia

Montenegro

Kosovo

Bulgaria

Black Sea

CAUCASUS MOUNTAINS

Georgia

Caspian

Azerbaijan

Armenia

Portugal

Spain

Vatican
City

Macedonia

Albania

Greece

Turkey

Ir

Mediterranean

Malta

Sea

Cyprus

Lebanon

Syria

Iraq

Coto Doñana
the delta of the
Guadalquivir River
page 173

Israel

Jordan

Kuw

Eilat

Migration Hotspot
Eilat, Israel
page 174

Red Sea

Saud

URAL MOUNTAINS

Russia

Kazakhsta

Arabi

Tropic of Cancer

In western Europe there are probably more "official" places to watch birds per square mile than anywhere else.

BIRDING IN

EUROPE & THE MIDDLE EAST

EUROPE HAS SOME EXCEPTIONAL BIRDS. FOR EXAMPLE, IT POSSESSES NUMEROUS large and imposing raptors with six-foot wingspans, like the Imperial Eagle, White-tailed Eagle, and Eurasian Griffon. It has the beautiful, widespread Black Woodpecker, a crow-size velvety black bird with a deep red crown. And, perhaps most exotically, it has the Eurasian Hoopoe, a kingfisher cousin that can be found over much of the continent. The hoopoe is one of the region's most distinctive and unmistakable birds—black, white, and sandy buff plumage, broad wings, a huge erectile crest, and a long, thin, downcurved bill. It is a true avian treat to witness this striking bird foraging on the ground and then flying low to disappear into its nest, usually a hole in a tree or some other natural cavity.

However, from the general standpoint of building a global bird list, Europe can be a relatively unprofitable destination. First, the total number of species that might be spotted—perhaps 500 in Europe proper, up to about 650 if the Middle East is included—is much less than that found in some other continental birding destinations such as South America, Asia, or Africa. Perhaps of greater significance, when compared to that on other continents, the birdlife is much less "foreign" to North American birders. This is because North America and Europe (and the Nearactic and Palearctic regions, in general) share many of the same bird families. Furthermore, many species range over both continents—some of the ducks, geese, hawks, grouse, and owls, not to mention songbirds such as Horned Lark, Bohemian Waxwing, Winter Wren, Gray-headed Chickadee, Common Raven, and Hoary Redpoll.

PREVIOUS PAGES: **Northern Gannet colony** St. Kilda—an isolated archipelago that is the westernmost part of the Outer Hebrides northwest of Scotland—is home to variety of nesting seabirds. The Northern Gannet colony (or gannetry) found here is the largest in the world, totaling 30,000 pairs or about 25 percent of the global population. *Scotland*

Many birders traveling internationally for their hobby are keen to maximize their potential for seeing a lot of species or lots of exotic, colorful birds. For these people, Europe may less appealing. Still, huge numbers of North Americans visit Europe annually for business or holidays (France, Spain, Italy, the United Kingdom, and Germany are among the world's top ten tourism destinations). Many of these travelers are birders, so they take along binoculars. Knowledgeable birdwatchers do indeed visit Europe specifically for birding, even if it is not usually their first choice among world destinations, to see birds or avian spectacles they cannot see easily elsewhere.

What is of prime birder interest in Europe? First, the European avifauna is complex in that it has influences of several regions. This is especially true of northern Asia, which is contiguous with northern Europe and shares with it several ecological zones

Italian Alps Although much of Europe is heavily settled and the primeval forests are long gone, most of the higher elevations of the Alps remain in a natural state. *Italy*

and habitats, and of Africa, which is adjacent to southern Europe in the Mediterranean region. Thus, birding Europe can provide a small introduction to these other, more "foreign" zones. Good examples here are two mainly African groups, the bee-eaters and rollers. Each has a single, brightly colored, broadly distributed representative in Europe, the European Bee-eater and the European Roller—species sufficiently grand and gaudy that birders from anywhere would be most delighted to see them.

Second, although many of the European bird families will be familiar, some of them are particularly diverse, with myriad novel species to see. This is true particularly among the shorebirds and waterbirds (many of which breed during summer in Eurasia's Arctic region and then migrate southward to winter in temperate or tropical areas), as well as raptors, larks, pipits and wagtails, and the bunting and sparrow group.

Third, there are exhilarating concentrations of birds to experience, such as the huge colonies of seabirds and shorebirds characteristic of the Outer Hebrides island group, which lies just west of the Scottish mainland. Here, birds such as Leach's Storm-Petrel, Northern Fulmar, Northern Gannet, Dunlin, Eurasian Golden-Plover, and Atlantic Puffin breed in profusion. Wading birds and waterfowl congregate in huge numbers along the wild and remote North Sea coast of the Netherlands and Germany (an area known as the Waddenzee) to feed in the region's rich marshes and mudflats. Birders visit national parks and other sites here to see the tens of thousands of Red Knots, Eurasian Oystercatchers, and Bar-tailed Godwits among other shorebirds; and Barnacle Geese, Common Eiders, and other waterfowl. There are several points in Europe, such as Falsterbo in southern Sweden, where birders gather seasonally to watch thousands of hawks pass over in their mass migrations.

Yellow-billed Chough These bold and inquisitive members of the crows and jays family are alpine specialists. Flocks are often seen expertly soaring around mountaintops and steep cliffs; around Alpine villages and ski resorts they can become quite tame and approachable. Also known as Alpine Chough. *Germany*

The Middle East is covered here in conjunction with Europe because the composition of its avifauna is similar to Europe's. Scholarly books that deal with birds in this part of the world often consider Europe and the Middle East together, as do some field guides.

TRAVELING IN THE AREA

There are attractions to birding Europe that have nothing to do with the birds themselves. These concern Europe's fine tourist and birding infrastructure and the feeling of safety one has in traveling the roads and wandering the countryside in a continent now largely free and peaceful. Guides are not necessary over most of Europe, as long as you have the wherewithal to handle various languages and navigate the transportation systems. Public transport, especially the excellent railway system, is an efficient way to get around, but in most situations you will need a rental car to reach the best birding locations. Reaching Europe now can be fairly inexpensive, but accommodations in some regions are often pricey.

In western Europe there are probably more "official" places to watch birds per square mile than anywhere else. Britain's Royal Society for the Protection of Birds (RSPB) has more than 150 nature reserves dotting that nation's wilder areas. Germany, Sweden, Norway, France, and Spain have many national parks. For those who like the comradeship of the birding fraternity, Europe enjoys a very high birder density not only in Britain, with its long and popular history of birdwatching, but also in countries such as Ireland, Sweden, Denmark, and the Netherlands. In fact, when pursuing birds in places like Asia and Africa, it is usually these European birders whom one is most likely to bump into.

One final point of interest: Even though there has been an international push to standardize English common names of birds, Europeans (especially the British) often use common names that differ from the names typically employed by North Americans for the same species. Examples are Goosander, which is the European name for Common Merganser; Kentish Plover, used for our Snowy Plover; Great Gray Shrike for Northern Shrike; and Common Crossbill for Red Crossbill. When in doubt, check the bird's scientific name, which should be the same on both continents. Because all or most of Europe possesses only a single representative of some bird groups, the common names typically used there are shorter, without preceding modifiers: Ptarmigan is used for Rock Ptarmigan, Kingfisher for Common Kingfisher, Wren for Winter Wren, and Nuthatch for Eurasian Nuthatch. ∎

Bluethroat This species, an Old World flycatcher (but more recently placed in the thrush family), has a huge breeding range that extends across the Palearctic and south into China, India, and the Middle East. It even reaches northern Alaska, the only reliable place you can add it to your North American life list. *Europe*

OPPOSITE: **Common Kingfisher** A bright and beautiful species found throughout Europe. It perches motionless on the lookout for small fish, which are caught after a vertical plunge into the water. Its nest is located in a tunnel dug into a sandy bank. *England*

BIRDS OF THE REGION SIGNIFICANT GROUPS

DUCKS, GEESE, AND SWANS | HAWKS, EAGLES, AND KITES | GROUSE AND PTARMIGANS | OWLS | WOODPECKERS | PIPITS AND WAGTAILS | HYPOCOLIUS | ACCENTORS | OLD WORLD WARBLERS | OLD WORLD FLYCATCHERS

The selection of significant families of Europe detailed below—with a few exceptions—will be familiar to many readers. This is because Europe and North America, both being Northern Hemisphere continents, feature quite similar avifaunas and share many types of birds. Even some of the less familiar groups—the Old World warblers and Old World flycatchers, for instance—have a few North American representatives. Only two, the Hypocolius and the accentors, may seem totally "foreign."

■ Ducks, Geese, and Swans

Ducks, geese, and swans are familiar to birders the world over and need not be defined or described here. The family Anatidae is well represented in the region. This is especially true for Europe, where about 40 species are seen regularly—about the same number as in North America. Moreover, waterfowl (or "wildfowl," as ducks, geese, and swans are collectively called by the British) are important in Europe as a symbol of conservation. Much long-term work in the region has gone into preserving this group of birds and the wetlands they need to sustain healthy populations.

Of the larger members of the family, Europe has three swans. Two of them are shared with North America: the Tundra Swan, called Bewick's Swan in Europe, which looks slightly different and is a separate subspecies, and the Mute Swan, which is native to Eurasia but

not to North America. The Whooper Swan is wholly Eurasian. Nine goose species in Europe include the rare and threatened Lesser White-fronted Goose and the somewhat common Graylag Goose, made famous by mid-20th-century studies of behavioral imprinting.

Of the smaller waterfowl, many species will be familiar to first-time visitors from North America. Some species with a European distribution, but not normally occurring in North America include: Common Shelduck, Ruddy Shelduck, Garganey, Marbled Duck, Red-crested Pochard, Common Pochard, Ferruginous Duck, Smew, and White-headed Duck. Of

OPPOSITE: **Whooper Swan** The white swans of the Northern Hemisphere—Mute, Trumpeter, Whooper, and Tundra—are closely related. Whoopers have a wide breeding range in the Palearctic, extending from Iceland to easternmost Russia. *Finland*

these only the two shelducks and the Marbled Duck have no close relatives in North America. Shelducks are large, goose-like ducks that feed extensively on land or near the water's edge.

■ Hawks, Eagles, and Kites

The hawk, eagle, and kite family Accipitridae occurs worldwide except in Antarctica and is richly represented in Europe and the Middle East. Just as in their home countries, traveling birders often thrill to watch these majestic predatory birds soaring over field, forest, mountain, and desert. The approximately 40 species in the region include a number of large, striking birds that birdwatchers often especially want to see. These include the White-tailed Eagle, Eurasian Griffon, Imperial Eagle, and Lammergeier. Just as in North America, a popular birding activity in Europe is to gather at certain places that funnel hawks along

White-tailed Eagle An impressive, heavily built eagle that is a close relative of the Bald Eagle of North America. In Europe, this uncommon eagle is found around seacoasts and large rivers and lakes. *Finland*

their migration routes, or "corridors," to gawk at and marvel over the large numbers of passing raptors. Great hawk-watching locations are located in Falsterbo at the southern tip of Sweden, Gibraltar, the Black Sea region, and Israel, among others.

Two facts for North American birders to keep in mind when in Europe: First, some European raptors are the same species as those found in North America, such as the Golden Eagle, Northern Goshawk, and Rough-legged Hawk (known in Europe as Rough-legged Buzzard), although they are often classified as different subspecies. Second, the vultures in this part of the world, such as the Egyptian and Cinereous Vultures, as well as those in Asia and Africa, belong with the hawks and eagles in the family Accipitridae. They are essentially eagles with bare-skinned heads. These vultures are not closely related to the New World vultures such as the Turkey Vulture and Andean Condor, which constitute the separate family Cathartidae.

■ Grouse and Ptarmigans

The grouse and ptarmigans, chicken-like birds of Eurasia and North America, were formerly considered to be part of the pheasant family but are now separated as a self-contained unit of 19 species in the family Tetraonidae. Six of these occur in Europe, some of them with broad distributions. Most are difficult to see because they are very wary. For instance, spotting the Eurasian Capercaillie—the male an almost turkey-size black bird—is a challenge: It is widely distributed but scarce over most of its range and is extremely shy. The best time to look for most grouse and ptarmigans is in spring when the males are calling and displaying. The springtime displays of the male Eurasian Capercaillie and Black Grouse are spectacular events; local birders may know about the locations of the performance arenas (or leks).

Eurasian Capercaillie The blackish, male capercaillie (shown) is almost twice the size of the mottled brown female. During the courtship period (March to May) the males gather at dawn to display at hidden forested sites. *Sweden*

■ Owls

Owls, family Strigidae, comprise about 200 species worldwide species. The family is absent only in Antarctica and on some remote oceanic islands. North America has 19 owls (including the Barn Owl, which is in a separate family), and Europe and the Middle East combined have about the same number. North American birders will find some familiar birds here. Great Gray, Snowy, and Northern Hawk Owls, as well as Long-eared, Short-eared, and the Barn Owl are the same species as back home. There are several species

of scops-owls in Europe and the Middle East. They are among a large group of small owls widely distributed in the Old World and closely related to the New World screech-owls.

Your chance of seeing any of these species is greatly reduced unless you go "owling" at night in the proper habitat. Often the first indication of an owl's presence is its vocalizations, which can also be very helpful in making a nighttime identification. Daytime observations are usually chance encounters with a roosting bird.

Eurasian Eagle-Owl This very large owl—larger than the related Great Horned Owl of North America—is a fearsome predator of small mammals and birds up to the size of ducks and gulls. It is resident across the Palearctic and into China and the Middle East. *Finland*

Woodpeckers

Woodpeckers, family Picidae, occur everywhere there are trees except in Australia. They are one of the bird groups considered especially characteristic of Europe and the Middle East. There are about 12 species in the region, many of them widespread and fairly abundant. One of them is a small (six-inch) brown and gray bird known as the Eurasian Wryneck, two are green, one is the Black Woodpecker, and the others are black and white (pied) woodpeckers. Among the last group are three that overlap in distribution in some areas, look much alike (all in genus *Dendrocopos*), but differ in size: the Lesser Spotted, Middle Spotted, and Great Spotted Woodpeckers. As with the Hairy and Downy

Woodpeckers in North America, size helps birders distinguish the three species.

Discounting the aberrant Eurasian Wryneck, to North Americans the two "green woodpeckers" will seem the most unusual—their green plumage is a mossy olive-yellow color. The most widespread European species is known simply as the Green Woodpecker. It is a common bird of open woodlands, parks, and gardens that favors deciduous trees and also spends much time on the ground feeding on ants. The other species, Gray-faced Woodpecker, is decidedly less common and reaches higher elevations than the Green Woodpecker. It is absent from most of southern Europe and is not found in the British Isles. It is interesting to note that Ireland has no woodpeckers at all.

Pipits and Wagtails

Pipits and wagtails are small, slender, ground-dwelling songbirds that are probably most recognized for their incessant tail wagging. As they walk or run along, they constantly move their tails up and down. The family Motacillidae, with about 66 species, is also noted for its almost worldwide distribution. Pipits and wagtails spend most of their time on the ground feeding, pursuing insects and other small arthropod prey. Pipits tend to be open-country birds; wagtails have a close association with water and are often seen along streams, ditches, and in waterlogged meadows. About ten pipit species are found in Europe and the Middle East, as are four wagtails.

Pipits are notorious among birdwatchers because so many species look alike—most are streaky brownish birds with pale underparts—and are difficult to identify. Clues in the field sometimes lie in minor differences in their displays and flight calls. Pay close attention to the head pattern, leg color, and the

Great Spotted Woodpecker A common woodpecker throughout Europe; found in woodlands, gardens, and parks. This is a male; the female lacks the red spot on the back of the head. *England*

commonly occur in Europe are White Wagtail, Yellow Wagtail, Citrine Wagtail, and Gray Wagtail.

◼ Hypocolius

The Hypocolius is an uncommon, mid-size, grayish songbird largely restricted to the Middle East, chiefly Iraq, Jordan, and Arabia. It is one of those unusual birds that appears to have no close relatives, so ornithologists have placed it in its own family Hypocoliidae. About nine inches long, the Hypocolius has a short, wide bill, long tail, and short legs. The species inhabits open areas—scrublands, shrubby areas, and gardens. Usually occurring in small groups, these birds forage for small fruits and berries and occasional insects.

White Wagtail In Europe, this is the most common wagtail. Often noticed by non-birders, it is a conspicuous bird when seen running on the ground and it frequently nests around human habitations. *Europe*

Hypocolius This sleek, long-tailed species from the Middle East and western India has soft, satiny plumage similar to a waxwing and lives in brushy, semi-desert areas. Males (like the one shown here) have a black, shrike-like mask that the females lack. *India*

amount of streaking on the upperparts, and consult your field guide. The five most common species found in Europe are: Tawny Pipit, Tree Pipit, Meadow Pipit, Rock Pipit, and Water Pipit.

The wagtails found in Europe are an altogether different cup of tea. They are conspicuous, brightly marked birds, either black and white, or with mixtures of black, white, gray, and yellow. In structure, they appear slender and very long-tailed, and although they are closely related to pipits they are very unlikely to be confused with them. In contrast to pipits, the plumage of most wagtail species varies between the sexes and seasonally. The wagtails are mainly limited to the Old World, but two species have crossed the Bering Strait and also breed in Alaska. The four species that

Accentors

Accentors are small, drably colored, sparrow-like songbirds of Europe, Asia, and Northern Africa. There are 13 species in the family Prunellidae. All are called accentors except one: the common Dunnock (sometimes called European Hedge Sparrow), which is distributed broadly in Europe and parts of western Asia. Accentors are recognized for their unusual Old World distribution only in the temperate zone and their almost universal confinement to mountainous environments. The Dunnock is the only species that occurs in lowland areas in addition to inhabiting higher elevation sites in, for instance, the Alps and Pyrenees.

Accentors are approximately six to seven inches long. They have slender, pointed bills and shortish legs. Their thick plumages are brown and/or gray above, often streaked, and grayish or tawny below. Birders unfamiliar with accentors often initially mistake them for sparrows, finches, or buntings. Birds mainly of high-altitude scrub and brush, mountain slopes, and Alpine meadows, some accentors, such as the Alpine and Himalayan Accentors, routinely breed up to 16,500 feet and have been observed much higher. Members of this family tend to feed on the ground, but also in undergrowth and shrubs. Accentors like the Dunnock and Alpine Accentor are not difficult to locate in appropriate habitats.

Old World Warblers

Old World warblers are small, mostly plain, inconspicuous songbirds that make their livings chiefly by moving actively through dense foliage seeking insects. Many are undistinguished-looking brown birds, naturally leading most North American birdwatchers who first see them to conclude quickly that they are the difficult-to-identify "LBJs" (little brown jobs) of the Old World. The family Sylviidae, with about 290 species, is distributed widely across Eurasia and Africa but also occurs in the Australian region. Only the Arctic Warbler breeds in the New World, in Alaska. About 50 species inhabit Europe and the Middle East.

Most of these slim-bodied birds are four to six inches long. Chiefly brown, olive, or yellow, often with darker streaks, they typically have slender, pointed bills and some have longish tails. Old World warblers occur in a wide variety of habitats, from forests and woodlands to grasslands, thickets, shrublands, croplands, marshes, and mangroves. They are mainly arboreal insect-eaters, pulling bugs off foliage, flowers, and bark, but also take some seeds and other plant materials.

Dunnock This common garden bird is a year-round resident in most of western Europe. It was introduced to New Zealand in the late 1800s and now breeds throughout that country. *England*

wheatears. Old World flycatchers are widely distributed in Europe, Africa, and Asia. Only two, the Bluethroat and Northern Wheatear, make it to the New World. (Note: the American Ornithologists' Union places these two species in the thrush family.)

Old World flycatchers vary considerably in shape, color, and size. Most are small, 4 to 6 inches long, but some in the group range up to 12 inches. Many come in dull browns or grays, but some are black and white, or black and yellow, or blue and white, or have reddish chests. Many perched flycatchers compulsively flick their tails. These birds chiefly inhabit forests and woodlands, often staying in the canopy, but others

Blackcap A rather large warbler named for the male's black cap, which is rusty red in the female (shown). It is a common breeding bird in most of Europe and favors parks and gardens, especially those areas with dense undergrowth. *Finland*

■ Old World Flycatchers

Old World flycatchers are predominantly forest and woodland songbirds that feed by catching flying insects. Many are drab and fairly inconspicuous, but others are brighter and more easily noticed. Some, such as the European Pied Flycatcher, are common residents of parks and gardens. The family Muscicapidae has a checkered classification history. It is often considered to encompass about 270 species, including not only a multitude of flycatchers, but also a major subgroup that in the past was often considered part of the thrush family Turdidae. The Muscicapidae includes nightingales, rubythroats, redstarts, forktails, cochoas, chats, scrub-robins, stonechats, and

Collared Flycatcher Where this species overlaps with two very similar ones—European Pied and Semicollared Flycatchers—the identification of females and immatures is a challenge. The adult male in the photograph has a broad white collar that the other two species lack. *Turkey*

are birds of forest edges and clearings. Some, such as many chats and wheatears, are open-country birds. A few species dwell among rocks of fast-moving streams and rivers. About 30 Old World flycatchers occur in Europe and the Middle East.

Northern Europe possesses some fine birdlife. Several groups such as seabirds and waterbirds are abundant and often occur in big concentrations.

NORTHERN EUROPE

NORTHERN EUROPE—THE SECTION OF EUROPE CONTAINING BRITAIN, GERmany, and the Scandinavian nations, among other countries—each year attracts millions of cultural and leisure tourists from around the world, not least from the United States and Canada. Only a small fraction of these visitors realize that this region is also a gem of a birding destination.

A prime attraction is waterfowl. For birders who grow restless after year upon year of seeing the same ducks, geese, and swans in North America, northern Europe boasts a selection of novel species. In many cases, these are present in large numbers along coasts, in inland wetlands, and in wet fields and pastures in the region's plentiful agricultural districts. They include the large Whooper Swan, the shy, plain-looking Bean Goose, the rare Lesser White-fronted Goose, the Brant-like Barnacle Goose, and the Smew, a handsome diving duck that breeds in forests of the far north.

For those not satisfied by waterfowl, there is a variety of other water-associated birds in the region: seabirds such as shearwaters, storm-petrels, gannets, and alcids (auks and puffins); almost 40 species of shorebirds (waders) breeding or passing through on their migrations; myriad gulls and terns, along with four species of skuas (three of which are called "jaegers" in North America). Landbirds of interest usually include hawks, grouse, owls, woodpeckers, and some charming small birds such as kinglets and tits.

Which northern European countries tend to attract global birders? Britain, the Scandinavian nations, the Netherlands, and Germany are among the biggest draws.

Britain has innumerable top birding spots, including the wild Shetland Islands and Outer Hebrides for seabirds and the Scottish Highlands for pine forest species.

OPPOSITE: **Atlantic Puffin** These well-known seabirds are favorites of birders and non-birders alike. This colony on the Shetland Islands is located far to the north, but there are easier-to-visit summer breeding colonies of puffins located in the south of England. *Scotland*

Ruff The Ruff is a shorebird "of a different color." The males in breeding plumage (shown) exist in seemingly infinite patterns and colors. Displaying males gather on leks (May–June) to win the right to mate with as many females as they can. Scandinavia has a sizable population of breeding birds. *Europe*

LOCAL BIRDING & CONSERVATION ORGANIZATIONS

■ **BIRDLIFE FINLAND** (www.birdlife.fi) organization of Finnish bird societies; promotes bird conservation and birding

■ **DUTCH BIRDING ASSOCIATION** (www.dutchbirding.nl) stimulates birding by disseminating information about birds, especially rare ones

■ **ROYAL SOCIETY FOR THE PROTECTION OF BIRDS** (www.rspb.org.uk) large British organization dedicated to the conservation of birds

■ **SWEDISH ORNITHOLOGICAL SOCIETY** (www.sofnet.org) society interested in bird conservation, research, and the promotion of birding

■ **WILDFOWL & WETLANDS TRUST** (www.wwt.org.uk) promotes the conservation of wetlands and birds worldwide; operates wetlands visitor centers in Britain

Norfolk, a coastal county in eastern England with many nature reserves, is considered perhaps the country's best overall birding site (with more than 350 species observed, many of them migrants).

In Norway, the Arctic north is a frequent birder destination. In Finland, lakes and forests around the capital, Helsinki, are good for birding, as are areas in the northeastern region. Bavaria is a popular birding spot in Germany. Other countries in northern Europe popular with birders are Iceland, Austria, Switzerland, and, more recently, Poland, Romania, and Bulgaria.

The best times to visit northern Europe vary by region. Britain, for example, can be birded in any month: Late spring and summer have breeding birds, winter has wintering birds, and fall is great for migrants. Visiting Arctic portions of the region or mountain ranges in the temperate portion needs to be timed to avoid harsh weather and, in the high latitudes, summer insect swarms.

GEOGRAPHY AND HABITATS

Northern Europe as considered here comprises Iceland, the United Kingdom, Ireland, Scandinavia, and the other European countries that do not border the Mediterranean

Sea. Russia is excluded. Major geographical features in this region include several mountain ranges such as the Scandinavian Mountains running through the Scandinavian Peninsula, the Alps from eastern France to Austria, and the Carpathians from Romania to the Czech Republic; and rivers such as the Danube, Rhine, and Elbe. Most of the main habitats of northern Europe are similar to those of North America. There is tundra in Scandinavia's far north, which pokes above the Arctic Circle, but much of this region is covered by northern (boreal) coniferous forest. Farther south on the European mainland, temperate broadleaf and temperate mixed forests predominate. Much of the region's temperate forest has been replaced with open agricultural lands and settlements. The only extensive areas of steppe, or grassland, in northern Europe are in Romania and Hungary (where global birders travel to see grassland birds in such places as Hungary's Hortobágy National Park).

BIRDLIFE

Northern Europe possesses some fine birdlife. Several groups such as seabirds and waterbirds are abundant and often occur in big concentrations, but the overall variety

BIRDING THE FLAMBOROUGH HEAD BIRD CLIFFS IN YORK, BRITAIN

The most northerly coastal chalk cliffs in Britain extend for seven miles along the east coast on a large headland, Flamborough Head, jutting out into the sea. They are located just over 35 miles east of the city of York and near the town of Bridlington. During most of the year, there is little activity on the cliffs, but from April to August the cliff faces are packed with nesting seabirds. Because most seabird colonies are on remote islands, the mainland location of Flamborough makes watching and photographing breeding seabirds readily accessible at short distances.

About 2,000 pairs of Atlantic Puffins breed on these rock faces between May and the end of July. By August, the young puffins have left the cliffs to spend the fall and winter on the North Sea. Near Bempton is the largest mainland gannet colony (gannetry) in England, with more than 2,500 pairs.

From the cliff tops looking out to sea you can watch the Northern Gannets hovering and then diving from heights of up to about 120 feet, entering the sea at up to 60 mph to catch fish below the water's surface. Of the other six species of seabirds nesting here, Black-legged Kittiwakes are the most numerous, with more than 45,000 pairs jammed onto the cliffs. Also present are Northern Fulmar, European Herring Gull, Common Murre, and Razorbill. Because it projects so far into the sea, Flamborough Head is also an ideal place in spring and fall to watch for migrant seabirds streaming by, especially on days with strong easterly winds. On stormy winter days, this area is popular for birders seeking errant vagrants. —D.P.

Black-legged Kittiwake Around the sea cliffs where they breed, the kittiwakes' shrill cries of *kitt-i-waake* (hence their name) bounce off the rock walls in a cacophony of noise—a great birding spectacle. *Norway*

is relatively low. Good birders willing to move around a lot on a two- or three-week trip can probably see between 150 and 200 species in places such as Finland and Norway, Britain, Hungary, Poland, and Bulgaria.

Northern Europe lacks many "flagship" species—highly charismatic species that birders especially come to see, such as the Resplendent Quetzal, toucans, and motmots in Central America. Only one bird species is endemic to northern Europe as defined in this chapter: the Scottish Crossbill. This finch occurs only in Scottish pine forests and looks like the common, wide-ranging Red Crossbill, so it hardly qualifies as a major attraction.

Given the lack of endemics, it is no surprise that there are no Endemic Bird Areas (EBAs) in northern Europe. Rather, what northern Europe offers the global birder is good, safe access to a variety of bird groups characteristic of the Palearctic realm, such as owls, woodpeckers, tits, creepers, and representatives of the jay and crow family. Birders who particularly prize raptors will certainly be satisfied with the region's collection of seven eagles, two kites, four harriers, and various buzzards and accipiters, not to mention eight falcons. Birders especially interested in

Black Woodpecker A male is depicted in the photograph— notice how the red crown continues down to the bill. In the female the red is limited to a patch on the hindcrown. *Finland*

SPOTTING THE BLACK WOODPECKER

Not all momentous birding experiences revolve around rare or endemic species. The Black Woodpecker has a broad geographical range, yet it remains perhaps the most memorable bird I have seen in Europe. Being the size of a crow, with all-black plumage punctuated by a bright red crown, certainly renders it striking and attractive. But for me its significance is more its use as a barometer of changing forestry practices and its importance in supporting many other unrelated species. During the last century this woodpecker has disappeared from many parts of its range where extensive forest and large trees were cleared or severely thinned, but it has recently expanded back into central and western Europe. In the areas where the Black Woodpecker has returned, forest patches have been replanted and selective cutting of old snags and larger trees has been controlled. The Black Woodpecker has become a sensitive biological assessment, or "bioindicator," species of habitat change.

The return of this woodpecker to former parts of its range also reveals its importance in the survival and range extension into these new forests of many other species of birds and of some mammals. It is the only animal in this part of the world capable of constructing large holes in trees, and it makes new holes almost every year for its nests. Many other cavity-nesting bird species and mammals need these holes to be protected from nest predators, but they cannot make the tree holes themselves. If there are no Black Woodpeckers and, thus, no abundance of excavated tree holes, many other species apparently cannot survive in the forest. The Black Woodpecker, therefore, is also a "keystone species," one whose presence or absence affects much of the rest of the species community. —D.P.

Old-growth Forest The old-growth forests of Europe, like this one, are largely gone and the bird species that depend on them are greatly reduced in number. Remnants exist in protected areas, and larger tracts occur in northern countries. *Norway*

FIELD GUIDE & SITE GUIDE BOOKS

■ *Birds of Europe, 2nd ed.* (2010)
K. Mullarney, L. Svensson, D. Zetterström, and P. J. Grant
Princeton University Press

■ *Birds of Europe: With North Africa and the Middle East* (1999)
L. Jonsson
Christopher Helm Publishers

■ *A Field Guide to the Birds of Britain and Europe, 5th ed.* (2001)
R.T. Peterson, G. Mountfort, and P.A.D. Hollum
Houghton Mifflin

■ *Pocket Guide to the Birds of Britain and North-West Europe* (2002)
C. Kightley, S. Madge, and D. Nurney
Christopher Helm Publishers

■ *Where to Watch Birds in Europe and Russia* (2000)
N. Wheatley
Princeton University Press

waterfowl or shorebirds, will likewise be pleased with their variety and abundance in northern Europe.

As in northern portions of North America, a significant fraction of the bird species that breed in northern Europe migrate in the autumn to escape harsh winter conditions that make finding food difficult or impossible. They travel primarily to southern Europe or to northern and other parts of Africa. Some manage to remain all year in their northern haunts, including insect-eaters that can find sufficient food: woodpeckers, titmice, nuthatches, creepers. An interesting facet of northern European birds (and, to a slightly lesser extent, the European avifauna in general) is that these are among the most scrutinized birds on Earth—perhaps from a birdwatching viewpoint but also from scientific and conservation perspectives. These species are continually censused and studied, poked, and prodded. A result is that the health status of bird populations here are known precisely, as well as whether the populations of each and every species are increasing in numbers, stable, or declining.

Significant Species of Northern Europe

ABOUT 64 FAMILIES FOUND IN THIS REGION

■ **DUCKS, GEESE, AND SWANS** (Anatidae), **about 35 species**

Whooper Swan *Cygnus cygnus*
large, all-white swan restricted to the Old World

Bean Goose *Anser fabalis*
big, mainly gray-brown goose; breeds throughout northern Eurasia in tundra and boreal forest zones

Pink-footed Goose *Anser brachyrhynchus*
closely related and very similar to the Bean Goose; occurs only in Greenland, Iceland, and northwestern Europe

Smew *Mergellus albellus*
small diving duck (a merganser); male distinctly patterned in black and white

■ **HAWKS, EAGLES, AND KITES** (Accipitridae), **17 species**

European Honey-Buzzard *Pernis apivorus*
largish, fairly common hawk with variably colored plumage that breeds over much of northern Europe

Short-toed Eagle *Circaetus gallicus*
large, uncommon, long-winged eagle with light underparts

Montagu's Harrier *Circus pygargus*
broadly distributed, medium-size hawk; male gray and female brown

Greater Spotted Eagle *Aquila clanga*
brown eagle of central and eastern Europe and Asia

■ **GROUSE AND PTARMIGAN** (Tetraonidae), **5 species**

Eurasian Capercaillie *Tetrao urogallus*
the largest grouse, distributed from western Europe eastward to Siberia and Mongolia; now scarce in many regions

Black Grouse *Tetrao tetrix*
black grouse with an unusual lyre-shaped tail

Hazel Grouse *Bonasa bonasia*
small, plump, mainly gray, brown, and white grouse that prefers damp areas of forests

■ **SANDPIPERS AND ALLIES** (Scolopacidae), **about 25 species**

Spotted Redshank *Tringa erythropus*
long-billed, sooty gray shorebird with reddish legs; breeds in far northern regions of Eurasia

Temminck's Stint *Calidris temminckii*
small, brownish sandpiper; breeds as far south as Scotland

Broad-billed Sandpiper *Limicola falcinellus*
small, brown, uncommon sandpiper; breeds chiefly in Scandinavia and northern Russia

■ **OWLS** (Strigidae), **12 species**

Eurasian Eagle-Owl *Bubo bubo*
the largest owl of Europe, with a wide Eurasian range

Ural Owl *Strix uralensis*
large, uncommon, heavily streaked forest owl

Eurasian Pygmy-Owl *Glaucidium passerinum*
tiny gray-brown owl; found mainly in Scandinavia and other parts of northern Eurasia

■ **WOODPECKERS** (Picidae), **10 species**

Middle Spotted Woodpecker *Dendrocopos medius*
medium-size, black and white woodpecker; often scarce, found only in Europe, western Russia and parts of the Middle East

Black Woodpecker *Dryocopus martius*
Europe's largest woodpecker, all black with a red cap; fairly common

Gray-faced Woodpecker *Picus canus*
greenish woodpecker with a gray head; has a broad Eurasian range

■ **LARKS** (Alaudidae), **6 species**

Crested Lark *Galerida cristata*
typical lark with a spiky crest; has a wide Old World distribution

Wood Lark *Lullula arborea*
heavily streaked lark of various habitats but occurs often in forests; breeds over much of Europe

■ **WAGTAILS AND PIPITS** (Motacillidae), **10 species**

Meadow Pipit *Anthus pratensis*
common, typical pipit that breeds over much of northern Europe

Rock Pipit *Anthus petrosus*
dark pipit that breeds along northern Europe's rocky coasts

Citrine Wagtail *Motacilla citreola*
mainly yellow wagtail with a gray back; has a limited range in northern and central Europe but a larger range in Asia

■ **OLD WORLD WARBLERS** (Sylviidae), **about 25 species**

Icterine Warbler *Hippolais icterina*
common, widespread warbler, greenish above, pale yellow below; found in various habitats with trees

Barred Warbler *Sylvia nisoria*
largish gray warbler of thickets and shrublands

■ **OLD WORLD FLYCATCHERS** (Muscicapidae), **12 species**

Red-breasted Flycatcher *Ficedula parva*
smallest European flycatcher, gray above, whitish below; male has orange throat and upper breast

Bluethroat *Luscinia svecica*
small flycatcher, male has bright blue throat and upper chest; also breeds in northern Alaska

■ **CROWS, JAYS, AND MAGPIES** (Corvidae), **10 species**

Siberian Jay *Perisoreus infaustus*
jay of Scandinavia and northern Asia, typically found in dense coniferous forests; mainly gray-brown but with reddish brown wing patches

Eurasian Nutcracker *Nucifraga caryocatactes*
distinctive, predominantly brown bird heavily spotted with white; coniferous forests from Scandinavia to China

Yellow-billed Chough *Pyrrhocorax graculus*
black crow-like bird of mountainous regions, often seen around ski resorts; broad distribution

■ **FINCHES, SISKINS, AND CROSSBILLS** (Fringillidae), **20 species**

Parrot Crossbill *Loxia pytyopsittacus*
slightly bulkier than the Red Crossbill; occurs only in coniferous forests from Scandinavia to western Siberia

Scottish Crossbill* *Loxia scotica*
very similar to Red Crossbill but this somewhat common species is endemic to Scottish pine forests

Eurasian Bullfinch *Pyrrhula pyrrhula*
male of this beautiful finch gray and black above, reddish below; breeds form Britain across Eurasia to Japan

■ **BUNTINGS, SPARROWS, AND ALLIES** (Emberizidae), **11 species**

Ortolan Bunting *Emberiza hortulana*
bunting with grayish head and orange-brown belly; broadly distributed but usually sparse where found

Rustic Bunting *Emberiza rustica*
small and sparrow-like, with brown, black, and white plumage; breeds only in Scandinavia and northern Russia

Some Other Species Global Birders Often Seek

Great White Pelican *Pelecanus onocrotalus*
broadly distributed in Asia, Africa, but uncommon and localized in parts of eastern Europe

Black Stork *Ciconia nigra*
found in forested areas in northeastern Europe and other regions; black and white with reddish bill and legs

Common Crane *Grus grus*
brownish gray crane with black and white head that has a small red patch; broadly distributed in Scandinavia, also Germany and Poland

Corn Crake *Crex crex*
uncommon rail over much of northern Europe; brown and streaked, and very shy

Great Bustard *Otis tarda*
uncommon, very large ground bird of rolling grasslands; occurs in localized pockets of northern Europe

European Roller *Coracias garrulus*
handsome, largely pale blue or turquoise bird; found widely in Eurasia including in eastern and southern Europe

Goldcrest *Regulus regulus*
tiny, common songbird in the kinglet family; breeds over much of Europe

Alpine Accentor *Prunella collaris*
sparrow-like but with a finer bill; has a black and white barred throat; fairly common in mountain regions

Rufous-tailed Rock-Thrush *Monticola saxatilis*
small thrush of mountain regions and rocky environments; male has blue-gray head, brown wings, and burnt orange breast

Bearded Reedling *Panurus biarmicus*
member of the parrotbill family; very small, fairly common tit-like bird of reedy habitats

Long-tailed Tit *Aegithalos caudatus*
common small bird of forests, thickets, and gardens with broad Eurasian range; in same family as North America's Bushtit

Crested Tit *Lophophanes cristatus*
small, crested, chickadee-like bird of coniferous and mixed forests

Short-toed Treecreeper *Certhia brachydactyla*
very similar to North America's Brown Creeper; found over much of Europe south of Scandinavia

Eurasian Penduline-Tit *Remiz pendulinus*
very small songbird typically found in trees or bushes near water; in the same family as North America's Verdin

Restricted to Northern Europe

A good birder visiting some of the better birding sites in France or Spain during spring can expect to see perhaps 150 species in seven to ten days.

SOUTHERN EUROPE & THE MIDDLE EAST

Southern Europe is a heavily traveled tourist corridor, from Portugal and Spain in the west to Greece and Turkey in the east. Aside from wonderful cultural experiences, visitors are powerfully drawn to this region for its agreeable Mediterranean climate of warm, dry summers and mild, humid winters; for its attractive Mediterranean habitats, typically open, hilly, and scrubby; and for the Mediterranean Sea itself, with its often magnificent coastal scenery with water meeting rocks and cliffs. Birders come to southern Europe to find birds characteristic of the region's pleasing climate, habitats, and coasts. Many of these are water-associated birds of the region's coastal marshes, river deltas, and bays, including cormorants, herons, ibises, flamingos, ducks, rails, shorebirds, and gulls. Other birds often sought out are those typical of the Mediterranean region's dry shrubland and scrub habitats, especially some raptors, thrushes, Old World warblers and Old World flycatchers.

Southern Europe is also an excellent venue to observe migrating birds, both those that winter in the region and those that are passing through on their journeys elsewhere. Important southern Europe birding destinations are:

France, with such popular sites as the delta wetlands at Camargue, where the Rhône River joins the Mediterranean, the high-elevation forests of the French Pyrenees, and the coasts and mountains of the island of Corsica.

Spain, especially places such as Monfragüe National Park in the central-west, the Doñana Preserve in the southwest, which encompasses sprawling marshlands where the Guadalquivir River empties into the Atlantic, and the southern coast.

Portugal (the Algarve, the country's southernmost region), Gibraltar, and Greece (particularly the large island of Lesbos in the Aegean Sea).

OPPOSITE: **White Stork** Its long association with man has lent this species a variety of cultural associations—harbinger of spring, bringer of babies, and symbol of prosperity, to name a few. They often nest on man-made structures and return year after year to the same site. Eastern Europe and the Iberian Peninsula are its strongholds in Europe. *Spain*

Greater Flamingo In Europe, this species breeds in colonies around the Mediterranean basin. The marshes and shallow saline lagoons of the Camargue in southern France (the delta of the Rhône River) teem with birdlife and are home to a large number of these flamingos. *France*

LOCAL BIRDING & CONSERVATION ORGANIZATIONS

 **ITALIAN LEAGUE FOR THE PRESERVATION OF BIRDS**
(www.lipu.it)
dedicated to the conservation of birds and their habitats; operates nature centers and reserves

■ **ORNITHOLOGICAL SOCIETY OF THE MIDDLE EAST**
(www.osme.org)
started in 1978, encourages birding and interest in, and conservation of, Middle Eastern and Central Asian birds

■ **ORNITHOLOGICAL SOCIETY OF SPAIN**
(www.seo.org)
has worked on the conservation of birds and their habitats since 1954

■ **SOCIETY FOR THE PROTECTION OF NATURE IN ISRAEL**
(www.aspni.org)
Israel's largest environmental organization; operates major birding centers

The Middle East is included in this section of the book because it is more or less contiguous with southern Europe, and the two regions share much the same birdlife. Common birding destinations are Israel (with significant sites at Eilat, Mount Hermon, the Negev Desert, and the Dead Sea) and Turkey (particularly hills and marshes along the southern coast and high-elevation habitats in the Taurus Mountains). Birding in southern Europe can be accomplished at any time of year, but April through June are the best months in many areas when primary intentions are to see breeding birds.

GEOGRAPHY AND HABITATS

Southern Europe as treated here consists of the Iberian Peninsula and the countries that border the northern portion of the Mediterranean Sea. The large Mediterranean islands of Corsica, Sardinia, Sicily, Crete, and Cyprus, frequent tourist and sometimes birding destinations, are also included.

A good number of major habitat types occur in the region. Of principal concern to birders are the high-elevation mountain zones, the grasslands, the scrub habitats, the wetlands, and the marine areas. Mountain forests, often of conifers, and open Alpine habitats occur in such locations as the Pyrenees, in the French and Italian Alps, in southern Spain's Sierra Nevada, on the island of Corsica, and in southern

Turkey's Taurus Mountains. Grassland, or steppe, is characteristic of parts of Spain and Turkey.

The Mediterranean region of southern Europe is especially known for shrublands and scrub habitats, generally on dry, stony soils. These areas are common in southern Spain, southern France, coastal Italy, and Greece, and on the larger Mediterranean islands. The vegetation in some of these shrubby habitats is called maquis (similar to what is known as chaparral in California) and the Mediterranean area is one of the few regions of the world in which it occurs. Dominated by stands of low-growing evergreen shrubs with tough leaves, this vegetation is related to the Mediterranean climate. The shrubs' tough leaves are drought resistant, functioning well in both dry summers and wet winters.

BIRDLIFE

More than 450 bird species regularly occur in southern Europe and the Middle East. While this is not a huge number relative to bird numbers at many other global destinations, there are some fine birds here and many scenic, alluring places that are quite

BIRDING THE COTO DOÑANA, SPAIN

The Coto Doñana (the Doñana Preserve) is easily my favorite birding site in southern Europe. It is a vast wilderness of coastal marshes, dunes, forests, and scrublands situated in the delta of the Guadalquivir River, just southwest of Seville in Spain's southwest. The protected area is actually made up of a separate national park (with an area of 22 square miles) and natural park (21 square miles). I best remember driving into the preserve's headquarters with Egyptian Vulture and Eurasian Griffon running across the road in front of our vehicle. In nearby trees a pair of Spanish Eagles had built their immense stick nest. In the wetlands, Black Stork, Glossy Ibis, Marbled Teal, Ferruginous Pochard, White-headed Duck, Purple Swamphen, and Red-knobbed Coot were remarkable. Flocks of resident Greater Flamingo waded in estuaries and, because one doesn't usually associate flamingos with Europe, made me question whether I really was in that part of the world.

This corner of Europe gives a toehold to many species that otherwise occur mainly in Africa, such as Audouin's Gull, Red-necked Nightjar, Rufous-tailed Scrub-Robin, and Spectacled Warbler. In addition, as many as six million migratory birds use these protected habitats as stopover areas on their way to Scandinavia in the spring and Africa in the fall. Thus, habitat destruction, encroachment of beach resorts, and accidental release of mine tailings in the region impact not only this nature preserve but also the birds that pass through to nest or winter continents away. —D.P.

Azure-winged Magpie This mid-size member of the crows and jays family (Corvidae) is endemic to the Iberian Peninsula. An almost identical species that occurs in the Far East was, until recently, considered to be the same species. *Spain*

attractive as birding spots. A good birder visiting some of the better birding sites in France or Spain during spring can expect to see perhaps 150 species in seven to ten days. A lot of these will be waterbirds, especially if famous wetlands at locations such as Spain's Doñana Preserve and France's Camargue are on the itinerary. Some species are typically seen in great abundance while wintering in these areas. Many thousands of Greater Flamingos, Graylag Geese, Eurasian Teal, and Northern Pintail occur at Doñana. Multitudes of Greater Flamingos, Eurasian Teal, and Red-crested Pochards are present at Camargue. A number of seabirds of interest are found along coasts or around islands. These include two shearwaters that breed only in the Mediterranean: the Balearic and Levantine Shearwaters.

The region is also known for raptors such as Red Kite, Black Kite, Lammergeier, Egyptian Vulture, Eurasian Griffon, Cinereous Vulture, Short-toed Eagle, Spanish Eagle, and Booted Eagle; accentors, with three species in the region including Alpine and Radde's Accentors and Dunnock; Old World warblers, particularly those of the genus *Sylvia* that tend to breed in Mediterranean shrub and scrub habitats, such as the Sardinian, Spectacled, Dartford, and Marmora's Warblers; larks, with more than

Steppe Eagle Almost the entire population of this eagle that breeds in Russia and Central Asia migrates through the Middle East to spend the winter in sub-Saharan Africa. *Oman*

BIRDING IN EILAT, ISRAEL

Israel is a birder's paradise because it is on the only land bridge that connects Africa, Asia, and Europe, and migration routes converge from these three areas to force millions of birds through this crossroads twice a year. Of all the great birding areas in this country, the crown jewel is at Israel's southern tip at the Red Sea resort of Eilat. Small passerines as well as large, soaring hawks, eagles, and storks move through in immense flocks. By some estimates more than 500 million birds of 230 species stop over or pass through this area every year. Most of the world's populations of Levant Sparrowhawk and Steppe Eagle move through this regional bottleneck.

Eilat was once an extensive salt marsh of about five square miles, which flooded during the winter. Its salty soil content was perfect for desert-adapted flowers that grew high-quality fruits in spring and fall, just when migrants arrive after crossing hundreds of miles of ocean or desert without food. Because of development for tourism and agriculture, these salt marshes and native plants disappeared. Small passerine migrants had no place to refuel, and this impacted nesting and wintering populations throughout Europe, Asia, and Africa. Recent conservation efforts are restoring small portions of these salt marshes and their fruiting plants.

In addition to migratory species, local resident birds associated with the desert habitat contribute to the avian diversity here. They include Sand Partridge, Hume's Tawny Owl, Desert Lark, White-tailed Wheatear, and Tristram's Starling. The Ostrich was once native to Israel's desert regions but was hunted to extinction by the 1920s. A plan to reintroduce the bird to this area is now underway. —D.P.

European Roller One of the flashiest birds of Europe—it is a summer visitor (mostly May–August) to southern and eastern Europe and winters in parts of Africa. *Hungary*

ten species; and the Hypocolius, which occurs mainly in and around Iraq. Other birds of great interest are from families often associated with Africa and that are most diverse there, such as the bee-eater and roller mentioned in this chapter's introduction, and bustards (three species in the region), pratincoles and coursers (three species), and sandgrouse (five species).

Only a few birds are endemic to southern Europe. The Spanish Eagle, with a very small surviving population, occurs only in central and southern Spain. Marmora's Warbler is restricted to Corsica, Sardinia, and few other Mediterranean islands (with some individuals wintering in northern Africa). The Corsican Nuthatch is found only in mid-elevation pine forests on Corsica. Krueper's Nuthatch is mainly confined to Turkey. And the Citril Finch is limited to mountain coniferous forests in several regions of southern Europe. There are 10–15 species endemic to the Middle East, most confined to the Arabian Peninsula.

Southern Europe is both a common wintering location for birds breeding in northern Eurasia and a frequent stopover site for birds wintering to the south in Africa. Typical winter visitors include many ducks, thrushes, and Old World warblers. Many of the birds that stop on their way northward or southward, usually termed transients or passage migrants, are shorebirds. These species breed in the far north, often on tundra, and spend winters in warmer areas, for instance, along African coasts. Major sites for spotting migrant birds include Gibraltar, Camargue in France, the Greek island of Lesbos, Cyprus, Turkey's southern coastal marshes, and Israel.

FIELD GUIDE & SITE GUIDE BOOKS

■ *Birds of Europe, 2nd ed.* (2010)
K. Mullarney, L. Svensson, D. Zetterström, and P. J. Grant
Princeton University Press

■ *Birds of Europe: With North Africa and the Middle East* (1999)
L. Jonsson
Christopher Helm Publishers

■ *A Field Guide to the Birds of Britain and Europe, 5th ed.* (2001)
R.T. Peterson, G. Mountfort, and P.A.D. Hollum
Houghton Mifflin

■ *Field Guide to the Birds of the Middle East* (2004)
R.F. Porter, S. Christensen, and P. Schiermacker-Hansen
Princeton University Press

■ *Where to Watch Birds in Asia* (1996)
N. Wheatley
Princeton University Press

■ *Where to Watch Birds in Europe and Russia* (2000)
N. Wheatley
Princeton University Press

Significant Species
of Southern Europe and the Middle East
ABOUT 70 FAMILIES FOUND IN THIS REGION

■ **HAWKS, EAGLES, AND KITES** (Accipitridae), **about 30 species**

Eurasian Griffon *Gyps fulvus*
very large brown and black vulture, with bare-skin head and neck; uncommon, found in mountain zones

Lesser Spotted Eagle *Aquila pomarina*
medium-size dark eagle with a small reddish patch on the back of its neck; found in eastern Europe, the Balkan Peninsula, Turkey

Spanish Eagle* *Aquila adalberti*
large, rare eagle; endemic to the Iberian Peninsula

Bonelli's Eagle *Aquila fasciatus*
medium-size, generally rare eagle of hills and mountains

■ **FALCONS** (Falconidae), **11 species**

Eleonora's Falcon *Falco eleonorae*
scarce, medium-size falcon with long wings; breeds mainly on Mediterranean islands

Lanner Falcon *Falco biarmicus*
large, beautiful, and uncommon falcon mainly of dry plains, grasslands, and deserts

■ **PHEASANTS AND PARTRIDGES** (Phasianidae), **15 species**

Caspian Snowcock *Tetraogallus caspius*
grayish ground bird of mountainous regions of Turkey and Iran

Red-legged Partridge* *Alectoris rufa*
chicken-like bird of open country and grassy areas; widespread and common in western Europe

■ **SANDGROUSE** (Pteroclidae), **5 species**

Pin-tailed Sandgrouse *Pterocles alchata*
pigeon-like ground bird with long, tapering tail; found in grasslands and semi-desert in Spain, southern France, and the Middle East

Black-bellied Sandgrouse *Pterocles orientalis*
pigeon-like ground bird of dry grasslands and semi-desert; found over the Iberian Peninsula and Middle East

■ **LARKS** (Alaudidae), **about 15 species**

Dupont's Lark *Chersophilus duponti*
furtive, uncommon lark of dry grasslands, plains, and semi-desert in Spain and northern Africa

Calandra Lark *Melanocorypha calandra*
common lark of grassy areas and farmland; ranges broadly over southern Europe, Middle East, and northern Africa

■ **SWALLOWS** (Hirundinidae), **6 species**

Eurasian Crag-Martin *Ptyonoprogne rupestris*
large, heavy-bodied swallow of mountain areas, often found around cliffs and watercourses

Red-rumped Swallow *Cecropis daurica*
wide-ranging Old World swallow, similar to Barn Swallow

■ **WAGTAILS AND PIPITS** (Motacillidae), **11 species**

Tawny Pipit *Anthus campestris*
largish, typical pipit with only light streaking; breeds over much of Europe in open habitats

Water Pipit *Anthus spinoletta*
fairly common pipit that breeds in mountain zones above treeline; has a pinkish-tinged breast during breeding

■ **ACCENTORS** (Prunellidae), **3 species**

Alpine Accentor *Prunella collaris*
sparrow-like, but with a finer bill and a black and white barred throat; fairly common in mountain regions

Radde's Accentor *Prunella ocularis*
sparrow-like bird, found primarily in mountains of Turkey

■ **OLD WORLD WARBLERS** (Sylviidae), **about 40 species**

Rueppell's Warbler *Sylvia rueppelli*
breeds in the Mediterranean region, especially Greece and Turkey; male with black throat and white moustache stripe

Subalpine Warbler *Sylvia cantillans*
breeds over much of southern Europe on mountainsides and scrubby hills

Sardinian Warbler *Sylvia melanocephala*
widespread breeding bird in regions adjoining the Mediterranean Sea; male gray and black above, whitish below

■ **OLD WORLD FLYCATCHERS** (Muscicapidae), **about 30 species**

Rufous-tailed Scrub-Robin *Cercotrichas galactotes*
small, shy songbird of southern Europe, Middle East

Cyprus Wheatear *Oenanthe cypriaca*
mainly black and white bird of rocky, grassy, or lightly wooded sites; breeds only in Cyprus

■ **FINCHES, SISKINS, AND CROSSBILLS** (Fringillidae), **20 species**

Syrian Serin* *Serinus syriacus*
yellowish finch restricted to the Middle East, particularly Israel, Lebanon, and Syria

Corsican Finch* *Serinus corsicanus*
small finch, yellow below and with conspicuous yellow wing bars; found only on Corsica and Sardinia

■ **BUNTINGS, SPARROWS, AND ALLIES** (Emberizidae), **10 species**

Cretzschmar's Bunting *Emberiza caesia*
found on rocky slopes in Greece and the Middle East; has a blue-gray head and rust-colored belly

Some Other Species Global Birders Often Seek

Dalmatian Pelican *Pelecanus crispus*
large, rare pelican found in southeastern Europe and points eastward

Squacco Heron *Ardeola ralloides*
smaller, brownish heron with white wings; breeds mainly in southern Europe and the Middle East

White Stork *Ciconia ciconia*
huge white bird with large black wing patches; common in various parts of Europe including Iberian Peninsula, Greece, and Turkey

Eurasian Spoonbill *Platalea leucorodia*
large, uncommon white bird with flattened, spatula-like bill and long, black legs; found in southern Spain and southeastern Europe

Greater Flamingo *Phoenicopterus roseus*
tall, white and pinkish; occurs in localized areas around the periphery of the Mediterranean

White-headed Duck *Oxyura leucocephala*
rare duck of Spain, Turkey, and a few other areas; male reddish brown with a white head and blue bill

Red-knobbed Coot *Fulica cristata*
predominantly African coot that also breeds very locally in southern Spain

Little Bustard *Tetrax tetrax*
largish, stocky, sandy brown ground bird of France, Iberian Peninsula, and a few other sites; male with striking black and white neck

Pied Avocet *Recurvirostra avosetta*
beautiful, black and white shorebird with a long, upcurved bill; patchily distributed, locally common

Eurasian Thick-knee *Burhinus oedicnemus*
not uncommon, largish shorebird found in grasslands, farmlands, and semi-desert areas

Collared Pratincole *Glareola pratincola*
unusual shorebird, brown above with white belly, looks like tern in flight; breeds in parts of southern Europe

Audouin's Gull *Larus audouinii*
red-billed gull with gray-green legs; breeds only around the Mediterranean on rocky islands

Great Spotted Cuckoo *Clamator glandarius*
large, crested cuckoo of the Mediterranean region; light below, dark gray above with white spots

White-throated Kingfisher *Halcyon smyrnensis*
largish red-billed kingfisher with broad southern Asia distribution, including portions the Middle East

European Bee-eater *Merops apiaster*
Europe's sole bee-eater species; a flashy greenish blue, yellow, and reddish brown bird found mostly in open country and woodland edges

Eurasian Hoopoe *Upupa epops*
striking color pattern, long bill, and huge crest make this one of Europe's most recognizable birds; breeds over most of southern Europe

Syrian Woodpecker *Dendrocopos syriacus*
black, white, and red woodpecker; limited to southeastern Europe and the Middle East

White-throated Dipper *Cinclus cinclus*
blackish, brown, and white; Europe's only dipper, has a wide Old World range

Arabian Babbler* *Turdoides squamiceps*
large gray-brown babbler of the Middle East; occurs in Israel and surrounding areas

Corsican Nuthatch* *Sitta whiteheadi*
endemic to higher elevation pine forests on island of Corsica

Wallcreeper *Tichodroma muraria*
nuthatch-like, gray and reddish; fairly common in some mountain regions on cliff faces

Palestine Sunbird *Cinnyris osea*
only sunbird of this region, found in Israel and adjacent countries

Woodchat Shrike *Lanius senator*
handsome black and white shrike with reddish brown crown and nape; breeds over most of southern Europe, common in some regions

Tristram's Starling* *Onychognathus tristramii*
black starling with a large copper-colored wing patch; restricted to Middle East

Dead Sea Sparrow* *Passer moabiticus*
small brownish sparrow with gray, black, white, and yellow head; found in Turkey, Israel, and adjacent areas

*Restricted to Southern Europe and the Middle East

CHAPTER 6

AFRICA

ATLANTIC

OCEAN

Black Sea

Caspian Sea

M e d i t e r r a n e a n   S e a

Morocco

Tunisia

Algeria

L i b y a

Egypt

Tropic of Cancer

Western Sahara (Morocco)

S A H A R A

Red Sea

Mauritania

Mali

Niger

Chad

S u d a n

Eritrea

Cape Verde

Sengal

Djibouti

Gambia

Burkina Faso

Shoebill
near Murchison Falls
page 199

Guinea-Bissau

Guinea

Nigeria

Ethiopia

Sierra Leone

Côte d'Ivoire

Ghana

Togo

Benin

Cameroon

Central African Republic

Liberia

Gray-necked Rockfowl
Korup National Park
page 200

Equatorial Guinea

Sao Tome & Principe

Somalia

Equator

Gabon

Congo

Democratic

Uganda

Kenya

I N D I A N

ATLANTIC

Rwanda

Burundi

O C E A N

Republic

OCEAN

Cabinda (Angola)

of the Congo

Tanzania

Pitta-like Ground-Roller
Masoala National Park
page 207

Comoros

Angola

Malawi

Zambia

Madagascar

Mozambique

Zimbabwe

Réunion (France)

Tropic of Capricorn

Namibia

Botswana

Swaziland

Lesotho

South Africa

miles

0   500

0   750

kilometers

Pelagic Birding
off Cape Town
page 208

Cape Town

In addition to its great birds and myriad large mammals, Africa has something else for birders and other nature travelers: a pronounced element of adventure.

BIRDING IN

AFRICA

AFRICA HAS A LONG COLORFUL HISTORY OF PEOPLE FROM OTHER CONTInents visiting to see its wildlife. The current global trend to ecotourism, in fact, traces perhaps its deepest root to the East African nation of Kenya. Generations of Europeans and North Americans have traveled there to go "on safari" to view (and in the past to gun down) the region's array of large, charismatic, savanna-roaming mammals—from big cats to elephants, rhinos, buffalo, zebras, giraffes, and antelopes.

Africa's birds, which receive much less attention from the African tourism industry and from most visitors as well, are actually as astounding as their hairy, four-legged neighbors. Africa is a tremendous birding destination. The numbers are certainly there: Africa and its associated islands boast a more-than-ample 2,500 or so avian species, the majority of them endemic to the continent.

The reasons for this great bird diversity are largely the same as for South America, the continent with the most birds: Almost all of the African continent is tropical or subtropical, and there tend to be more bird species in these types of regions than in nontropical zones (see Chapter 2 for explanation); and Africa contains a rich variety of habitats, each supporting its own characteristic set of bird species. Adding to its large resident avifauna, Africa also supports a good number of seasonal migrants that breed to the north in Eurasia.

Aside from Africa's number of species, it is also the kinds of birds present and unique to the continent that amaze and make Africa a must-go birding location, even if only once in a lifetime. These birds range from the globe's largest and perhaps

PREVIOUS PAGES: **Masai Mara National Reserve** An African treasure, noted for the seasonal migration of millions of wildebeest, zebras, gazelles, and their attendant predators. The birdlife of the reserve is also impressive— over 450 species, including vultures, Secretary-birds, hornbills, Ostriches, and numerous raptors, among the larger species. *Kenya*

most outlandish species, the Ostrich, to a group of small, mousy, scurrying birds fittingly called mousebirds. Between these extremes are such fantastic animals as the Secretary-bird, which is essentially a terrestrial eagle, the Shoebill, a large, gray, stork-like swamp bird with a gigantic bill, and the turacos, big arboreal relatives of cuckoos with richly hued plumages.

In addition to its great birds and myriad large mammals, Africa has something else for birders and other nature travelers: a pronounced element of adventure almost everywhere and, in some areas, an additional tinge of danger. A personal case in point: In Kenya's Samburu National Reserve, I once stepped out of a small vehicle into the arid savanna to view a shrike. A few minutes later I got back into the vehicle, continued driving down the dirt track, and discovered nearby, behind a large bush, a pair of sleeping lions. After that incident, I decided to remain inside the vehicle at all times while in potentially dangerous areas—and you should, too.

Lesser Flamingo Although small in size, Lake Nakuru National Park is famous for the astonishing number of Lesser Flamingos that nest along its shores. At times, the lake's surface can be almost obscured by the shifting flocks of pink birds. *Lake Nakuru, Kenya*

Blue Coua The cuckoo family (Cuculidae) is a diverse assemblage of birds with a variety of often unfamiliar names such as koel, coucal, malkoha, and coua. The lovely Blue Coua is endemic to Madagascar, as are the other eight living species of coua. *Madagascar*

Where to go? Africa is huge, the second largest continent after Asia, and knowledgeable birders roam it far and wide. In northern Africa, Morocco is the easiest and safest destination, but it is also possible to birdwatch in Egypt, say, during an archaeologically inspired holiday. West Africa constitutes a huge area divided into many countries, large and small. Not all of them are suitable for the gentle pursuit of birding, but a few, such as Gambia, Cameroon, and Gabon, are good bets. For instance, in the protected lowland evergreen rain forests of Cameroon's Korup National Park birders can encounter more than five hornbill species, including White-thighed, Yellow-casqued, and Red-billed Dwarf Hornbills, and they can search for the rare, difficult-to-see, and ornithologically curious Gray-necked Rockfowl.

East Africa has an abundance of spots for great birding, including Ethiopia, Kenya, Uganda, and Tanzania. The sites in Kenya alone would keep any serious birder in avian ecstasy for many weeks. The grassy savanna, riverside forest, and marshes of Masai Mara National Reserve support such restricted-range species as

Yellow-throated Sandgrouse, Magpie Shrike, and Swahili Sparrow. Lake Nakuru National Park routinely exhibits in its large, shallow alkaline lake thousands, sometimes hundreds of thousands, of Greater and Lesser Flamingos. Mount Kenya's cool, high-elevation forests and boggy grasslands teem with exciting birds like Jackson's Francolin, Hartlaub's Turaco, and Golden-winged Sunbird.

Likewise, a number of countries in southern Africa provide excellent birding locations, such as South Africa, Namibia, Botswana, and Zambia. South Africa is easiest to navigate, and in this vast land there are almost limitless birding possibilities: the arid Kalahari savanna of the Northern Cape Province in the western portion of the country, the slopes and foothills of the southern Drakensberg Mountains, the forests, woodlands, and wetlands of the southeastern Mkuzi Game Reserve, the acacia savanna of the famed Kruger National Park in the northeast,

Red-billed Oxpecker and Impala The oxpeckers—there are two species, both endemic to sub-Saharan Africa—are named for their habit of perching on large mammals and eating parasites. Both species of oxpecker are common and overlap in parts of their ranges. *South Africa*

and the usually highly fruitful pelagic birding conducted in the waters not far off Cape Town. Finally, Madagascar, an island nation located in the Indian Ocean east of southern Africa, is an important birding location, especially due to the presence of several endemic families.

Northern Africa is not covered in detail in this chapter because most of its birds are identical to those in southern Europe (see Chapter 5). Common birding destinations in northern Africa include Morocco and Egypt. Popular spots in Morocco, which boasts the longest bird list of any northern African nation, include the forests of the Atlas Mountains, desert areas around the southeastern village of Merzouga, and coastal zones near the southern town of Agadir. In Egypt, frequent birding areas are the Sinai Peninsula in the northeast, Luxor in central Egypt, and Abu Simbel in the south. The latter two sites are also common archaeological tourism destinations. An almost legendary but way-out-of-the-way birding site in northern Africa is Banc D'Arguin National Park at the edge of the Sahara on Mauritania's northern coast. The mudflats and lagoons there support millions of wintering shorebirds as well as tens of thousands of gulls, terns, cormorants, and others. For ease of coverage, I divide the remainder of the African continent into only two birding sections, sub-Saharan Africa and Madagascar.

Saddle-billed Stork A huge stork with a colorful bill—males stand about five feet tall and have a wingspan of nine feet—that stalks lowland swamps and wetlands of sub-Saharan Africa. The bird pictured is a female; the male has dark eyes. *South Africa*

TRAVELING IN THE REGION

As a birding destination, Africa has a lot going for it: numerous and diverse birds, wonderful landscapes, intriguing habitats, and, in many sections, infrastructure dedicated to getting international visitors to wildlife-watching locations and accommodating them there. But Africa as a whole has a reputation for widespread poverty, a general low level of development, and also of political turmoil—so it is not a destination everyone embraces without serious thought beforehand. After deciding to go, one of the next questions any Africa-bound birder will likely consider is, "Can I do it on my own, or do I need a guided tour?" For most people, the answer is that a guided tour, arranged with an international nature tour company,

an American or British birding tour company, or a local, in-country "safari" tour company, will be the most efficient, most comfortable, and safest way to visit Africa's best birding sites.

Of course, independent birding travel in Africa is possible, and the adventurous have done it for decades. In South Africa especially, it's possible to plan a long trip to various parks and reserves, make advance accommodation reservations at a string of national parks, rent a car, get a map, and take off. But on most of the continent, the great majority of birders are going to feel much more comfortable being with a guide and leaving the logistics— and the driving—to others. If tours by United States or European companies are too pricey, then a good alternative is to find less expensive nature tours conducted by local tour companies in countries like Kenya. In Nairobi, for instance, many tour companies take tourists on, most commonly, three- to seven-day trips

to some of that country's great national parks and reserves. Prices are fairly low if one is willing to camp out in tents, and higher if more luxurious accommodation is desired. There are also specialty birding tour operators in places like Kenya and South Africa.

How is birding carried out in Africa in areas where wildlife might be dangerous? In many national parks and game reserves, all birding is conducted from vehicles, typically either Land Rover–type vehicles or minibuses that permit standing to watch and photograph wildlife in safety. There are walking tours in safer areas or with rifle-toting escorts. Even in more dangerous zones it is often possible to bird on foot around accommodations, campgrounds, and other places. Night driving along wildlife-viewing roads in national parks is often banned because it can be hazardous. Tolerating guided tours and long hours birding from vehicles can be very much worthwhile here. A very good birder spending three weeks in one of the more bird-diverse African countries, such as Kenya, Uganda, Tanzania, or Cameroon, can expect to see between 300 and 400 species. ■

Vulturine Guineafowl The six species of guineafowl (family Numididae) are endemic to Africa. The Vulturine is easily the most spectacular. Within its East African range it is a common bird usually seen in flocks. *Kenya*

OPPOSITE: **African Fish-Eagle** Fish-eagles in the genus *Haliaeetus* (which includes North America's Bald Eagle) occur around the globe. The African Fish-Eagle is common on many major rivers and lakes in sub-Saharan Africa. *Kenya*

BIRDS OF THE REGION SIGNIFICANT GROUPS

BUSTARDS | TURACOS | MOUSEBIRDS | BEE-EATERS | ROLLERS | BARBETS | HONEYGUIDES | SUNBIRDS | WEAVERS | INDIGOBIRDS

The significant African bird families described below are a varied lot, ranging from very large ground birds (bustards) to fairly large arboreal birds (turacos) to tiny aerial songbirds (sunbirds). A few of these families, such as the mousebirds and honeyguides, contain mainly drably plumaged species. However, many of the others are often spectacularly outfitted. In fact, some of the species in the turaco, bee-eater, roller, and sunbird families must be considered to be among the globe's gaudiest birds.

■ Bustards

Bustards are large ground birds of open landscapes. Twenty of the 26 species occur in Africa, the rest inhabiting Europe, Asia, and Australia. The family Otididae is in the order Gruiformes with the cranes and rails. Despite the size and frequent conspicuousness of some of the species, bustards are not a well-known group, and their drab coloration contributes to a general lack of appreciation. When bustards are recognized, it is usually for being game birds or for their role in reducing agricultural pests by consuming enormous numbers of insects and small rodents. Two species from southern Asia are called floricans, and in southern Africa many are called korhaans ("crowing hens") for their croaking, clattering calls—an example being South Africa's endemic Blue Bustard (or Korhaan).

Black Bustard This small dark bustard (or korhaan) is endemic to southernmost Africa. *South Africa*

OPPOSITE: **Kori Bustard and Southern Carmine Bee-eater** The bee-eater has hitched a ride on a Kori Bustard, sub-Saharan Africa's largest bustard, probably to feed on the insects stirred up by the strolling bird. *Botswana.*

Bustards are long necked and long legged, with stocky bodies and short, sharp bills. They range in length from 16 to 47 inches. The largest, Africa's Kori Bustard, weighs up to 40 pounds, making it one of the heaviest flying birds. Bustards prefer dry, open habitats, and they spend almost all their time on the ground. When disturbed, they stalk furtively away, only reluctantly taking flight when pressed. Smaller bustards are shy and usually very hard to spot or approach.

■ Turacos

Turacos are large, arboreal birds of forests, woodlands, and savannas. They are known for brilliant plumages and raucous, often repetitive calls, which are some of

Prince Ruspoli's Turaco A much sought-after Ethiopian endemic, this endangered turaco inhabits juniper forests and acacia-conifer woodlands. Its range is very small, and this species is threatened by habitat loss. *Ethiopia*

the most characteristic sounds of these habitats. The 23 turaco species are confined to Africa. The family Musophagidae is usually placed in order Cuculiformes with the cuckoos. Some of the turacos are called plantain-eaters, and others are known as go-away-birds, for their loud, distinctive *g'way, g'way* calls.

Turacos, all with conspicuous crests, are 16 to 29 inches long, and have short bills and long, broad tails. Many have bare, brightly colored patches of skin around their eyes. Most species are primarily a striking glossy blue, green, or purplish, but the go-away-birds and plantain-eaters are clad mostly in gray, brown, and white. Gregarious birds, turacos often congregate in large groups and fly from tree to tree in "strings," or single file. Most turacos specialize on eating fruit but also take some leaves, buds, and flowers, and the occasional insect. A few turacos are fairly easy to spot because they have adapted to wooded areas near large towns. For instance, Hartlaub's Turaco is seen in parks and gardens around Nairobi, while the Purple-crested Turaco is found in some of South Africa's suburban parks.

■ Mousebirds

Mousebirds are small, often conspicuous birds that inhabit forest edges, savanna, scrublands, and farms and gardens. They are perhaps best known for their copious consumption of fruits and vegetables, flowers and foliage, and for the resulting anger and frustration they arouse in farmers and gardeners. Their name arises from their mouse-like appearance (smallish and drab, with long tails) and their typical small-rodent-like behaviors of scuttling through vegetation, living in groups, and huddling together. There are only six mousebirds (called "colies" in some parts of Africa). Their family Coliidae is placed in its own order Coliiformes—the only order wholly endemic to Africa.

White-backed Mousebird A common species in South Africa that is often seen around human-altered habitats such as orchards and thickets bordering agricultural fields. *South Africa*

Mousebirds are 11 to 15 inches in length including their very long tails, with crests, short necks, and short bills. All are dully colored in gray or brownish hues. Several, such as the Red-faced and Blue-naped Mousebirds, have bare, colored skin around the eyes that forms a mask. Mousebirds are usually found in groups, often between five and eight birds, but dozens of mousebirds may gather to feed at trees full of ripe fruit. These birds are often spotted in town parks and gardens and in agricultural districts.

■ Bee-eaters

Bee-eaters are small to mid-size birds that feed on flying insects, primarily bees and wasps. Their elegant form and brilliantly colored plumages, combined with an animated, outgoing nature, typically make them birder favorites. Most of the 26 bee-eaters, family Meropidae, occur in Africa, while a few inhabit southern Europe, southern Asia, and Australia. The group is included in order Coraciiformes with the kingfishers.

Slender birds with long, thin, sharply pointed, downcurved bills, bee-eaters are often dazzling in their bright plumages of greens, blues, and reds. They range in length from 6 to 15 inches. Most have thick black eye stripes and long tails. In some, such as the common White-throated Bee-eater, the two central

Swallow-tailed Bee-eater With a diet made up almost exclusively of honeybees, this species lives up to the family name. Its forked tail is unique in the bee-eater family. *South Africa*

tail feathers grow very long, and these "streamers" can add up to four inches to a bird's length. Bee-eaters are often easily spotted by birders because they prefer open habitats such as woodlands, savanna, plantations, and forest edges and clearings, not to mention parks, gardens, and roadside utility wires. They are highly social, usually discovered in pairs or family groups, or, during the winter, in large flocks.

Lilac-breasted Roller A well-known and conspicuous bird of sub-Saharan Africa. It is easily seen in many national parks and game reserves. *Kenya*

Rollers

Rollers are handsome, colorful birds, often conspicuous as they sit on exposed perches to hunt insects and other small prey. They are called rollers because they "roll" in flight during their spectacular aerial territorial displays. The birds fly straight up, then dive toward the ground while twisting their body, beating their wings, and giving loud calls. Their vivid plumages of sky blue, purple-blue, blue-green, lilac, and russet brown also make them avian standouts. The family Coraciidae, classified in order Coraciiformes with the kingfishers and bee-eaters, contains 12 rollers, 8 occurring in Africa.

Stocky, medium-size birds (10 to 15 inches long), rollers have large heads and short necks. Some, such as southern Africa's Racket-tailed Roller, have long tail streamers. They prefer open country—woodlands, savannas, forest edges, and agricultural sites—but some species inhabit forests. They feed by sallying out from their perch to catch flying insects, or more often by flying to the ground to take terrestrial prey.

Barbets

Barbets are mainly tropical arboreal birds known for their colors, vocalizations, and fruit-centered diets. They are popular with birdwatchers because of their beauty, their sometimes melodic songs and duetting, and because they present interesting identification challenges. In some regions, several species look much alike, with only subtle differences in color

Yellow-breasted Barbet Uncommon but widespread from Ethiopia to western Africa, this barbet occupies dry woodlands and scrubby areas. *Ethiopia*

patterns. There are about 83 barbet species, half of them in Africa and the remainder distributed broadly in South America, Central America, and southern Asia. The family Capitonidae is usually placed in order Piciformes with the woodpeckers.

Rather husky, small and medium-size birds (ranging in length from 4 to 14 inches), barbets are big-headed and short-necked. Their colorful, often spotted and streaked plumages are usually combinations of black, white, yellow, red, or orange. Some species, especially in Africa, come in more inconspicuous browns—West Africa's mainly brown Naked-faced Barbet being a case in point. African tinkerbirds, named for their ringing calls, are diminutive barbets clad mainly in streaked browns, yellows, black, and white. The barbet name derives from the bristles that surround the base of the bill. Barbets are birds chiefly of forests and woodlands, although some of the African species prefer forest edges and more open areas such as scrublands and gardens.

■ Honeyguides

Honeyguides, smallish and rather drab, are named for the extraordinary guiding behavior of the Greater Honeyguide, which leads people to honeybee hives. The guiding is mutually advantageous: In some rural African communities, people obtain honey from the hives, and the guides get some of the beeswax, a main food for them. Aside from this intriguing relationship with people, honeyguides are known for their unusual breeding behavior. They are brood parasites, the females laying their eggs in the nests of other species, the "host" species then raising honeyguide young.

The 17 honeyguide species, family Indicatoridae, are placed in order Piciformes with the woodpeckers and barbets. Fifteen occur in sub-Saharan Africa, two in southern Asia. All are mostly dull gray, olive, or greenish brown. Ranging from four to eight inches long, honeyguides have small heads and short bills. Their skin is particularly thick, presumably to help protect them from bees angry about the birds raiding their hives. These birds mainly inhabit forests and woodlands. Their diet is centered on beeswax, the yellow substance secreted by honeybees and used for building honeycombs; but they also eat insects, spiders, and occasionally fruit.

Greater Honeyguide The immature (shown) of this species is dominant around bees' nests and is almost always the one that guides humans. Some adults never guide, but all ages make beeswax a staple of their diet. *South Africa*

■ Sunbirds

Sunbirds are very small to mid-size, often very pretty birds with long downcurved bills designed to penetrate flower parts to get nectar. Distributed mainly through sub-Saharan Africa and southern Asia, they are noted for the rapid, acrobatic way they flit in and out of flowering trees and shrubs as they search for flowers and insects. Because of their iridescent colors, bill shape, nectar-feeding behavior, and aggressiveness in defending feeding territories, sunbirds are considered to be the Old World "ecological equivalent" of the New World hummingbirds. However, the two groups are not closely related. The sunbird family Nectariniidae contains about 130 species, including 10 in Asia called spiderhunters.

Ranging from 3.5 to 8.5 inches long, sunbirds have relatively thin, downcurved bills that vary from fairly short to extremely long. The often spectacularly

Beautiful Sunbird Like others in its family, this sunbird is almost always seen in the vicinity of flowering plants. This species is common across central Africa from West Africa to Ethiopia and south into Kenya and Tanzania. *Gambia*

colorful sunbird males typically have patches of red, blue, and/or yellow, as in the Beautiful Sunbird from West and East Africa and Anchieta's Sunbird from south-central Africa. Females are much duller, usually shades of olive or yellow. Sunbirds occupy many habitats, including forests, forest edges, woodlands, mangroves, parkland, gardens, and more open areas such as agricultural sites.

■ Weavers

Weavers are small songbirds that primarily live in savannas, grasslands, and other open habitats of Africa and, to a lesser extent, southern Asia. They are most recognized for their construction of elaborate, woven, roofed grass nests. Because they typically breed in colonies, trees adorned with several hanging weaver nests are a common sight through many regions of Africa. The weaver family Ploceidae contains 116 species, variously named weaver, fody, malimbe, quelea, bishop, and widowbird. In addition to their nests, these birds are noted for their gregariousness and for

Vitelline Masked-Weaver The entrance to this almost completed nest is at the bottom. This species (male shown) is one of the "yellow weavers" that can be very difficult to identify—pay close attention to the shape of the mask, eye color, and back pattern. *Ethiopia*

their numbers. They sometimes gather into enormous groups, flocks so huge that, as they move, they resemble clouds of dark smoke. One of these flocking species, the Red-billed Quelea, is considered to be the world's most abundant wild bird—perhaps 1.5 billion individuals. Farmers in sub-Saharan Africa consider it to be a major, crop-stealing pest.

Weavers are chiefly 4.5 to 10 inches long (although widowbirds with long tails range up to 28 inches) and have short, stout bills. In many species, male and female differ markedly in appearance, especially during breeding, when males become more colorful or elaborate. The largest subgroup in the family is the yellow weavers such as the Village and Spectacled Weavers, in which males tend to have black heads or face masks. Fodies of the Madagascar region are red, brown, and black. Malimbes are red and black forest weavers. Male queleas are mostly brown and streaked, but during breeding have varying amounts of red on the head, chest, and bill. Male bishops during breeding adopt black and red or black and yellow plumages, while male widowbirds grow long, elaborate tail feathers and bright shoulder patches.

■ Indigobirds

Indigobirds and whydahs are small seed-eating birds restricted to Africa. Their family Viduidae encompasses 20 species and is recognized for its unusual breeding. All its members are brood parasites: They do not build nests, incubate eggs, or feed young. Rather, the "parasitic" females deposit their eggs in the nests of other species; the "host" parents then raise the indigobird or whydah young as their own. Whydahs are also noted for the males' elaborate, elongated tails when in their breeding plumages, in such species as the Long-tailed Paradise-Whydah and the Shaft-tailed

Whydah. Indigobirds are notorious among birders for their similar appearances. Many are little blackish (male) or streaked brownish (female) songbirds with small white bills, making them difficult to distinguish as to species. These birds are

Eastern Paradise-Whydah The breeding male (shown) is conspicuous and easy to identify. In nonbreeding plumage it loses its long tail streamers and closely resembles the streaky brown female. This species is a brood parasite on Green-winged Pytilia (one of the waxbills). *Tanzania*

only four to five inches long, but breeding male whydahs have long central tail feathers that add another six to ten inches. Whereas indigobirds are mainly blackish or brownish, breeding male whydahs are combinations of black, white, buff, and reddish brown; females and nonbreeding males are brown and streaked. Whydahs and indigobirds are mainly birds of woodlands and savannas but also live around human settlements.

A birding trip to sub-Saharan Africa will surely produce exposure to several endemic bird families, the sighting of many truly exotic individual species, a good long bird list, and almost certainly lifelong birding memories.

SUB-SAHARAN AFRICA

A TYPICAL NATURE TRAVELER IN SUB-SAHARAN AFRICA SPOTS LARGE, FOUR-legged mammals grazing on an expanse of green, tan, and brown savannah and cries out "zebras!" or "giraffes!" or "rhinos!" The global birder in the same situation fixates not on the zebras or giraffes but on the small songbirds moving over the mammals' bodies and cries out "oxpeckers!" The two species of oxpeckers, or "tickbirds," restricted to Africa, are gray-brown birds known for their habit of clinging to the hides of large, often hairy mammals and feeding on ticks and other parasites they find there (see p.184). The curious but common oxpeckers are just a tiny part of a large, thrilling avifauna that confronts any birder visiting sub-Saharan Africa.

The previous descriptions of significant African birds, as well as the photographs in this chapter, only hint at the potential richness of birding experiences here. A very brief list of must-see species might encompass such varied offerings as the Ostrich, plus the odd, stork-like Shoebill, the white-headed and white-tailed African Fish-Eagle, the Secretary-bird, a couple of the bustards, a few turacos, and the Lilac-breasted Roller (one of the continent's flashiest birds). The list might also include the Southern Ground-Hornbill (a turkey-size black bird with long legs and colorful throat wattles) and at least one of the two sugarbirds, which are peculiar nectar-eating birds restricted to southern Africa.

Aside from lots of great birds, habitat types contribute positively to birding in sub-Saharan Africa. This is because birding here tends to occur in fairly open habitats, including especially the area's vast expanses of open woodlands and savannas. In general, birds are more easily spotted and followed in these types of habitats than in habitats more densely vegetated, such as tropical rain forest with its "closed," or overhanging, leafy canopy.

OPPOSITE: **Namib Desert** Located in Namib-Naukluft Park, the largest conservation area in Africa, the huge red sand dunes at Sossusvlei make a spectacular backdrop. The surrounding area hosts many desert-adapted birds. A specialty of the area is the Dune Lark, a Namibian endemic. *Namibia*

A birding trip to sub-Saharan Africa will surely produce exposure to several endemic bird families, the sighting of many truly exotic individual species, a good long bird list, and almost certainly lifelong birding memories. Several countries within each of three main regions are traditional birding destinations because they are relatively safe, and because they have high bird diversity and fairly easy ways of reaching and remaining at birding sites. The following three paragraphs mention some sites in the three main regions of sub-Saharan Africa.

In West Africa, the tiny country of Gambia has a history of accommodating visiting birdwatchers and the availability of many indigenous bird guides (of varying cost and quality). The larger country of Cameroon has between 850 and 900 species and a set of good national parks in which to search for them.

In East Africa, the large number of popular birding spots includes Ethiopia, with the rolling savanna and plains of Awash National Park and the wet woodlands and high-elevation habitats of Bale Mountains National Park. In Kenya, oft-visited national parks and reserves greatly facilitate birding, including the two Tsavo National Parks, Lake Nakuru National Park, Masai Mara National Reserve, Mount Kenya, and the Kakamega Nature Reserve. In Uganda, where nature tourism is expanding, are such great birding spots as the Biwindi Impenetrable Forest National Park, where mountain gorillas reside, and Kibale National Park, where chimpanzees are often seen.

In southern Africa, Chobe National Park and the Okavango Delta in Botswana, Etosha National Park and Namib-Naukluft National Park in Namibia, and Kruger National Park, the Mkhuze Game Reserve, Drakensberg Park, and Hluhluwe-Umfolozi Park in South Africa all support wonderful birding. Sub-Saharan Africa spans a wide range of latitudes and climates, so the best time to visit varies.

GEOGRAPHY AND HABITATS

Sub-Saharan Africa spans an immense area that is almost all tropical except for South Africa and the southern portions of Namibia, Botswana, and Mozambique. The region's main river systems are the Niger, Congo, Zambezi, Limpopo, and the southern part of the Nile. Mountain zones include the Ethiopian Highlands, a huge area encompassing mainly Ethiopia and Eritrea. Much of the land there rises to above 5,000 feet. In the East African highlands, mountains reach great heights such as Kilimanjaro at 19,341 feet and Mount Kenya at 17,057 feet. Southern Africa's Great Escarpment traces a U-shape from western Namibia south to central South Africa (where it forms the Cape Fold Mountains and the Drakensberg Mountains) and then northward again into Mozambique.

LOCAL BIRDING & CONSERVATION ORGANIZATIONS

■ **AFRICAN BIRD CLUB** (www.africanbirdclub.org) British organization concerned with ornithology, birding, and avian conservation in Africa; its website provides country-by-country birding information

■ **BIRDLIFE SOUTH AFRICA** (www.birdlife.org.za) promotes birding and avian education and conservation in South Africa

■ **ETHIOPIAN WILDLIFE AND NATURAL HISTORY SOCIETY** (www.ewnhs.org.et) society that, since 1966, has focused on learning about and conserving Ethiopia's wildlife

■ **NATUREKENYA** (www.naturekenya.org) local organization that supports East African conservation and birding, especially in Kenya

■ **WILDLIFE CONSERVATION SOCIETY OF TANZANIA** (www.wcstarusha.org) promotes conservation in Tanzania and is especially interested in preserving the nation's avian diversity

Other major geographical features include the Great Rift Valley that supports wonderful savanna birding habitats in Kenya, Uganda, and Tanzania. Another feature is the string of alkaline and freshwater lakes known as Rift Valley lakes, which include Lake Tanganyika, one the world's deepest lakes; Lake Victoria, the world's second largest freshwater lake; and several of Kenya's smaller, famed wildlife-watching venues such as Lake Nakuru and Lake Naivasha.

Other significant features are the Congo Basin, the enormous lowland drainage area of the Congo River that contains huge tracts of rain forest; the Okavango Delta, the globe's largest inland river delta, located in Botswana; and the Kalahari Desert, centered in Botswana but extending into Namibia and South Africa. Three main habitat types or groups in sub-Saharan Africa cover huge regions: savanna and woodland, lowland rain forest, and semi-desert. The last habitat includes the sahel, which runs in an east-to-west band across the continent just south of the Sahara, and the karoo, a semi-desert shrubland characteristic of parts of southern Africa. Habitats covering smaller but significant areas include grassland, high-elevation forest, and desert, such as Namibia's coastal Namib Desert.

FINDING THE SHOEBILL

The large, gray, long-legged, swamp-dwelling Shoebill (or Shoe-billed Stork) is bizarre in both appearance and behavior. The Shoebill's placement on the avian family tree is confusing. Historically it has been considered closely related to storks, but recent molecular studies show that it may be more related to pelicans or perhaps to herons. Currently it is placed within its own single-species family Balaenicipitidae. The 5,000 to 8,000 individuals are restricted to marshes of northeastern Africa along the White Nile floodplain. A few occur in western Tanzania and Uganda, but the vast majority of the population is in southern Sudan. The bird's monstrous, voluminous bill seems to have several uses. Its sharp tip is used to pry lungfish, molluscs, reptiles, and carrion from muddy swamp bottoms; it is used to pour water over the birds' eggs to keep them cool on its large floating nests;

and during courtship, the males clap their bills shut to make a loud, hollow sound.

Because of long civil unrest in Sudan, the best place to find the Shoebill is in Uganda, especially along the Victoria Nile at Albert Nile Delta near Murchison Falls. Recently the Mabamba Swamp near Entebbe and the international airport has become a relatively reliable spot as well, but the population there is much smaller. I have found that for such a large bird, the Shoebill can be, at times, amazingly difficult to locate. A long boat ride through marshes and sometimes slogging on foot along muddy trails parallel to swamps is often required—part of a messy initiation rite here for birders. —D.P.

Shoebill This localized species was not described until 1850, and there is still much to be learned about it. The main conservation concern is the destruction of the papyrus swamplands it inhabits to make room for cattle. *Lake Albert, Uganda*

BIRDLIFE

Sub-Saharan Africa roughly corresponds to the zoogeographic region known as the Afrotropical, or Ethiopian Zone. More than 2,000 bird species can be found here, various authorities offering different totals depending on which seabirds, migrants, and islands are included. Perhaps 1,400 species are endemic to the area. Part-time residents, or migrants, are an important part of the avifauna, with many Palearctic species spending their winters wholly or partly in sub-Saharan Africa.

Sub-Saharan Africa is known among ecologists for its diversity of ground-living species and seed-eaters. Also well represented in sub-Saharan Africa are birds of prey, sandgrouse, pigeons and doves, cuckoos, swifts, kingfishers, hornbills, swallows, bulbuls, thrushes, babblers, and starlings. Relatively poorly represented are parrots, trogons, with only three species, broadbills, with four species, and pittas, with two.

In addition to the ten significant families detailed earlier, there are many other interesting bird families and species, some of them endemic. The following is a small sampling. Nonpasserine families or species of particular interest include: the Ostrich; the Hamerkop (single-species endemic family); the Shoebill (single-species family

Gray-necked Rockfowl This bird was photographed on Mount Cameroon, above Etome, in the same area as Korup National Park. *Cameroon*

SPOTTING THE GRAY-NECKED ROCKFOWL

Rockfowl, also commonly called picathartes, are strange, no matter how they are viewed. They are slim, crow-size birds with long legs, bare heads, and bizarre vocalizations that make it difficult even for scientists to classify them. Now they are installed in their own family. The two populations of rockfowl, Gray-necked mainly in Cameroon and Nigeria, and White-necked mostly farther west in Ghana to Sierra Leone, are now classified as two closely related species.

Birds of dense, dark lowland forest, the rockfowl populations are sparse and scattered. The only reasonably assured way to see this bird is to visit a nesting colony during early courtship season.

Seven of us hiked into Korup National Park in southwestern Cameroon to one of the few known nesting sites for the Gray-necked Rockfowl. The forest is spectacular, and the hike is over flat ground under a tall closed canopy. Congo Serpent-Eagle, Bare-cheeked Trogon, Yellow-casqued Hornbill, African Pitta, as well as numerous greenbuls, filled the six-mile hike to a small isolated rise in the forest that was covered with house-size boulders. Three of these huge boulders formed a grotto where several mud nest platforms had been started. We arrived late in the afternoon and sat motionless in the shade with our backs to the far-side boulder. All of a sudden we heard a loud hissing sound, and the first rockfowl came bounding in from the adjacent forest. Then three others came in, and they bounced around like jumping jacks on their long legs with no obvious goal for a full 20 minutes—barely 25 feet from us. As night fell, their activity lessened, and we slipped quietly away, elated. When nesting begins in April, this area is closed to tourists (to protect the birds). —D.P.

FIELD GUIDE & SITE GUIDE BOOKS

■ *Birds of Africa South of the Sahara* (2004)
I. Sinclair and P. Ryan
Princeton University Press

■ *The Birds of East Africa: Kenya, Tanzania, Uganda, Rwanda, Burundi* (2002)
T. Stevenson and J. Fanshawe
Princeton University Press

■ *Birds of Eastern Africa, rev. ed.* (2009)
B. van Perlo
Princeton University Press

■ *Birds of the Horn of Africa: Ethiopia, Eritrea, Djibouti, Somalia, and Socotra* (2009)
N. Redman, T. Stevenson, and J. Fanshawe
Princeton University Press

■ *Birds of Southern Africa* (2009)
B. van Perlo
Princeton University Press

■ *Birds of Southern Africa, 3rd ed.* (2002)
I. Sinclair, P. Hockey, and W. Tarboton
Princeton University Press

■ *Birds of Western Africa* (2005)
N. Borrow and R. Demey
Princeton University Press

endemic to central Africa), the Secretary-bird (single-species endemic family); guinea-fowl; pratincoles and coursers; and woodhoopoes and scimitar-bills (endemic family of eight species).

Passerine families or species that have a strong or uniquely African distribution include: larks (about 70 species in sub-Saharan Africa); cisticolas, prinias, and apalises (very common in Africa and sometimes called "African warblers"); wattle-eyes and batises (endemic family of 31 species); rockfowl (endemic family of 2 species found in western Africa); rockjumpers (3 unusual babblers; endemic to southern Africa); sugarbirds (endemic family of 2 species found in southern Africa); shrikes, helmet-shrikes, and bushshrikes (the last family endemic to Africa); and waxbills.

Several countries in sub-Saharan Africa sustain avifaunas that exceed a thousand species, especially Kenya, Tanzania, and Uganda. The Democratic Republic of the Congo, formerly Zaire, heads the list of African countries in avian richness, with more than 1,100 species. However, few birders would go there, given the country's recent deadly wars in which millions of people may have died. A second tier of country destinations, each with between 800 and 900 species, includes Cameroon, Nigeria, Ethiopia, and South Africa. The sub-Saharan mainland contains about 25 Endemic Bird Areas (EBAs) plus a few others on nearby islands. A few of the larger EBAs are the Upper Guinea forests and the Cameroon and Gabon lowlands in West Africa, the Central Ethiopian highlands, the Serengeti Plains in East Africa, and the southern African grasslands in South Africa and Lesotho.

Significant Species
of Sub-Saharan Africa

ABOUT 98 FAMILIES FOUND IN THIS REGION

■ **BUSTARDS** (Otididae), **17 species**

Kori Bustard* *Ardeotis kori*
largest bustard, three feet tall and weighing up to
40 pounds; occurs in East and southern Africa

Black Bustard* *Eupodotis afra*
common, strikingly marked smaller bustard; endemic
to South Africa

■ **PRATINCOLES AND COURSERS** (Glareolidae), **12 species**

Three-banded Courser* *Rhinoptilus cinctus*
handsome, plover-like terrestrial shorebird of dry scrub
and bushy grassland in East and southern Africa

■ **SANDGROUSE** (Pteroclidae), **10 species**

Four-banded Sandgrouse *Pterocles quadricinctus*
small sandgrouse of dry savannas and cultivated areas
of West and East Africa

■ **TURACOS*** (Musophagidae), **23 species**

Great Blue Turaco* *Corythaeola cristata*
large gray-blue or greenish blue turaco with a black
crest and black-tipped tail; main range in West and
central Africa

Violet Turaco* *Musophaga violacea*
violet-blue turaco with a red crown; inhabits forests
and woodlands of West Africa

Gray Go-away-bird* *Corythaixoides concolor*
common savanna and woodland species endemic
to southern Africa

■ **MOUSEBIRDS*** (Coliidae), **6 species**

Red-faced Mousebird* *Urocolius indicus*
mainly gray, long-tailed bird with a red, bare-skin face;
common over southern Africa in savanna, woodlands,
orchards, and gardens

■ **BEE-EATERS** (Meropidae), **19 species**

Northern Carmine Bee-eater* *Merops nubicus*
large, striking red or pinkish bee-eater with green
patches; from the savannas of West and East Africa

Boehm's Bee-eater* *Merops boehmi*
small, mainly green East African bee-eater of
woodlands, scrub areas, and thickets

■ **ROLLERS** (Coraciidae), **8 species**

Lilac-breasted Roller* *Coracias caudatus*
multicolored roller with two long tail streamers; common
in woodlands and grasslands of East and southern Africa

Blue-bellied Roller* *Coracias cyanogaster*
white-headed and white-chested roller common in woodlands in portions of West and Central Africa

■ **HORNBILLS** (Bucerotidae), **about 25 species**

White-crested Hornbill* *Tockus albocristatus*
black hornbill with a white bushy crest and very long,
white-tipped tail, from West and Central Africa

Hemprich's Hornbill* *Tockus hemprichii*
brown and white hornbill with a dark red bill, from East
Africa's Ethiopian Highlands region

Trumpeter Hornbill* *Ceratogymna bucinator*
black and white hornbill with a blackish bill and casque;
present in forests of East and southern Africa

Southern Ground-Hornbill* *Bucorvus leadbeateri*
largest hornbill, a terrestrial species present in savanna
and woodlands of southern Africa, but also as far north
as southern Kenya

■ **BARBETS** (Capitonidae), **41 species**

Yellow-rumped Tinkerbird* *Pogoniulus subsulphureus*
very small barbet of forests and woodlands; common
over much of sub-Saharan Africa

Vieillot's Barbet* *Lybius vieilloti*
distinctive brown and yellow barbet with a red head;
found in West and Central Africa

Chaplin's Barbet* *Lybius chaplini*
largely white and brown barbet endemic to Zambia

■ **HONEYGUIDES** (Indicatoridae), **15 species**

Greater Honeyguide* *Indicator indicator*
honeyguide that can lead people to bees' nests; brown
above and whitish below, and male has a pinkish bill

■ **CISTICOLAS AND ALLIES** (Cisticolidae), **about 90 species**

Rudd's Apalis* *Apalis ruddi*
small songbird of forests and thickets; endemic to
eastern coasts of southern Africa

■ **SUNBIRDS** (Nectariniidae), **about 80 species**

Beautiful Sunbird* *Cinnyris pulchellus*
very small sunbird from West and East Africa; male sports long tail streamers and is mainly a metallic green with a wide red chest band with yellow sides

Orange-breasted Sunbird* *Anthobaphes violacea*
common sunbird endemic to southern South Africa's shrublands; male has a greenish head and orange-yellow chest

■ **WEAVERS** (Ploceidae), **about 100 species**

Jackson's Widowbird* *Euplectes jacksoni*
endemic to Tanzania and Kenya; breeding male has a very long, curved tail

Social Weaver* *Philetairus socius*
endemic to the savanna and scrub habitats of southern Africa; brown above and white below, with black markings

■ **WAXBILLS AND ALLIES** (Estrildidae), **about 80 species**

Violet-eared Waxbill* *Granatina granatina*
striking small savanna and woodland songbird from southern Africa; male brownish with red bill, purplish cheeks, and blue rump

Pink-throated Twinspot* *Hypargos margaritatus*
small finch with a white-spotted black belly; endemic to thickets and scrub in southeastern Africa

■ **INDIGOBIRDS*** (Viduidae), **20 species**

Long-tailed Paradise-Whydah* *Vidua interjecta*
West African finch; breeding male has an extremely long, broad tail, perhaps twice its body length

Purple Indigobird* *Vidua purpurascens*
male black, female brownish and streaked; found in East and southern Africa

Some Other Species Global Birders Often Seek

Ostrich *Struthio camelus*
largest bird; the Somali subspecies (*molybdophanes*) is sometimes considered a separate species

Jackass Penguin* *Spheniscus demersus*
medium-size penguin endemic to coastal areas of Namibia and South Africa

Hamerkop *Scopus umbretta*
unique stork-like bird of wetlands with a backward-pointing crest, found in Africa, Madagascar, and Arabia

Saddle-billed Stork* *Ephippiorhynchus senegalensis*
large, uncommon black and white stork with reddish patches on its bill and legs

Shoebill* *Balaeniceps rex*
large, stork-like swamp bird with a massive bill, endemic to eastern and central Africa

Cape Griffon* *Gyps coprotheres*
large vulture endemic to southern Africa, occurring mainly in grassland and savanna regions

Martial Eagle* *Polemaetus bellicosus*
huge, crested eagle, dark above with a light, spotted belly; inhabits many open environments

Secretary-bird* *Sagittarius serpentarius*
raptor of grasslands, savanna, and woodlands that forages and spends most of its time on the ground

Gray Crowned-Crane* *Balearica regulorum*
mainly gray crane with a tall crest of yellow feathers, from East and southern Africa

African Finfoot* *Podica senegalensis*
unusual waterbird of Africa's densely vegetated rivers and streams; one of the globe's three finfoots

Bar-tailed Trogon* *Apaloderma vittatum*
one of Africa's three trogons, this species occurs mainly in wet evergreen forests at higher elevations

Green Woodhoopoe* *Phoeniculus purpureus*
blue-green, predominantly arboreal bird with a long, red, downcurved bill; the most widespread of the six woodhoopoe species

Ground Woodpecker* *Geocolaptes olivaceus*
largish gray-brown and pinkish woodpecker found on the ground in open habitats; endemic to southern Africa

Green-breasted Pitta* *Pitta reichenowi*
rain forest species and one of Africa's two pittas

Chorister Robin-Chat* *Cossypha dichroa*
common forest inhabitant, dark gray above, orangish below; endemic to South Africa

Gray-necked Rockfowl* *Picathartes oreas*
large, rare, limited-range bird of West African rain forests; one of only two rockfowl, or picathartes, species

Orange-breasted Rockjumper* *Chaetops aurantius*
striking, long-tailed, blackish and orange ground-dwelling babbler; endemic to rocky slopes in South Africa

Cape Sugarbird* *Promerops cafer*
one of two sugarbirds; long billed and very long-tailed, endemic to South African shrublands

Uluguru Bushshrike* *Malaconotus alius*
endangered bushshrike, black and olive above, yellowish below; endemic to wet forests of the Uluguru mountains of central Tanzania

Golden-breasted Starling* *Lamprotornis regius*
very handsome open-country starling, greenish blue above and golden yellow below; endemic to East Africa

Restricted to Sub-Saharan Africa

In Madagascar, the greatest prizes for international birders are sure to be sightings of any and all of the species of mesites, ground-rollers, asities, and vangas.

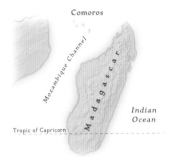

Comoros

Mozambique Channel

Madagascar

Indian Ocean

Tropic of Capricorn

MADAGASCAR

Reaching Madagascar from North America can cost thousands of dollars and entail a minimum of three or four flights. This island country also can be an expensive place to stay and has had its share of political strife. Nevertheless, most global birders place this distant destination somewhere near the top of their travel wish lists and endeavor to visit it at least once. The reason is that the place is a hot spot of endemic species—birds and many other kinds of animals, not to mention plants. The high level of endemism is a consequence of Madagascar's history: This largely tropical island off southeastern Africa has been separated from the African mainland for perhaps 150 million years, and in that long period of isolation an incredible array of unique species developed.

Many people interested in nature recognize that the primitive primates known as lemurs are endemic to Madagascar (a couple of species appear also on nearby smaller islands, perhaps introduced), but a much smaller number of people know of Madagascar's unique birds. These include five families restricted to the island, or almost so. From the bird fancier's perspective, it's imperative to say that among these birds are some of the world's most striking and exotic. Certainly included would be the Pitta-like Ground-Roller, a secretive, green-winged ground bird with a blue and white head and throat; the Cuckoo-Roller, a crow-size tree-canopy species, whose male is a metallic green above and gray and white below; the Helmet Vanga, a black and brown forest bird with a huge, humped, pale blue bill; and the Sickle-billed Vanga, a forest and savanna resident, black and white with an exceedingly long, thin, downcurved bill.

Efforts to add these and some of Madagascar's more than one hundred other endemic bird species to life lists tend to involve going with a tour group or locating

OPPOSITE: **Anjajavy Coastal Forest** This dry deciduous forest in the northwest part of the country supports a number of endemic bird species and lemurs. Two species of baobab trees are visible in the photograph. *Madagascar*

Cuckoo-Roller This unusual species (male shown) is placed in its own family (Leptosomatidae) and is endemic to Madagascar and the Comoro Islands. It is widespread in suitable habitat and often noticed flying over the forest that it inhabits. *Madagascar*

LOCAL BIRDING & CONSERVATION ORGANIZATIONS

■ **AFRICAN BIRD CLUB** (www.africanbirdclub.org) British organization concerned with ornithology, birding, and avian conservation in Africa, including Madagascar and some other Indian Ocean islands

■ **ASITY MADAGASCAR** (www.asitymadagascar.org) relatively new organization dedicated to the conservation of Madagascar's biodiversity, birds in particular

a local guide with whom to travel. Independent birding is certainly possible, but in-country transportation can be difficult or expensive, roads can be troublesome (and impassible during rainier seasons), Malagasy and French are dominant languages, and, as of this writing, relations with the U.S. government are far from cordial; and therefore, as with many areas in and around Africa, most birders likely will be more comfortable traveling around Madagascar with area experts or knowledgeable locals.

National parks and reserves are scattered throughout the country. For instance, the relatively new Masoala National Park, taking up most of the Masoala Peninsula in the northeastern portion of the island, has forest species like the critically endangered Madagascar Serpent-Eagle as well as the Red-breasted Coua, Scaly Ground-Roller, Helmet Vanga, and Bernier's Vanga. Small parks and wetlands in and around Madagascar's capital, Antananarivo, in the center of the island, sport such endemics and near-endemics as Madagascar Kestrel, Madagascar Coucal, Madagascar Swamp-Warbler, and Madagascar White-eye.

Cloud forests of Andasibe-Mantadia National Park in central-eastern Madagascar, not far from the capital and often visited by international tourists, provide habitat for endemics like Madagascar Rail, Red-fronted Coua, Rufous-headed Ground-Roller, Short-legged Ground-Roller, Velvet Asity, Sunbird Asity, Red-tailed Newtonia (an Old World warbler), and Coral-billed Nuthatch. Rain forests of Ranomafana National Park in the southeast have many endemics including Brown Mesite, Blue Coua, Pitta-like Ground-Roller, and Yellow-bellied Asity.

This mainly tropical country can be visited at most times of the year, but a birder's optimal season is during September and October.

GEOGRAPHY AND HABITATS

Madagascar, the globe's fourth-largest island, more than 1,000 miles long and 300 miles wide, lies in the Indian Ocean directly east of Mozambique. Several small Indian Ocean islands near Madagascar include the Comoro Islands, Aldabra Island, Mauritius, and Réunion, and some of these share certain bird species with the larger island.

A main geographic feature of Madagascar is a centrally situated higher elevation region that runs in a north-south axis through the island. Much of these central highlands are at 2,500 to 4,500 feet elevation, and several peaks rise to 7,500 feet and more. In the east, the highlands fall in a steep escarpment, but in the west, the decline in elevation toward the sea is more gradual. Madagascar has five large lakes. The largest, Lake Alaotra, in the east, is quite shallow, and it and adjoining marsh areas and irrigated agricultural lands make up a significant wetland area important for aquatic birds. Most of the other large lakes are also important for water-associated birds.

BIRDING MASOALA NATIONAL PARK, MADAGASCAR

In 1993 I was invited to consult on identifying the boundaries of a newly proposed national park in Madagascar. I had heard horror stories of the devastation of natural habitats on the island, but I was eager to see some of the many unique plants and animals that occur there and nowhere else in the world. We took a short domestic flight from the capital, Antananarivo, to the small airport in Maroantsetra on the northeast coast. A three-hour boat ride across Antongil Bay then brought us to the Masoala Peninsula, the site of the proposed park. Because of the lack of roads, this is one of the few places in Madagascar where there is relatively untrammeled forest, from the edge of the beach to the tops of the mountains. In the early 1990s there were no tourist facilities, so we gathered our tents and supplies and hiked up to a campsite on top of the low mountains that form the spine of the peninsula. The forest was spectacular, and the frogs, lemurs, butterflies, birds, and orchids were a biologist's dream. I awoke at dawn to a cacophony of unfamiliar primate, bird, and frog sounds. The most startling was from a beautiful Pitta-like Ground-Roller that had its bright blue and white head halfway into the opening of my tent. Apparently I had placed my tent within its territory.

Finally established in 1997, Masoala National Park is now Madagascar's largest protected area. The park boasts ten lemur species, including the endemic red ruffed lemur and the elusive aye-aye. Many of Madagascar's endemic bird species are easily found here, including the extremely rare Madagascar Serpent-Eagle, the Madagascar Red Owl, and the Helmet Vanga. Several tourist lodges have now been constructed on the peninsula. —D.P.

Pitta-like Ground-Roller
Of the five species of ground-rollers (all endemic to Madagascar), this one is the most widespread and common. Even so, its secretive nature can make it very difficult to see. *Madagascar*

Major habitat types of Madagascar are evergreen rain forests, with primary forest surviving chiefly in the eastern part of the island, seasonally dry deciduous forest in the west, and grasslands and savannas in both the east and west. Perhaps Madagascar's most unique and celebrated habitat occurs in the south and southwest, where the arid, harsh climate and poor soils combine to produce large tracts of dry thorn scrub, often referred to as "spiny forest." This dense, unusual habitat has many weird endemic plants such as several species of baobab trees, many euphorbias, as well as shrubs and even trees that look like spiny cacti. Due to the large number of unusual, rare, and endemic birds, some birders consider Madagascar's spiny forest habitat to be among the Earth's most intriguing birding locations.

BIRDLIFE

Madagascar's birdlife is exceptional not for its number of species but for its degree of endemism. In fact, given the island's large size, varied habitats, and nearness to the African mainland's rich avifauna, it might be expected to harbor even more than

Yellow-nosed Albatross
Of all pelagic seabirds, the albatrosses are probably the most sought-after. Pelagic birding trips off southern Africa often find multiple species of albatross, including this one. *off South Africa*

BIRDING OFFSHORE OF CAPETOWN, SOUTH AFRICA

No other pelagic area except perhaps parts of Antarctica can challenge a pelagic trip off the South African city of Cape Town for spotting incredible numbers of individuals and species of seabirds. The large numbers are because of the presence of the nutrient-rich Benguela Current, which originates in the icy waters of Antarctica. The concentration of bird numbers is greatly enhanced behind a fishing trawler, where 5,000 or more birds of 20 or 30 species can congregate in the boat's wake.

Winter (May–September) is generally the most awesome season for pelagic birds in this region, as Antarctic species move north to escape the ice and snow of their nesting areas. A thousand individuals of seven species of albatross are not unheard of on a single daylong pelagic trip. Antarctic Giant Petrel, Hall's Giant Petrel, Southern Fulmar, Cape (or Pintado) Petrel, White-chinned Petrel, Broad-billed Prion, Sooty Shearwater,

Wilson's Storm-Petrel, and Cape Gannet are all regular at this time of year.

In summer (October–April), smaller numbers of individuals are typical. These are mainly more northerly breeding species wintering here, such as Great-winged Petrel, Soft-plumaged Petrel, Cory's Shearwater, Greater Shearwater, White-bellied Storm-Petrel, and European Storm-Petrel.

Rarities and vagrants add spice to many trips with species such as Light-mantled Albatross, White-headed Petrel, Atlantic Petrel, Blue Petrel, Gray Petrel, Kerguelen Petrel, and White-faced Storm-Petrel. Reasonably priced day trips, led by experienced local leaders and using radar to detect trawlers on the continental shelf, 20 to 25 miles offshore, depart from Simon's Town and Hout Bay harbors at least once a month. Be ready for cancellations and delays because sea conditions often become too rough to go out on the day of your scheduled trip. —D.P.

the number of species that do live there. That number, including offshore seabirds of the area, is about 280. Of these, about 210 breed regularly in Madagascar. Approximately 50 percent of the 210 are endemic to the island—the highest proportion of endemic birds found among any of the globe's relatively large countries.

What kind of birds are Madagascar's endemics? Generally speaking, they are dense-habitat forest birds, with only about 10 percent of them existing in habitats that might be termed "open," such as grassland or scrub. The greatest prizes for international birders are sure to be sightings of any and all of the species of mesites, ground-rollers, asities, and vangas. Three of the former groups are endemic, whereas the vangas and also the Cuckoo-Roller are shared with nearby smaller islands such as the Comoro Islands.

The three species of mesites (family Mesitornithidae, included in order Gruiformes with the rails) are mid-size ground birds of forests, woodlands, and thickets. All are brownish or grayish with lighter underparts, and they have long, thick tails. They eat seeds, insects, and fruit. In the past, some were thought to be flightless, but all can fly, albeit weakly.

Ground-rollers (family Brachypteraciidae, closely related to the roller family) are a group of five species of medium-size, skulking, mostly terrestrial birds with large heads, stout, short bills, and longish legs. Some are drab, others fairly colorful. Most are forest inhabitants, but one lives in woodland and scrub areas. All eat chiefly insects and other small invertebrates.

The four species of asities (passerine family Philepittidae) are small, stout forest birds with very short tails, recognized for their bright colors and remarkable bill shapes. Two, the Sunbird Asity and Yellow-bellied Asity, have very long, slim, downcurved bills, used to gather nectar from flowers. The other two are fruit-eaters and have relatively short bills.

Vangas (family Vangidae) are small and mid-size, somewhat shrike-like songbirds restricted mainly to Madagascar. Vanga bills vary widely, from smallish but wide and mostly straight, to stout but compressed side to side, to long, humped, and hooked, to long, thin, and highly curved. These are arboreal, primarily canopy birds, inhabiting forests, woodlands, and, in drier regions, semi-desert scrub. They eat insects but also spiders and small vertebrates.

Finally, the Cuckoo-Roller (single-species family Leptosomatidae, related to rollers) occupies many habitats and eats insects and small lizards. In addition to its endemic families, Madagascar is usually credited for having good numbers of rails and cuckoos. One subgroup of nine cuckoos, called couas, is endemic to the island and on most birders' must-see lists. Couas are pigeon-size, fairly colorful, and have long, stiff tails and naked, often bluish skin around their eyes.

FIELD GUIDE & SITE GUIDE BOOKS

■ *Birds of the Indian Ocean Islands* (2003)
I. Sinclair and O. Langrand
Struik Publishers

■ *Guide to the Birds of Madagascar* (1990)
O. Langrand
Yale University Press

■ *Where to Watch Birds in Africa* (2000)
N. Wheatley
Princeton University Press

Significant Species
of Madagascar

ABOUT 70 FAMILIES FOUND IN THIS REGION

■ **HAWKS, EAGLES, AND KITES** (Accipitridae), **13 species**

Madagascar Cuckoo-Hawk* *Aviceda madagascariensis*
secretive forest hawk that takes insects and small
reptiles

Madagascar Fish-Eagle* *Haliaeetus vociferoides*
Madagascar's largest raptor, found along coasts and
waterways

Madagascar Serpent-Eagle* *Eutriorchis astur*
large brown raptor of Madagascar's rain forests; critically
endangered and almost extinct

Reunion Harrier *Circus maillardi*
long-legged raptor of Madagascar plus some of its
nearby islands; eats small vertebrates

■ **MESITES*** (Mesitornithidae), **3 species**

White-breasted Mesite* *Mesitornis variegatus*
skulking ground bird of dry forests, one of three mesites
in this endemic family

■ **RAILS AND RELATIVES** (Rallidae), **11 species**

Madagascar Flufftail* *Sarothrura insularis*
very small, shy rail found in marshes but also around
rain forest edges

Madagascar Rail* *Rallus madagascariensis*
medium-size secretive rail of marshes and moist
woodlands

■ **CUCKOOS** (Cuculidae), **12 species**

Giant Coua* *Coua gigas*
large terrestrial bird, bronze-green above, tan and
brownish below; at 24 inches long, the largest coua

Crested Coua* *Coua cristata*
large, crested, arboreal cuckoo with a long blue tail

Madagascar Coucal* *Centropus toulou*
large black bird with reddish brown wings; found in
Madagascar and the island of Aldabra

■ **GROUND-ROLLERS*** (Brachypteraciidae), **5 species**

Pitta-like Ground-Roller* *Atelornis pittoides*
striking, shy, terrestrial rain forest bird

Long-tailed Ground-Roller* *Uratelornis chimaera*
mostly brown and white ground bird with sky blue
patches on the wings and on its very long tail

■ **ASITIES*** (Philepittidae), **4 species**

Velvet Asity* *Philepitta castanea*
small, stocky, rain forest bird; breeding male blackish
with blue or green fleshy growths over its eyes and on
its forehead

Yellow-bellied Asity* *Neodrepanis hypoxantha*
very small rain forest canopy bird, metallic dark blue
above, yellow below, with a long, thin, downcurved bill

■ **VANGAS** (Vangidae), **15 species**

Hook-billed Vanga* *Vanga curvirostris*
larger vanga, black and white; found in forests, woodlands, and mangroves

Sickle-billed Vanga* *Falculea palliata*
one of the most unusual vangas with a long, thin bill;
this species occupies various habitats including dry
forests and savannas

Blue Vanga *Cyanolanius madagascarinus*
small forest bird, blue above and white below; the only
vanga that also occurs outside of Madagascar (in the
Comoro Islands)

Coral-billed Nuthatch* *Hypositta corallirostris*
small, secretive rain forest vanga; male all blue-gray
with reddish bill; like a nuthatch, looks for food on tree
trunks and large branches

Some Other Species Global Birders Often Seek

Madagascar Ibis* *Lophotibis cristata*
mainly reddish brown ibis of Madagascar's woodlands

Gray-headed Lovebird* *Agapornis canus*
small, green parrot with a gray head; one of Madagascar's three parrots; found in savanna and woodland
habitats

Vasa Parrot *Coracopsis vasa*
the bigger of two species of fairly large, gregarious,
dark brown parrots in Madagascar; also occurs in the
Cormoro Islands

White-browed Owl* *Ninox superciliaris*
medium-size nocturnal owl, brown above, whitish and
barred below; occurs in various wooded habitats

Cuckoo-Roller *Leptosomus discolor*
large, arboreal forest bird comprising a single-species family; one of Madagascar's most sought-after birds

Madagascar Hoopoe* *Upupa marginata*
one of the globe's two hoopoe species; looks very like the widespread Eurasian Hoopoe

Appert's Greenbul* *Phyllastrephus apperti*
rare, plain-looking bulbul (also called Appert's Tetraka); olive, yellow, gray, and white, endemic to the dry forests of southwestern Madagascar

Madagascar Paradise-Flycatcher *Terpsiphone mutata*
broadly distributed flycatcher; male has very long tail streamers and comes in two forms: black and white or black and reddish brown

Wedge-tailed Jery* *Hartertula flavoviridis*
one of four species of small, insect-eating Madagascar babblers called jeries that are chiefly forest birds

White-throated Oxylabes* *Oxylabes madagascariensis*
fairly secretive, brown forest bird with a white throat; one of two Madagascar babblers known as oxylabes

Madagascar White-eye *Zosterops maderaspatanus*
typical white-eye; resident in Madagascar but also on various nearby islands

*Restricted to Madagascar

Helmet Vanga This outstanding bird is only found in primary rain forest in northeast Madagascar. Despite its gaudy appearance, it can be difficult to locate—it is secretive and spends long periods perched quietly in the sub-canopy. *Madagascar*

CHAPTER 7
ASIA

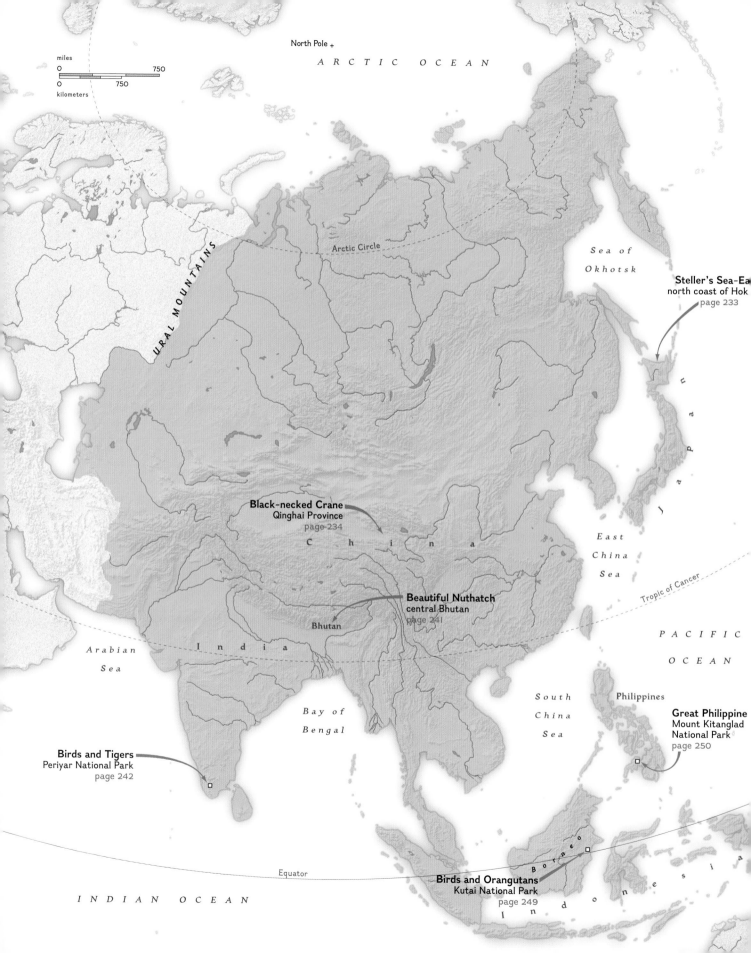

miles
0 — 750
0 — 750
kilometers

North Pole +

A R C T I C   O C E A N

Arctic Circle

URAL MOUNTAINS

Sea of
Okhotsk

Steller's Sea-Ea
north coast of Hok
page 233

Black-necked Crane
Qinghai Province
page 234

C h i n a

East
China
Sea

Beautiful Nuthatch
central Bhutan
page 241

Bhutan

Tropic of Cancer

P A C I F I C

O C E A N

Arabian
Sea

I n d i a

South
China
Sea

Philippines

Great Philippine
Mount Kitanglad
National Park
page 250

Bay of
Bengal

Birds and Tigers
Periyar National Park
page 242

Borneo

Equator

Birds and Orangutans
Kutai National Park
page 249

I n d o n e s i a

I N D I A N   O C E A N

BIRDING IN

ASIA

SOME OF THE MOST DAZZLING BIRDS ON EARTH ARE HEADQUARTERED IN ASIA, making this, the largest continent, a frequent destination for the serious global birder. About a quarter of the world's bird species occur here, many of them beautiful and amazing, so it's no easy task to single out just a few to use as examples. But if I think back to a recent trip, a number of bird types and individual species stand out. Hornbills, shared mainly between southern Asia and Africa, are true avian stars, large, charismatic, and on every birder's wish list. Hearing the loud *whoosh...whoosh...whoosh* sounds these birds make with their huge wings as they fly overhead, skirting the treetops, is just plain exhilarating, as is the sight of these big birds perched in trees, pulling fruits with their massive bills. Asia is particularly known for its pheasants, and some of them are truly spectacular. One I saw that was unforgettable—a once-in-a-lifetime bird—was the Lady Amherst's Pheasant in southern China. The male, strutting about a dim forest floor in early morning and then moving out into a sunny clearing for a better view, had a three-foot-long tail and was clad in a riotously colorful plumage, with green crown topped with red-orange crest, blue-green upper breast and upper back, yellow lower back and rump, blue-purple wings, and red elongated feathers surrounding its tail base. Two absolutely exquisite smaller birds seen on the same trip were both Old World flycatchers: The first was the common White-capped Redstart, the male black above and reddish brown below but with a pure white crown that catches the eye as the bird perches on wet rocks in its typical habitat of Tibetan mountain streams; and the second was the Grandala, a thrush-like, high-elevation bird in which the male is almost totally bright blue but with black wings

PREVIOUS PAGES:
Ruddy Shelduck A flock of shelducks accompanied by a few Bar-headed Geese flies over high-altitude Qinghai Lake located in a remote region of west-central China. *China*

and tail. The Grandala, viewed at eye level on a hillside as it investigated the feeding possibilities around dried yak droppings, was one of the most brilliantly hued birds I've seen. It is a gross understatement to say that visiting Asia with binoculars in hand and time to explore will yield most satisfactory birding experiences.

Mammoth Asia spans the terrestrial world from Turkey in the west to Japan in the east, and Russia in the north to Indonesia in the south; of necessity, in this chapter we can touch only lightly on this huge region. The continent actually spans two zoogeographic regions, northern Asia being part of the Palearctic Zone and southern Asia forming most of the Oriental Zone. Russia occupies the major portion of northern Asia but will get little mention here. The vast expanse of this country is still relatively little-visited by birders because independent travel there can be difficult,

White Eared-Pheasant
In summer, this pheasant occurs in alpine meadows as high as 15,000 feet, where it feeds on roots and tubers. The bird in the photograph has temporarily perched on the roof of the Xiongse Nunnery in Tibet. *China*

good birding sites are often in very remote, hard-to-access places, and many of its birds can be seen elsewhere (because they are shared with Europe or migrate to winter in more southerly sites). The Middle East is treated in the chapter on Europe because the birds of those two regions are similar. China, covering a large swath of Asia, is increasingly thought of as a must-go birding destination, with its large avifauna (more than 1,200 species), mix of tropical and temperate birds, and rapidly improving infrastructure beckoning. It is treated here as part of northern Asia even though its southern reaches are physically part of the Oriental Zone. As China has sought to increase international tourism, it has opened itself to birding tours and even to independent nature travelers. Yet few visitors proceed to rural areas without guides—especially since some natural areas are still off-limits to foreigners or require special permits. Contemporary birding in China can be traced back to the 1980s, when ecotourists first started visiting the Wolong Nature Reserve in southern China's Sichuan Province to observe giant pandas in their natural habitat and brought binoculars along. Birding tours still routinely stop at this reserve, where about 300 species have been spotted. Other popular birding spots in northern Asia include Japan and South Korea, both having modern infrastructures, and, these days, even central Asia's Kazakhstan and Uzbekistan.

Grandala The glistening blue Grandala (male shown) is one of Asia's real stunners. This high-mountain species is often seen in large flocks. It forages for invertebrates on rocky slopes and alpine meadows from Kashmir to Tibet and China. *China*

Much of India's international reputation rests on its huge population, bustling cities, rapid economic growth, and widespread poverty. Among nature travelers, this large country is probably most often known as the best place, indeed one of the only places, left to see a tiger in the wild. However, somewhat surprisingly, India boasts a large number of national parks and wildlife reserves that protect not only a threatened population of tigers, but a rich avifauna. About 1,200 bird species occur in India, making it a center of southern Asian birding. The Himalayan countries of Nepal and Bhutan, to India's north, have diverse birdlife and are often targeted by birders, although political violence in Nepal and restrictions on international tourism in Bhutan sometimes limit birding. Another frequent birding destination in southern Asia is Sri Lanka, located off India's southern coast.

A final region to address here is Southeast Asia, which is very popular with global birders. This tropical area boasts wonderful birds and several countries where travel

and exploration are easy and relatively safe. First there is Thailand, where tourism is a major component of the economy and the infrastructure in many areas is excellent. This friendly country might be renowned for its southern beaches and northern hill trekking, but it also excels at providing amazing bird habitats at places such as Doi Inthanon National Park in its northern reaches, Khao Yai National Park in its central area, not far from Bangkok, and Kaeng Krachan National Park in its peninsular region. Malaysia, adjacent to Thailand, is a bit more difficult to navigate but also has many good birding sites, including its famed Taman Negara National Park and various forested, highland "hill stations." Some of these are resort areas located not far from the capital, Kuala Lumpur. Cambodia, home to the splendid Angkor Wat temple complex that is now heavily visited by international tourists, can be birded, as can neighboring Laos. Even Vietnam, for many years effectively closed to Americans, has now opened its borders to birders from all over the world. Birders also roam the main and more remote islands of Indonesia and the Philippines. Only Myanmar, formerly Burma, is generally off-limits, due to its unhappy relations with the West.

BIRDING IN THE AREA

With more than 2,600 species, Asia is second among the continents only to South America in avian richness. Thus, there are a great many birds here to add to life lists. A few well-chosen locations and a few weeks of effort can yield hundreds of species. Six families are endemic. You must visit Asia to see them. These are the Ibisbill (family Ibidorhynchidae), leafbirds (Chloropseidae), ioras (Aegithinidae), the Hypocolius (Hypocoliidae), Philippine creepers (or rhabdornises; Rhabdornithidae), and fairy-bluebirds (Irenidae). Asia is also well known for its cranes, pigeons, frogmouths, hornbills, broadbills, pittas, larks, pipits, bulbuls, accentors, babblers, parrotbills, tits, sunbirds, flowerpeckers, and corvids (jays, crows, and magpies).

The bulbuls and babblers are particularly diverse groups in Asia. They are dominant in the avifauna in the sense that, in many regions, representatives of these two families are very common and often seem to compose a large fraction of the birds observed. In fact, in Southeast Asia, a traveling birder may sometimes feel that he or she is more successful at "bulbul-watching" than birdwatching. But at least bulbuls, even if ultra-common, are in many cases easy to identify to species. On the other hand, babblers and a few other groups contain multiple species that look much alike, making identification quite challenging. Somewhat analogous to the situation with North America's warblers, Asia has myriad Old World warblers (family Sylviidae), many of them, especially the abundant leaf warblers, difficult to tell apart. For instance, the India region has more than 20 of these small, arboreal insect-eaters that

OPPOSITE: **Black Kite** This raptor is very common in India and often seen flying over urban areas, such as here in New Delhi. *India*

share olive-colored upperparts, lighter underparts, and light eye lines. And Asia has so many look-alike lark species that field guides sometimes include special sections giving micro-details of bird morphology in an attempt to assist birders in distinguishing these birds in the field. For most of us, the only way we are going to successfully distinguish some of these birds is by standing next to a helpful expert or, failing that, DNA analysis!

The large number of similar-looking species among the Asian larks, pipits, babblers, warblers, and others raises the question of birding guides. A guide with knowledge of local birds and local languages is a real help in many areas of Asia. Not only are the birds sometimes confusing, the local environs can be. Getting around on one's own can be difficult, especially if you have a limited amount of time for your trip and don't want to waste precious birding hours on seeking directions and finding appropriate routes. Even in a more developed country like Thailand, road signs, once away from urban areas, can be lettered solely in the local language, not English—making driving problematic. So all but the very adventurous and independent will typically want to engage guides. Some areas are obvious exceptions, places that are relatively easy to navigate for English speakers, such as Japan, Hong Kong, Singapore and Taiwan. Many global birders will visit Asia on organized birding tours with accompanying

Painted Stork The distinctive pink tertial feathers that overhang the folded wings give them their name and help make them a favorite with birders and the general populace. Painted Storks are widely distributed in Asia south of the Himalaya. *India*

guides, but note that local guides are often available in destination countries. In places like China, India, Thailand, and Vietnam, a search of the Internet, and the consultation of birding websites, will yield names, references, and contact information for local guides. These are often individuals or small companies that can plan itineraries to birding sites, make all arrangements, provide vehicles, do the driving and, if you're interested, assist you with finding and identifying birds. The prices for such services vary considerably among regions and with the expertise of the guides. If you want a birding trip with the British guide who lives in Southeast Asia and coauthored a major field guide to the region, well, it is pricey, but very possible. If you want to go with the small birding tour company in Vietnam run by a local college biologist in Ho Chi Minh City who speaks pretty good English but knows his Vietnamese birds, the cost is less. The trips put together by such local companies can be excellent and memorable, especially for the tidbits of cultural information that can be imparted by a local guide. Even if you navigate to a national park or other birding area on your own, hiring a guide or park ranger for that particular site, who might know the local trail network and preferred birding locations, is often a smart move.

Chestnut-capped Laughingthrush The 52 species of laughingthrushes are an Asian conglomeration of attractively patterned, medium-size babblers (family Timaliidae). The Chestnut-capped Laughingthrush is a forest bird found in peninsular Malaysia and on the island of Sumatra. *Malaysia*

As for Asian birdwatchers, their numbers are rising. In addition to Japan, where birding is somewhat popular and well-off Japanese birders travel the world in search of bird sightings, India has its resident birders, as do places like Malaysia and Thailand. It's quite an experience to be slogging through a muddy trail in a Thai national park and stumble across a Thai family, mom, pop, and offspring, all outfitted in the latest branded outdoor clothing, and toting backpacks, binoculars, and spotting scope. China is a special case, where birding by the new middle class is just starting to take off. Estimates by experienced local birders put the number of Chinese birders at between 2,000 and 10,000 (out of 1.3 billion). In Malaysia, a local bird tour leader placed the number of birders in his country at about 300. In Vietnam, while wandering through Cat Tien National Park, I asked my local guide how many serious birders there were in his country. His precise answer: "Eleven: six guys in our birding club and five expats from the embassies in Hanoi and Ho Chi Minh City." ■

BIRDS OF THE REGION SIGNIFICANT GROUPS

PHEASANTS AND PARTRIDGES | CRANES | HORNBILLS | BROADBILLS | PITTAS | BULBULS | LEAFBIRDS | BABBLERS | PARROTBILLS | SUNBIRDS AND SPIDERHUNTERS

The significant families of Asian birds discussed below are of two main types, larger nonpasserines and then a variety of generally smaller passerine, or perching, birds. Among the former are pheasants, cranes, and hornbills, all three of which are virtually certain to be near the pinnacle of every birder's viewing wish list while visiting Asia. And many of the passerines here will not be far behind in interest, including the unusual broadbills, the curious and often gorgeous pittas, and the endemic leafbirds.

◼ Pheasants and Partridges

Pheasants and partridges are known in the Western Hemisphere mainly as fairly drab-looking game birds, but the family of these chicken-like birds, Phasianidae, with a natural Old World distribution, actually contains some of the globe's most visually striking larger birds. These include, among others, the Silver Pheasant, the male of which is a brilliant bright white above and glossy blue-black below; the Crested Fireback, the male of which has a blue face, dark purplish blue body and fiery red-yellow back; the incredibly ornate Indian Peafowl and Green Peafowl; and the Lady Amherst's Pheasant. The Phasianidae family contains about 155 species, including partridges, francolins, junglefowl, Old World quail, and pheasants. Several species were introduced to North America as game birds and are now common there, such as Chukar and Ring-necked

Pheasant. Birds in this group are stocky and have short, thick, chicken-like bills, long, heavy toes with claws adapted for ground-scratching, and short or long tails. Some of the pheasants have tails up to five feet long.

Pheasants are generally birds of forests; partridges tend to be in forest undergrowth or in nearby open areas. In Asia, these birds are often among the most eagerly anticipated sightings for traveling birders. Unfortunately, pheasants and partridges, being ground birds, are usually very wary, and flee and hide at the slightest disturbance. Trying to get good looks at forest-dwelling pheasants, in particular, can be an especially frustrating pursuit.

OPPOSITE: **Red-crowned Crane** This endangered crane has a wild population of less than 2,000 individuals. It breeds mainly in northeast China and adjacent Russia and migrates to Korea and east-central China for the winter. A population of more than 500 birds is resident on the Japanese island of Hokkaido. *Japan*

Blood Pheasant This high-mountain species resides in India, Nepal, Bhutan, and China. The male (shown) has blood red feathering on the head, breast, and tail; both sexes have red feet and legs and red skin around their eyes. *India*

■ Cranes

Cranes are very tall, long-necked, long-legged wading birds that have been admired by people for millennia. China and Japan especially have long associated cranes with positive attributes and emotions—longevity, happiness, luck, and, more recently, peace. Crane characteristics that attract human attention are their size (some approach the height of people), their graceful movement and elegant appearance (Africa's crowned cranes being particularly beautiful), their soaring flight capabilities, and their renowned courtship "dances." There are 15 species of cranes (family Gruidae), and they occur on all the continents except South America and Antarctica. Eight are found in Asia.

Cranes range in length from three to more than five feet; the largest, the Sarus Crane, has a wingspan up to nine feet. Colored mainly gray, white, and black, most cranes have a patch of red, naked skin on top of their head. Bills generally are longish but relatively delicate, especially when compared with those of the similar-looking storks. Primarily wetland and open-country birds, cranes forage by walking slowly and steadily in water or on swampy ground, searching for food; they eat plant materials and small animals—just about anything they can swallow. They are particularly attracted to grain-growing areas after harvesting, feeding in fields on grain spillage. Many of the cranes have small and declining populations. However, as a consequence of their large size, areas where they breed or winter are often reliably known, and persistent birders

Sarus Crane At almost six feet the Sarus Crane is the tallest flying bird. It is a nonmigratory wetland species found in the Indian subcontinent, Southeast Asia, and northern Australia. The largest population is in India where these cranes are revered and often live in close proximity to humans. *India*

can often spot them—albeit usually from a distance, as they nest on distant lakeshores, feed in large fields, or soar high above the ground.

Hornbills

Hornbills are among the Old World's most distinctive and intriguing birds, and birders who travel to southern Asia (or to Africa or the New Guinea region, where they also occur) often place them at or near the top of their must-see lists. The hornbills' massive, curved, frequently colorful bills suggest a kinship with toucans, but the two groups are not closely related (although both may have developed big bills for the same reason, to cut down and manipulate tree fruit). Rather, the hornbill family Bucerotidae, with 57 species, is placed in order Coraciiformes with the kingfishers, whereas the toucans are in order Piciformes with the woodpeckers.

Medium-size to very large birds (one to four feet long), hornbills have long tails, shortish legs, and patches of bare skin on their face and throat that are often brightly colored. Their immense bills, often in vibrant reds or yellows, are usually topped with a "casque," an extra ridge; in some, the casque is large, in others, reduced. Bills appear heavy but are actually constructed of a sponge-like substance covered by a thin horn-like material, and are very light.

Hornbills are forest, woodland, and savanna birds, usually seen in pairs or small family groups. Many species spend most of their time in the canopy of forests, but will move lower to exploit a good food supply; some will come to the ground to hunt insects. Spotting hornbills often involves luck, when they are sighted flying overhead or in the distance, or brought to your attention by their loud croaking and booming calls. Alternatively, staking out large fruit trees—fig trees in Southeast Asia, for example—where hornbills are known to gather for meals frequently produces positive results.

Rhinoceros Hornbill One of the largest hornbills, this rain forest species lives in the Malay Peninsula, Sumatra, Java, and Borneo. In flight, the loud sound generated by the air coursing over its wings is often the first indication of its presence. *Thailand*

Broadbills

Broadbills are tropical passerine birds, thickset and often exquisitely marked. They are renowned and named for their large, flat, hooked bills and very wide gapes, which aid in capturing and consuming animal prey. Also noted for their coloring, which ranges from striking red and black to bright green, these beautiful birds tend to be favorites of globe-trotting birdwatchers. The family Eurylaimidae has 15 species, 11 in Southeast Asia and 4 in Africa. From about 5 to 11 inches long, broadbills have largish heads, big eyes, and strong feet. Not all are brightly colored; some are solid brown or streaked brown and white.

Birds chiefly of forests, some broadbills venture into more open habitats such as woodlands, forest edges, bamboo stands, and even scrub areas. Most take whatever small animals they can find, mainly insects, but also spiders, snails, tree frogs, and lizards; some also eat small fruits and berries. Three mostly green species of Southeast Asia primarily eat fruit, and through evolution they have "lost" their broad bills, no longer

Long-tailed Broadbill A forest bird of the Himalaya and Southeast Asia, this species has a shrill call and usually moves around in noisy flocks. *India*

required for catching small animals. Many broadbills are gregarious, occurring in flocks of up to ten or more individuals. Often, broadbills are difficult to find because they are typically shy and tend to perch quietly for long periods in obscuring tree foliage.

Pittas

Pittas are medium-size ground birds of Old World tropical forests. Owing to their secretiveness, relatively little is known about them—but it is clear they are among nature's most dazzling avian creations. It is their coloring that most attracts; some of them are luminous in bright reds, sky blues, mustard yellows, and forest greens. At one time, owing to their radiance, they were called "jewel-thrushes." Their beauty, elusiveness, and typical rarity combine to create a mystique that renders the pittas perennial favorites of birders—"favorite" in this case meaning "highly sought-after but rarely spotted." Unfortunately, they can be reliably seen only by the playback of recorded vocalizations. Seeing one of these birds, such as the Bar-bellied Pitta I observed crossing a trail in Vietnam, is a wonderful birding experience.

The pitta family, Pittidae, includes about 30 species distributed from West Africa through India, Southeast Asia and parts of Australia. Most occur in Southeast Asia. Ranging in length from 6 to 11 inches, pittas appear stocky and almost tailless, and have longish, stout legs. Their bright colors are often difficult to appreciate because they are mainly on the birds' underparts and because of the dark shadows of the deep-forest floor that these birds inhabit. Easily overlooked because of their forest settings and shyness, pittas are usually almost invisible to people except for their haunting call notes and whistles; they are far more often heard than seen. Pittas, usually found alone or in pairs, hop about on the ground, tossing and turning leaves with their bills, searching for insects, snails, worms, and small frogs and lizards.

Blue-winged Pitta Some pittas are migratory; the Blue-winged breeds in mainland Southeast Asia and migrates as far south as Sumatra and Borneo for the winter. *Singapore*

Bulbuls

Bulbuls are small to mid-size, mainly forest-dwelling songbirds, usually with conspicuous crests, which are widely distributed throughout much of southern Asia and Africa. They are known generally as highly success-

Red-vented Bulbul One of the most familiar species of the Indian subcontinent, usually conspicuous and often seen in noisy flocks outside of the breeding season. *India*

ful, adaptable birds, as manifested by their diversity (the family Pycnonotidae contains about 130 species) and their abilities to adjust to new lands when people have transported them from their native regions. For anyone who birds in southern Asia, bulbul diversity and abundance quickly become clear—some days most of the birds one sees are bulbuls, often many varieties within the same forest habitat. As for their adaptability, the best example is the Red-whiskered Bulbul, a native of southern Asia that now, through human transportation, is a thriving inhabitant of such far-flung sites as Australia, Florida, Hawaii, and various Indian Ocean islands. Because of their singing abilities, bulbuls are also popular cage birds in many parts of their range.

Bulbuls, five to nine inches in length and slender, have narrow, often slightly downcurved bills and longish tails. Most are dull in subdued grays, browns, or greens. Although chiefly forest birds, bulbuls sometimes favor forest edges, woodlands, thickets, or even more open sites, including parks and gardens. Many forest bulbuls are shy and skulking. Most bulbuls are gregarious, traveling in noisy family groups or joining mixed-species feeding flocks. They principally eat fruits, including berries, but some also take insects or probe flowers for nectar.

Leafbirds

Leafbirds are brightly colored, arboreal songbirds of forested regions of southern Asia. They are mainly green but some, such as the Golden-fronted and Orange-bellied Leafbirds, are so striking that catching them with binoculars in just the right light is a traveling birdwatcher's absolute delight. Their beauty often lands them on the covers of bird books that deal with Asia. Some of the leafbirds are accomplished mimics of other birds' songs. A single pair hidden high in a tree's dense foliage at times spews forth sufficiently varied vocalizations to convince a person on the ground that the tree must contain a multi-species flock. The family, Chloropseidae, contains eight species and is one of only a few bird families unique to Asia.

Leafbirds are six to nine inches long and have slender, slightly downcurved bills. Males are more colorful than females, tending to have glossy black and blue throat patches that females lack. Leafbirds are found primarily in the mid-levels and canopy of forests. Most of their food is fruit and seeds taken from fruit, but some insects are also eaten. These birds search energetically for food among leaves in dense foliage, often hanging at odd angles to reach the best bits. Although quite striking and obvious when centered

Orange-bellied Leafbird All the other leafbirds have green underparts except the male (shown) of this species, making it easy to identify. This species is resident from northern India to southern China and south to the Malay Peninsula. *Singapore*

in your binocular's field of view, leafbirds can be difficult to spot as their overall green color often melds them seamlessly into their leafy green surroundings.

■ Babblers

Babblers are often some of the most frequently seen species on Asian birding trips. The babbler family Timaliidae contains more than 270 species of babblers, laughingthrushes, barwings, fulvettas, minlas, illadopsises, and yuhinas, among others. The group is distributed through Eurasia and Africa, with most occurring in tropical southern Asia. This immense assemblage of often nondescript songbirds is recognized for its ecological diversity, gregarious behavior, and vocalizations. In some regions such as India and Southeast Asia babblers are extremely diverse and abundant, and are common park and garden birds. They are generally noisy, often engaging in long, boisterous bouts of babbling, chattering, or chuckling songs, sometimes in group choruses. Many babblers stick to dense undergrowth and tend to be heard more often than seen.

Babblers, 3.5 to 12.5 inches long, typically are rather robust looking and usually have narrow bills

that, depending on subgroup, are slightly to extremely downcurved. Most are brown or olive above and lighter, often with dark streaks, below, but a few Asian forest-dwellers such as the Red-billed Leiothrix are more boldly colored. Although most common in forests and dense brushy areas, babblers actually occupy a variety of habitats, from rain forests to scrubby deserts and treeless, high-elevation areas. Many are arboreal but some are semi- or mainly terrestrial, foraging by hopping about lower levels of forests, bushes, or on the ground. Most consume insects and other small invertebrates, but many also eat fruits, seeds, or nectar. Babblers are often found together in family groups of three to 30 that huddle together when resting or roosting.

Streak-breasted Scimitar-Babbler The scimitar-babblers have long downcurved bills that are used to poke into leaves on the forest floor. This species is found from northern India to China and northern Indochina. *India*

Parrotbills

Parrotbills are mostly brownish Eurasian songbirds with unusual, somewhat parrot-like bills. Often yellow, the bills are stubby but broad, slightly bulging, and powerful—sometimes used to strip bamboo stalks. There are 20 parrotbill species, family Paradoxornithidae. Most occur in China, Nepal, and eastern India. Parrotbills are 3.5 to 11 inches long, with generally longish tails and strong legs and feet. Plumage, soft and loose looking, is mostly brown, buff, and gray. Many species have black markings on their head and/or throat.

Spot-breasted Parrotbill In the proper habitat—scrubby abandoned fields and bamboo thickets—this species is fairly common from northeast India to China and northern Indochina. It forages in small groups and sometimes joins mixed feeding flocks. *Thailand*

Birds mainly of reeds, tall grasses, dense scrub, and, especially, bamboo thickets, some parrotbills also inhabit forests, although usually the lower parts. Many occur in mountainous regions, some up to 12,000 feet in the Himalaya. They feed chiefly on insects, but also on berries, seeds, and some other plant materials such as buds and shoots. They are gregarious, foraging in small to largish parties. These pretty, small birds, with their parrot-like bills and charming behavior of hanging at odd angles to feed, are often favorites of birdwatchers.

They typically are skulking birds, so getting good looks at them can be an accomplishment.

Sunbirds and Spiderhunters

Birders in southern Asia often spot small, fast-moving birds with long, thin bills that are frequently mistaken for hummingbirds. However, hummingbirds are restricted to the New World—so what are these hummingbird look-alikes? They are sunbirds, which, although they resemble hummingbirds in several respects, are not even closely related to them. (Hummingbirds are nonpasserines, most closely related to swifts; sunbirds are passerines.) Like hummingbirds, sunbirds are small, often very pretty arboreal birds with long bills used to probe and penetrate flower parts to get nectar. They are notable, like hummingbirds, for the rapid, acrobatic way they flit in and out of flowering trees. Sunbirds are distributed mainly in southern Asia and sub-Saharan Africa. The family Nectariniidae contains about 130 species, including 10 in Asia called spiderhunters.

Ranging from about four to eight inches long, sunbirds have relatively thin, downcurved bills that vary in length among subgroups. Some have shorter, sharper bills suitable for a more insect-centered diet; spiderhunters, essentially large sunbirds, have extremely long, curved bills. Species such as Asia's Fire-tailed Sunbird, have very long central tail feathers. The often spectacularly colorful sunbird males typically have patches of red, blue, and/or yellow, and many have metallic green or blue iridescence that sparkles in the sun. Females are much duller, usually shades of olive or yellow. Spiderhunters have dull olive or yellow plumage, and their sexes look alike. Sunbirds occupy an array of habitat types, including forests, forest edges, woodlands, mangroves, parkland, gardens, and more open areas such as scrublands and agricultural sites.

A few days in the mountains of Sichuan and Qinghai Provinces can yield sightings of such striking birds as Tibetan Snowcock, Tibetan Partridge, and Temminck's Tragopan.

NORTHERN ASIA
CHINA, KOREA, JAPAN

Traveling all the way to northern Asia for mere birdwatching might at first glance seem a bit odd. But there are magnificent birds to see here—lots of gorgeous pheasants and cranes, to mention just two of this region's famous avian families—and plenty of safe and accessible sites in which to search for them. The truth of the matter is that today, versus perhaps 50 years ago, travel to Asia for pleasure or business has become routine. When we hear of a retired couple or a college student traveling in, say, Japan or China, or a neighbor temporarily stationed by his employer in Shanghai or Seoul, it hardly rates a raised eyebrow.

Where do birders tend to go? Well, China, with more than 1,200 bird species, is the largest and greatest destination here. Although undemocratic and with usually tight control of foreign visitors, China is nonetheless a frequent host to global birders, both organized groups and independent travelers. To the uninitiated, this massive, complex country might at first seem a daunting birding challenge. But birders actually flock to just a few prominent sites that are somewhat easy to reach and navigate, and where the locals have become used to binocular-toting foreigners (or "big-noses," as the usual Chinese slang term for Westerners translates). These include especially the large southern province of Sichuan, home to spicy hot foods but also mountain forests that provide habitat for many of China's endemic bird species. The Wolong Nature Reserve, or "Panda Reserve," is located here, as are other birding hot spots such as the Jiuzhaigou Nature Reserve and Omei Shan and Wawu Shan (Omei Mountain and Wawu Mountain). Another stop on many birding trips in China is Beidaihe, a coastal resort town in Hebei Province, only a few hours east of Beijing. The seaside and upland habitats here are frequent stopover points for birds migrating

OPPOSITE: **Tibetan Plateau** This location with typical grassland valleys and rugged hills is near the Chinese border with India. *China*

Blue-and-white Flycatcher Northern Asia has a diverse and beautiful selection of Old World flycatchers to search for. This species—one of the many with blue plumage—breeds in Japan, Korea, and nearby areas of China and Russia; it winters in Southeast Asia. *Japan*

LOCAL BIRDING & CONSERVATION ORGANIZATIONS

■ **CHINA ORNITHOLOGI-CAL SOCIETY**
(www.chinabird.org) promotes bird conservation and research on Chinese birds. China also now has several local birding societies, including the Wild Bird Society of Shanghai and the Shenzhen Bird Watching Society (see www .chinabirdnet.org).

■ **HONG KONG BIRD WATCHING SOCIETY**
(www.hkbws.org.hk) established in 1957, this organization encourages the appreciation and conservation of Hong Kong's birds

■ **WILD BIRD SOCIETY OF JAPAN**
(www.wbsj.org or www.jeef .or.jp/ASIA/japan/WBSJ. html)
started in 1934, is involved with conservation and protection of birds and runs many wildlife sanctuaries

■ **WILD BIRD SOCIETY OF TAIPEI**
(www.wbst.org.tw) established in 1973, is dedicated to the appreciation, research, and protection of wild birds and their habitats; manages several nature reserves

northward in spring toward their Russian or Arctic breeding sites or in fall to their more southerly wintering sites in Indonesia and other areas. Birders gather seasonally in Beidaihe to see species, including many shorebirds, that are difficult to catch sight of anywhere else. Beidaihe is especially interesting to visit because it is a town that high-ranking Communist Party members visit regularly for summer beach holidays, with large sections closed seasonally for the exclusive use of top officials. Birding other locations in China, such as the Tibetan Plateau, is very possible but usually involves deeper planning and is definitely more adventurous.

Japan is also a natural destination for birders interested in this region of the world. The major islands can be explored by train, with the northernmost and least developed main island, Hokkaido, being a great self-drive location. There, the forests of Daisetsu National Park yield many woodpeckers, pipits, and buntings; the rocky shores of Shiretoko National Park are home to wintering Steller's Sea-Eagles; and the marshes of Kushiro Shitsugen National Park harbor a population of Red-crowned Cranes. On inter-island ferries from Hokkaido, birders spot seabirds such as Short-tailed Albatross and Streaked Shearwater, not to mention assorted alcids that occur solely in that part of the world, including Spectacled Guillemot and Japanese Murrelet. South Korea has several good birding locations such as the famous Sorak-San National Park in the eastern part of the country. Even tiny Hong Kong boasts an important wetland birding site, the Mai Po Nature Reserve, where migrating waterbirds and shorebirds stop to feed in mangroves, swamps, and ponds.

GEOGRAPHY AND HABITATS

Northern Asia is a huge region, dominated by China in the south and Siberia, the massive central and eastern portions of Russia, in the north. Also included are such countries and regions as Mongolia, Kazakhstan, the Korean Peninsula, and Japan. Habitats over this enormous area vary from frozen tundra in the high Arctic regions of Russia to subtropical forests of southern China. Deciduous forests occur in most of the temperate areas, with broadleaf evergreen forests common in warmer regions. Grasslands, semi-deserts, deserts, and many freshwater habitats occur in parts of northern Asia, including some of the globe's largest river systems such as China's Yangtze. A typical feature of better birding sites in China, with its long history of development and large human population, is that they exist only where agriculture or other development is difficult. Thus, China's birding locations are often in remote mountainous areas or, when near cities or large towns, on isolated mountaintops.

The Tibetan Plateau can be singled out here as especially interesting geographically and ornithologically. Covering a major portion of central and western China, this massive plateau often has its *lower* elevations bottom out at 12,000 or 13,000 feet above sea

SPOTTING THE STELLER'S SEA-EAGLE

The Steller's Sea-Eagle is one of the largest raptors in the world, and there are perhaps 5,000 left. These eagles breed on the coast of southwestern Russia, and more than half the population winters in Japan, mainly on the northern island of Hokkaido. Fish, ducks, and carrion are their main food. Historically, the supply of fish in northern Japan was more than adequate to support large concentrations of this eagle, but overfishing in recent years has so reduced this food supply that nearly 35 percent of wintering Steller's Sea-Eagles now use mountain areas for at least some period. Here they scavenge the carcasses of deer killed by hunters. Even with these recent changes, large numbers of these huge eagles can be found wintering on the north coast of Hokkaido, where they sit on ice, beaches, and other perches waiting for dead fish to float by, especially in areas where fish are cast off by fishermen or, more recently, by hotel owners trying to attract nature-loving tourists during the winter off-season. The sight of a flock of beautiful Steller's Sea-Eagles on ice floes, with perhaps a White-tailed Eagle nearby, is one that no birder or wildlife photographer will ever forget. —D.P.

Steller's Sea-Eagle Although most birders go to Japan's northern island of Hokkaido to see this spectacular eagle, these birds were photographed farther north, on Russia's Kamchatka Peninsula. *Russia*

level. Roads wind over high mountain passes above 16,000 feet, which sometimes means exiting vehicles to chase birds in very low oxygen conditions—not for the faint-hearted. Much of the land that is not high mountains consists of arid grassland that provides grazing habitat for herds of domestic yak and assorted wild herbivores. The cold and remoteness of this high-elevation region have so far prevented much development, and so many birds thrive here. The diversity of the birdlife at such high altitudes may be relatively low, but the number of individuals is often high, providing exciting birding experiences.

Taiwan, a large island lying off of southeastern China and straddling the Tropic of Cancer, is also included in this section of the book. The western portion of Taiwan is relatively flat and is where most of the population lives. The eastern two-thirds of the island is mountainous, with extensive areas of evergreen broadleaf forest and many natural areas of interest to birders.

BIRDLIFE

The pheasants of northern Asia are among the region's most sought-after birds. This is because this group is quite diverse here, many of the species are colorful

Black-necked Crane In winter, these cranes move to lower elevation river valleys where they can forage in unfrozen grain fields after the harvest. *China*

SPOTTING THE BLACK-NECKED CRANE

In 1876, the Black-necked Crane became the last species of crane to be formally described. The remoteness of its breeding and wintering ranges had kept it hidden from ornithologists. The world population of 5,000 breeds mainly in the high-altitude Qinghai-Tibetan Plateau in China, and winters in lower parts of the plateau to Bhutan and northeastern India.

One summer a number of years ago, four of us decided to take a break from research on small mammals in northern China and explore the eastern portion of the Tibetan plateau, with seeing Black-necked Crane as one of our primary goals. These large, handsome birds nest in high-altitude wetlands and feed in shallow marshes, streams, and pastures. Black-necked Cranes are remarkably tolerant of people and regularly feed near domestic livestock, perhaps because local Buddhist beliefs protect them.

With amazingly good highways but deplorable places to spend the nights, we drove hundreds of miles from the city of Xining, Qinghai's provincial capital, southwest to where there were few cities and people. The wildlife and vistas were remarkable, with rolling 11,000-foot-altitude grasslands and isolated mountain peaks rising above the plain. Birds included Tibetan Snowcock, Tibetan Sandgrouse, Mongolian Lark, Crested Tit-Warbler, Mongolian Ground-Jay, and Przewalski's Rosefinch. After several days, we finally came to extensive marshlands, and in the first marsh we found three pairs of Black-necked Cranes. Throughout the next week we continued to find a pair or two in almost every large marshy area we encountered, an amazing feat back then, but now one almost anyone can accomplish with a rental car and a fairly adventurous spirit. —D.P.

and attractive, and most are challenging to locate and get good looks at. Birders in China may spend a lot of time scanning mountainsides, looking for pheasants in grassy openings among shrubs or trees. A few days in the mountains of Sichuan and Qinghai Provinces can yield sightings of such striking birds as Tibetan Snowcock, Tibetan Partridge, Temminck's Tragopan, and both White and Blue Eared-Pheasants. Nine pheasant species occur at the Wolong Nature Reserve alone, including the beautiful Chinese Monal and Golden Pheasant, both of which are endemic to China. Japan has the endemic Green and Copper Pheasants.

After pheasants, cranes may be on the most wish lists in northern Asia. Eight species occur in the area, including the endangered Siberian and Red-crowned Cranes. A number of large raptors are often highly anticipated birds of this region, including such stunners as Pallas' Fish-Eagle, White-tailed Eagle, Steller's Sea-Eagle, and Crested Serpent-Eagle. Owls are another diverse group here, with several larger species represented, including northeastern Asia's endangered Blakiston's Fish-Owl. Among the passerine groups that are diverse and frequently encountered are larks, pipits, wagtails, accentors, babblers, parrotbills, and tits. The last group, in the same family as the New World chickadees, includes a host of delightful small birds, with many species often seen in the same area—for instance, I have spotted Great, Green-backed, Marsh, White-browed, and Rufous-vented Tits all in the same locality in southern China.

A few eagerly sought species characteristic of the high-elevation Tibetan Plateau are the Ibisbill, a unique gray, black, and white shorebird with a long downcurved bill, which is the sole member of family Ibidorhynchidae; the Wallcreeper, an exceptional nuthatch-like bird of rock walls that is a striking black, gray, and maroon and is usually considered one of Eurasia's most spectacular small birds (sometimes classed as the sole species of family Tichodromidae); the truly striking blue Grandala; and Hume's Groundpecker, a small brownish songbird found only on the Tibetan Plateau, where it runs around the grassy, rocky ground, perpetually digging with its bill for insects.

As far as endemics go, China has more than 50 species, about half of which occur in Sichuan and adjacent provinces. There are 12 Endemic Bird Areas, many of which center on the Tibetan Plateau and the mountain regions of Sichuan. Japan, where more than 500 species have been spotted, has only 12 endemics. South Korea, with about 400 total species, has no endemics. The best time to bird northern Asia is from April through August, covering the breeding period of most species.

FIELD GUIDE & SITE GUIDE BOOKS

■ *Birds of East Asia: China, Taiwan, Korea, Japan and Russia* (2009)
M. Brazil
Princeton University Press

■ *Birds of Europe, Russia, China, and Japan: Non-Passerines: Loons to Woodpeckers* (2009)
N. Arlott
Princeton University Press

■ *Birds of Europe, Russia, China, and Japan: Passerines: Tyrant Flycatchers to Buntings* (2007)
N. Arlott
Princeton University Press

■ *The Birds of Hong Kong and South China* (2005)
C. Viney, K. Phillips, and L.C. Ying.
Hong Kong Government Information Services

■ *A Field Guide to the Birds of China* (2000)
J. MacKinnon and K. Phillips
Oxford University Press

■ *A Field Guide to the Birds of Russia and Adjacent Territories* (1989)
V.E. Flint, et al.
Princeton University Press

■ *A Photographic Guide to the Birds of Japan and North-East Asia* (2008)
T. Shimba
Yale University Press

■ *Where to Watch Birds in Asia* (1996)
N. Wheatley
Princeton University Press

Significant Species
of Northern Asia

ABOUT 100 FAMILIES FOUND IN THIS REGION

■ **DUCKS AND GEESE** (Anatidae), **about 60 species**

Swan Goose* *Anser cygnoides*
northern Asia goose with a black and white neck

Baikal Teal* *Anas formosa*
Russian-breeding duck that winters in China and Japan

■ **HAWKS, EAGLES, AND KITES** (Accipitridae), **about 50 species**

Steller's Sea-Eagle* *Haliaeetus pelagicus*
huge, dark eagle with white shoulders; found usually in coastal northeastern Asia

Lammergeier *Gypaetus barbatus*
large vulture of mountain ranges in Eurasia and Africa

Himalayan Griffon *Gyps himalayensis*
large, pale brown vulture largely restricted to the Himalayan region and parts of western China

■ **PHEASANTS AND PARTRIDGES** (Phasianidae), **about 65 species**

Temminck's Tragopan *Tragopan temminckii*
chicken-like bird of subalpine forests, mainly in China; the male is reddish with blue facial skin

Blue Eared-Pheasant* *Crossoptilon auritum*
large pheasant restricted to mountain foests of north-central China; male mostly bluish gray

Copper Pheasant* *Syrmaticus soemmerringii*
long-tailed brown pheasant endemic to Japan's coniferous and mixed broadleaf/coniferous forests

Lady Amherst's Pheasant *Chrysolophus amherstiae*
striking, colorful, long-tailed pheasant found in southwestern China, Tibet, Myanmar

■ **CRANES** (Gruidae), **9 species**

Siberian Crane *Grus leucogeranus*
critically endangered; breeds in Arctic Russia

Black-necked Crane *Grus nigricollis*
large crane with a black head; occurs primarily on the Tibetan Plateau in China and adjacent portions of India

■ **AUKS, MURRES, AND PUFFINS** (Alcidae), **16 species**

Spectacled Guillemot *Cepphus carbo*
blackish brown, limited to waters off northeastern Asia

Japanese Murrelet* *Synthliboramphus wumizusume*
restricted to ocean waters around Japan and Korea

■ **LARKS** (Alaudidae), **13 species**

Mongolian Lark *Melanocorypha mongolica*
uncommon grassland lark of southern Russia, Mongolia, northern China

■ **ACCENTORS** (Prunellidae), **10 species**

Himalayan Accentor *Prunella himalayana*
breeds in alpine meadows in northern and central Asia; also known as Altai Accentor

Japanese Accentor* *Prunella rubida*
accentor restricted mainly to Japan

■ **OLD WORLD WARBLERS** (Sylviidae), **about 105 species**

Marsh Grassbird* *Megalurus pryeri*
occurs only in scattered localities in southeastern Russia, northeast China, and Japan

Asian Desert Warbler *Sylvia nana*
small, plain-looking warbler that breeds in central Asia and western China

■ **OLD WORLD FLYCATCHERS** (Muscicapidae), **about 95 species**

White-tailed Rubythroat *Luscinia pectoralis*
bird of bushes and thickets in mountain regions; the male has a glittering red throat

Grandala *Grandala coelicolor*
bird of alpine meadows; male a stunning, bright blue

Little Forktail *Enicurus scouleri*
small black and white bird of rocky streams in mountain forests

■ **BABBLERS** (Timaliidae), **about 130 species**

Barred Laughingthrush* *Garrulax lunulatus*
inhabits bamboo forests, endemic to central China

Hwamei *Garrulax canorus*
celebrated singer and cage bird; found in China, Taiwan, and parts of southeastern Asia

Gray-faced Liocichla* *Liocichla omeiensis*
gray-olive babbler with a reddish wing patch, restricted to mountain forests in two of China's provinces

Tibetan Babax* *Babax koslowi*
cinnamon-colored babbler usually on or near the ground; endemic to the Tibetan region

■ **PARROTBILLS** (Paradoxornithidae), **21 species**

Spectacled Parrotbill* *Paradoxornis conspicillatus*
found in bamboo areas of mountain forests in central
China

Reed Parrotbill* *Paradoxornis heudei*
occurs only in reed beds in limited parts of southeastern
Russia and eastern China

■ **TITS AND CHICKADEES** (Paridae), **22 species**

Green-backed Tit *Parus monticolus*
fairly common tit with greenish upperparts, in the Himalayan region, China, and parts of southeastern Asia

■ **CROWS, JAYS, AND MAGPIES** (Corvidae), **about 30 species**

Sichuan Jay* *Perisoreus internigrans*
gray, relatively short-tailed jay found only in central China

Mongolian Ground-Jay* *Podoces hendersoni*
brown, black, and white, desert jay found in Kazakhstan,
Mongolia, and northern China

Hume's Groundpecker *Pseudopodoces humilis*
small sandy-gray bird of grassy plains and yak pastures
in the Tibetan Plateau and Himalayan region

■ **SISKINS, CROSSBILLS, AND ALLIES** (Fringillidae), **55 species**

Asian Rosy-Finch* *Leucosticte arctoa*
a mostly Russian-breeding blackish brown finch with
wintering sites in China and Japan

Japanese Grosbeak* *Eophona personata*
large grayish and black finch with a large bill

■ **BUNTINGS, SPARROWS, AND ALLIES** (Emberizidae), **31 species**

Ochre-rumped Bunting* *Emberiza yessoensis*
reed bunting, the male has a black head; endemic to
northeast Asia

Yellow-throated Bunting *Emberiza elegans*
attractive woodland bunting; male with a black crest and
yellow and black head

Some Other Species Global Birders Often Seek

Swinhoe's Storm-Petrel *Oceanodroma monorhis*
all-dark species; breeds only on islands off Japan, Korea
and southeastern Russia

Schrenck's Bittern *Ixobrychus eurhythmus*
brown above, white below; breeds in eastern Asia

Oriental Stork *Ciconia boyciana*
endangered stork, white with black markings; breeds in
southern Russia and China

Black-faced Spoonbill *Platalea minor*
endangered and one of the rarest birds in Asia

Amur Falcon *Falco amurensis*
striking small falcon, male mostly gray with large white
wing patches

Ibisbill *Ibidorhyncha struthersii*
unusual shorebird, gray, brownish, black and white
with long reddish bill; only species in family
Ibidorhynchidae

Saunders' Gull *Larus saundersi*
rare gull, restricted largely to coastal eastern Asia

Tibetan Sandgrouse* *Syrrhaptes tibetanus*
sandgrouse of desert areas and rocky hillsides; found in
central Asia and Tibetan Plateau

White-bellied Pigeon *Treron sieboldii*
mostly green forest pigeon of Japan, Taiwan, eastern
China, and parts of southeastern Asia; also known as
Japanese Green-Pigeon

Blakiston's Fish-Owl* *Ketupa blakistoni*
huge brown owl, now endangered; occurs in eastern
Russia, northeastern China, Japan

Japanese Woodpecker* *Picus awokera*
green-backed woodpecker with a gray head, endemic
to Japan

Fairy Pitta *Pitta nympha*
scarce pitta with bright green wings; breeds in Japan,
Korea, eastern China, and Taiwan

Rosy Pipit *Anthus roseatus*
high-elevation pipit of grassy meadows that breeds in
China and some surrounding regions

Japanese Waxwing* *Bombycilla japonica*
crested and gray-brown with a red-tipped tail; breeds in
eastern China and eastern Russia, and winters particularly in Japan

Brown Dipper *Cinclus pallasii*
plump and all brown; found in and around rivers

Japanese Paradise-Flycatcher *Terpsiphone atrocaudata*
uncommon monarch flycatcher; male black and white
with extremely long tail streamers

Snowy-browed Nuthatch* *Sitta villosa*
nuthatch restricted to parts of Russia, China, and Korea

Wallcreeper *Tichodroma muraria*
nuthatch-like gray and maroon bird found on rock
walls in mountainous areas; only species of family
Tichodromidae

Fork-tailed Sunbird *Aethopyga christinae*
greenish above with a yellow rump, the male with
maroon throat; occurs in southeastern China and Vietnam

Przewalski's Rosefinch* *Urocynchramus pylzowi*
endemic to western China and Tibet; sole species in
family Urocynchramidae

*Restricted to Northern Asia

More than 1,300 species reside year-round or spend winters in southern Asia.

SOUTHERN ASIA

SOUTHERN ASIA MIGHT NOT BE ONE OF THE FIRST PLACES YOU THINK OF AS A destination for an exotic birding adventure, but knowledgeable birders with global perspectives know that the region harbors a large array of species and that, once reached, can be quite welcoming and inexpensive to explore. There are also a lot of spectacular birds here. To name just a few: Painted and Woolly-necked Storks; Demoiselle and Common Cranes; bustards such as the Indian Bustard and Bengal Florican; the common and widespread Indian Gray Hornbill; the large, gray and white Crested Kingfisher; and the multihued Indian Pitta.

With around 1,200 species, huge India is southern Asia's main birding destination. Several regions in the country are prime birding targets, including Gujarat state in the west; the Western Ghats, a mountainous area the runs along the western side of India; and especially north-central India where the capital, New Dehli, is located. Three famous birding spots within a few hundred miles of New Dehli are Corbett National Park and Ranthembhore National Park, which are among India's most famous parks, and the Keoladeo National Park, which used to be called the Bharatpur Bird Sanctuary.

The former two parks have bird lists exceeding 500 and 250 bird species, respectively; because both have active tiger populations, most birding there is done from vehicles or elephant back. (There are instances of birders on foot concentrating so intently on birds through binoculars that tigers were able to approach and attack them.) The big attraction of Keoladeo National Park is its wetlands that attract huge numbers of waterbirds, both resident and migratory, including pelicans, cormorants, darters, ducks, geese, cranes, and jacanas. All told, about 400 species have

OPPOSITE: **Rufous-necked Hornbill** This spectacular hornbill is uncommon to rare throughout its range. The female seals herself into the nest hole (see the slot in tree trunk) where she remains for about three months, emerging only when her chick is ready to fledge. The male (shown) provides food through the slotted entrance hole. This photograph was taken at Eaglenest Wildlife Sanctuary in Arunachal Pradesh, a superb birding location. *India*

Taktshang Monastery Known as the "Tiger's Nest," this famous Buddhist site clings to its sheer cliff location in Bhutan. Much of the Bhutanese countryside is protected and wildlife there is flourishing under the enlightened protection of the monarchy. *Bhutan*

LOCAL BIRDING & CONSERVATION ORGANIZATIONS

▓ **BIRD CONSERVATION NEPAL**
(www.birdlifenepal.org) involved with several bird projects, including a long-term program aimed at vulture conservation

▓ **BOMBAY NATURAL HISTORY SOCIETY**
(www.bnhs.org) largest non-governmental conservation organization in the Indian subcontinent, started in 1883

▓ **FIELD ORNITHOLOGY GROUP OF SRI LANKA**
(www.fogsl.net) founded in 1976, promotes conservation of Sri Lankan birds through education and research

▓ **THE ORIENTAL BIRD CLUB**
(www.orientalbirdclub.org) UK organization that promotes and encourages conservation of birds of the Oriental region

been seen in the area, which includes shallow lakes, dry forest, savanna, and scrub habitats. The best time for birding over many regions of India, especially in the north, is the winter, November through March when it is cooler and there is less rain. Some parks, in fact, close during the monsoon season.

Nepal is also a frequent birding destination with a high number of bird species for a small country. Chitwan National Park, an area of wet forests and marshy grasslands at the base of the Himalaya that is now popular with ecotourists, has recorded more than 450 bird species within its boundaries. Nepal's Himalayan scenery is beautiful and, although trekking in the high mountains is not for everyone, birding here can be very rewarding. Sri Lanka, a tropical island nation off India's southern coast, is another small country with a large avifauna of more than 400 species. Sri Lanka, Nepal, and India often experience political or religious violence, but tourists and nature travelers are rarely affected.

GEOGRAPHY AND HABITATS

The term "southern Asia," as used here, refers mainly to the Indian subcontinent, which includes Pakistan, India, Nepal, Bhutan, Bangladesh, and Sri Lanka. The southern half of India lies in the tropics, as does Sri Lanka and the southern half of Bangladesh. Although much of India's original forest cover has been cut for timber or firewood or degraded by grazing or development, some extensive forest zones still exist. These include areas of deciduous forest in the center and south of the country, some of it tropical wet forest, some drier forest. Dry thorn forest occurs over large sections of India, especially in the western region and also in the southern, tropical region, in the rain shadow of the Western Ghats, a mountain range. Other major Indian habitats are scrublands, desert (only in the far western portion of the country), and wetlands, which include inland lakes and reservoirs, seasonal pools that fill with the monsoon rains, and mangrove swamps. Many of India's major parks and reserves occupy land that in the past was exploited for commercial purposes, be it logging, grazing, or farming. In some of these areas the natural vegetation is recovering. The Himalayan region, in northern India and in Nepal and Bhutan, has mixtures of forest types, including coniferous forest, rhododendron forest, and broadleaf forest. Sri Lanka is mainly a low-elevation island. It has major dry and wet zones, with tropical evergreen forests predominating in the moister regions, and scrub areas and secondary forests in the drier zones. Little primary forest remains, but there are several wild areas and national parks.

SPOTTING THE BEAUTIFUL NUTHATCH

There are some bird species that are very rare and have no reliable sites to find them, so you have to prepare yourself for the inevitable: that you will never see them. The Beautiful Nuthatch of the eastern Himalaya is one such bird and is considered by some to be the rarest nuthatch in the world. It has a small, declining, severely fragmented population as a result of cutting and fragmentation of evergreen and semi-evergreen forest along mid-elevation mountain slopes from Bhutan to northern Vietnam. While birding in central Bhutan, I was happy that we had such a successful trip so far. We had found rare but regular specialties, such as Ward's Trogon, Yellow-rumped Honeyguide, Rufous-throated Wren-Babbler, Green Shrike-Babbler, Fire-tailed Myzornis, and Fire-tailed Sunbird. While searching through yet another mixed flock and trying to filter out the common yuhinas and other "nuclear" species of the flock, someone yelled, "Beautiful Nuthatch overhead!" There, only 20 feet up in a tall broadleaf tree, was a pair of these nuthatches following on the fringe of the mixed-species flock. They acted like any other nuthatch I had seen before, clambering headfirst down trunks and on the undersides of large branches. But they looked like no other nuthatch I had ever seen. Their orangish breasts were combined with deep blue backs that were streaked with white and had bold stripes of powder blue. We kept them in sight for several minutes, and then they were gone. I remember thinking: If I could see a nearly impossible species, what might be next? —D.P.

Beautiful Nuthatch
Populations are known to exist in a number of protected areas including Thrumshing La National Park in Bhutan and Eaglenest Wildlife Sanctuary and Buxa Tiger Reserve in India. Its range extends to southeast China and northern Southeast Asia, including Myanmar, Vietnam, and Laos. *India*

BIRDLIFE

More than 1,300 species reside year-round or spend winters in southern Asia. India, of course, is the main destination and has the largest avifauna, about 1,200 species. Many birders who travel to India manage to spot 300 or so species in, say, a three-week trip—especially if their time is concentrated in the country's north. The two small Himalayan countries that border India—Nepal and Bhutan—also are bird rich, with more than 700 species found in Nepal and more than 500 in Bhutan. There are several reasons for the large numbers of species in this region of the world. One is that, although southern Asia forms a large part of the Oriental zoogeographic zone and possesses birds characteristic of this region, it also enjoys some avian influences from two other zoogeographic zones. For example, the accentors, a small family (Prunellidae, with 13 species) of sparrow-like songbirds known for living in mountainous terrain at high elevations, are mainly typical of the Palearctic zone. But nine accentor species also occur in southern Asia—in northern India, Nepal, and Bhutan—at the southern extreme of their ranges. And southern Asia also shares some types of birds that are more typical of the Afrotropical zone, including honeyguides

BIRDING PERIYAR NATIONAL PARK IN KERALA, INDIA

White-cheeked Barbet This common forest species, which is endemic to India, excavates its own nest hole in a soft-wooded tree trunk. Like other Asian barbets its diet consists mainly of fruit. *India*

Periyar National Park, located in the Cardamom Hills of eastern Kerala state, is one of India's largest parks. It is readily accessible, has good lodging, and is a great place to see more than half of the 24 endemic bird species of the Western Ghats (a major mountain range along India's western side). More than 315 bird species have been recorded at Periyar, including many passage migrants and wintering species from northern Asia. The rainy monsoon season, which lasts from about May to August, makes for a wet time and lots of land leeches. Other times of the year are considerably drier. Periyar is a tiger reserve (there are 27 tiger reserves in India), and there are many other large mammals including leopard and elephant, so you must make sure always to have a local guide with you.

Most tourists focus on the large lake, known as Periyar Lake. There are boat tours available here, but this part of the park is the most crowded. The forest is where you will see the most bird species. On our first trip, we birded each day for hours along well-maintained forest paths and jeep trails. In a short time we found Gray Junglefowl, Nilgiri Wood-Pigeon, Malabar Parakeet, Malabar Trogon, Malabar Gray Hornbill, White-cheeked Barbet, Black-and-rufous Flycatcher, Wynaad Laughingthrush, Crimson-backed Sunbird, White-bellied Treepie, and many other, more widespread, species.

In the higher elevations of the park are grasslands with indigenous forest patches called sholas. Here other endemics occur, such as Broad-tailed Grassbird and Nilgiri Flycatcher. If you go out owling at night Collared Scops-Owl, Spot-bellied Eagle-Owl, Brown Fish-Owl, and Ceylon Frogmouth are often found. —D.P.

Gould's Sunbird The male (shown) is a brilliant, long-tailed bird that is always a birding highlight. Females of most sunbird species are shades of olive and can be very challenging to identify. *India*

FIELD GUIDE & SITE GUIDE BOOKS

■ *Birds of India, Pakistan, Nepal, Bangladesh, Bhutan, Sri Lanka, and the Maldives* (1999)
R. Grimmett, C. Inskipp, and T. Inskipp
Princeton University Press

■ *Birds of Nepal* (2000)
R. Grimmett, C. Inskipp, and T. Inskipp.
Princeton University Press

■ *Birds of South Asia, The Ripley Guide, Vol. 1: Field Guide* (2005)
P.C. Rasmussen and J.C. Anderton
Smithsonian Institution and Lynx Edicions

■ *A Birdwatcher's Guide to India* (2001)
K. Kazmierczak and R. Singh
Prion

■ *A Field Guide to the Birds of the Indian Subcontinent* (2000)
K. Kazmierczak
Yale University Press

■ *A Field Guide to the Birds of Sri Lanka* (1999)
J. Harrison
Oxford University Press

■ *Pocket Guide to the Birds of the Indian Subcontinent* (2002)
C. Inskipp, T. Inskipp, and R. Grimmett
Christopher Helm Publishers

(family Indicatoridae), sunbirds (Nectariniidae), and weavers (Ploceidae). Another explanation for the great species richness of southern Asia is that the variable climates of the region, from tropical wet in the south to temperate cool in the north, and its great elevational range, from sea level to the high Himalaya, conspire to provide many different habitats in which birds can live.

Among the bird families or groups that can be considered significantly represented in southern Asia are the pheasants, herons and egrets, kingfishers, hornbills, barbets, woodpeckers, leafbirds, dippers, babblers, laughingthrushes, and drongos. Some of these are quite diverse here, with 21 herons and egrets, 11 hornbills, 33 woodpeckers, and more than a hundred babblers and laughingthrushes. Among smaller, more obscure groups, southern Asia boasts two of the world's four iora species (family Aegithinidae), four of the eight long-tailed tits (Aegithalidae, of which North America's Bushtit is a member), and five of the eight treecreepers (Certhiidae, of which North America's Brown Creeper is a member). About 140 species are endemic to the Indian subcontinent, or about 10 percent of its avifauna. India itself has 40 endemics, Sri Lanka has 24, and Nepal, but 2.

Significant Species of Southern Asia

ABOUT 100 FAMILIES FOUND IN THIS REGION

■ **STORKS** (Ciconiidae), **9 species**

Painted Stork *Mycteria leucocephala*
white stork with orangish face and reddish legs, common in the India region

Greater Adjutant* *Leptoptilos dubius*
large, mainly bluish gray stork; now endangered and very rare

■ **HAWKS, EAGLES, AND KITES** (Accipitridae), **about 50 species**

Pallas' Fish-Eagle *Haliaeetus leucoryphus*
brown eagle with a sandy-buff-colored head and broad white tail band; occurs in central and southern Asia

Changeable Hawk-Eagle *Spizaetus cirrhatus*
eagle of southern and southeastern Asia that varies by region in coloring and in presence or absence of a crest

■ **PHEASANTS AND PARTRIDGES** (Phasianidae), **about 45 species**

Satyr Tragopan* *Tragopan satyra*
chicken-like bird of the Himalaya; the male has a red neck, white-spotted red underparts, and blue facial skin

Himalayan Monal *Lophophorus impejanus*
large Himalayan pheasant; male an iridescent metallic green, bronze and purple

■ **CRANES** (Gruidae), **5 species**

Demoiselle Crane *Anthropoides virgo*
small gray crane that winters in southern Asia

Sarus Crane *Grus antigone*
large crane with a red head and reddish legs, common in some areas of southern Asia

■ **PIGEONS AND DOVES** (Columbidae), **about 30 species**

Nilgiri Wood-Pigeon* *Columba elphinstonii*
large forest pigeon with a black and white checkerboard neck pattern; endemic to southern India

Orange-breasted Pigeon *Treron bicinctus*
small green pigeon of forest areas; male with gray markings and an orange breast

■ **OWLS** (Strigidae), **about 30 species**

Spot-bellied Eagle-Owl *Bubo nipalensis*
very large owl of forest regions; found in various parts of southern Asia including India, Nepal, Bhutan, and Sri Lanka

Asian Barred Owlet *Glaucidium cuculoides*
small, heavily barred owl of the Himalayan region; fairly common

■ **HORNBILLS** (Bucerotidae), **10 species**

Malabar Pied-Hornbill* *Anthracoceros coronatus*
medium-size black and white species; endemic to India and Sri Lanka

Great Hornbill *Buceros bicornis*
very large black and white hornbill; occurs in forests in various parts of southern Asia

■ **BARBETS** (Capitonidae), **10 species**

Golden-throated Barbet *Megalaima franklinii*
barbet of Himalayan forests; has yellow, red, and white head patches

Crimson-fronted Barbet* *Megalaima rubricapillus*
beautiful, small barbet of southern India and Sri Lanka, with a red face, throat, and chest

■ **LARKS** (Alaudidae), **22 species**

Greater Hoopoe-Lark *Alaemon alaudipes*
generally uncommon desert lark of Pakistan and western India

Malabar Lark* *Galerida malabarica*
lark of grassy and agricultural areas; endemic to the Indian Western Ghats region

■ **BULBULS** (Pycnonotidae), **20 species**

Yellow-browed Bulbul* *Iole indica*
olive-green above, bright yellow below; endemic to India's Western Ghats and Sri Lanka

■ **THRUSHES** (Turdidae), **about 35 species**

Malabar Whistling-Thrush* *Myophonus horsfieldii*
black and blue thrush that lives along forested streams; endemic to India

Gray-winged Blackbird *Turdus boulboul*
large, dark thrush of Himalayan forests

■ **OLD WORLD WARBLERS** (Sylviidae), **about 80 species**

Bristled Grassbird* *Chaetornis striata*
shy, streaky brown bird of grasslands, paddy-field and swampy areas; endemic to the subcontinent

■ **OLD WORLD FLYCATCHERS** (Muscicapidae), **about 85 species**

Nilgiri Flycatcher* *Eumyias albicaudatus*
small blue flycatcher, endemic to India's Western Ghats

Golden Bush-Robin *Tarsiger chrysaeus*
small flycatcher of the Himalayan region; male orange and black

■ **BABBLERS** (Timaliidae), **about 115 species**

Ashy-headed Laughingthrush* *Garrulax cinereifrons*
brown babbler with a gray head; endemic to Sri Lankan moist forests and bamboo thickets

Spiny Babbler* *Turdoides nipalensis*
skulking brownish babbler, endemic to scrub areas of Nepal

Fire-tailed Myzornis *Myzornis pyrrhoura*
small, uncommon, mainly emerald green Himalayan bird; male with reddish patches on wings, tail, and chest

■ **PARROTBILLS** (Paradoxornithidae), **9 species**

Great Parrotbill *Conostoma oemodium*
uncommon Himalayan species; the largest parrotbill

■ **CROWS, JAYS, AND MAGPIES** (Corvidae), **23 species**

Black-headed Jay *Garrulus lanceolatus*
very long-tailed blue and white jay with a black head; found in mountain forests

White-bellied Treepie* *Dendrocitta leucogastra*
very long-tailed black, white and brown bird endemic to the Indian Western Ghats region

■ **STARLINGS AND MYNAS** (Sturnidae), **17 species**

Common Hill Myna *Gracula religiosa*
large black songbird with yellow wattles, yellowish bill, and white wing patches

White-faced Starling* *Sturnia albofrontata*
Sri Lankan forest starling, dark gray above and white-streaked light gray below

Some Other Species Global Birders Often Seek

Spot-billed Pelican *Pelecanus philippensis*
pelican of lakes, reservoirs and estuaries, with dark spots on its upper bill

White-bellied Heron *Ardea insignis*
large, gray, very rare, endangered heron found in Bhutan and some adjacent regions

Indian Bustard* *Ardeotis nigriceps*
uncommon bustard; endemic to India

Greater Painted-snipe *Rostratula benghalensis*
one of only three painted-snipe species; widespread in India, Pakistan and often fairly common

Crab Plover *Dromas ardeola*
large white shorebird with black markings; the only species in family Dromadidae

Ibisbill *Ibidorhyncha struthersii*
unusual bird, gray, brown, black and white with a long reddish bill; the sole member on family Ibidorhynchidae

Malabar Parakeet* *Psittacula columboides*
beautiful blue, green and blue-gray parrot endemic to India's Western Ghats region

Red-faced Malkoha* *Phaenicophaeus pyrrhocephalus*
large, long-tailed, black-and-white cuckoo with a red face patch and green bill; endemic to Sri Lanka

Ceylon Frogmouth* *Batrachostomus moniliger*
nocturnal, insect-eating bird endemic to India's Western Ghats region and Sri Lanka

Malabar Trogon* *Harpactes fasciatus*
one of three trogons of southern Asia and the only one endemic to the Indian subcontinent

Blue-bearded Bee-eater *Nyctyornis athertoni*
large, green bee-eater with a blue throat and chest

Great Slaty Woodpecker *Mulleripicus pulverulentus*
huge slate-gray woodpecker found in southern Asia in the Himalayan region

Indian Pitta* *Pitta brachyura*
green-backed pitta with bold head stripes; the only pitta endemic to the Indian subcontinent

White-tailed Iora* *Aegithina nigrolutea*
small, yellow and olive-greenish songbird with black wings; one of four ioras and the only one endemic to the subcontinent

Hypocolius *Hypocolius ampelinus*
the only member of single-species family Hypocoliidae; breeds in the Middle East but winters as far eastward as western India

Rufous-breasted Accentor *Prunella strophiata*
small, streaked-brown songbird that breeds at up to about 17,000 feet elevation in the Himalaya

Beautiful Nuthatch *Sitta formosa*
large, rare nuthatch with blue and black upperparts that occurs in eastern India and Bhutan

Wallcreeper *Tichodroma muraria*
gray and maroon bird found on rock walls in mountainous areas; the only species of family Tichodromidae

Fire-tailed Sunbird *Aethopyga ignicauda*
sunbird confined to the Himalayan region and northern Myanmar; breeding male is multicolored with a long tail

Restricted to Southern Asia

Southeast Asia is, mile for mile, one of the richest, most diverse bird areas on the planet, with most of the countries possessing between 600 and 1,000 species.

SOUTHEAST ASIA

T HE EASIEST ACCESS TO TROPICAL ASIAN BIRDS LIES IN SOUTHEAST ASIA. A NON-stop, sometimes fairly inexpensive flight from either of the North American coasts can land you in, say, Bangkok, Thailand, or Kuala Lumpur, Malaysia, placing you within only a couple of hours' drive of magnificent birding. The day after arrival you could be walking along a forest track, spotting, or at least trying to spot, such exciting birds as hornbills, barbets, broadbills, and pittas, not to mention the bewildering array of local bulbuls and babblers. Some of the birds here are so alien, yet so interesting, that it is quite wonderful just to see them—even if they are fairly common. The Greater Racket-tailed Drongo comes to mind. It is a denizen of the region's forests and is often seen above forest openings, chasing its insect food or other birds. It is all black, crested, and has two very long, thin feather shafts streaming back from the end of its forked tail, each one capped by a twisted racket-shaped portion of feather. It is so odd looking in the air that when you first spot it, you do a double take and then quickly review in your mind the alternative possibilities to its being a bird at all.

What's also fun is that, because you're now in Asia, perhaps for the first time, you don't have to travel far or to remote regions to see novel birds. For instance, just driving around the agricultural areas on the outskirts of Bangkok, one can stop at paddy fields, ponds, and marshes and see all kinds of interesting water birds including the Chinese Pond-Heron, Cinnamon Bittern, Asian Openbill (a stork), and Pheasant-tailed and Bronze-winged Jacanas. Southeast Asia can be a magical birding destination and for those not afraid of the heat—and occasional other challenges like leeches, cobras, and encounters with wild elephants—it is a region not to be

OPPOSITE: **Great Philippine Eagle** The adult male (right) is feeding a juvenile at its rain forest nest site on Mount Kitanglad, Mindanao Island. *Philippines*

Canopy Walkway This spectacular birding location allows birders to experience treetop birding in the rain forest of Danum Valley, Sabah, Borneo. *Malaysia*

missed. Best times to visit are usually during the drier seasons, for instance December through April in Thailand and April through September in Indonesia.

GEOGRAPHY AND HABITATS

Southeast Asia, as defined here, consists of mainland and island portions. The mainland section, located east of India and south of China, contains the countries of Myanmar (Burma), Thailand, Laos, Cambodia, Vietnam, and Malaysia. The island groups, situated south and southeast of the mainland region, consist chiefly of Indonesia and the Philippines, with the large of island of Borneo being split between Malaysia and Indonesia. Singapore is a small island nation located off the southern tip of mainland Malaysia. Another name associated with this region is Indochina, which often refers either to the mainland section of Southeast Asia or solely to the areas formerly under French control—Vietnam, Laos, and Cambodia.

When trying to visualize natural areas of Southeast Asia, most people probably imagine endless lowland tropical forest, and this type of environment does predominate in the region. But there are highland areas here as well, with mountainous zones in all the Southeast Asian countries. Higher elevations are usually in the 3,000- to 6,000-foot range, but peaks can be much higher—for example, Mount Kinabalu in Malaysian Borneo reaches more than 13,400 feet. Major habitats include deciduous forests, mainly in lowland areas of Cambodia, Thailand, and Myanmar; broad-leaved evergreen forests, both at low and higher elevations; and, in lesser amounts and often in small pockets, swamp forest, pine forests, bamboo forest, and coastal mangrove forest. Only limited grassland zones now exist, as most of these have been developed for settlements or agriculture. Likewise, freshwater wetlands in the area, in the forms of lakes, marshes, and rivers, are often drained or overexploited by local people, reducing their quality as bird habitat. The major river in the region is the Mekong, which flows through or adjacent to Myanmar, Thailand, Laos, Cambodia, and Vietnam on its way to the South China Sea. Southeast Asia has abundant coastal marine/beach habitat and many small islands that are birding destinations. West of peninsular Thailand, for instance, lie the Andaman and Nicobar Islands, where birders seek such species as the Nicobar Scrubfowl, one of the mound-building megapodes, and the large, mainly terrestrial Nicobar Pigeon.

BIRDLIFE

Southeast Asia is, mile for mile, one of the richest, most diverse bird areas on the planet, with most of the countries possessing between 600 and 1,000 species. For instance, Thailand and Myanmar each have between 900 and 1,000 species, and Malaysia and Vietnam each have between 700 and 800. The birdlife of the region is phenomenal, and birders new to the region are sure to be pleased with the number and variety of

BIRDING KUTAI NATIONAL PARK IN BORNEO, INDONESIA

In 1974, my wife and I flew from Jakarta to Balikapapan on the east coast of Indonesian Borneo. Here we had to buy all our food and supplies for a three-month stay along the Sangatta River, some 75 miles north. At this time there were no roads, so we had to take a water taxi on a 24-hour ride to Samarinda and then a motorized canoe to our hut on the river's edge. When the canoe left us, we were on our own and nine miles from the nearest village. The canopy of this pristine forest soared to about 110 feet. Wild orangutans called from over our hut every morning, and the beauty, solitude, and excitement of being in such a pristine forest made us forget about our isolation. My research here quickly turned up birds such as Wallace's Hawk-Eagle, Sunda Scops-Owl, Short-toed Coucal, five species of hornbills including the huge Rhinoceros Hornbill, ten species of woodpeckers, five

species of broadbills, Blue-headed Pitta, Garnet Pitta, and the peculiar Bornean Bristlehead, now considered to be in a family (Pityriaseidae) of its own.

Shortly after we left, an area of 740,000 acres was officially protected and declared the Kutai Game Reserve. This protection did not prevent one-third of the forest from being cut down in subsequent years. In an attempt to prevent a further decline, in 1982 the Indonesian government established 495,000 acres of the remaining forest as the Kutai National Park. However, extensive fires destroyed 60 percent of the protected forest in 1982–1983. The recovering burned forest and remaining primary forest of Kutai presently constitute the largest area of native dipterocarp lowland forest in Indonesian Borneo. It is now accessible by road, and 270 species of birds can yet be found there. —D.P.

Red-bearded Bee-eater This large bee-eater frequents the edges of dense forest where it sits motionless for long periods. Unlike most other bee-eaters that are colonial, this one is solitary or occurs in pairs. *Borneo, Indonesia*

species they can spot and add to their life lists. To take Thailand as an example, a good birder could expect to see over 300 species on a three- or four-week trip that takes in national parks in the north, central, and southern parts of this Texas-size country.

Good numbers of species, as well as spectacular species, are typically seen in many families of birds. Highlights among nonpasserines include the pheasants (especially the Silver Pheasant, the male of which is an amazingly beautiful bird when seen in the wild) and the Red Junglefowl, which is the wild ancestor of domestic chickens. Pigeons include several species of large imperial-pigeons as well as more than ten species of smaller, gorgeously clad green-pigeons. Among the cuckoos are several handsome, long-tailed, arboreal malkohas, some larger terrestrial species like the common Greater Coucal, and the uncommon but quite striking Coral-billed Ground-Cuckoo. Other highlights are frogmouths (with 8 of the world's 12 species), trogons, hornbills (about 25 different species), barbets, and woodpeckers. Passerines well represented here include broadbills, pittas, cuckoo-shrikes and minivets, bulbuls, leafbirds, ioras, babblers, drongos, and mynas. Most of these latter groups may be initially unfamiliar to many birders, but in Southeast Asia all except the pittas can be regularly seen.

Great Philippine Eagle These huge eagles require a home range of up to 50 square miles to breed successfully. *Philippines*

SPOTTING THE GREAT PHILIPPINE EAGLE

One of the largest raptors in the world, the Great Philippine Eagle, endemic to the Philippines, occurs on four major islands, but the majority of the population is on Mindanao. It feeds primarily on large animals, such as flying lemurs, squirrels, civets, hornbills, and monkeys. Thus each pair needs an immense area of forest to have adequate prey available, and a pair breeds only every other year. Because of habitat destruction, this eagle is critically endangered, with fewer than 500 birds surviving.

A group of us flew to northern Mindanao and then drove to the base of Mount Kitanglad National Park, one of the most accessible places to look for this bird. Unfortunately, it was an off year for breeding by the pair known to be on this mountain, so we were going to have to find another eagle, on our own. We hiked the relatively easy three miles up to our staging area, and early the next morning we hiked farther up the mountain into the known territory of a pair of eagles. Unlike the first trail, this one was often steep, muddy, and sprinkled with land leeches. On the way up Kitanglad, racquet-tail parrots flew over, and we saw other Philippine endemics such as McGregor's Cuckoo-shrike, Mount Apo Sunbird, Mindanao White-eye, and Apo Myna. At a clearing overlooking a deep forest canyon high on the mountainside, we began searching. Two hours in the hot sun went by, and as we were about to leave, one of our group spotted a large raptor soaring over the ridge in back of us. Its huge bill and monstrous wingspan, even at a distance, made it clear that once again a great bird had been pulled out of the hat. Our spirits were high, and the leeches and mud, though present, seemed to be much less pressing problems on the hike down the mountain. —D.P.

Coral-billed Ground-Cuckoo
This shy, ground-dwelling
cuckoo—endemic to
Thailand, Laos, Cambodia,
and Vietnam—can be
difficult to find; it usually
keeps to forests with dense
undergrowth and runs
away from any disturbance.
Thailand

FIELD GUIDE & SITE GUIDE BOOKS

■ *Birds of Southeast Asia*
(2005)
C. Robson
Princeton University Press

■ *A Field Guide to the*
Birds of South-East Asia
(1982)
B. King, M. Woodcock, and
E. C. Dickinson
HarperCollins

■ *A Guide to the Birds*
of the Philippines (2000)
R. S. Kennedy, et al.
Oxford University Press

■ *A Guide to the Birds*
of Thailand (1991)
B. Lekagul and P. D. Round
Saha Karn Bhaet, Ltd.,
Bangkok

■ *A Photographic Guide*
to the Birds of Indonesia
(2003)
M. Strange
Princeton University Press

■ *A Photographic Guide*
to the Birds of Southeast
Asia (2003)
M. Strange
Princeton University Press

Two Southeast Asian countries deserve special mention because they consist solely of large chains of islands and, related to that geography, have many endemic birds. The Philippines, comprising more than 7,000 islands (the largest being Luzon and Mindanao), supports more than 570 bird species, with about 190 of them endemic to this island group. Indonesia is a complex amalgam of more than 17,000 large and small islands, some with familiar names such as Java and Bali, others, like Sulawesi, less familiar. The country is especially intriguing ornithologically, with more than 350 of its 1,500 bird species being endemic.

Of great interest to ornithologists and knowledgeable birders is that one of the more abrupt transitions from one zoogeographic zone to another occurs in western Indonesia. Known as Wallace's Line, after Alfred Russel Wallace, who initially drew it, the boundary snakes between the large islands of Borneo and Sulawesi and then south, between the smaller islands of Bali and Lombok (see map p. 45). The Oriental zone, with its species-rich avifauna, lies to the west of the line, and the relatively bird-poor Australian zone lies to the east. The boundary is not absolutely sharp, of course, and over time, some animal groups have spread across the line, from one region to the other. Still, a journey to this region, with time spent in both Borneo and Sulawesi because of their characteristically different faunas, would yield a great diversity of bird sightings. Sulawesi, in fact, is included in Wallacea, the faunal subregion named after Wallace that includes three major island groups (Sulawesi, the Moluccas, and the Lesser Sunda Islands) and is among the ornithologically least known and most exotic places on Earth (supporting about 700 bird species, 250 of them endemic).

Significant Species of Southeast Asia

ABOUT 108 FAMILIES FOUND IN THIS REGION

■ **PHEASANTS AND PARTRIDGES** (Phasianidae), **about 50 species**

Crested Fireback* *Lophura erythrophthalma*
large pheasant of Malaysia, Indonesia, and southern Thailand; male blackish with an orangish lower back

Mountain Peacock-Pheasant* *Polyplectron inopinatum*
brown and grayish black chicken-like bird endemic to peninular Malaysia

Great Argus* *Argusianus argus*
large pheasant from the Malay Peninsula, Sumatra, and Borneo; male with a bare, blue-skin face and incredibly long tail

■ **PIGEONS AND DOVES** (Columbidae), **about 70 species**

Nicobar Pigeon *Caloenas nicobarica*
stocky dark pigeon with unusual long feathers that hang from its neck area

Flame-breasted Fruit-Dove* *Ptilinopus marchei*
uncommon Philippines dove of higher elevation forests, with red-orange crown and chest patch

Gray-headed Imperial-Pigeon* *Ducula radiata*
large pigeon endemic to Sulawesi, Indonesia

■ **PARROTS** (Psittacidae), **about 35 species**

Green Racquet-tail* *Prioniturus luconensis*
small green parrot from the Philippines with two long, extended tail feathers that have racquet-shaped tips

Vernal Hanging-Parrot *Loriculus vernalis*
tiny, green, fruit-eating parrot with reddish bill, rump, and feet

■ **CUCKOOS** (Cuculidae), **about 45 species**

Black-bellied Malkoha* *Phaenicophaeus diardi*
large, long-tailed forest cuckoo found in the Malay Peninsula and Indonesia

Coral-billed Ground-Cuckoo* *Carpococcyx renauldi*
large ground bird of Thailand, Cambodia, Laos, and Vietnam; gray and black above with reddish bill

■ **KINGFISHERS** (Alcedinidae), **about 30 species**

Indigo-banded Kingfisher* *Alcedo cyanopectus*
tiny, uncommon kingfisher endemic to freshwater streams in the Philippines

Lilac Kingfisher* *Cittura cyanotis*
largish, distinctive kingfisher with lilac-colored cheeks; found in parts of Indonesia

■ **HORNBILLS** (Bucerotidae), **about 20 species**

Rhinoceros Hornbill* *Buceros rhinoceros*
black and white hornbill with a large, usually upturned, "casque" on its bill; Malay Peninsula and Indonesia

Rufous Hornbill* *Buceros hydrocorax*
reddish and brown hornbill; endemic to the Philippines

Bushy-crested Hornbill* *Anorrhinus galeritus*
medium-size, dark brown hornbill from the Malay Peninsula and Indonesia

■ **BARBETS** (Capitonidae), **about 20 species**

Fire-tufted Barbet* *Psilopogon pyrolophus*
green mountain barbet in Malaysia and Indonesia; has a small tuft of red feathers at the base of its bill

Bornean Barbet* *Megalaima eximia*
small green barbet endemic to Borneo

■ **BROADBILLS** (Eurylaimidae), **10 species**

Green Broadbill* *Calyptomena viridis*
small, iridecent green forest bird found mainly in Thailand, Malaysia, and Indonesia

Black-and-red Broadbill* *Cymbirhynchus macrorhynchos*
forest bird; black above, reddish below, with a blue and yellow bill

■ **PITTAS** (Pittidae), **25 species**

Gurney's Pitta* *Pitta gurneyi*
critically endangered pitta that occurs only in southern Thailand and perhaps in Myanmar

Garnet Pitta* *Pitta granatina*
beautiful small pitta, mainly blue, red, and black; from the Malay Peninsula and Indonesia

Whiskered Pitta* *Pitta kochi*
red-bellied pitta endemic to higher elevation forests in the Philippines

■ **CUCKOO-SHRIKES** (Campephagidae), **about 35 species**

Cerulean Cuckoo-Shrike* *Coracina temminckii*
species endemic to Sulawesi, Indonesia

Scarlet Minivet *Pericrocotus flammeus*
striking, common bird; male all red and black

■ **BULBULS** (Pycnonotidae), **about 50 species**

Crested Finchbill *Spizixos canifrons*
green bulbul with a grayish, crested head and yellow bill

White-headed Bulbul* *Hypsipetes thompsoni*
gray bulbul with a white head and reddish bill, found
only in Myanmar and Thailand

■ **LEAFBIRDS** (Chloropseidae), **8 species**

Yellow-throated Leafbird* *Chloropsis palawanensis*
Philippine endemic, common in forests and forest edges

Orange-bellied Leafbird *Chloropsis hardwickii*
one of Asia's prettiest birds, the male is bright green
above with an orangish belly and turquoise-blue
shoulder patches

■ **OLD WORLD FLYCATCHERS** (Muscicapidae), **about 105 species**

Sunda Forktail* *Enicurus velatus*
forktail endemic to mountain streams in Indonesia

Green Cochoa *Cochoa viridis*
striking green flycatcher with blue crown and tail
and silver-blue markings on its black wings

■ **BABBLERS** (Timaliidae), **about 200 species**

Falcated Wren-Babbler* *Ptilocichla falcata*
secretive, brownish, streaked bird found usually on
the ground; endemic to the Philippines

Black-backed Sibia* *Heterophasia melanoleuca*
babbler of broadleafed evergreen forests

■ **SUNBIRDS AND SPIDERHUNTERS** (Nectariniidae), **about 35 species**

Mount Apo Sunbird* *Aethopyga boltoni*
sunbird with yellow underparts; endemic to mountain
forests in the Philippines

Whitehead's Spiderhunter* *Arachnothera juliae*
white-streaked brown bird with a long, downcurved bill
and yellow rump; endemic to Borneo

■ **OLD WORLD ORIOLES** (Oriolidae), **16 species**

Maroon Oriole *Oriolus traillii*
widely distributed forest species; male maroon
and black, female brown above and white below
with dark streaks

■ **CROWS, JAYS, AND MAGPIES** (Corvidae), **about 25 species**

Green Magpie *Cissa chinensis*
bright green bird with a broad black stripe through
its eye; occurs widely in Southeast Asia

Ratchet-tailed Treepie* *Crypsirina temia*
genuinely strange-looking, largish black bird with
a long, broad, spiky-edged tail

Some Other Species Global Birders Often Seek

Asian Openbill *Anastomus oscitans*
grayish and black stork with an obvious gap between
the upper and lower parts of its bill

Storm's Stork* *Ciconia stormi*
stork of fresh water in forest zones; blackish with red bill
and legs

Great Philippine Eagle* *Pithecophaga jefferyi*
rare, critically endangered eagle endemic to forests
in the Philippines

Black-thighed Falconet* *Microhierax fringillarius*
very small, fairly common falcon of forest edges
and clearings

Maleo *Macrocephalon maleo*
one of the chicken-like megapodes, or mound-
builders; black and whitish with a knobbed head;
found in Sulawesi, Indonesia

Masked Finfoot *Heliopais personatus*
large, grebe-like river bird with a yellow bill; one of
the globe's three finfoot species

Spoon-billed Sandpiper *Eurynorhynchus pygmeus*
small sandpiper with a strangely shaped bill; breeds
in Siberia and winters in Southeast Asia

Edible-nest Swiftlet* *Aerodramus fuciphagus*
small, dark swift; constructs a saliva nest used in bird's
nest soup

Asian Paradise-Flycatcher *Terpsiphone paradisi*
crested monarch flycatcher with a bluish bill; extremely
long tail in male

Stripe-breasted Rhabdornis* *Rhabdornis inornatus*
one of three rhabdornis (or Philippine creeper) species;
endemic to the Philippines

Asian Fairy-Bluebird *Irena puella*
broadly distributed forest bird with brilliant blue
and black coloring; one of two fairy-bluebirds
(family Irenidae)

Greater Racket-tailed Drongo *Dicrurus paradiseus*
distinctive black bird with very long tail streamers
with racket-shaped ends

Bornean Bristlehead* *Pityriasis gymnocephala*
predominantly black and red bird with a huge bill;
endemic to forests of Borneo; the sole species of
family Pityriaseidae

Restricted to Southeast Asia

CHAPTER 8

AUSTRALASIA & THE TROPICAL PACIFIC

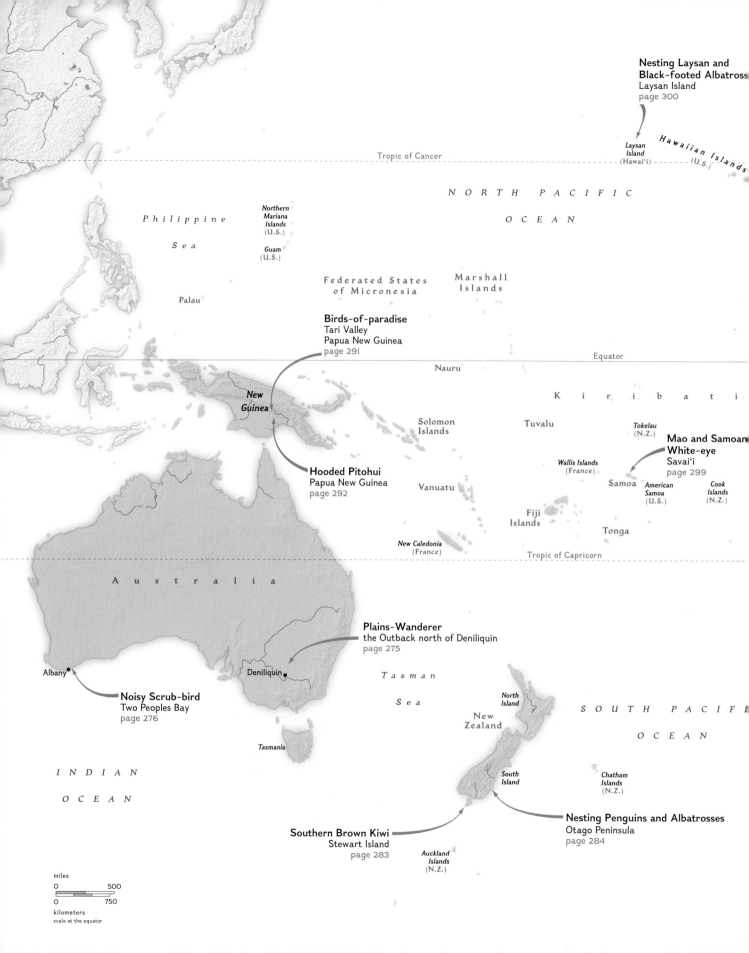

Nesting Laysan and Black-footed Albatross
Laysan Island
page 300

Hawaiian Islands (U.S.)

Laysan Island (Hawaiʻi)

Tropic of Cancer

NORTH PACIFIC OCEAN

Philippine Sea

Northern Mariana Islands (U.S.)

Guam (U.S.)

Federated States of Micronesia

Marshall Islands

Palau

Birds-of-paradise
Tari Valley
Papua New Guinea
page 291

Equator

Nauru

K i r i b a t i

New Guinea

Solomon Islands

Tuvalu

Tokelau (N.Z.)

Mao and Samoan White-eye
Savaiʻi
page 299

Hooded Pitohui
Papua New Guinea
page 292

Wallis Islands (France)

Samoa

American Samoa (U.S.)

Cook Islands (N.Z.)

Vanuatu

Fiji Islands

Tonga

A u s t r a l i a

New Caledonia (France)

Tropic of Capricorn

Plains-Wanderer
the Outback north of Deniliquin
page 275

Deniliquin

T a s m a n S e a

North Island

SOUTH PACIFIC OCEAN

Albany

Noisy Scrub-bird
Two Peoples Bay
page 276

New Zealand

South Island

Chatham Islands (N.Z.)

Tasmania

I N D I A N

O C E A N

Nesting Penguins and Albatrosses
Otago Peninsula
page 284

Southern Brown Kiwi
Stewart Island
page 283

Auckland Islands (N.Z.)

miles
0   500

0   750
kilometers
scale at the equator

BIRDING IN

AUSTRALASIA & THE TROPICAL PACIFIC

THEY'RE FAR AWAY, CAN TAKE AGES TO GET TO, AND MAY BUST YOUR BIRD-ing budget for years, but they're worth it. From an Ameri-centric world-view, taking a birding trip to the Australasian or the Pacific region can be considered journeying to some of the farthest corners of the Earth—and from a global birding standpoint, to some of the most exotic corners. For our pur-poses, the Australasian region includes Australia, New Zealand, and New Guinea, and the Pacific region includes the island groups of the tropical western and central Pacific Ocean. Some 1,700 bird species occur in the combined areas. This is a good deal fewer than in some other continents or faunal regions (South America's 3,100 species, for example), but what is lost in diversity is more than made up in exotic beauty, interest, and in many cases, ease of observation.

Australia and New Zealand are the main birding destinations here, especially Aus-tralia, with its larger, continental-size avifauna, its mix of temperate and tropical spe-cies, and its large complement of colorful birds. New Guinea and the small islands of the tropical Pacific are also included in this chapter. For various reasons—difficult to access, difficult to explore, and/or having relatively small avifaunas—most of them are less common birding destinations.

A large proportion of international travelers interested in animals and other nat-ural attractions visit Australia. This continent's vast open spaces, sunshine, bright colors, and stunning wild scenery—rain forests and open eucalyptus forests in the east, desert and grasslands in the outback—are powerful attractions. But it is mainly the unique fauna that makes a trip to this distant land a life goal for many people

PREVIOUS PAGES: **Simpson Desert** This desert covers parts of Queensland, South Australia, and the Northern Territory. It features a wide range of plants and animals in a varied landscape of dunes, dry lakes, spinifex grasslands, and acacia woodlands. *Australia*

Red-collared Myzomela
The island of New Guinea has an abundance of endemic species such as this honeyeater—a tiny but conspicuous bird of mountain forests.
Papua New Guinea

interested in birds and other wildlife. A prime attraction is its celebrity mammals: the diverse and abundant marsupials—kangaroos, koalas, and wombats, to mention a few—and the primitive, egg-laying mammals, platypus and echidna.

But the birds are wonderful and almost always easier to see. Some of the stand-outs are the parrots, including the large and amazing cockatoos; the large flightless Emu and Southern Cassowary; the beautiful bowerbirds, which build elaborate stick structures to attract mates; and the megapodes, or mound-builders, which construct enormous mounds of decaying vegetation to incubate their eggs.

Also deserving of mention are an abundance of large monitor lizards, crocodiles, lots of snakes, and the Great Barrier Reef—a collection of thousands of individual reefs along northeastern Australia's continental shelf that provides easy access to an enormous and thrilling marine fauna.

New Zealand's chief natural attractions are its magnificent scenery and fine outdoor recreational activities. The country has particularly beautiful mountain and coastal scenery, and views of its plentiful bays and remote fiords are prime tourist draws. Another major attraction is the country's bountiful zones of volcanic and geothermal activity—especially areas of geysers and boiling mud. Hikers come for the rugged mountains, pristine rain forests, and cross-country bushwalking, while others come for rock climbing, bungee jumping, sea kayaking, or white-water rafting.

But birds and other wildlife are also major attractions. Owing to New Zealand's remote location and island form, most of its native wildlife, particularly its birds, is endemic. Globe-trotting birders travel to New Zealand to see such groups as penguins (several species including the rare Yellow-eyed Penguin are easily spotted), huge seabirds (such as nesting Royal Albatrosses), and fascinating endemic landbirds such as kiwis (flightless birds that are the symbol of New Zealand) and the Kea (a large alpine parrot).

Westland Tai Poutini National Park Located on New Zealand's South Island, the park includes the highest peaks of the Southern Alps, spectacular glaciers, and stretches of remote coastline. New Zealand endemic birds found in the park include Okarito Brown Kiwi, Blue Duck, and Kea among many others. *New Zealand*

TRAVELING IN THE AREA

Birding in Australia and New Zealand is as safe and straightforward as birding in the United States or Canada. Both are developed nations with modern infrastructures. Thus, these are ideal destinations for birders who want to travel extensively, see lots of exotic birds, and add significantly to their life lists, but also enjoy planning do-it-yourself trips and exploring on their own.

As long as appropriate cautions are exercised in remote, wild areas—the same care you would consider taking in wilderness regions almost anywhere—all will be fine. Special precautions need to be taken when birding the remote Australian outback, the great arid and semi-arid inland portion of the continent. Generally all-wheel-drive vehicles toting spare parts, emergency radios, and survival supplies are considered essential. Australian and New Zealand birdwatchers are common, and there are local birding organizations with chapters in all major cities.

The large island of New Guinea is divided politically between Indonesia (whose half of the island is now called Papua or West Papua, formerly Irian Jaya or Western New Guinea) and the independent nation of Papua New Guinea (PNG). Indonesia sometimes makes it difficult for outsiders to visit Papua; special travel permits can be required. Many regions in both the Indonesian and PNG sections are still fairly primitive, and there is some violent crime. Only the most intrepid attempt solo birding outside of town areas. Few national parks exist, and most lands are the property of various tribal groups. Local permission is traditionally obtained before using land for any purpose—even for birding. For those wishing to visit and bird Papua or PNG, organized tours with accompanying local guides are the best and safest bets.

The islands of the tropical Pacific vary tremendously in ease of access and safety as birding destinations, from the broad accessibility and security of Hawaii to places like the Solomon Islands (located between Papua New Guinea and Fiji), where long-term political instability, security problems, and occasional ethnic violence make birding an uncertain and sometimes unsafe enterprise. A few of the more commonly visited and safer islands and island groups are mentioned on pages 297–303. ■

Comb-crested Jacana This denizen of freshwater wetlands has greatly elongated toes to support its weight on floating vegetation. These two adults are involved in a territorial dispute at Kakadu National Park, Northern Territory. *Australia*

OPPOSITE: **Ora Resurgence Cave** This spectacular location on the island of New Britain where the Ora River emerges from underground is very remote. There are now a number of eco-lodges in Papua New Guinea that offer excellent birding. *Papua New Guinea*

BIRDS OF THE REGION SIGNIFICANT GROUPS

RATITES | MEGAPODES | PIGEONS | PARROTS | KINGFISHERS AND KOOKABURRAS | LYREBIRDS | FAIRYWRENS | HONEYEATERS | HAWAIIAN HONEYCREEPERS | BOWERBIRDS | BIRDS-OF-PARADISE

The regions of the world covered in this chapter possess a wealth of significant bird families. This selection encompasses several that most birders would quickly associate with the Australasian region because they are restricted, or almost restricted, to that zone. A few families such as the parrots and kingfishers have much broader distributions but are particularly diverse here. Finally, the Hawaiian honeycreepers are special due to their extremely limited range that is wholly within U.S. jurisdiction.

■ Ratites

The world has 12 surviving species of ratites, which are birds with flat, keel-less, raft-like ("ratite") sternums, and most of them occur in the Australian region. Ratites are flightless birds that run along the ground. Their classification is controversial but most agree that there are five families: Struthionidae (the Ostrich of Africa), Rheidae (the Greater and Lesser Rheas of South America), Casuariidae (three species of cassowary—one in Australia and all three in the New Guinea region), Dromaiidae (the Emu of Australia), and Apterygidae (the five species of kiwi, endemic to New Zealand). Most ratites are huge, Ostrich-like birds. Emus, for instance, stand about five feet tall and weigh up to 110 pounds, but the kiwis are much smaller, on the order of 3 to 6 pounds.

Emus, which occur over most of mainland Australia except in heavily settled or thickly forested areas, are seen alone, in pairs, or in small groups. These big birds, which can move along at a quite respectable 30 miles per hour when hurried, are often nomadic wanderers with no real territories. They move frequently, following food availability—chiefly grasses in season and other lush vegetation. Emus are usually shy, but can be quite curious and have been known to approach or follow people. Almost anyone driving through Australia's vast ranchlands or tramping through its national parks will eventually spot these large, shaggy-looking birds. It's a discombobulating experience—and a bit scary—to be walking and birding on a trail and stumble across such huge avian creatures.

OPPOSITE: **Laughing Kookaburra** Neophyte birders may not realize that the kookaburra (an Aboriginal name) is a species of kingfisher, but just about everyone has heard of it. The photograph shows a bird looking out of its nest hole in a termite mound. *Australia*

Southern Cassowary There are three species of cassowary—Southern, Dwarf, and Northern—but only this one occurs in Australia. The other two are found in New Guinea and the nearby islands of New Britain and Yapen. *Australia*

Cassowaries are mainly fruit-eaters, and when wild fruit is scarce, they often enter orchards and gardens to eat cultivated fruit such as bananas. They may use the bony crest on their head as a shovel to turn over soil and leaf litter on the rain forest floor, in search of fallen fruit, and it may help them push their way through dense, tangled vegetation. These large birds are fairly sedentary, not moving over long distances unless forced by lack of food. Cassowaries can be aggressive, especially when breeding, and have one very long, sharp claw on each foot that can do considerable damage. Spotting a cassowary in the wild is difficult. Their populations are not large, particularly in Australia, and typically they are very wary. Some

people do catch occasional glimpses of them, often at dawn or dusk, at the edge of a forest clearing, or when one crosses a road or trail, but their distinctive footprints and droppings are all that most people ever see of wild individuals.

Kiwis, rotund terrestrial birds, are generally nocturnal. They inhabit forests but also scrub and agricultural areas and eat insects, spiders, worms, and fruit. They are generally uncommon and much more often heard than seen.

◼ Megapodes

Some of the most intriguing birds on Earth are the megapodes, or mound-builders, which are distributed mainly in Australia, New Guinea, elsewhere in Melanesia, and on some tropical Pacific islands. These birds (family Megapodidae) are also known as mound-birds, incubator birds, and in Australia as scrubfowl and brush-turkeys. They are placed in the order Galliformes with chickens, turkeys, pheasants, and partridges. Their classification is frequently revised, but there seem to be about 20 species.

Australian Brush-turkey Although resembling North America's Wild Turkey, it is not closely related. A relatively common Australian endemic, it is found from northern Queensland to New South Wales. *Australia*

They are mostly dull brownish birds with small crests and measure about 20 inches long. But the ones known as brush-turkeys are bigger and black, with bare heads and necks and large folded tails. Several in the family construct enormous mounds of soil and vegetation (up to 35 feet across and more than 10 feet high), and lay their eggs in tunnels in the mounds. The heat emitted by the decaying plant material is the main source of warmth for incubation. Males attending the mounds regulate the temperature toward one that is best for their eggs' development by scratching more matter onto the mounds or taking some of it off.

Other megapode species do not build mounds but lay their eggs in sandy soil or in holes dug on beaches, and let the sun incubate them. They are all ground-dwelling birds, seldom flying unless given no other choice. Although usually shy and inconspicuous, individuals in parks and other public areas often become used to people, and show themselves readily. This is particularly true for the Orange-footed Scrubfowl and Australian Brush-turkey, which birders spot easily in many parts of northern and northeastern Australia.

■ Pigeons

Worldwide, the pigeon family is represented, often in large numbers, almost everywhere on dry land except for Antarctica and some oceanic islands. The family Columbidae includes approximately 300 species. About 25 species occur in Australia, where half of them are endemic. Approximately 30 species, many endemic to one or a few islands, occupy most of the forested islands of the tropical Pacific. But New Guinea has an impressive 45 species, including about 14 species of fruit-doves that are small and colorful, 10 imperial-pigeons that are large and arboreal, and three crowned-pigeons that are huge, crested ground-dwellers.

Pigeons worldwide vary in size from the dimensions of a sparrow or robin to those of a small turkey. Smaller species generally are called doves and larger ones, pigeons. The soft, dense plumages of most pigeons and doves come in understated grays and browns, although some have bold patterns of black lines or spots and many have splotches of iridescence, especially on necks and wings. But some groups, such as the fruit-doves, are easily among the most gaily colored of birds. Some pigeons have conspicuous crests, many in the Australian region being good examples.

Victoria Crowned-Pigeon This large, ground-dwelling species, with its decorative, airy fan of head plumes, resides in lowland forests of New Guinea and surrounding islands. *Captive*

Pigeons inhabit almost all kinds of habitats, from arid grasslands to tropical rain forests to higher elevation mountainsides. Most species are at least partly arboreal, but some spend their time in and around cliffs, and still others are primarily ground-dwellers. They eat seeds, ripe and unripe fruit, berries, and the occasional insect, snail, or other small invertebrate. In the Australian region, pigeons partially fill the ground seedeater niche that pheasants, grouse, and partridges occupy on other continents. Pigeons are often easier to see than many other kinds of birds, especially when they come to the ground. But some types can be difficult to spot, and even the brightly colored fruit-doves, owing to their heavy emphasis on green, can disappear easily into green tree canopies.

Parrots

The 370 or so species in the parrot order Psittaciformes are globally distributed across the tropics, with some species extending into subtropical and even temperate-zone areas such as New Zealand. The order has a particularly diverse and abundant presence in the Australian region. South America has more parrot species, but from a birding point of view, Australia enjoys a great advantage. Most South American parrots are rain forest species that can be difficult to see in the forest canopy, whereas many Australian species live in more open habitat such as eucalyptus forests and scrub areas, typically making viewing and identification much easier.

There are two main parrot groups. The cockatoos, family Cacatuidae, are medium- to large-size parrots with crests that they can erect. The world's 21 species occur in the Australian and Indonesia regions, with 14 in Australia (11 endemic) and 3 in New Guinea.

Australian King-Parrot A forest-dwelling parrot, the male (shown) is intensely red on the head and body; the female has a green head and breast. The species is found in eastern Australia. *Australia*

The family includes cockatoos, corellas, and such common Australian residents as the Galah and the Cockatiel. Many cockatoo vocalizations are loud, harsh, and carry long distances, and birders are often alerted to the birds' presence by these sounds. Although many cockatoos tend to spend much of their time perched high in trees, some forage on the ground, which contributes to the ability of birders to locate and get good looks at these impressive birds.

The rest of the parrots are in the family Psittacidae. More than 40 species (three-quarters of them endemic) occur in Australia, including rosellas, the Budgerigar, and 6 species of lorikeets. The lorikeets are a distinct subgroup of brilliantly colored parrots, confined to the Australia, New Guinea, Indonesia, and Pacific island areas. They specialize in eating nectar and pollen. The larger species are known as lories. New Guinea also can be considered a center of parrot diversity, with more than 40 species, including many lorikeets. New Zealand has six native parrots—most of which are endemic—including the only flightless parrot, the endangered Kakapo. In the Pacific islands, parrots (mostly lorikeets and lories) occur in the Solomons and Vanuatu region and in Polynesia. Only a single species resides in Micronesia, and Hawaii has no native parrots.

Kingfishers and Kookaburras

Kingfishers are handsome, bright birds of rain forests and woodlands that, in some parts of the world, make their living chiefly by diving into fresh water or salt water to catch fish. However, most of the Australian region's kingfishers, along with those of the tropical Pacific, including the famous kookaburras, hunt on land. Classified with the bee-eaters and rollers in order Coraciiformes, the approximately 90 kingfisher species (family Alcedinidae) range over most of the temperate and tropical areas of the globe. Ten species,

Blue-winged Kookaburra The "other" kookaburra, it is bluer than the Laughing Kookaburra and has a more northerly distribution, including parts of New Guinea. Three other kookaburra species—Rufous-bellied, Spangled, and Shovel-billed—also reside on New Guinea. *Australia*

including the Laughing and Blue-winged Kookaburras, occur in Australia, and they range in size from a small, fish-eating species at 5 inches, to the largest kingfisher in the world, the Laughing Kookaburra, at up to 18 inches long. New Guinea has 22 kingfishers (including 3 kookaburras), about ten species occur in the tropical Pacific, and New Zealand has but one. Kingfishers, though varying in size, are all of a similar form: large heads with very long, robust, straight bills, short necks, short legs, and, on some, noticeable crests. These birds are usually quite colorful, but in the Australian region, blue and white, along with chestnut-orange, predominate.

Kingfishers of the region mainly eat insects and their larvae, vertebrates such as small reptiles and

mice, and, when near water, freshwater and saltwater crustaceans. Usually seen hunting alone, they perch motionless on a tree branch, fence post, or telephone wire, staring down at the ground. When they detect prey, they glide smoothly down, grab with their bill, and then return to a perch to eat. Kookaburras specialize in small snakes, lizards, and rodents, but also take a lot of larger insects. Kingfishers are highly territorial, aggressively defending their territories from other members of their species with noisy, chattering vocalizations, chasing, and fighting. Some of the most indelible memories many birders take away from the Australian region originate with kookaburra encounters, frequently in the form of a chunky, stoic-looking kookaburra suddenly diving to the ground to snatch up a lizard or frog. Hearing kingfishers' raucous vocalizations—especially the famous, maniacal-sounding call of the Laughing Kookaburra—is also a treat.

Lyrebirds

Lyrebirds (family Menuridae, with only two species) attract birder interest because they are endemic to Australia, occur over a fairly small area, and have spectacular long tails (that resemble a Greek lyre, a musical instrument) that are used in courtship displays. They are large, brownish, secretive, ground-dwelling forest birds with big, powerful feet. Males and females look much alike, but females are a bit smaller and their tails are less elaborate.

Lyrebirds forage on the forest floor either alone or in small groups. They use their large feet to dig into the earth, exposing worms, spiders, insects, insect larvae, and millipedes, among other invertebrates, which they gobble up. They will also tear apart rotting wood on the forest floor, looking for food. The brown lyrebirds are well camouflaged when on the ground, which further protects them in their shy ways. When

Superb Lyrebird The male's elegant tail is inverted over his head during courtship display. The two outer tail feathers are lyre-shaped, flanked by two guard plumes, and twelve filamentous feathers fill the center. *Australia*

alarmed, they tend to run speedily away; they are weak flyers, usually managing only short, clumsy flights. They do, however, roost overnight in trees, but usually they jump up, branch by branch, to these high roosts.

Male lyrebirds are famous for their courtship displays in which they sing and display their gaudy tails. The central part of the long tail is held, spread fan-like, over the head, and two large, boldly patterned side feathers point outward to either side. When a female approaches, the male quivers the tail feathers, and there is much jumping and circling. After mating, the female departs to nest on her own. Males sing long, loud songs that often superbly mimic the vocalizations of such birds as whipbirds, kookaburras, rosellas, cockatoos, currawongs, magpies, and eagles. The Superb Lyrebird is still fairly common in parts of southeastern Australia, and persistent birders are usually rewarded with sightings. Albert's Lyrebird has a very restricted range, is considered a vulnerable species, and is very difficult to see.

▣ Fairywrens

Fairywrens, family Maluridae, are about 27 species of small insect-eaters that mainly inhabit shrubs, thickets, and undergrowth. There are three distinct groups, known as fairywrens, emuwrens, and grasswrens. Most members of the family occur in Australia, but four species are endemic to New Guinea. They are highly social, living in small communal groups. They forage on the ground and in shrubs, hopping as they search for their insect food. A few species are common denizens of forest edges, parklands, and picnic grounds, and are commonly seen.

Superb Fairywren Found throughout southeastern Australia, this species has adapted well to human-altered landscapes and is common in suburban Sydney, Canberra, and Melbourne. *Australia*

These birds, with small bills and long tails that are usually held stiffly upward, often stand out because the males have patches of varying sizes of bright, iridescent blue. Male Splendid Fairywrens in Australia, for instance, and male Broad-billed Fairywrens in New Guinea, are mostly blue. These are considered by bird-lovers to be among the world's most beautiful small birds. Females in the group are usually brownish, some having blue tails. Average Australians often class together all fairywrens as "blue wrens," and this group is among the most widely identifiable there among non-birders.

Honeyeaters

An interesting facet of the ecology of the Australian region is the large number of birds that feed mainly on plant nectar. One very successful group, the honeyeaters, is especially numerous in Australia and New Guinea. In fact, in some areas on some days, it seems as if all the birds you see are honeyeaters. The reason for this group's great success in the region is related to its chief food source: plant nectar, which is mostly a sugar water solution and is superabundant in most habitats across Australia and New Guinea. For instance, it is estimated that a single large eucalyptus tree, during its peak flowering period, can support about 15 honeyeaters for one to two months.

This large family, Meliphagidae, contains 175 species that are distributed mostly in Australia (72 species), New Guinea (65 species), and Solomons/Vanuatu (15 species), but they also occur in New Zealand (3 species) and on some other tropical Pacific islands (8 species). Honeyeaters are small or medium-size birds with slender bodies and long, slim, downcurved bills. Most are attired in dull gray, greenish olive, or brown, often with streaks—not the most visually glamorous of birds. Many, such as friarbirds, have areas of bare colored skin on the face, and some, such as wattlebirds, have protuberances that hang from near the ear or eye.

Honeyeaters are mainly birds of forests, but some occupy more open habitats. Gregarious, they forage in flowering trees and shrubs usually in small parties. Most honeyeaters have very long tongues that can be thrust deep into long, tubular flowers to collect nectar

and into cracks between pieces of tree bark to gather other fluid foods. The tongue has a brush-like tip that soaks up nectar like a mop.

Macleay's Honeyeater This honeyeater is endemic to northeastern Queensland, where it forages for insects and nectar. Here it is nectaring on the flower of a native bottlebrush tree. *Australia*

Hawaiian Honeycreepers

Birdwatchers who visit the Hawaiian Islands are typically eager to seek out the little birds known as Hawaiian honeycreepers. Most of these colorful birds, also called Hawaiian finches, are difficult to find because they have small and declining populations and inhabit

Iiwi This individual was photographed on the Big Island of Hawaii. The species is also common on Maui and Kauai, but rare on Molokai and Oahu. Look for it around flowering trees. *Hawaii*

remote mountain forests. The reason for their general rarity is that since human colonization of the islands some 1,600 years ago, these pretty birds have been persecuted. They were hunted for their decorative feathers, their forest homes were cleared for agriculture, their eggs and young were eaten by introduced nest predators such as rats and mongooses, and their immune systems were overwhelmed by introduced diseases. Only a few species remain, many of them endangered and now confined mainly to patches of protected high-elevation wet forests on Kauai, Maui, and the Big Island of Hawaii. Of the 45 or more Hawaiian honeycreeper species present on the islands when people first settled there, perhaps 18 species still exist in family Drepanididae.

Hawaiian honeycreepers are small birds, mostly four to five inches long. Many are greenish or green and yellow, but some are bright red or orangish, or brownish, and one surviving member is black. As a group, the birds' most distinctive physical trait is their bills, which vary from short and straight to very long and highly downcurved. Fortunately, a few of the honeycreepers are common enough to be located by almost any birder who visits Hawaii.

■ Bowerbirds

Bowerbirds, some of which are spectacularly colored, are celebrated for their elaborate courtship activities. The males build "bowers"—stick structures—and sometimes decorate them elaborately. One species might specialize in decorative piles of blue objects; in other species, items such as berries, small stones, snail shells, or leaves of a certain color are selected. All this activity—the diligent males spend months building, decorating, and rearranging their properties—is to attract females and convince them to mate.

Males of some species erect walls of twigs that are stuck into the ground. The walls form a structure that resembles an actor's stage or a marriage bower, and may even be "painted" by the male with his saliva that has been colored with compounds such as charcoal. With his bower constructed, a male vocalizes to attract passing females. A female approaches, evaluates his bower and his antic courtship displays, and, if convinced that he is a high-quality individual, mates. Few would argue that this complex behavior places the bowerbirds among the world's most interesting bird groups.

Regent Bowerbird Fortunately for birders, this lovely species (male is shown) remains common throughout its range, which is limited to the rain forests of eastern Queensland and New South Wales. *Australia*

Bowerbirds are medium-size to largish birds, chunky, with shortish wings, tails, and legs. Some of them are quite stunning, with Australia's black and yellow male Regent Bowerbird and New Guinea's orange and yellow male Flame Bowerbird, for example, being among the bird world's true jewels. Bowerbirds are mostly denizens of rain forests and other wet forests. There are only 20 bowerbird species (family Ptilonorhynchidae). Ten occur in Australia; eight are endemic and two are shared with New Guinea, where the remaining species in the family are situated. Some bowerbirds are quite common and frequently seen, such as Australia's Green Catbird and Satin Bowerbird. Many others are inconspicuous and regularly seen only at their bowers.

Birds-of-paradise

Many birders consider the birds-of-paradise to be the most beautiful of the world's birds. Many of them are fantastically colored, and males in some species have bizarre plumages—tremendously long tail feathers and sometimes head plumes. Females are usually comparatively plain. These mid-size to largish birds are also celebrated for the breeding displays that males perform to attract and convince females to mate with them. During the breeding season, males spend most of each day—whenever they are not feeding—at display sites, usually a horizontal branch high in a large tree. They vocalize and display to attract the attention of passing females. Displays usually involve the male moving his head up and down, stretching his neck, rhythmically swaying his body, hopping side to side, and extending his wings. When a female approaches, a male's antics increase in intensity. If the female is convinced the displaying male is of high quality, she mates with him and then leaves to nest on her own. The male returns to his mate-attraction displays and will mate with as many females as he can.

Magnificent Bird-of-paradise This male is in full courtship display. The plumage is so complex that it can be hard to tell what is what. In this case, the bird is facing forward and has expanded his iridescent green breast shield. *Papua New Guinea*

Birds-of-paradise occur only in rain forest and a few other densely vegetated forest habitats. Hunting for fruits, berries, and insects, they usually fly from fruiting tree to fruiting tree, staying in the higher canopy, and often hanging at odd angles to reach tasty morsels. But they will also fly down to feed at tree trunks, stumps, and fallen logs. In most species, males seem to hold territories year-round, feeding and displaying for females within these territories. There are 44 species of birds-of-paradise, and almost all are restricted to the Australian region. Thirty-eight species occur in New Guinea and its surrounding small islands, two reside in Indonesia's Moluccan Islands, and four (known as riflebirds and manucodes) are found in eastern Australia. Many of New Guinea's birds-of-paradise are uncommon or very wary around settled areas because they are hunted for their feather plumes, which are, even today, worn during traditional ceremonies. Outside of settled areas, some species, such as the Raggiana Bird-of-paradise, are common and birders usually are able to locate them.

*Ecologically, Australia's landbirds are known for
their sedentary lifestyles, communal breeding,
and long breeding seasons.*

AUSTRALIA

AUSTRALIA, THE WORLD'S SMALLEST CONTINENT OR LARGEST ISLAND, IS AMONG the globe's most intriguing travel destinations and one of its premier birding locations. Encompassing both tropical and temperate regions, it has amazing, colorful birdlife, including 55 parrot species. Even within cities and suburbs you can see such stunners as Sulphur-crested Cockatoos (which are locally considered "pest" birds) and Rainbow Lorikeets (multicolored parrot beauties). Simply put, an amazing place for birds—don't miss it.

Australia is a parliamentary democracy allied with the British Commonwealth, and among the safest places in the world to travel (aside from the driving-on-the-wrong-side-of-the-road problem). More than 90 percent of Australians live in and around the few major cities or along the country's eastern coast, leaving huge portions of the continent underpopulated or unpopulated, making birding here even more attractive. It is difficult to believe, but as recently as the 1970s, land was so available and inexpensive in Australia that one recommendation in local birdwatching books was that, if readers wanted a good, regular birding site, they should simply find a pleasing, pristine bit of "the bush" (as Australians call all rural landscapes), and purchase it! Birders can experience wonderful birds in Australia at any time of year, but the period from August through January (late winter through summer) may be best because most birds there breed during this period, particularly passerines.

GEOGRAPHY AND HABITATS

Australia is about 2,500 miles wide (east to west) and 2,000 miles "tall" (north to south), and has an area roughly the size of the United States excluding Alaska. The

OPPOSITE: **Uluru-Kata Tjuta National Park** This famous park in the country's center encompasses both Uluru (Ayers Rock) and its sister formation Kata Tjuta (Mount Olga, depicted). In addition to the scenery and cultural significance of the area there are also birds of interest, for example, Pied Butcherbird, Black-faced Woodswallow, and Crimson Chat. *Australia*

Eucalyptus forest Eucalyptus trees are a major component of Australia's forests—there are over 700 species. Many birds are tied to these forests, for instance, the honeyeaters that rely on nectar produced by eucalyptus flowers. *Australia*

LOCAL BIRDING & CONSERVATION ORGANIZATIONS

■ **AUSTRALIAN BIRD STUDY ASSOCIATION**
(www.absa.asn.au)
organization with individual, institutional, and corporate members that supports bird study and conservation

■ **BIRD OBSERVATION & CONSERVATION AUSTRALIA**
(www.birdobservers.org.au; boca.org.au)
formerly known as the Bird Observers' Club of Australia, organizes birding activities and trips and works in bird conservation and education

■ **BIRDING NSW**
(www.birdingnsw.org.au)
New South Wales Field Ornithologists Club; promotes birding and bird conservation in the state of New South Wales, where Sydney is located

■ **BIRDS AUSTRALIA**
(www.birdsaustralia.com.au)
Formerly known as the Royal Australasian Ornithological Union, the premier Australian ornithological organization and the country's oldest national conservation organization

country spans more than 30 degrees of latitude, with its northern 40 percent located in the tropics and the remainder in the south temperate zone. It is divided politically into seven states: Queensland (northeast), New South Wales (southeast), Victoria (southeast), Tasmania (an island south of Victoria), South Australia (south-central), Western Australia (west), and the Northern Territory (north-central; not formally considered a state).

Australia holds the title of flattest continent. Most of it lies at elevations of less than 1,000 feet above sea level, much of it below 650 feet. The average elevation is about 900 feet, compared to a worldwide average terrestrial elevation of about 2,300 feet. Most of the higher areas are distributed along or near the coasts. The only fairly high mountains are in the Great Dividing Range, which runs parallel to the eastern coast, 30 to 250 miles inland. West of the Great Dividing Range, all the way to the Indian Ocean, Australia is mainly flat and dry, with only occasional small outcroppings of higher terrain (such as the famous Ayers Rock and the MacDonnell Ranges near Alice Springs). Most of this land is monotonous, flat plains, barren semi-desert, and grasslands used extensively for livestock grazing. Between the Great Dividing Range and the Pacific Ocean is a narrow, fertile strip of land on which most of Australia's people live and work.

Main habitat types include rain forest in small patches along the east coast; large areas of open eucalyptus forest and woodland; shrubland (with shrubs up to 12 feet high) along eastern coastal areas; low shrubland (with plants up to 6 feet tall) in the south and west; heathland (open areas of evergreen shrubs usually less than 6 feet high) covering some coastal lowlands and some subalpine and alpine areas; and grasslands, including huge regions of hummock and tussock grassland in the central and western sections of the country.

BIRDLIFE

About 750 bird species occur in Australia, slightly more than the number that regularly occur in North America north of Mexico. More than 300 of these species are endemic to Australia. Many of the remainder are birds that migrate or wander over long distances and many continents—such as shorebirds and seabirds. Some well-known, wide-ranging bird groups are absent from Australia, including flamingos, Old World vultures, hummingbirds, woodpeckers, true wrens, nuthatches, shrikes, true finches, titmice, and buntings.

SPOTTING THE PLAINS-WANDERER

Some birders, knowing that seeing all the world's birds is likely impossible, have instead set a goal of seeing at least one member species of each of the 200-odd bird families. Even this objective is difficult, especially because taxonomists seem to be constantly rearranging the bird families. For example, until recently the enigmatic and endangered Plains-wanderer was considered an unusual type of buttonquail (family Turnicidae). Now, however, this quail-like bird is regarded as the only species in its own family (Pedionomidae). Although it occurs in native grasslands and stubble fields throughout broad swaths of the southeastern Australian interior, it is always erratic there and found only with great luck—except north of the town of Deniliquin in the outback region of the state of New South Wales. Here, in a private stubble field, the land's owner has worked with local bird guide Phil Maher to make the Plains-wanderer a more or less reliable sighting.

With only five bird families left to reach my goal, I excitedly arranged a search for the Plains-wanderer. Along with others I drove in the darkness along interminable country roads and arrived on time at the gate to THE field. Our two Land Rovers then started crisscrossing the field using the headlights to illuminate the stubble. We spotted Stubble Quail and an occasional Inland Dotterel had our hearts pumping. Finally, after three hours of searching, a female Plains-wanderer, as if by magic, suddenly appeared running on the ground only a few yards away. Two males, less colorful than the female, showed up about five minutes later. For now, traveling to this field is the primary way to add this family and species to your list. But be forewarned: No refunds if you miss finding the bird. —D.P.

Plains-wanderer The male (shown) is smaller and more cryptically colored than the female. It is the male who incubates and cares for the young. *Australia*

Ecologically, Australia's landbirds are known for their sedentary lifestyles, communal breeding, and long breeding seasons. Most of Australia's birds don't make the kind of long migrations that are a regular feature of birds in North America and Europe. Only 17 percent of Australian bird species are migratory, whereas about 70 percent in Europe and 55 percent in North America are migratory. Communal breeding, in which a group of birds (not just a single pair, though usually related) contributes to a single nest, is considered relatively rare among the world's birds, but is fairly common in Australia where 34 percent of the landbirds are communal breeders.

Breeding seasons for Australia's temperate-zone birds are usually longer than for comparable-size birds in temperate areas on other continents; incubation and fledgling periods, in particular, are often longer. Reasons for these ecological differences are not completely known, but researchers believe that they may relate to the birds' food supplies. Most food is obtained year-round from evergreen eucalyptus forests, with only weak seasonal changes in availability. Nectar-feeders are especially diverse and abundant in Australia; one group, the honeyeaters (family Meliphagidae) is Australia's largest bird family, with 72 species. Honeyeaters are everywhere on the

Two Peoples Bay Nature Reserve Other rare birds inhabit the reserve: Ground Parrot, Western Bristlebird, and Western Whipbird. *Australia*

SPOTTING THE NOISY SCRUB-BIRD

The Noisy Scrub-bird is endemic to extreme southwestern Australia and is a member of an ancient family (Atrichornithidae) that contains only one other species. This small brownish bird with a white throat was first described in the mid 1800s and then "disappeared" around 1890. Presumed extinct for 70 years, a small population was rediscovered in 1961 at Two Peoples Bay on the southern coast of Western Australia. This area was quickly turned into a nature reserve, and since then the population has grown to about a thousand individuals in several locations along the coast.

The Noisy Scrub-bird is a sneaky dweller of thick coastal undergrowth. If it weren't for the male's ear-piercing song, it might never have been rediscovered. To see the bird is very difficult, even when its voice lets you know exactly which hillside it is occupying. When I visited Two Peoples Bay I found that, luckily, this rare bird was attracted to squeaking noises I made by "kissing" my fingers. These sounds apparently resemble distress signals made by birds struggling in the talons of a hawk. Even using this attractant, the Noisy Scrub-bird's close approach was cautious and elusive. I never saw the bird as a whole but, instead, amid the vegetation, I viewed its various body parts one by one. First I saw an eye, then a patch of breast, then a cocked tail. Before I knew it, my five-second viewing opportunity ended as the bird scampered back into thicker vegetation. But in my mind's eye I was able to assemble the glimpses I'd had of the partial bird into a whole and, to my great satisfaction, was able to add a check to my life list for both a new family and a new species. —D.P.

Emu One of Australia's iconic birds. Emus are imposingly large, flightless birds related to Ostriches, rheas, cassowaries, and kiwis. They are common over much of the continent, but avoid dense forest and extremely arid areas. *Australia*

continent, occupying essentially all terrestrial habitats. These arboreal birds are so abundant and successful that in many woodland areas ten or more species are present, sometimes at densities of up to eight individuals per species per acre.

Australia has about 55 species of parrots, and some of the largest and most spectacular in the world. Many are common and easy to see. Indeed, it is a rare day in Australia when you will not encounter them. In addition to their occurrence in wild areas, they are seen low in shrubs and even on the ground in urban and suburban parks and backyards. Your first good looks at Crimson Rosellas, Rainbow Lorikeets, Sulfur-crested Cockatoos, black-cockatoos (multiple species), and even Galahs will be unforgettable experiences. All of them are so common that many Australians regard them as pests.

Aside from parrots and honeyeaters, Australian landbirds eagerly anticipated by international birders include two large flightless species (Emu, Southern Cassowary), megapodes (mound-builders), birds-of-paradise, and bowerbirds. Australia also boasts numerous sites for those interested in spotting hordes of migrant shorebirds, including easily accessed beaches and mudflats at or near Darwin, Cairns, Brisbane, and Sydney. Finally, for seabird lovers, many claim that pelagic birding trips out of Wollongong, just south of Sydney, are among the world's best. More than 90 species of oceangoing birds can be seen in the area, about one-third of all the globe's pelagic species.

FIELD GUIDE & SITE GUIDE BOOKS

■ *Birds of Australia, 8th ed.* (2010)
K. Simpson and N. Day
Princeton University Press

■ *Field Guide to Australian Birds* (2004)
M. Morcombe
Steve Parish Publishing

■ *The Field Guide to the Birds of Australia, 8th ed.* (2007)
G. Pizzey
HarperCollins

■ *Where to Watch Birds in Australasia and Oceania* (1998)
N. Wheatley
Princeton University Press

Significant Species of Australia

85 FAMILIES FOUND IN THIS REGION

■ **CASSOWARIES** (Casuariidae), **1 species**

Southern Cassowary *Casuarius casuarius*
endangered, blackish, Ostrich-like bird of northeastern rain forests; also occurs in New Guinea.

■ **EMU*** (Dromaiidae), **1 species**

Emu* *Dromaius novaehollandiae*
brownish, shaggy-looking, Ostrich-like bird of open areas; ranges widely over the continent

■ **PENGUINS** (Spheniscidae), **about 3 species**

Little Penguin *Eudyptula minor*
world's smallest penguin; common along Australia's southern shores

■ **MEGAPODES** (Megapodidae), **3 species**

Orange-footed Scrubfowl *Megapodius reinwardt*
common, relatively small megapode of Australia's northern reaches; brown above, gray below, with a little crest

Malleefowl* *Leipoa ocellata*
large, scarce, potentially threatened megapode of arid shrublands, woodlands, and scrub areas

Australian Brush-turkey* *Alectura lathami*
common, large, dull blackish megapode of Australia's east; it has a bare reddish head and neck

■ **PIGEONS AND DOVES** (Columbidae), **about 25 species**

Spinifex Pigeon* *Geophaps plumifera*
striking reddish brown pigeon with thin, tall crest; inhabits dry grasslands

Chestnut-quilled Rock-Pigeon* *Petrophassa rufipennis*
dark brown with lighter spots; occurs mainly in sandstone cliff areas in the north-central part of Australia

Wompoo Fruit-Dove *Ptilinopus magnificus*
brightly colored rain forest pigeon

■ **COCKATOOS** (Cacatuidae), **14 species**

Palm Cockatoo *Probosciger aterrimus*
large, black rain forest cockatoo with prominent crest; occurs in Cape York Peninsula and New Guinea

Red-tailed Black-Cockatoo* *Calyptorhynchus banksii*
large, common, sooty black cockatoo of Australia's forests and woodlands

Pink Cockatoo* *Cacatua leadbeateri*
smaller, pink and white, crested cockatoo; also known as Major Mitchell's Cockatoo

■ **PARROTS** (Psittacidae), **about 40 species**

Rainbow Lorikeet *Trichoglossus haemotodus*
abundant, multicolored, nectar-eating parrot common in woodlands, shrublands, parks, and gardens

Golden-shouldered Parrot* *Psephotus chrysopterygius*
colorful, endangered parrot of Australia's northeastern savanna woodlands; feeds mainly on the ground

Crimson Rosella* *Platycercus elegans*
abundant parrot of forests, parks, and agricultural districts; fantastically attired in red, blue, and black

Eclectus Parrot *Eclectus roratus*
large, bulky parrot of the northeast; the male is mainly green, the female red and blue

■ **KINGFISHERS** (Alcedinidae), **10 species**

Laughing Kookaburra* *Dacelo novaeguineae*
world's largest kingfisher and Australia's most famous bird; broadly distributed in the east and southwest

Blue-winged Kookaburra *Dacelo leachii*
almost as large as, and similar to, the Laughing Kookaburra; occurs in open forests and woodlands of the northern half of the continent

■ **LYREBIRDS*** (Menuridae), **2 species**

Superb Lyrebird* *Menura novaehollandiae*
famous endemic of southeastern forests and woodlands; brown above, gray below; male with a long, unusual tail used in display

■ **AUSTRALASIAN ROBINS** (Petroicidae), **20 species**

Red-capped Robin* *Petroica goodenovii*
very small, black and white, with red cap and breast; broad distribution over the southern half of Australia

Dusky Robin* *Melanodryas vittata*
small, olive-brown songbird endemic to Tasmania

■ **WHIPBIRDS AND QUAIL-THRUSHES** (Eupetidae), **8 species**

Eastern Whipbird* *Psophodes olivaceus*
crested songbird of eastern Australia; has an amazing, loud *whip-crack* call

Cinnamon Quail-thrush* *Cinclosoma cinnamomeum*
brown, black, and white bird of stony deserts

■ **FAIRYWRENS** (Maluridae), **about 20 species**

Splendid Fairywren* *Malurus splendens*
male is a gorgeous little blue bird, the female duller; widely distributed in central and western Australia

Red-winged Fairywren* *Malurus elegans*
endemic to swamps and other thick-vegetation habitats of southwestern Australia

■ **THORNBILLS, SCRUBWRENS, AND ALLIES** (Acanthizidae), **about 45 species**

Fernwren* *Oreoscopus gutturalis*
small brown bird with a restricted range in northeastern mountain rain forests

Weebill* *Smicrornis brevirostris*
tiny and yellowish, resident in Australia's drier forests and woodlands; the smallest Australian bird

■ **AUSTRALIAN CHATS*** (Epthianuridae), **5 species**

Crimson Chat* *Epthianura tricoclor*
small, pretty songbird restricted mainly to open woodlands, grasslands, and scrub zones of interior Australia

■ **AUSTRALASIAN TREECREEPERS** (Climacteridae), **6 species**

White-throated Treecreeper* *Cormobates leucophaea*
small, common, upright bird that clings to tree bark; found in forests and woodlands of eastern Australia

■ **HONEYEATERS** (Meliphagidae), **about 70 species**

Pied Honeyeater* *Certhionyx variegatus*
black and white honeyeater from arid savanna and scrubland habitats of central Australia

New Holland Honeyeater* *Phylidonyris novaehollandiae*
black, white, and yellow honeyeater common over many portions of southern Australia

■ **BUTCHERBIRDS AND CURRAWONGS** (Cracticidae), **9 species;** **also called bellmagpies**

Pied Butcherbird* *Cracticus nigrogularis*
large black and white bird of woodlands, scrublands and agricultural areas; widely distributed over the continent

Black Currawong* *Strepera fuliginosa*
large, black, and crow-like with white wing and tail tips; endemic to Tasmania and nearby islands

■ **BIRDS-OF-PARADISE** (Paradisaeidae), **4 species**

Paradise Riflebird* *Ptiloris paradiseus*
bird-of-paradise with long downcurved bill and several iridescent patches; restricted to rain forest patches of central-eastern Australia

■ **BOWERBIRDS** (Ptilonorhynchidae), **10 species**

Regent Bowerbird* *Sericulus chrysocephalus*
males a striking black and yellow, females mainly mottled brown; occurs in eastern rain forests, orchards

Satin Bowerbird* *Ptilonorhynchus violaceus*
males glossy blue black, females greenish and brown; found in rain forest areas of the east and northeast

Green Catbird* *Ailuroedus crassirostris*
common bowerbird of temperate rain forest zones of the southeastern portion of the continent

Some Other Species Global Birders Often Seek

Magpie Goose *Anseranas semipalmata*
black and white goose with a knobbed head; found in northern Australia and New Guinea

Black Swan* *Cygnus atratus*
world's only all-back swan; wide-ranging in Australia and introduced to New Zealand

Wedge-tailed Eagle *Aquila audax*
largest Australian raptor, usually very dark, with a long, wedge-shaped tail; most habitats except rain forest

Brolga *Grus rubicunda*
tall, grayish crane with bare red skin on the head; shared only with New Guinea

Plains-wanderer* *Pedionomus torquatus*
uncommon to rare quail-like ground bird; the only member of endemic family Pedionomidae

Rainbow Pitta* *Pitta iris*
beautiful, endemic bird of the far north; found in thick scrub, rain forest, and mangrove edges

Noisy Scrub-bird* *Atrichornis clamosus*
rare, brown bird with a tiny coastal range; one of two scrub-bird species of endemic family Atrichornithidae

Hall's Babbler* *Pomatostomus halli*
brown and white bird with downcurved bill; one of Australia's four species of pseudo-babblers

Southern Logrunner* *Orthonyx temminckii*
small bird of rain forest floors; one of Australia's two members of the logrunner family (Orthonychidae)

Varied Sitella *Neositta chrysoptera*
small nuthatch-like forest bird; one of two sittella species

Gouldian Finch* *Chloebia gouldiae*
one of the world's most strikingly marked small birds; endemic to woodlands and grasslands of northern Australia

Restricted to Australia

Of intense birder interest are New Zealand's few species of native parrots, especially the Kakapo, Kea, and New Zealand Kaka.

NEW ZEALAND

EVEN THOUGH IT IS EXPENSIVE TO REACH FROM ALMOST EVERYWHERE, NEW ZEALAND is a wonderful travel destination. Indeed, many visitors believe its natural beauty to be unmatched—at least on this planet. As a birding destination, however, the country can best be said to be idiosyncratic. This is because its terrestrial avifauna is not extensive, but what does exist is interesting, sometimes spectacular, and usually endemic. Perhaps to make up for the comparative dearth of landbirds in New Zealand, many seabirds, shorebirds, and other water-associated birds are common and easily seen. About the size of Colorado in land area, New Zealand is a stable country, democratic, and, like nearby Australia, part of the British Commonwealth. Its international reputation is that of a beautiful, safe, out-of-the-way spot with tough environmental policies and a strong stance with respect to wildlife conservation. Self-travel in New Zealand is easy and, compared with many other international destinations, mid-priced. A good time to visit is October through February, when many of the local birds are breeding.

GEOGRAPHY AND HABITATS

New Zealand is positioned in the southern Pacific Ocean, more than 1,200 miles southeast of Australia. For the most part, the country consists of two large islands, North Island and South Island. The northern tip of North Island is approximately 1,000 miles from the southern tip of South Island. Many smaller islands, located at various distances from the main islands, are also part of New Zealand. These include the subtropical Kermadec Islands to the main islands' north, the temperate-zone Chatham Islands to the east, and the subantarctic Campbell Island group to the

OPPOSITE: **Lake Wakatipu** The scenery in New Zealand is often spectacular. Lake Wakatipu is located on South Island near Fiordland National Park. *New Zealand*

south. Some of these distant smaller islands are eagerly visited by birders to spot the few endemic species living there, but the information presented here concentrates on New Zealand's main islands.

North Island, somewhat smaller than South Island but with a larger human population, consists mainly of lower elevation areas; however, there are mountains in its central and southern expanses. Auckland, the country's largest city, is in the northern part of the island and Wellington, the capital, is in the south. The northern portion of the island, or Northland, is famous for its beaches, estuaries, and tall forests. Just south of Auckland, a large, shallow bay known as the Firth of Thames is a renowned sanctuary for migrant wading birds. Rotorua, an area popular with tourists for its hot springs and bubbling mud pools, is located near the center of North Island, and Urewera National Park, which contains North Island's largest area of intact forest and is one of New Zealand's largest national parks, lies on this island's eastern side.

South Island, however, is home to most of the stunning mountains, rugged fiords, and tranquil lakes typically seen in New Zealand travel advertising. The island is dominated by the Southern Alps, which form a lengthwise spine across this rectangular island. Substantial areas of South Island have been set aside as national parks and nature reserves, many of them still containing true wilderness areas. Outside of these preserves, much of the level land in South Island has been converted to ranching and farming. Important habitats in New Zealand are its abundant and always nearby coastal zones, freshwater wetlands including lakes and rivers, forests, and extensive alpine zones above the tree line in mountainous regions.

BIRDLIFE

The main thing to know about New Zealand's birdlife is that, like birdlife on many other of the world's islands, it has been significantly reduced in diversity and distribution ever since people arrived. Aside from the negative effects of habitat alterations caused by human settlements, logging and farming, the main injury to birdlife has been introduced predators that prey on birds and their nests. The list of predators brought to New Zealand by people, especially since the British arrived in the 1800s, is long. It includes rats, cats, dogs, ferrets, stoats, and weasels. These predators drove some species to extinction, a few as recently as the 1900s, and severely reduced the populations of many others.

Today, some of New Zealand's bird's survive only on small coastal or offshore islands, and only as a consequence of intensive conservation efforts that include the painstaking elimination of most predators. Examples are the Kakapo, a large, flightless, nocturnal parrot; the Stitchbird, a small black, brown, and yellow honeyeater;

LOCAL BIRDING & CONSERVATION ORGANIZATIONS

■ **MIRANDA SHOREBIRD CENTRE, NORTH ISLAND** (www.nzbirds.com/birding/miranda.html) shorebird information center, research outpost and birding lodge located on the Firth of Thames, a key migratory shorebird stopover site

■ **ORNITHOLOGICAL SOCIETY OF NEW ZEALAND** (www.osnz.org.nz) started in 1939 to encourage fieldwork on birds and now the country's premier bird organization

■ **FOREST & BIRD** (www.forestandbird.org.nz) founded in 1923, now helps protect New Zealand's native wildlife and wild areas

and the Saddleback, a striking forest songbird, and one of two species of an endemic family, the wattlebirds. Some of these islands are restricted nature reserves, usually closed to the public.

New Zealand's landbirds are largely resident, with no real seasonal changes in their distributions. Some species do show minor movement with season, either locally or altitudinally. Many of the wading birds present seasonally do migrate, to Australia or to the Northern Hemisphere for breeding.

Currently there are roughly 70 landbirds on and near New Zealand's main islands, of which about 40 are native; the rest are introduced from Australia, Asia, or Europe. About 25 of the landbird species are endemic. Other New Zealand birds total somewhat more than 100 species, and include seabirds, shorebirds, and waterbirds such as ducks, grebes, and rails. More than 30 of these are endemic to New Zealand or its nearby ocean waters. Some parts of New Zealand sport incredibly high densities of seabirds. For example, the Snares Islands, located off the southern tip of South Island and covering a total of about 1.5 square miles of dry land, are known globally for the density of their breeding seabirds, including millions of Sooty Shearwaters.

SPOTTING THE SOUTHERN BROWN KIWI

Although familiar icons of New Zealand, kiwis are very difficult to see in the wild. The Southern Brown Kiwi is the most common of the five kiwis, but even with this species, one's chances of seeing it are low. However, they do call loudly, and if you want to settle for hearing one, their vocalizations in the late austral winter (June–August) can be heard readily at numerous forest sites on both North and South Islands. The most reliable place to see them, however, may be on the beaches of Stewart Island (located off South Island's southern tip), where the population is estimated to be about 25,000. Although kiwis are mainly nocturnal, here they can also be active during the day.

The remote beaches of Mason Bay and Ocean Beach are accessible via hiking or boat. Instead of the hours-long hike to Mason Bay, we decided to take a boat at night to Ocean Beach. The sand here was covered with myriad kiwi tracks, reflecting the large numbers that emerge from the forest floor from twilight to dawn to feed on large sand insects. With the light from a powerful flashlight we swept the moonlit beach for no more than five minutes before a waddling Southern Brown Kiwi was interrupted in mid-grab at an insect. After a half hour more of slowly walking along the beach we spotted four more kiwis, none of which seemed upset at our presence. A few stocky brown birds cruising a beach—an unforgettable experience to a global birder. —D.P.

Southern Brown Kiwi This photograph was taken at Mason Bay on Stewart Island, home of the *lawryi* subspecies of Southern Brown Kiwi. *New Zealand*

Kiwis—now usually separated into five species—may be New Zealand's most famous avian inhabitants, but many visiting birders never spot these flightless brownish ground birds in the wild. This is because kiwis are now uncommon or rare, depending upon species, and have very limited distributions. They are also generally nocturnal, so one can understand why they are sometimes heard but not often seen. Birders look for them on Tiritiri Matangi Island (a small, tightly protected island 20 miles northeast of Auckland), on the western coast of South Island, on Kapiti Island near Wellington, and on Stewart Island, which is a larger island just off South Island's southern tip. The latter site may be the easiest place to see wild kiwis. About 25,000 Southern Brown Kiwis live on the island, and some of them often emerge onto beaches at night, where they can be spotted.

A key group for birders is the endemic passerines, especially some that are sufficiently common to be located by nonexperts. These include the Rifleman, Gray Gerygone (locally called Gray Warbler), Fernbird, Pipipi (or Brown Creeper), Whitehead, Tomtit, New Zealand Robin, Tui, and New Zealand Bellbird. Another group of intense birder interest is New Zealand's few species of native parrots, especially the Kakapo, Kea, and New Zealand Kaka, all of which are fairly large birds. The first

Yellow-eyed Penguin The nest of this species is a shallow bowl made of twigs, grass, and leaves, often concealed at the base of a tree or in dense vegetation. *New Zealand*

BIRDING THE OTAGO PENINSULA, SOUTH ISLAND

New Zealand's Otago Peninsula is an easily reached site where any birder can readily see two spectacular species: Yellow-eyed Penguin and Royal Albatross. The peninsula, just beyond the modest town of Dunedin in the southern portion of New Zealand's South Island, is one center of the country's conservation and nature tourism efforts. The Royal Albatross, the globe's largest albatross, breeds only on some New Zealand islands and at Taiaroa Head on Otago Peninsula. Here, an interpretive center and bird-viewing blind has been constructed, so that when these large birds nest, birders can approach fairly closely and gawk not only at the flying birds but at nest-tending individuals as well. The Royal Albatross Centre (http://www.albatross.org.nz/) is run by the nonprofit Otago Peninsula Trust. Albatross nesting activities can often be seen all year because young that hatch from eggs laid in October through December don't fledge until about eight months old.

The Yellow-eyed Penguin is a New Zealand endemic that breeds on some smaller islands off South Island and on South Island itself. Small colonies of this endangered species, which has a total population perhaps under 10,000, make their homes on the coast of the Otago Peninsula. Groups of individuals, after a hard day's fishing, emerge from the ocean in the late afternoon or early evening and waddle to their beachside nests or sheltering spots. These "penguin parades" are a treat to watch, and on the Otago Peninsula there are commercial viewing enterprises where you can watch the processions from the protection of a blind. Breeding is in September through March. —L.B.

Kea Bold and inquisitive, "cheeky" Keas are large alpine parrots found only on South Island. Their curiosity often leads them to pry apart the rubber parts of unattended cars and to carry off unguarded items of clothing. *New Zealand*

is very rare and difficult to see. The other two are more common and many visitors see them—the Kea in the alpine zone of South Island, and the New Zealand Kaka at, among other places, the Karori Wildlife Sanctuary not far from downtown Wellington or on Stewart Island.

First among New Zealand seabirds on many birders' wish lists are penguins. Several species occur in the country's surrounding waters and a few come ashore to breed. Three are New Zealand endemics, the Fiordland, Snares, and Yellow-eyed Penguins; the latter species is often easily seen (see sidebar, opposite). Other sought-after seabirds here include myriad tubenoses, including seven albatrosses typically seen only during pelagic birding cruises (the smaller ones are locally called mollymawks), several endemic cormorants (often called shags), and a few endemic shorebirds. One of the latter, a small gray and white wader with a black chest band is known as the Wrybill. It breeds on South Island and winters on North Island, and looks pretty uninteresting through a spotting scope until you realize that the tip of its black bill curves noticeably to the right—it's a truly unique bird!

A couple of large endemic and flightless rails also attract birder attention: the Weka, which is locally common, and the Takahe, now quite rare and endangered. A last group to point out is the sizable cohort of introduced birds, many from Europe or Australia. They don't really belong to New Zealand, but they're present, so birders unfamiliar with them can take advantage of the situation. These include a few Australian parrots, a European owl, and a bunch of European songbirds including the Eurasian Blackbird, Song Thrush, Dunnock, Eurasian Skylark, Chaffinch, Common Redpoll, European Goldfinch, European Greenfinch, and Yellowhammer.

FIELD GUIDE & SITE GUIDE BOOKS

■ *Hand Guide to the Birds of New Zealand* (2001)
H. Robertson and
B.D. Heather
Oxford University Press USA

■ *The Reed Field Guide to New Zealand Birds* (1999)
G. Moon
Stackpole Books

■ *Where to Watch Birds in New Zealand* (2007)
K. Ombler
New Holland Publishers

Significant Species
of New Zealand

ABOUT 50 FAMILIES FOUND IN THIS REGION

■ KIWIS* (Apterygidae), 5 species

North Island Brown Kiwi* *Apteryx mantelli*
endangered kiwi, flightless, restricted to isolated populations on North Island and some small offshore islands.

Great Spotted Kiwi* *Apteryx haastii*
uncommon kiwi of South Island, living in mountainous forest and subalpine zones; the largest kiwi

■ PENGUINS (Spheniscidae), 6 species

Snares Penguin* *Eudyptes robustus*
locally common endemic species with yellow crest; breeds on Snares Islands, south of South Island

Yellow-eyed Penguin* *Megadyptes antipodes*
endangered New Zealand endemic penguin; breeds on South Island and some other New Zealand islands

Little Penguin *Eudyptula minor*
fairly common penguin and the smallest penguin, found around New Zealand and southern Australia

■ ALBATROSSES (Diomedeidae), 7 species

Royal Albatross *Diomedea epomophora*
endemic breeder in New Zealand, but this huge seabird roams southern oceans

Shy Albatross *Thalassarche cauta*
locally common albatross, breeds on New Zealand subantarctic islands and Tasmania islands; also called Shy Mollymawk

■ PETRELS AND SHEARWATERS (Procellariidae), 25 species

Buller's Shearwater *Puffinus bulleri*
common endemic breeder with striking markings; migrates to the Northern Hemisphere in the austral winter

Sooty Shearwater *Puffinus griseus*
abundant dark shearwater, breeds in New Zealand, Australia, southern South America; also called Muttonbird

Fairy Prion *Pachyptila turtur*
small gray seabird, abundant in some of New Zealand's coastal areas

■ CORMORANTS (Phalacrocoracidae), 11 species

Spotted Shag* *Phalacrocorax punctatus*
slender gray cormorant with conspicuous black and white markings, yellowish feet; locally common

■ RAILS, CRAKES, AND COOTS (Rallidae), 7 species

Weka* *Gallirallus australis*
large flightless rail found in various habitats including forests, grasslands, and scrub; brownish and streaked

■ PARROTS, (Psittacidae), 6 species

Kea* *Nestor notabilis*
celebrated olive-colored parrot of high-elevation forests and alpine habitats of South Island

New Zealand Kaka* *Nestor meridionalis*
brownish or olive-colored forest parrot with reddish patches and white crown; locally common in some regions

Yellow-fronted Parakeet* *Cyanoramphus auriceps*
small, long-tailed yellow-green forest parrot; widespread but fairly uncommon

■ NEW ZEALAND WRENS* (Acanthisittidae), 2 species

Rifleman* *Acanthisitta chloris*
tiny forest songbird, New Zealand's smallest bird; male greenish and white, female brownish

South Island Wren* *Xenicus gilviventris*
uncommon small bird of alpine rocky areas on South Island

■ AUSTRALASIAN ROBINS (Petroicidae), 3 species

Tomtit* *Petroica macrocephala*
small, common, black and white songbird of forests and scrub areas

New Zealand Robin* *Petroica australis*
dark gray forest bird with an upright stance; generally uncommon

■ WHISTLERS AND ALLIES (Pachycephalidae), 3 species

Whitehead* *Mohoua albicilla*
small North Island songbird with a whitish head and underparts, pale brown upperparts; locally common

Pipipi* *Mohoua novaeseelandiae*
small, brown South Island songbird with gray face and neck; also called Brown Creeper

■ HONEYEATERS (Meliphagidae), 3 species

Tui* *Prosthemadera novaeseelandiae*
mid-size dark iridescent bird with white throat tufts; found in forests, parks, and gardens

Stitchbird* *Notiomystis cincta*
rare, striking, black, yellow, and brownish North Island songbird; now found only on small, predator-free islands

New Zealand Bellbird* *Anthornis melanura*
common greenish bird with a dark, forked tail; found widely on both main islands

■ **WATTLEBIRDS*** (Callaeidae), **2 species**

Kokako* *Callaeas cinereus*
endangered bluish gray bird with hanging blue wattles

Saddleback* *Philesturnus carunculatus*
rare black bird with a large brown back patch and rump

Some Other Species Global Birders Often Seek

New Zealand Grebe* *Poliocephalus rufopectus*
endemic small grebe; occurs only on North Island, mainly in lakes and ponds

Blue Duck* *Hymenolaimus malacorhynchos*
uncommon blue-gray duck with a pale bill; found chiefly in fast-flowing, high-elevation rivers and streams

New Zealand Falcon* *Falco novaeseelandiae*
medium-size falcon of forests and adjacent grasslands and agricultural areas; the country's only falcon

Black Stilt* *Himantopus novaezelandiae*
all-black stilt with reddish legs; fairly rare endemic species

Red-breasted Dotterel* *Charadrius obscurus*
endemic plover, often seems quite tame; also called New Zealand Dotterel

Wrybill* *Anarhynchus frontalis*
unusual, fairly common, endemic plover with right-curved bill tip

Black-billed Gull* *Larus bulleri*
common, pale gull endemic to New Zealand; found both coastally and inland

New Zealand Pigeon* *Hemiphaga novaeseelandiae*
New Zealand's largest and only endemic pigeon; metallic green above, white below

Long-tailed Koel *Eudynamys taitensis*
brown streaky and barred cuckoo with a long tail; also called Long-tailed Cuckoo

Fernbird* *Megalurus punctatus*
small brown-streaked wetland songbird that typically keeps to dense vegetation; an Old World Warbler, family Sylviidae

Gray Gerygone* *Gerygone igata*
common, small, gray songbird of forests, parks, and gardens; in family Acanthizadae; also called Gray Warbler

*Restricted to New Zealand

New Zealand Fantail Flitting from perch to perch, always on the lookout for flying insects, the fantail is not a shy bird and will often approach people. This New Zealand endemic is found on both North and South Islands. *New Zealand*

New Guinea's amazing avifauna is spearheaded by birds-of-paradise, with more than 30 of the family's 44 species occurring on the main island and most of the remainder on the small surrounding islands.

NEW GUINEA

SURELY ONE OF THE MOST EXCITING AND UNIQUE BIRDING DESTINATIONS WORLD-wide is the green, forested island of New Guinea. In the number and kinds of birds that can potentially be seen, and in the high degree of endemism, it is hard to beat. Because it is sometimes difficult to visit the western, or Indonesian, half of New Guinea, and the existing tourist infrastructure there is still relatively primitive, this account focuses mainly on the eastern half of the island, which is occupied by the Independent State of Papua New Guinea (PNG), a parliamentary democracy and a part of the British Commonwealth.

Before 1980, few international birdwatchers reached PNG, which meant that few were able to feast their eyes on most species of the avian world's most gorgeous representatives—the birds-of-paradise. Tourist services were primitive or nonexistent. Besides hotels in the capital, Port Moresby, and in some larger towns, there were few places to stay, and birding tours were almost unknown. Those who managed to birdwatch there were mainly limited to researchers, who stayed at established research stations or camped, government workers, and well-off travelers who could organize their own mini-expeditions of guides, porters, small-aircraft flights, and ground vehicles. Furthermore, there was little land set aside for nature observation; most of the island was divided into communal tribal areas where permission of tribal elders or councils was required for even modest land usage or passage—including for birdwatching. Outside of towns, local life was still fairly primitive, and there was occasional violence.

By the mid 1990s conditions for birders improved as some in PNG discovered their land's potential for ecotourism. Now, eco-lodges in various parts of the country

OPPOSITE: **Mountain Rain Forest** New Guinea's incredible biodiversity is due to a combination of its tropical location and varied topography. The early morning mist rises from this valley near Mount Hagen in Enga Province. *Papua New Guinea*

Crested Berrypecker This large, high-mountain species is placed in its own family (Paramythiidae) with one other New Guinea endemic, the Tit Berrypecker. *Papua New Guinea*

LOCAL BIRDING & CONSERVATION ORGANIZATIONS

■ **THE NATURE CON-SERVANCY PAPUA NEW GUINEA PROGRAM**
(www.nature.org/wherewe work/asiapacific/papuanew guinea/)
worldwide conservation organization; works with local PNG communities to protect threatened habitats

■ **RESEARCH AND CON-SERVATION FOUNDATION OF PAPUA NEW GUINEA**
(www.rcf.org.pg)
established in 1986 and now PNG's largest conservation organization; works on environmental education and conservation

■ **THE WILDLIFE CONSER-VATION SOCIETY**
(www.wcs.org)
with a global mission to preserve wildlife and wild place, helps establish environmental organizations in Papua New Guinea and also works to train future conservation leaders there

cater to nature travelers and there are a few local bird tour leaders. Many of the eco-lodges offer rustic accommodations (less-than-pristine thatched-roof cottages) and are fairly expensive, but they often have hiking and birding trails on their properties that provide birding access to a land that was previously off-limits to most global birders. Many birds-of-paradise breed from August through January, so that is a propitious period for birders to visit.

Other than Varirata National Park just outside Port Moresby, there are still few national parks or well-established wildlife reserves in PNG, so a lot of birding, even when conducted under the aegis of pricey professional birding tours, occurs along main roads. Be aware that there are problems with law and order in the country, official corruption is rife, a major road system is lacking, and a great many different languages are spoken. All but the most adventurous birders who want to visit PNG (or Papua) and birdwatch outside of main towns or resort areas should probably do so only as part of an organized tour group. Still, birders who make it to this exotic destination are usually richly rewarded with sightings of beautiful birds and many endemics, and the trip itself is sure to provide many lifelong travel memories.

AUSTRALASIA & THE TROPICAL PACIFIC

GEOGRAPHY AND HABITATS

The huge island of New Guinea, 1,600 miles long and 317,000 square miles in area (the size of Texas plus Iowa), is situated in the Pacific Ocean just north of Australia and south of the Equator. The country of Papua New Guinea, at 179,000 square miles (a little larger than California), occupies the eastern half of the island. The land is mostly mountainous, about 65 percent at elevations above 1,000 feet and about 15 percent above 5,000 feet. New Guinea, with one mountain peak rising to about 16,500 feet, is the "highest" island on Earth. The tallest mountains, along with their passes and valleys, constitute a broad highland region that runs east to west across the island's center. Lowland regions, including broad river floodplains and abundant swamplands, predominate in the southern portion of the island and in coastal areas. Rain forest covers more than 70 percent of the island, from lowlands to about 10,000 feet in elevation. In addition to rain forest, other major habitat types are swamp forest, mangrove forest along the coasts (complete with plentiful saltwater crocodiles), open woodlands, and subalpine meadows. Also, grasslands occur in and around long-settled regions, including the mountain valley areas.

BIRDING THE TARI VALLEY

Tari is a village in a remote valley of Papua New Guinea's Southern Highlands Province. People there, the Huli, have only been exposed to the outside world for a generation. Although thousands of years of cultivation have modified many parts of the valley, spectacular native birds occur in the valley's forest patches as well as in nearby extensive forest at higher elevations.

Because of a long practice of intensive hunting in the area, birds tend to be extremely shy and reclusive. Thus, birding here and, in fact, in much of Papua New Guinea, is often more difficult than in most other tropical forests. Nevertheless, in forest patches of the village environs are Superb Bird-of-paradise, Blue Bird-of-paradise and Lawes' Parotia (also a bird-of-paradise). Higher up in the area, on the forested ridges of the Müller Range, Mount Kerewa, and the Doma Peaks, there are another 12 species

of birds-of-paradise as well as hundreds of additional highland species, many of them endemic.

At the Ambua Lodge, an ecolodge situated at 6,800 feet and overlooking the Tari Valley, the forest is full of parrots, doves, flycatchers, and babblers. Specialties here include New Guinea Eagle, Feline Owlet-Nightjar, Shovelbilled Kookaburra, Papuan Whipbird, and several birds-of-paradise including Ribbon-tailed Astrapia, Princess Stephanie's Astrapia, King-of-Saxony Bird-of-paradise, Black Sicklebill and Brown Sicklebill. Even higher in the mountains nearby, in an area called the Tari Gap, are grasslands and forest patches with even more endemics and specialties. It's simply a terrific region for birding. —D.P.

King-of-Saxony Bird-of-paradise The male's head plumes are some of the most extraordinary in the bird world. This bird is on his display perch. *Papua New Guinea*

291

BIRDLIFE

About 800 bird species are found on and around the large island of New Guinea and its nearby satellite islands (excluding the Bismarck Archipelago and Solomon Islands), and about half are endemic. PNG has more than 700 species, about 75 endemic to PNG itself. Of the 800 New Guinea birds, about 650 are breeding land-birds or freshwater birds and 40 are seabirds. The remainder are migrants, either those that arrive from more northerly breeding zones to spend the winter, such as many shorebirds, or those coming from Australia to spend nonbreeding periods. Birds in the latter group include both waterbirds such as egrets and ibises, and land-birds including bee-eaters, kingfishers, cuckoos, and pittas.

Like Australian birds, New Guinea's birds are known for their sedentary lifestyles, although at times some species leave their territories to wander. For example, some of the pigeons and fruit-doves, as well as some lories and lorikeets, are known to roam in flocks from place to place as they search seasonally for food resources such as flowers and fruits. Also like the Australian avifauna, New Guinea's birds include a lot of nectar-eaters. These encompass more than 20 species of lories and lorikeets, small

Hooded Pitohui Found from mid-elevations to lowland areas on New Guinea and Yapen Island, this species usually hides in thickets. *Papua New Guinea*

SPOTTING THE HOODED PITOHUI, THE POISON BIRD

There are six species of pitohuis, all are endemic to New Guinea. These birds (members of the Australasian whistler family Pachycephalidae) are relatively common forest inhabitants and travel in small flocks. While studying bird ecology in lowland Papua New Guinea, I removed a Hooded Pitohui from one of my mist nets. After I had weighed and measured the bird, I let it go. A few minutes later, my fingers started to tingle. For years people handling these birds have complained of numbness and tingling sensations. A chemical analysis in 1992 of three of these species showed that their skin and feathers contained a powerful poison, homobatrachotoxin, which is part of the same family of steroidal alkaloid chemicals found in the poison-arrow frogs of Central and South America.

Apparently the Hooded Pitohui acquires its poison from poisonous beetles it eats.

Like many other poisonous animals, this bird advertises its defensive chemicals by being obvious, in this case by having a strong smell and bright orange and black plumage. With these strong signals, even predators that are not too smart can learn to avoid the Hooded Pitohui after a single close encounter. Similar coloration and smells in the other two species of poisonous pitohuis may be of mutual advantage: a predator only has to learn the noxiousness of these birds from encountering one individual, and the lesson can be extended to the other poisonous species because they are so similar in form and color. Some scientists think these poisons may also repel feather mites and other parasites from these birds. One other New Guinea bird, the Blue-capped Ifrita (of the quail-thrush family Eupetidae), is now known to have this poison in its skin as well. —D.P.

and medium-size parrots that feed primarily on nectar and pollen, and more than 60 species of honeyeaters. Another interesting characteristic of the New Guinea avifauna is the presence a large number of bird species that eat only fruit—which is fairly rare in the bird world. Most notable among the fruit-eaters are approximately 15 species of fruit-doves (genus *Ptilinopus*), attractive green pigeons, often with patches of red and yellow in their plumage.

New Guinea's amazing avifauna is spearheaded by birds-of-paradise, with more than 30 of the family's 44 species occurring on the main island and most of the remainder on the small surrounding islands. This cohort of birds-of-paradise often overshadows all other New Guinea birds; bird tours to the region strongly emphasize finding and watching them.

But a host of other kinds of birds, including many glorious ones, are found here. For instance, bowerbirds are strongly represented in New Guinea, with 12 of the family's 20 species present, including the group's most flamboyant member, the Flame Bowerbird. Other important New Guinea bird groups that strongly attract birder interest are cassowaries, with all three existing species found on the island; megapodes (or mound-builders), with 7 of the world's 21 species occurring on the island; and the three crowned-pigeon species, spectacularly large pigeons with bushy crests. Parrots are particularly well represented in New Guinea, with about 45 species. These include tiny pygmy-parrots only 3.5 inches in length, large cockatoos, and the world's four species of tiger-parrots, smallish parrots of higher elevation sites that are mainly green with black barring. Kingfishers are another group characteristic of New Guinea, with more than 20 species, including several paradise-kingfishers that have striking long tails, and four of the globe's five kookaburra species.

Among the passerine birds, aside from the super-charismatic birds-of-paradise and bowerbirds, significant groups include honeyeaters and fairywrens as well as other families limited to the Australasian region. Some of these families are: Australasian robins (Petroicidae), Australasian treecreepers (Climacteridae), logrunners (Orthonychidae), Australo-Papuan babblers (Pomatostomidae), thornbills (Acanthizidae), a family that includes mouse-warblers, scrubwrens, and numerous gerygones.

Finally, there are two wholly endemic bird families in New Guinea. They are little known, and their classification is controversial. Melanocharitidae contains six species of berrypeckers and four called longbills. Paramythiidae contains the Crested and Tit Berrypeckers. They range in length from the tiny Pygmy Longbill at 2.8 inches, to the Crested Berrypecker at 8 inches. Most are plainly marked, but the Crested and Tit Berrypeckers are brightly colored. Berrypeckers occupy forested habitats, from lowlands to high altitudes; most flit about the forest understory or favor forest edges.

**FIELD GUIDE
& SITE GUIDE BOOKS**

■ *Birds of New Guinea, 2nd ed.* (2010)
B. Beehler, T.K. Pratt, and D.A. Zimmerman
Princeton University Press

■ *Birds of New Guinea and the Bismarck Archipelago: A Photographic Guide* (2001)
B.J. Coates and W.S. Peckover
Dove Publications

Significant Species
of New Guinea

82 FAMILIES FOUND IN THIS REGION

■ **CASSOWARIES** (Casuariidae), **3 species**

Dwarf Cassowary* *Casuarius bennetti*
large, Ostrich-like bird, the smallest of the three cassowaries; found in forests of hills and mountains

■ **MEGAPODES** (Megapodidae), **9 species**

Wattled Brush-Turkey* *Aepypodius arfakianus*
blackish megapode of mountain areas; during breeding
male has a bright red comb and neck wattle

Black-billed Brush-Turkey* *Talegalla fuscirostris*
common but secretive megapode of rain forest areas;
mainly black and grayish

New Guinea Scrubfowl* *Megapodius affinis*
megapode of low and middle-elevation rain forests;
fairly widespread and common

■ **PIGEONS AND DOVES** (Columbidae), **about 45 species**

Pheasant Pigeon* *Otidiphaps nobilis*
large, chicken-like ground pigeon with a tail unique for
a pigeon, compressed side-to-side

Victoria Crowned-Pigeon* *Goura victoria*
huge, spectacularly crested pigeon of lowland forests
and swamps

Orange-fronted Fruit-Dove* *Ptilinopus aurantiifrons*
small pigeon of lowland forests and woodlands; green
with orange forehead and white throat

Collared Imperial-Pigeon* *Ducula mullerii*
large lowland rain forest pigeon usually found near
water or mangroves

■ **PARROTS** (Psittacidae), **about 45 species**

Papuan Lorikeet* *Charmosyna papou*
mountain parrot with a long streamer tail; green above,
red and black below

Pesquet's Parrot* *Psittrichas fulgidus*
large red and black parrot of middle-elevation forests

Edward's Fig-Parrot* *Psittaculirostris edwardsii*
small, chunky, fig-eating parrot of lowlands and foothills;
green with yellow, blue, and red markings

Madarasz's Tiger-Parrot* *Psittacella madaraszi*
small forest parrot of middle elevations; male green
with a brown head, female has a black-and-green-
barred back

■ **OWLET-NIGHTJARS** (Aegothelidae), **7 species**

Barred Owlet-Nightjar* *Aegotheles bennettii*
small owl-like nocturnal bird of lowland forests; vermicu-
lated dark brown above, lighter below

■ **KINGFISHERS** (Alcedinidae), **22 species**

Rufous-bellied Kookaburra* *Dacelo gaudichaud*
widespread, striking, blue-winged kingfisher with black
head, white neck and throat, reddish brown chest

Shovel-billed Kookaburra* *Clytoceyx rex*
large, heavy-bodied kingfisher with massive bill; occurs
predominantly in middle-elevation wet forests

Blue-black Kingfisher* *Todiramphus nigrocyaneus*
generally uncommon; strikingly marked lowland kingfisher
of blue, back, and white

Hook-billed Kingfisher* *Melidora macrorrhina*
mostly brown kingfisher with a particularly heavy, hooked
bill; common and widespread

Brown-headed Paradise-Kingfisher* *Tanysiptera danae*
smaller, very long-tailed, particularly attractive kingfisher;
forest resident of extreme eastern New Guinea

■ **AUSTRALASIAN ROBINS** (Petroicidae), **about 25 species**

Lesser Ground-Robin* *Amalocichla incerta*
small brownish bird of mountain forest floors; generally
uncommon and difficult to locate

White-winged Robin* *Peneothello sigillata*
small mountain robin, predominantly black with white wing
patches; fairly common

■ **AUSTRALASIAN WHISTLERS AND ALLIES** (Pachycephalidae),
about 25 species

Golden-backed Whistler* *Pachycephala aurea*
small, mainly black and yellow bird inhabiting vegetation
around lakes and rivers

Hooded Pitohui* *Pitohui dichrous*
small, fairly common, forest songbird, reddish brown with
black head, wings, tail

■ **WHIPBIRDS AND QUAIL-THRUSHES** (Eupetidae), **7 species**

Papuan Whipbird* *Androphobus viridis*
rare, little-known, olive-green bird of mountain forests;
occurs only in widely scattered localities in New Guinea

Painted Quail-thrush* *Cinclosoma ajax*
rain forest ground-dweller that occurs only in a few
regions of New Guinea; generally shy and difficult to find

Chestnut-backed Jewel-babbler* *Ptilorrhoa castanonota*
striking, fairly common but elusive forest bird in blue,
white, reddish brown, and black

■ **BERRYPECKERS AND LONGBILLS*** (Melanocharitidae), **10 species**

Black Berrypecker* *Melanocharis nigra*
common, widely distributed berrypecker, chiefly of lowland rain forests; male black above, dark gray below

Slaty-chinned Longbill* *Toxorhamphus poliopterus*
forest bird of middle and higher elevations; mainly olive-
green and gray with very long, thin, downcurved bill

■ **CRESTED AND TIT BERRYPECKERS*** (Paramythiidae), **2 species**

Crested Berrypecker* *Paramythia montium*
colorful berrypecker of high mountain areas; occurs in
mossy forests and alpine thickets

■ **HONEYEATERS** (Meliphagidae), **about 60 species**

Red Myzomela *Myzomela cruentata*
very small rain forest honeyeater; male all red, female
mostly brownish

Belford's Melidectes* *Melidectes belfordi*
large, long-billed honeyeater with blue eye patch, from
the mountain forests of central New Guinea

■ **BIRDS-OF-PARADISE** (Paradisaeidae), **38 species**

Ribbon-tailed Astrapia* *Astrapia mayeri*
highland species, dark and iridescent; male sports
incredibly long, white tail streamers

Carola's Parotia* *Parotia carolae*
dark bird-of-paradise of middle elevation forests; male
has long, thin head plumes, yellowish "whiskers," and
iridescent breast shield

King Bird-of-Paradise* *Cicinnurus regius*
small species of lowland rainforest; male red and white
with long tail "wires"

Twelve-wired Bird-of-Paradise* *Seleucidis melanoleucus*
shy lowland species of dense rain forests; male
blackish and yellow with 12 wire-like feather shafts trail-
ing behind it

Raggiana Bird-of-Paradise* *Paradisaea raggiana*
common, widespread bird-of-paradise of lowland forests; male has long, ostentatious, reddish side plumes

■ **BOWERBIRDS** (Ptilonorhynchidae), **12 species**

Flame Bowerbird* *Sericulus aureus*
generally uncommon bird of forests of southern New
Guinea; male mainly orange and yellow, female brownish and yellow

Fire-maned Bowerbird* *Sericulus bakeri*
mid-elevation forest species found only in a northern
corner of New Guinea; male black with orangish frilly
"cape" and yellow wing patch

Some Other Species Global Birders Often Seek

Forest Bittern* *Zonerodius heliosylus*
little-known species, endemic to lowland forest streams
and rivers; also called New Guinea Tiger-Heron

Salvadori's Teal* *Salvadorina waigiuensis*
uncommon alpine duck found in lakes and streams,
often above 10,000 feet

New Guinea Eagle* *Harpyopsis novaeguineae*
large, broad-winged, mainly rain forest raptor with an
erectile crest; dark above, light below

New Guinea Flightless Rail* *Megacrex inepta*
large, dark ground bird of lowland wet thickets, swamp
forests; has a robust bill and long, heavy legs

Long-billed Cuckoo* *Rhamphomantis megarhynchus*
rare forest cuckoo found in scattered localities on the
island of New Guinea

Moustached Treeswift *Hemiprocne mystacea*
beautiful, widespread swift-like bird with long scissor-
tail; one of only four treeswift species

Blyth's Hornbill *Aceros plicatus*
New Guinea's only hornbill (also called Papuan Hornbill), fairly common; black with a white tail

Red-bellied Pitta *Pitta erythrogaster*
colorful, secretive bird of the forest floor; also found in
Philippines, parts of Indonesia, Australia

Northern Logrunner* *Orthonyx novaeguineae*
small forest ground bird of middle and some higher
elevations; generally scarce and hard to find

Wallace's Fairywren* *Sipodotus wallacii*
inconspicuous rain forest fairywren with a reddish brown
back; one of five fairywrens in New Guinea

Black Sitella* *Neositta miranda*
small bird of high mountain forests; mainly black with
red or pinkish forehead and chin; one of two species in
the sitella family

Torrent-lark* *Grallina bruijni*
black and white bird found near fast-flowing streams at
mid elevations in forest and grassland areas; one of two
species in the mudnest-builders family

Lowland Peltops* *Peltops blainvillii*
small, striking, large-headed bird, black with white and
red patches; member of the butcherbird family

Restricted to New Guinea

The forest-dwelling honeycreepers are Hawaii's most sought-after birds.

HAWAII & OTHER TROPICAL PACIFIC ISLANDS

T HE PACIFIC OCEAN COVERS OVER ONE THIRD OF THE EARTH'S SURFACE. Within this vast expanse of water there are scattered about 10,000 islands. None of the tropical Pacific islands are very large and many are very small—the largest is the Big Island of Hawaii, which is about twice the size of Delaware. Many seabird species are found across the region, but most of the native landbirds have very restricted ranges (often a single island) and are nonmigratory.

HAWAII

The Hawaiian Islands, of course, constitute one of the capitals of mass tourism, with beach resorts, water sports and scenic coastal vistas as main attractions. But these heavily visited tropical islands also have many wonderful natural areas that can be reached and enjoyed with only minor effort. What's more, because most tourists to these islands tend to remain on or near the ocean beaches, many of the native forests and other splendid habitats that attract birders are relatively lightly visited.

Among the most spectacular of Hawaii's natural sites, and great birding locations, are three parks: Kauai's Kokee State Park has trails with sweeping views and access to stunning high-elevation habitats, which are among the best places to see some of Hawaii's native forest songbirds—small brightly-colored birds, many them highly endangered, that live nowhere else on Earth. Maui's Haleakala National Park features gorgeous high-elevation tropical forest habitats. The Big Island's Hawaii Volcanoes National Park has striking volcanic landscapes, hiking trails that cross still steaming volcanic craters, an active volcanic vent chugging out lava, and all-but-deserted trails through native forests packed with endemic wildlife.

OPPOSITE: **Kokee State Park** In addition to spectacular views of the Kalalau Valley, the higher elevations of this park, located on the island of Kauai, offer great birding for native Hawaiian song-birds. *Hawaii*

Add to these amazing natural sites the facts that reaching Hawaii, for many people, is relatively inexpensive and that accommodations in the state span the range of prices, and you can begin to see why visiting Hawaii for birding might be an attractive option. Hawaii's forest birds breed in late winter through spring, its seabirds breed from February/March through August/September, and migrant ducks and shorebirds are seen mainly during winter—so birders can have a splendid time in Hawaii at almost any time of year.

OTHER TROPICAL PACIFIC ISLANDS

Aside from Hawaii, birders visit a number of other islands or island groups in the tropical Pacific, where they enjoy wonderful surroundings and can search for island endemics. A few examples: Independent State of Samoa (Western Samoa) has endemics including Tooth-billed Pigeon, Flat-billed Kingfisher, Samoan Triller, Samoan Fantail, Samoan Flycatcher, and Samoan White-eye. Fiji features endemics including Golden Dove, Peale's Imperial-Pigeon, Collared Lory, Masked Shining-Parrot, Long-legged Warbler, Silktail (a monarch flycatcher), Kadavu Honeyeater, and Fiji Parrotfinch. New Caledonia's endemics include Caledonia Goshawk, Kagu (an endangered flightless species placed in its own family), Cloven-feathered Dove, New Caledonian Imperial-Pigeon, New Caledonian Parakeet, New Caledonian Friarbird, and New Caledonian Crow.

GEOGRAPHY AND HABITATS

Few terrestrial sites on this planet are more isolated than the Hawaiian Islands, which arose relatively recently in the middle of the Pacific Ocean owing to underwater volcanic activity. They are more than 2,000 miles from North America, 3,500 miles from Japan, and 1,800 miles from their nearest island neighbors (the Marquesas). The Hawaiian archipelago runs from northwest to southeast in a chain approximately 1,550 miles long, straddling the Tropic of Cancer, the northernmost limit of the tropics.

Most of the islands are in the northwestern portion of the chain (called the Northwestern Hawaiian Islands). They include such out-of-the-way spots as Midway Atoll, Laysan Island, French Frigate Shoals, and Kure Atoll that barely rise above the waves. The Northwestern Hawaiian Islands are known mainly to birders interested in seeing seabirds such as the albatrosses and shearwaters that nest there.

The Hawaiian Islands in total encompass a land area of 6,425 square miles. The Northwestern chain, now a U.S. wildlife refuge, occupies less than one percent of Hawaii's landmass, while more than 99 percent is contained within the eight main islands that lie at the southeastern end of the chain. These eight include two very

LOCAL BIRDING & CONSERVATION ORGANIZATIONS

■ **BISHOP MUSEUM** (www.bishopmuseum.org) a center of biological research and conservation; many online seminars and publications

■ **HAWAII AUDUBON SOCIETY** (www.hawaiiaudubon.com) Hawaii's Audubon chapter; website recommends birding sites and tour companies

■ **HAWAII NATURAL HISTORY ASSOCIATION** (www.hawaiinaturalhistory .org) supports Hawaii's national parks, particularly by operating gift/bookshops at the parks

■ **THE NATURE CONSERVANCY OF HAWAII** (www.nature.org/hawaii; http://ice.ucdavis .edu/~robyn/tnch.html) works to protect Hawaii's native wildlife and plants; operates nature reserves and gives guided hikes at its reserves

small ones that few nonresidents reach and six larger islands that tourists regularly visit: Oahu, Molokai, Lanai, Maui, Kauai, and the Big Island of Hawaii. The latter three are the important birding destinations because Hawaii's surviving native bird species are mainly restricted to higher elevation sites on these islands.

Major Hawaiian habitat types are: lowland wet forests, found on all the main islands; lowland dry forests, heavily disturbed by the islands' human residents for more than a thousand years and now often sites for resorts and golf courses; and middle- and higher elevation forests, generally wet, but with rainfall not quite great enough to produce true "wet forest" habitat. Some of these middle- and higher elevation forests are the chief homes of Hawaii's remaining native songbirds.

On Maui and the Big Island there is striking subalpine scrub habitat and even true alpine zones around the uppermost sections of the highest peaks: Maui's Haleakala and the Big Island's Mauna Kea, Mauna Loa, and Hualalai. Open, grassy areas and shrublands are also found on portions of all the main islands. There is relatively little freshwater habitat in Hawaii.

BIRDING THE INDEPENDENT STATE OF SAMOA

Of all the islands of the Pacific I have visited, the Independent State of Samoa (Western Samoa), a former colony of New Zealand, comes closest, I believe, to providing a feeling of what natural Polynesia might have been like a hundred or more years ago. There are only 30 landbird species here, but almost half of them are endemic, including the spectacular Tooth-billed Pigeon (a dark, fruit-eating pigeon with a massive, hooked, orange bill). Three-quarters of the people of this country live on the small island of Upolu, and most of them are in the capital city of Apia. It is not difficult on Upolu to find forest patches in the higher elevations that have both undergrowth birds and canopy birds, but if you really want to take a step back in time and see what early explorers to Polynesia likely experienced, visit the island of Savai'i.

Savai'i is the third largest island in Polynesia after New Zealand and Tahiti, and there are daily flights and a ferry from Upolu. The facilities here tend toward basic, but the birdlife and natural areas are breathtaking. Although I found Samoans extremely friendly and welcoming, the one problem I did have in the country was an irritating habit of many young men: slinging small rocks at me for practice with their slingshots. They thought it was funny when I jumped, but they waved with friendly smiles as I disappeared into the forest looking for Samoan White-eye and Mao, an endemic Samoan honeyeater. —D.P.

Mao A blackish honeyeater that is found only on the islands of Savai'i and Upolu. The world population is thought to number about 500 birds. *Samoa*

BIRDLIFE

The great majority of Hawaii's 130 or so bird species can be divided into four main groups: 1) waterbirds and seabirds, 2) game birds, 3) non-native songbirds, and 4) native songbirds, including the famous Hawaiian honeycreepers.

Waterbirds and seabirds: Native—both resident and migratory—water-associated birds are seen along the islands' coasts and in nearshore and offshore areas This is varied group that includes the shorebirds, such as plovers, and a few freshwater marsh and pond birds such as herons, ducks, and geese. Seeing the endangered Nene, or Hawaiian Goose, that lives at high elevations on the islands of Hawaii and Maui is a desire of many visiting birders and usually easy to accomplish. The seabirds include, among other, albatrosses, frigatebirds, tropicbirds, terns, and noddies.

Game birds: Ten or more species of chicken-like landbirds live in Hawaii, including quail, pheasant, francolin, and turkey. All were introduced to the islands as game or ornamental birds, and some of them are now quite common.

Non-native songbirds: About 30 species of introduced perching birds, a few of them forest birds but many of them birds of open habitats, occupy the islands. Most of the

Laysan Albatross The main breeding colonies are on Midway and Laysan Islands, where pairs raise a single chick. When not breeding, this albatross ranges across the North Pacific. *Midway, Hawaii*

BIRDING LAYSAN ISLAND

When I was a university undergraduate I was invited to join a Smithsonian expedition to Laysan Island to band seabirds, one of my most exciting bird adventures ever. Laysan is only one mile wide and 1.5 miles long, and it has a salty lake at its center, one of only five natural lakes in all of the Hawaiian Islands. In the 19th and early 20th centuries, the huge numbers of seabirds here attracted guano miners ("guano" is the term used for old bird dropping deposits) and feather hunters. Besides killing thousands of birds, poachers also introduced rabbits to the island. These greedy herbivores quickly wiped out much of the vegetation and turned the island into a sand desert with periodic dust storms. In response, President Theodore Roosevelt in 1909 declared the island a part of the Hawaiian Islands Bird Reservation.

This preservation effort was too late to save three of the island's endemic landbirds

from extinction: Laysan Honeycreeper, Laysan Millerbird (an Old World warbler), and the flightless Laysan Rail. But still surviving is one of the avian world's truly spectacular sights: thousands of nesting Black-footed Albatross, Laysan Albatross, Christmas Shearwater, Wedge-tailed Shearwater, Masked Booby, Red-footed Booby, Magnificent Frigatebird, Sooty Tern, and White Tern. Laysan Island is also a wintering area for Bristle-thighed Curlew and Ruddy Turnstone. Years of pest elimination and exotic weed control on the island have helped native vegetation recover, and these native seabirds and shorebirds have prospered. In addition, two endemic landbirds survive, the Laysan Finch and Laysan Duck. The duck is particularly interesting; it is capable of flight but spends most of its time running up and down the salty lake's edge scooping up beaks-full of shore flies. —D.P.

Apapane This is the most abundant native songbird in the Hawaiian Islands and occurs in mountain forests on all the main islands. The flowering tree, called Ohia-lehua, often attracts honeycreepers like the Apapane. *Kauai, Hawaii*

songbirds routinely seen around Hawaiian towns and resorts were introduced to the islands during the past 150 years. Many of these species are securely established, and now permanently occupy the former habitats of native birds. In fact, Hawaii's most frequently seen songbirds—such as the Japanese White-eye and Common Myna—are aliens. Think of them as "bonus birds." Some, such as the White-rumped Shama, Red-billed Leiothrix, and Red Avadavat, are gorgeous species well worth seeking out.

Native songbirds: This group includes, among others, the forest-dwelling honey-creepers—Hawaii's most sought-after birds. These honeycreepers arose, apparently, when a single species of a finch-like bird long ago—perhaps more than three million years ago—left the North American mainland and, perhaps blown off course by a storm, eventually spotted Hawaii's volcanic islands jutting from the sea and settled there. There may have been no other forest-dwelling songbirds on the islands, so there may have been a complete lack of competition for resources and a wide assortment of "unfilled" ecological niches. That hypothetical single finch species, over evolutionary time, diverged into many different species, each suited to a different ecological niche, particularly with respect to feeding specializations.

The most obvious manifestation of this is the variety of bill shapes these birds developed to aid them in their foraging. Seed-eaters developed strong, stout, almost parrot-like bills, like the Palila; others that ate only insects, developed mid-size or longish downcurved bills to probe and grab bugs and their larvae on and under tree bark, like the Maui Parrotbill and Akipolaau; and some, feeding mostly on nectar but also grabbing some insects, developed long to short, narrow, downcurved bills, like the Iiwi and Apapane. Few of these birds are still common and widespread, but at least three, Apapane, Hawaii Amakihi, and Kauai Amakihi, are sufficiently abundant that all birders should be able to find them with minimal effort.

FIELD GUIDE & SITE GUIDE BOOKS

■ *The Birdwatcher's Guide to Hawai'i* (1996)
Rick Soehren
University of Hawaii Press

■ *Enjoying Birds and Other Wildlife in Hawai'i* (2002)
H. Douglas Pratt and Jacob Faust
Mutual Publishing

■ *A Field Guide to the Birds of Hawaii and the Tropical Pacific* (1987)
H. Douglas Pratt, et al.
Princeton University Press

■ *Hawaii's Birds, 5th ed.* (1997)
Hawaii Audubon Society

■ *Hawaii: Travellers' Wildlife Guide* (2006)
Les Beletsky
Interlink Books

Significant Species
of Hawaii

42 FAMILIES FOUND IN THIS REGION

■ **ALBATROSSES** (Diomedeidae), **3 species**

Laysan Albatross *Phoebastria immutabilis*
albatross most often seen from shore and commonest
albatross of the north Pacific; breeds in northwestern
Hawaiian Islands and elsewhere

■ **PETRELS AND SHEARWATERS** (Procellariidae), **9 species**

Newell's Shearwater* *Puffinus auricularis newelli*
endemic seabird; a subspecies of Townsend's
Shearwater that breeds only in Hawaii's high mountains

Hawaiian Petrel *Pterodroma sandwichensis*
endangered seabird that breeds in the crater of Maui's
Haleakala volcano and at similar sites in Hawaii; comes
to land at night

■ **TROPICBIRDS** (Phaethontidae), **2 species**

Red-tailed Tropicbird *Phaethon rubricauda*
coastal and pelagic seabird with very long red tail
streamers; breeds on small oceanic islands

White-tailed Tropicbird *Phaethon lepturus*
coastal and pelagic seabird of the tropics with very long
white tail streamers

■ **BOOBIES** (Sulidae), **3 species**

Red-footed Booby *Sula sula*
coastal and pelagic tropical seabird; usually nests and
roosts in trees

Brown Booby *Sula leucogaster*

coastal and pelagic seabird, but often found closer to
land than other boobies; nests on bare, rocky islands

■ **FRIGATEBIRDS** (Fregatidae), **1 species**

Great Frigatebird *Fregata minor*
large seabird with long wings and forked tail that soars,
sometimes in flocks, high over coastal zones

■ **GEESE AND DUCKS** (Anatidae), **15 species**

Nene* *Branta sandvicensis*
Hawaii's endangered endemic goose; also known
as Hawaiian Goose

Hawaiian Duck* *Anas wyvilliana*
endangered, female Mallard-like duck; restricted
to Oahu, Kauai, and the Big Island

■ **TERNS AND NODDIES** (Sternidae), **5 species**

Brown Noddy *Anous stolidus*
tern that nests in cliffs, trees, and on the ground; occurs
on and around many tropical and subtropical islands

Black Noddy *Anous minutus*
striking tern found along shorelines; nests in sea cliffs but
also on trees and bushes

White Tern *Gygis alba*
small all-white tern with a black bill; found in Hawaii both
coastally and inland

■ **THRUSHES** (Turdidae), **2 species**

Omao* *Myadestes obscurus*
native thrush, brownish above with a gray chest and belly;
found only on Hawaii's Big Island

■ **MONARCH FLYCATCHERS** (Monarchidae), **1 species**

Elepaio* *Chasiempis sandwichensis*
small, mainly brown and white songbird; Hawaii's only
native monarch flycatcher

■ **WAXBILLS** (Estrildidae), **10 species**

Lavender Waxbill *Estrilda caerulescens*
very small and bluish gray with a deep red rump; occurs
on the Big Island; introduced from Africa

Red Avadavat *Amandava amandava*
very small grassland and agricultural-area bird, introduced
from Asia; the male is reddish with white spots

■ **HAWAIIAN HONEYCREEPERS*** (Drepanididae), **about 17 species**

Palila* *Loxioides bailleui*
endangered yellow and gray Hawaiian honeycreeper

Maui Parrotbill* *Pseudonestor xanthophrys*
endangered Hawaiian honeycreeper with a parrot-like bill;
occurs in native forests at higher elevations on the Big
Island

Hawaii Amakihi* *Hemignathus virens*
common Hawaiian honeycreeper, small and yellowish
green; occurs at middle and higher elevations on several
of Hawaii's main islands

Anianiau*
tiny yellow or yellowish green Hawaiian honeycreeper
found only in native wet forests of Kauai

Akiapolaau* *Hemignathus munroi*
endangered honeycreeper with unique bill: the upper part is long, thin, and downcurved, while the lower part is shorter, thicker, and straight

Akepa* *Loxops coccineus*
very small Hawaiian honeycreeper from the Big Island and Maui; the male is reddish or orangish, the female greenish

Iiwi* *Vestiaria coccinea*
red and black Hawaiian honeycreeper with a long orange bill; occurs in native wet forests on all of Hawaii's main islands

Akohekohe* *Palmeria dolei*
endangered black honeycreeper found only on the slopes of the Haleakala volcano on Maui

Apapane* *Himatione sanguinea*
abundant, easily spotted honeycreeper, mostly red and blackish; found on all of Hawaii's main island.

Some Other Species Global Birders Often Seek

Hawaiian Hawk* *Buteo solitarius*
the islands' only native breeding raptor; typically occurs only on the Big Island of Hawaii

Hawaiian Coot* *Fulica alai*
endemic species similar to American Coot; found in lakes, ponds, marshes, estuaries on main islands

Pacific Golden-Plover *Pluvialis fulva*
overwintering Arctic breeder; favors grassy fields, lawns, golf courses on all main islands

Red-whiskered Bulbul *Pycnonotus jocosus*
introduced crested bulbul from Asia, now found on Oahu in parks, gardens, forests, suburbs

White-rumped Shama *Copsychus malabaricus*
introduced Asian species, an Old World flycatcher, family Muscicapidae; common on Kauai and Oahu

Red-billed Leiothrix *Leiothrix lutea*
beautiful small greenish bird with yellow throat and red markings; introduced Asian babbler

Yellow-fronted Canary *Serinus mozambicus*
small greenish and yellow finch of open woodlands and parks; introduced from Africa

Red-crested Cardinal *Paroaria coronata*
handsome gray and white cardinal with red head and crest; introduced from South America

*Restricted to Hawaii

Kauai Amakihi The Alakai Swamp (where this photograph was taken) is a protected highland area on the island of Kauai, and a stronghold for a number of Hawaii's endangered honeycreepers. *Kauai, Hawaii*

Appendix

SCIENTIFIC NAMES OF SPECIES MENTIONED IN THE TEXT

This appendix lists all the species mentioned in the text with their scientific names as they appear in *The Clements Checklist of Birds of the World*, 6th edition (Cornell University Press, 2007). It does not repeat the names of the birds that appear only in the Significant Species lists at the end of each sub-region. The scientific names for those species appear within those lists. The bolded entries indicate species that are illustrated with a photograph and the number of the page where that photograph appears. For ease of use, there is a separate list for each chapter, and the entries are alphabetized by each bird's English name.

■ **CHAPTER 1: BIRDING FROM A GLOBAL PERSPECTIVE**

Blackbird, Red-winged *Agelaius phoeniceus*
Blackbird, Yellow-headed *Xanthocephalus xanthocephalus*
Bowerbird, Regent *Sericulus chrysocephalus*
Condor, California *Gymnogyps californianus*
Coquette, Tufted *Lophornis ornatus* PAGE 13
Cowbird, Brown-headed *Molothrus ater*
Crane, Whooping *Grus americana* PAGE 13
Crow, American *Corvus brachyrhynchos*
Crow, Mariana *Corvus kubaryi*
Eagle, Bald *Haliaeetus leucocephalus*
Falcon, Peregrine *Falco peregrinus*
Grackle, Common *Quiscalus quiscula*
Hawk, Broad-winged *Buteo platypterus*
Hawk, Red-shouldered *Buteo lineatus*
Hornbill, Great *Buceros bicornis*
Kakapo *Strigops habroptila* PAGE 15
Kingfisher, Belted *Megaceryle alcyon*
Kingfisher, Malagasy *Alcedo vintsioides* PAGES 6-7
Liocichla, Bugun *Liocichla bugunorum* PAGE 23
Macaw, Hyacinth *Anodorhynchus hyacinthinus* PAGE 17
Macaw, Red-and-green *Ara chloropterus* PAGE 14
Owl, Great Horned *Bubo virginianus*
Owl, Snowy *Bubo scandiacus*
Parrot, Golden-shouldered *Psephotus chrysopterygius*
Penguin, King *Aptenodytes patagonicus* PAGE 20-21
Quetzal, Resplendent *Pharomachrus mocinno*
Robin, American *Turdus migratorius*
Roller, Indian *Coracias benghalensis* PAGE 19
Toucan, Keel-billed *Ramphastos sulfuratus* PAGE 12
Turkey, Wild *Meleagris gallopavo*
Warbler, Golden-winged *Vermivora chrysoptera* PAGE 11
Woodpecker, Pileated *Dryocopus pileatus*

■ **CHAPTER 2: THE GEOGRAPHY OF BIRDS**

Bellbird, Three-wattled *Procnias tricarunculatus* PAGE 30
Bowerbird, Golden *Prionodura newtoniana* PAGE 37
Broadbill, Green *Calyptomena viridis* PAGE 29
Bushshrike, Four-colored *Telophorus viridis* PAGE 31
Canastero, Dusky-tailed *Asthenes humicola*

Chilia, Crag *Ochetorhynchus melanurus*
Cockatoo, Palm *Probosciger aterrimus*
Crow, American *Corvus brachyrhynchos*
Emu *Dromaius novaehollandiae*
Falcon, Peregrine *Falco peregrinus*
Firecrown, Juan Fernandez *Sephanoides fernandensis*
Firecrown, Juan Fernandez *Sephanoides fernandensis* PAGE 40
Frigatebird, Great *Fregata minor* PAGE 24-25
Grackle, Great-tailed *Quiscalus mexicanus*
Gull, Swallow-tailed *Creagrus furcatus* PAGE 32
Huet-huet, Chestnut-throated *Pteroptochos castaneus*
Macaw, Hyacinth *Anodorhynchus hyacinthinus*
Mesia, Silver-eared *Leiothrix argentauris* PAGE 47
Mockingbird, Chilean *Mimus thenca*
Osprey *Pandion haliaetus*
Ostrich *Struthio camelus* PAGE 26
Parrot, St. Lucia *Amazona versicolor* PAGE 46
Penguin, Yellow-eyed *Megadyptes antipodes*
Plantcutter, Peruvian *Phytotoma raimondii* PAGE 39
Rayadito, Masafuera *Aphrastura masafuerae*
Secretary-bird *Sagittarius serpentarius* PAGE 38
Sparrow, House *Passer domesticus*
Spoonbill, Eurasian *Platalea leucorodia* PAGE 42
Starling, European *Sturnus vulgaris*
Swallow, Barn *Hirundo rustica*
Tapaculo, Ochre-flanked *Eugralla paradoxa*
Tapaculo, White-throated *Scelorchilus albicollis*
Tinamou, Chilean *Nothoprocta perdicaria*
Tit-tyrant, Juan Fernandez *Anairetes fernandezianus*
Tui *Prosthemadera novaeseelandiae* PAGE 41
Turca, Moustached *Pteroptochos megapodius*
Vanga, Chabert *Leptopterus chabert* PAGE 34
Woodpecker, Red-bellied *Melanerpes carolinus*
Wren, Carolina *Thryothorus ludovicianus*
Wren, South Island *Xenicus gilviventris* PAGE 33

■ **CHAPTER 3: MEXICO, CENTRAL AMERICA & THE WEST INDIES**

Aracari, Fiery-billed *Pteroglossus frantzii* PAGE 55
Bananaquit *Coereba flaveola*
Becard, Rose-throated *Pachyramphus aglaiae*

Blackbird, Cuban *Dives atroviolaceus*
Blackbird, Jamaican *Nesopsar nigerrimus*
Bobwhite, Black-throated *Colinus nigrogularis*
Booby, Blue footed *Sula nebouxii* **PAGE 68**
Booby, Brown *Sula leucogaster* **PAGE 68**
Brush-Finch, Rufous-capped *Atlapetes pileatus*
Bunting, Blue *Cyanocompsa parellina* **PAGE 71**
Bunting, Orange-breasted *Passerina leclancherii* **PAGE 75**
Cacique, Scarlet-rumped *Cacicus uropygialis* **PAGE 56**
Chachalaca, Plain *Ortalis vetula*
Chat, Gray-throated *Granatellus sallaei*
Chat, Red-breasted *Granatellus venustus* **PAGE 67**
Coquette, Short-crested *Lophornis brachylophus*
Crossbill, Hispaniolan *Loxia megaplaga*
Cuckoo, Bay-breasted *Coccyzus rufigularis*
Cuckoo, Squirrel *Piaya cayana*
Curassow, Great *Crax rubra* **PAGE 81**
Donacobius, Black-capped *Donacobius atricapilla*
Emerald, Cozumel *Chlorostilbon forficatus*
Euphonia, Antillean *Euphonia musica*
Euphonia, Scrub *Euphonia affinis*
Falcon, Laughing *Herpetotheres cachinnans*
Finch, Peg-billed *Acanthidops bairdii*
Flycatcher, Flammulated *Deltarhynchus flammulatus*
Flycatcher, Tufted *Mitrephanes phaeocercus*
Gnatwren, Long-billed *Ramphocaenus melanurus* **PAGE 66**
Grosbeak, Crimson-collared *Rhodothraupis celaeno*
Ground-Dove, Common *Columbina passerina*
Hawk, Crane *Geranospiza caerulescens*
Hawk, Roadside *Buteo magnirostris*
Heron, Boat-billed *Cochlearius cochlearius* **PAGE 70**
Hummingbird, Amethyst-throated *Lampornis amethystinus*
Hummingbird, Blue-capped *Eupherusa cyanophrys*
Hummingbird, Cinnamon *Amazilia rutila*
Hummingbird, Fiery-throated *Panterpe insignis*
Hummingbird, Ruby-topaz *Chrysolampis mosquitus* **PAGE 86**
Hummingbird, White-tailed *Eupherusa poliocerca*
Hummingbird, Xantus's *Hylocharis xantusii* **PAGE 73**
Ibis, Scarlet *Eudocimus ruber* **PAGE 57**
Jay, Dwarf *Cyanolyca nana* **PAGE 80**
Jay, San Blas *Cyanocorax sanblasianus*
Jay, Silvery-throated *Cyanolyca argentigula*
Jay, Tufted *Cyanocorax dickeyi* **PAGE 72**
Jay, White-throated *Cyanolyca mirabilis*
Jay, Yucatan *Cyanocorax yucatanicus*
Junco, Volcano *Junco vulcani*
Kingbird, Gray *Tyrannus dominicensis*
Kingbird, Tropical *Tyrannus melancholicus*
Kingfisher, Belted *Megaceryle alcyon*
Macaw, Military *Ara militaris*
Macaw, Scarlet *Ara macao*
Magpie-Jay, Black-throated *Calocitta colliei*

Manakin, Red-capped *Pipra mentalis* **PAGE 78**
Motmot, Blue-crowned *Momotus momota* **PAGE 63**
Motmot, Russet-crowned *Momotus mexicanus*
Motmot, Turquiose-browed *Eumomota superciliosa*
Nightingale-Thrush, Russet *Catharus occidentalis*
Night-Heron, Black-crowned *Nycticorax nycticorax*
Oriole, Martinique *Icterus bonana*
Oriole, Montserrat *Icterus oberi*
Palmchat *Dulus dominicus* **PAGE 91**
Palm-Tanager, Black-crowned *Phaenicophilus palmarum*
Parakeet, Green *Aratinga holochlora*
Parakeet, Socorro *Aratinga brevipes*
Parrot, Imperial *Amazona imperialis*
Parrot, Lilac-crowned *Amazona finschi*
Parrot, Maroon-fronted *Rhynchopsitta terrisi* **PAGE 58**
Parrot, Puerto Rican *Amazona vittata* **PAGE 87**
Parrot, Red-crowned *Amazona viridigenalis*
Parrot, Rose-throated *Amazona leucocephala*
Parrot, St. Lucia *Amazona versicolor*
Parrot, St. Vincent *Amazona guildingii*
Parrot, Thick-billed *Rhynchopsitta pachyrhyncha*
Parrot, Yellow-headed *Amazona oratrix*
Parrotlet, Mexican *Forpus cyanopygius*
Parula, Tropical *Parula pitiayumi*
Potoo, Common *Nyctibius griseus* **PAGE 60**
Potoo, Northern *Nyctibius jamaicensis*
Quail, Montezuma *Cyrtonyx montezumae*
Quail, Scaled *Callipepla squamata* **PAGE 60**
Quail-Dove, White-fronted *Geotrygon leucometopia*
Quetzal, Eared *Euptilotis neoxenus*
Quetzal, Resplendent *Pharomachrus mocinno* **PAGE 79**
Robin, Clay-colored *Turdus grayi*
Seedeater, Blue *Amaurospiza concolor*
Shrike-Vireo, Green *Vireolanius pulchellus* **PAGE 66**
Silky-flycatcher, Gray *Ptilogonys cinereus* **PAGE 53**
Snowcap *Microchera albocoronata* **PAGE 61**
Solitaire, Rufous-throated *Myadestes genibarbis*
Sparrow, Sierra Madre *Xenospiza baileyi*
Sparrow, Striped *Oriturus superciliosus*
Swallow, Golden *Tachycineta euchrysea*
Swallow, Mangrove *Tachycineta albilinea*
Swift, White-naped *Streptoprocne semicollaris*
Tanager, Red-headed *Piranga erythrocephala*
Tanager, Rose-throated *Piranga roseogularis*
Thrasher, Cozumel *Toxostoma guttatum*
Thrasher, Gray *Toxostoma cinereum*
Thrush, La Selle *Turdus swalesi*
Thrush, Red-legged *Turdus plumbeus*
Tiger-Heron, Bare-throated *Tigrisoma mexicanum*
Tinamou, Thicket *Crypturellus cinnamomeus*
Tityra, Masked *Tityra semifasciata*
Tody, Broad-billed *Todus subulatus*

Puffbird, White-whiskered *Malacoptila panamensis* **PAGE 107**

Rhea, Lesser *Rhea pennata*

Sapayoa, Broad-billed *Sapayoa aenigma*

Screamer, Horned *Anhima cornuta* **PAGE 105**

Screamer, Northern *Chauna chavaria*

Screamer, Southern *Chauna torquata*

Sharpbill *Oxyruncus cristatus*

Sheathbill, Snowy *Chionis albus*

Skua, Brown *Stercorarius antarcticus*

Skua, South Polar *Stercorarius maccormicki*

Steamerduck, Flightless *Tachyeres pteneres*

Stork, Maguari *Ciconia maguari*

Stork, Wood *Mycteria americana*

Sunbittern *Eurypyga helias*

Swan, Black-necked *Cygnus melanocoryphus*

Tanager, Paradise *Tangara chilensis* **PAGE 113**

Tapaculo, Ocellated *Acropternis orthonyx* **PAGE 110**

Tern, Antarctic *Sterna vittata*

Tern, Arctic *Sterna paradisaea*

Toucan, Toco *Ramphastos toco*

Trumpeter, Gray-winged *Psophia crepitans* **PAGE 106**

Woodcreeper, Montane *Lepidocolaptes lacrymiger* **PAGE 108**

Woodpecker, Magellanic *Campephilus magellanicus*

■ **CHAPTER 5: EUROPE & THE MIDDLE EAST**

Accentor, Alpine *Prunella collaris*

Accentor, Himalayan *Prunella himalayana*

Accentor, Radde's *Prunella ocularis*

Bee-eater, European *Merops apiaster*

Blackcap *Sylvia atricapilla* **PAGE 161**

Bluethroat *Luscinia svecica* **PAGE 153**

Capercaillie, Eurasian *Tetrao urogallus* **PAGE 157**

Chickadee, Gray-headed *Poecile cincta*

Chough, Yellow-billed *Pyrrhocorax graculus* **PAGE 151**

Coot, Red-knobbed *Fulica cristata*

Crossbill, Red *Loxia curvirostra*

Crossbill, Scottish *Loxia scotica*

Duck, White-headed *Oxyura leucocephala*

Dunlin *Calidris alpina*

Dunnock *Prunella modularis* **PAGE 160**

Eagle, Booted *Aquila pennatus*

Eagle, Golden *Aquila chrysaetos*

Eagle, Imperial *Aquila heliaca*

Eagle, Short-toed *Circaetus gallicus*

Eagle, Spanish *Aquila adalberti*

Eagle, Steppe *Aquila nipalensis* **PAGE 174**

Eagle, White-tailed *Haliaeetus albicilla* **PAGE 156**

Eagle-Owl, Eurasian *Bubo bubo* **PAGE 157**

Eider, Common *Somateria mollissima*

Finch, Citril *Serinus citrinella*

Flamingo, Greater *Phoenicopterus roseus*

Flycatcher, Collared *Ficedula albicollis*

Flycatcher, European Pied *Ficedula hypoleuca*

Flycatcher, Semicollared *Ficedula semitorquata*

Fulmar, Northern *Fulmarus glacialis*

Gannet, Northern *Morus bassanus* **PAGE 146-147**

Garganey *Anas querquedula*

Godwit, Bar-tailed *Limosa lapponica*

Golden-Plover, Eurasian *Pluvialis apricaria*

Goose, Barnacle *Branta leucopsis*

Goose, Bean *Anser fabilis*

Goose, Graylag *Anser anser*

Goose, Lesser White-fronted *Anser erythropus*

Griffon, Eurasian *Gyps fulvus*

Gull, Audouin's *Larus audouinii*

Gull, European Herring *Larus argentatus*

Hawk, Rough-legged *Buteo lagopus*

Hoopoe, Eurasian *Upupa epops*

Hypocolius *Hypocolius ampelinus*

Ibis, Glossy *Plegadis falcinellus*

Kingfisher, Common *Alcedo atthis* **PAGE 152**

Kite, Black *Milvus migrans*

Kite, Red *Milvus milvus*

Kittiwake, Black-legged *Rissa tridactyla* **PAGE 165**

Knot, Red *Calidris canutus*

Lammergeier *Gypaetus barbatus*

Lark, Desert *Ammomanes deserti*

Lark, Horned *Eremophila alpestris*

Magpie, Azure-winged *Cyanopica cyanus* **PAGE 173**

Merganser, Common *Mergus merganser*

Murre, Common *Uria aalge*

Nightjar, Red-necked *Caprimulgus ruficollis*

Nuthatch Corsican *Sitta whiteheadi*

Nuthatch, Eurasian *Sitta europaea*

Nuthatch, Krueper's *Sitta krueperi*

Ostrich *Struthio camelus*

Owl, Barn *Tyto alba*

Owl, Great Gray *Strix nebulosa*

Owl, Long-eared *Asio otus*

Owl, Northern Hawk *Surnia ulula*

Owl, Short-eared *Asio flammeus*

Oystercatcher, Eurasian *Haematopus ostralegus*

Pipit, Meadow *Anthus pratensis*

Pipit, Rock *Anthus petrosus*

Pipit, Tawny *Anthus campestris*

Pipit, Tree *Anthus trivialis*

Pipit, Water *Anthus spinoletta*

Plover, Snowy *Charadrius alexandrinus*

Pochard, Common *Aythya ferina*

Pochard, Ferruginous *Aythya nyroca*

Pochard, Red-crested *Netta rufina*

Ptarmigan, Rock *Lagopus muta*

Puffin, Atlantic *Fratercula arctica* **PAGE 162**

Raven, Common *Corvus corax*
Razorbill *Alca torda*
Redpoll, Hoary *Carduelis hornemanni*
Roller, European *Coracias garrulus* **PAGE 175**
Ruff *Philomachus pugnax* **PAGE 164**
Scrub-Robin, Rufous-tailed *Cercotrichas galactotes*
Shearwater, Balearic *Puffinus mauretanicus*
Shearwater, Levantine *Puffinus yelkouan*
Shelduck, Common *Tadorna tadorna*
Shelduck, Ruddy *Tadorna ferruginea*
Shrike, Northern *Lanius excubitor*
Smew *Mergellus albellus*
Sparrowhawk, Levant *Accipiter brevipes*
Starling, Tristram's *Onychognathus tristramii*
Stork, Black *Ciconia nigra*
Stork, White *Ciconia ciconia* **PAGE 170**
Storm-Petrel, Leach's *Oceanodroma leucorhoa*
Swamphen, Purple *Porphyrio porphyrio*
Swan, Mute *Cygnus olor*
Swan, Tundra *Cygnus columbianus*
Swan, Whooper *Cygnus cygnus* **PAGE 154**
Teal, Marbled *Marmaronetta angustirostris*
Vulture, Cinereous *Aegypius monachus*
Vulture, Egyptian *Neophron percnopterus*
Wagtail, Citrine *Motacilla citreola*
Wagtail, Gray *Motacilla cinerea*
Wagtail, White *Motacilla alba* **PAGE 159**
Wagtail. Yellow *Motacilla flava*
Warbler, Dartford *Sylvia undata*
Warbler, Marmora's *Sylvia sarda*
Warbler, Sardinian *Sylvia melanocephala*
Warbler, Spectacled *Sylvia conspicillata*
Wheatear, Northern *Oenanthe oenanthe*
Wheatear, White-tailed *Oenanthe leucopyga*
Woodpecker, Black *Dryocopus martius* **PAGE 166**
Woodpecker, Gray-faced *Picus canus*
Woodpecker, Great Spotted *Dendrocopos major* **PAGE 158**
Woodpecker, Green *Picus viridis*
Woodpecker, Lesser Spotted *Dendrocopos minor*
Woodpecker, Middle Spotted *Dendrocopos medius*
Wren, Winter *Troglodytes troglodytes*
Wryneck, Eurasian *Jynx torquilla*

■ **CHAPTER 6: AFRICA**

Albatross, Light-mantled *Phoebetria palpebrata*
Albatross, Yellow-nosed *Thalassarche chlororhynchos* **PG. 208**
Asity, Sunbird *Neodrepanis coruscans*
Asity, Velvet *Philepitta castanea*
Asity, Yellow-bellied *Neodrepanis hypoxantha*
Barbet, Naked-faced *Gymnobucco calvus*
Barbet, Yellow-breasted *Trachyphonus margaritatus* **PAGE 192**

Bee-eater, Southern Carmine *Merops nubicoides* **PAGE 188**
Bee-eater, Swallow-tailed *Merops hirundineus* **PAGE 191**
Bee-eater, White-throated *Merops albicollis*
Bustard, Black *Eupodotis afra* **PAGE 189**
Bustard, Blue *Eupodotis caerulescens*
Bustard, Kori *Ardeotis kori* **PAGE 188**
Coua, Blue *Coua caerulea* **PAGE 183**
Coua, Red-breasted *Coua serriana*
Coua, Red-fronted *Coua reynaudii*
Coucal, Madagascar *Centropus toulou*
Cuckoo-Roller *Leptosomus discolor* **PAGE 206**
Fish-Eagle, African *Haliaeetus vocifer* **PAGE 186**
Flamingo, Greater *Phoenicopterus roseus*
Flamingo, Lesser *Phoenicopterus minor* **PAGE 182**
Francolin, Jackson's *Francolinus jacksoni*
Fulmar, Southern *Fulmarus glacialoides*
Gannet, Cape *Morus capensis*
Ground-Hornbill, Southern *Bucorvus leadbeateri* **PAGE 201**
Ground-Roller, Pitta-like *Atelornis pittoides* **PAGE 207**
Ground-Roller, Rufous-headed *Atelornis crossleyi*
Ground-Roller, Scaly *Brachypteracias squamiger*
Ground-Roller, Short-legged *Brachypteracias leptosomus*
Guineafowl, Vulturine *Acryllium vulturinum* **PAGE 187**
Hamerkop *Scopus umbretta*
Honeyguide, Greater *Indicator indicator* **PAGE 193**
Hornbill, Red-billed Dwarf *Tockus camurus*
Hornbill, White-thighed *Ceratogymna albotibialis*
Hornbill, Yellow-casqued *Ceratogymna elata*
Kestrel, Madagascar *Falco newtoni*
Lark, Dune *Calendulauda erythrochlamys*
Masked-Weaver, Vitelline *Ploceus vitellinus* **PAGE 194**
Mesite, Brown *Mesitornis unicolor*
Mousebird, Blue-naped *Urocolius macrourus*
Mousebird, Red-faced *Urocolius indicus*
Mousebird, White-backed *Colius colius* **PAGE 191**
Newtonia, Red-tailed *Newtonia fanovanae*
Nuthatch, Coral-billed *Hypositta corallirostris*
Ostrich *Struthio camelus*
Owl, Madagascar Red *Tyto soumagnei*
Oxpecker, Red-billed *Buphagus erythrorhynchus* **PAGE 184**
Paradise-Whydah, Eastern *Vidua paradisaea* **PAGE 195**
Paradise-Whydah, Long-tailed *Vidua interjecta*
Petrel, Antarctic Giant *Macronectes giganteus*
Petrel, Atlantic *Pterodroma incerta*
Petrel, Blue *Halobaena caerulea*
Petrel, Cape *Daption capense*
Petrel, Gray *Procellaria cinerea*
Petrel, Great-winged *Pterodroma macroptera*
Petrel, Hall's Giant *Macronectes halli*
Petrel, Kerguelen *Aphrodroma brevirostris*
Petrel, Soft-plumaged *Pterodroma mollis*
Petrel, White-chinned *Procellaria aequinoctialis*

Petrel, White-headed *Pterodroma lessonii*
Pitta, African *Pitta angolensis*
Prion, Broad-billed *Pachyptila vittata*
Pytilia, Green-winged *Pytilia melba*
Quelea, Red-billed *Quelea quelea*
Rail, Madagascar *Rallus madagascariensis*
Rockfowl, Gray-necked *Picathartes oreas* **PAGE 200**
Rockfowl, White-necked *Picathartes gymnocephalus*
Roller, Lilac-breasted *Coracias caudatus* **PAGE 192**
Roller, Racket-tailed *Coracias spatulatus*
Sandgrouse, Yellow-throated *Pterocles gutturalis*
Serpent-Eagle, Congo *Dryotriorchis spectabilis*
Serpent-Eagle, Madagascar *Eutriorchis astur*
Shearwater, Cory's *Calonectris diomedea*
Shearwater, Greater *Puffinus gravis*
Shearwater, Sooty *Puffinus griseus*
Shoebill *Balaeniceps rex* **PAGE 199**
Shrike, Magpie *Corvinella melanoleuca*
Sparrow, Swahili *Passer suahelicus*
Stork, Saddle-billed *Ephippiorhynchus senegalensis* **PAGE 185**
Storm-Petrel, European *Hydrobates pelagicus*
Storm-Petrel, White-bellied *Fregetta grallaria*
Storm-Petrel, White-faced *Pelagodroma marina*
Storm-Petrel, Wilson's *Oceanites oceanicus*
Sunbird, Anchieta's *Anthreptes anchietae*
Sunbird, Beautiful *Cinnyris pulchellus* **PAGE 194**
Sunbird, Golden-winged *Drepanorhynchus reichenowi*
Swamp-Warbler, Madagascar *Acrocephalus newtoni*
Trogon, Bare-cheeked *Apaloderma aequatoriale*
Turaco, Hartlaub's *Tauraco hartlaubi*
Turaco, Prince Ruspoli's *Tauraco ruspolii* **PAGE 190**
Turaco, Purple-crested *Tauraco porphyreolophus*
Vanga, Bernier's *Oriolia bernieri*
Vanga, Helmet *Euryceros prevostii* **PAGE 211**
Vanga, Sickle-billed *Falculea palliata*
Weaver, Spectacled *Ploceus ocularis*
Weaver, Village *Ploceus cucullatus*
White-eye, Madagascar *Zosterops maderaspatanus*
Whydah, Shaft-tailed *Vidua regia*

■ **CHAPTER 7: ASIA**
Albatross, Short-tailed *Phoebastria albatrus*
Barbet, White-cheeked *Megalaima viridis* **PAGE 242**
Bee-eater, Red-bearded *Nyctyornis amictus* **PAGE 249**
Bittern, Cinnamon *Ixobrychus cinnamomeus*
Bristlehead, Bornean *Pityriasis gymnocephala*
Broadbill, Long-tailed *Psarisomus dalhousiae* **PAGE 226**
Bulbul, Red-vented *Pycnonotus cafer* **PAGE 227**
Bulbul, Red-whiskered *Pycnonotus jocosus*
Bushtit *Psaltriparus minimus*
Bustard, Indian *Ardeotis nigriceps*

Chukar *Alectoris chukar*
Coucal, Greater *Centropus sinensis*
Coucal, Short-toed *Centropus rectunguis*
Crane, Black-necked *Grus nigricollis* **PAGE 234**
Crane, Common *Grus grus*
Crane, Demoiselle *Anthropoides virgo*
Crane, Red-crowned *Grus japonensis* **PAGE 222**
Crane, Sarus *Grus antigone* **PAGE 224**
Crane, Siberian *Grus leucogeranus*
Creeper, Brown *Certhia americana*
Cuckoo-shrike, McGregor's *Coracina mcgregori*
Drongo, Greater-Racket-tailed *Dicrurus paradiseus*
Eagle, Great Philippine *Pithecophaga jefferyi* **PAGES 246, 250**
Eagle, White-tailed *Haliaeetus albicilla*
Eagle-Owl, Spot-bellied *Bubo nipalensis*
Eared-Pheasant, Blue *Crossoptilon auritum*
Eared-Pheasant, White *Crossoptilon crossoptilon* **PAGE 216**
Fireback, Crested *Lophura erythrophthalma*
Fish-Eagle, Pallas' *Haliaeetus leucoryphus*
Fish-Owl, Blakiston's *Ketupa blakistoni*
Fish-Owl, Brown *Ketupa zeylonensis*
Florican, Bengal *Houbaropsis bengalensis*
Flycatcher, Black-and-rufous *Ficedula nigrorufa*
Flycatcher, Blue-and-white *Cyanoptila cyanomelana* **PAGE 232**
Flycatcher, Nilgiri *Eumyias albicaudatus*
Frogmouth, Ceylon *Batrachostomus moniliger*
Goose, Bar-headed *Anser indicus* **PAGES 213-213**
Grandala *Grandala coelicolor* **PAGE 217**
Grassbird, Broad-tailed *Schoenicola platyurus*
Ground-Cuckoo, Coral-billed *Carpococcyx renauldi* **PAGE 251**
Ground-Jay, Mongolian *Podoces hendersoni*
Groundpecker, Hume's *Pseudopodoces humilis*
Guillemot, Spectacled *Cepphus carbo*
Hawk-Eagle, Wallace's *Spizaetus nanus*
Honeyguide, Yellow-rumped *Indicator xanthonotus*
Hornbill, Indian Gray *Ocyceros birostris*
Hornbill, Malabar Gray *Ocyceros griseus*
Hornbill, Rhinoceros *Buceros rhinoceros* **PAGE 225**
Hornbill, Rufous-necked *Aceros nipalensis* **PAGE 238**
Hypocolius *Hypocolius ampelinus*
Ibisbill *Ibidorhyncha struthersii*
Jacana, Bronze-winged *Metopidius indicus*
Jacana, Pheasant-tailed *Hydrophasianus chirurgus*
Junglefowl, Gray *Gallus sonneratii*
Junglefowl, Red *Gallus gallus*
Kingfisher, Crested *Megaceryle lugubris*
Kite, Black *Milvus migrans* **PAGE 218**
Lark, Mongolian *Melanocorypha mongolica*
Laughingthrush, Chestnut-capped *Garrulax mitratus* **PAGE 221**
Laughingthrush, Wynaad *Garrulax delesserti*
Leafbird, Golden-fronted *Chloropsis aurifrons*
Leafbird, Orange-bellied *Chloropsis hardwickii* **PAGE 228**

Leiothrix, Red-billed *Leiothrix lutea*
Monal, Chinese *Lophophorus lhuysii*
Murrelet, Japanese *Synthliboramphus wumizusume*
Myna, Apo *Basilornis mirandus*
Myzornis, Fire-tailed *Myzornis pyrrhoura*
Nuthatch, Beautiful *Sitta formosa* **PAGE 241**
Openbill, Asian *Anastomus oscitans*
Parakeet, Malabar *Psittacula columboides*
Parrotbill, Spot-breasted *Paradoxornis guttaticollis* **PAGE 229**
Partridge, Tibetan *Perdix hodgsoniae*
Peafowl, Green *Pavo muticus*
Peafowl, Indian *Pavo cristatus*
Pheasant, Blood *Ithaginis cruentus* **PAGE 224**
Pheasant, Copper *Symaticus soemmerringii*
Pheasant, Golden *Chrysolophus pictus*
Pheasant, Green *Phasianus versicolor*
Pheasant, Lady Amherst's *Chrysolophus amherstiae*
Pheasant, Ring-necked *Phasianus colchicus*
Pheasant, Silver *Lophura nycthemera*
Pigeon, Nicobar *Caloenas nicobarica*
Pitta, Bar-bellied *Pitta elliotii*
Pitta, Blue-headed *Pitta baudii*
Pitta, Blue-winged *Pitta moluccensis* **PAGE 226**
Pitta, Garnet *Pitta granatina*
Pitta, Indian *Pitta brachyura*
Pond-Heron, Chinese *Ardeola bacchus*
Redstart, White-capped *Chaimarrornis leucocephalus*
Rhabdornis, Stripe-breasted *Rhabdornis inornatus*
Rosefinch, Przewalski's *Urocynchramus pylzowi*
Sandgrouse, Tibetan *Syrrhaptes tibetanus*
Scimitar-Babbler, Streak-breasted *Pomatorhinus ruficollis* **PG 228**
Scops-Owl, Collared *Otus lettia*
Scops-Owl, Sunda *Otus lempiji*
Scrubfowl, Nicobar *Megapodius nicobariensis*
Sea-Eagle, Steller's *Haliaeetus pelagicus* **PAGE 233**
Serpent-Eagle, Crested *Spilornis cheela*
Shearwater, Streaked *Calonectris leucomelas*
Shelduck, Ruddy *Tadorna ferruginea* **PAGE 212-213**
Shrike-Babbler, Green *Pteruthius xanthochlorus*
Snowcock, Tibetan *Tetraogallus tibetanus*
Stork, Painted *Mycteria leucocephala* **PAGE 220**
Stork, Woolly-necked *Ciconia episcopus*
Sunbird, Crimson-backed *Leptocoma minima*
Sunbird, Fire-tailed *Aethopyga ignicauda*
Sunbird, Gould's *Aethopyga gouldiae* **PAGE 243**
Sunbird, Mount Apo *Aethopyga boltoni*
Tit, Great *Parus major*
Tit, Marsh *Poecile palustris*
Tit, Rufous-vented *Periparus rubidiventris*
Tit, White-browed *Poecile superciliosa*
Tit-Warbler, Crested *Leptopoecile elegans*
Tragopan, Temminck's *Tragopan temminckii*

Treepie, White-bellied *Dendrocitta leucogastra*
Trogon, Malabar *Harpactes fasciatus*
Trogon, Ward's *Harpactes wardi*
Wallcreeper *Tichodroma muraria*
White-eye, Mindanao *Lophozosterops goodfellowi*
Wood-Pigeon, Nilgiri *Columba elphinstonii*
Wren-Babbler, Rufous-throated *Spelaeornis caudatus*

■ **CHAPTER 8: AUSTRALASIA & THE TROPICAL PACIFIC**
Akipolaau *Hemignathus munroi*
Albatross, Black-footed *Phoebastria nigripes*
Albatross, Laysan *Phoebastria immutabilis* **PAGE 300**
Albatross, Royal *Diomedea epomophora*
Amakihi, Hawaii *Hemignathus virens*
Amakihi, Kauai *Hemignathus kauaiensis* **PAGE 303**
Apapane *Himatione sanguinea* **PAGE 301**
Astrapia, Princess Stephanie's *Astrapia stephaniae*
Astrapia, Ribbon-tailed *Astrapia mayeri*
Avadavat, Red *Amandava amandava*
Bellbird, New Zealand *Anthornis melanura*
Berrypecker, Crested *Paramythia montium* **PAGE 290**
Berrypecker, Tit *Oreocharis arfaki*
Bird-of-paradise, Blue *Paradisaea rudolphi*
Bird-of-paradise, King-of-Saxony *Pteridophora alberti* **PG. 291**
Bird-of-paradise, Magnificent *Cicinnurus magnificus* **PAGE 271**
Bird-of-paradise, Raggiana *Paradisaea raggiana*
Bird-of-paradise, Superb *Lophorina superba*
Blackbird, Eurasian *Turdus merula*
Booby, Masked *Sula dactylatra*
Booby, Red-footed *Sula sula*
Bowerbird, Flame *Sericulus aureus*
Bowerbird, Regent *Sericulus chrysocephalus* **PAGE 270**
Bowerbird, Satin *Ptilonorhynchus violaceus*
Bristlebird, Western *Dasyornis longirostris*
Brush-turkey, Australian *Alectura lathami* **PAGE 264**
Budgerigar *Melopsittacus undulatus*
Butcherbird, Pied *Certhionyx variegatus*
Cassowary, Southern *Casuarius casuarius* **PAGE 264**
Catbird, Green *Ailuroedus crassirostris*
Chaffinch *Fringilla coelebs*
Chat, Crimson *Epthianura tricolor*
Cockatiel *Nymphicus hollandicus*
Cockatoo, Sulfur-crested *Cacatua galerita*
Crow, New Caledonian *Corvus moneduloides*
Crowned-Pigeon, Victoria *Goura victoria* **PAGE 265**
Curlew, Bristle-thighed *Numenius tahitiensis*
Dotterel, Inland *Peltohyas australis*
Dove, Cloven-feathered *Drepanoptila holosericea*
Dove, Golden *Ptilinopus luteovirens*
Duck, Blue *Hymenolaimus malacorhynchos*
Duck, Laysan *Anas laysanensis*

Dunnock *Prunella modularis*
Eagle, New Guinea *Harpyopsis novaeguineae*
Emu *Dromaius novaehollandiae* **PAGE 277**
Fairy-wren, Broad-billed *Malurus grayi*
Fairy-wren, Splendid *Malurus splendens*
Fairywren, Superb *Malurus cyaneus* **PAGE 268**
Fantail, New Zealand *Rhipidura fuliginosa* **PAGE 287**
Fantail, Samoan *Rhipidura nebulosa*
Fernbird *Megalurus punctatus*
Finch, Laysan *Telespiza cantans*
Flycatcher, Samoan *Myiagra albiventris*
Friarbird, New Caledonian *Philemon diemenensis*
Frigatebird, Magnificent *Fregata magnificens*
Galah *Eolophus roseicapilla*
Gerygone, Gray *Gerygone igata*
Goldfinch, European *Carduelis carduelis*
Goshawk, Caledonia *Accipiter haplochrous*
Greenfinch, European *Carduelis chloris*
Honeyeater, Kadavu *Xanthotis provocator*
Honeyeater, Macleay's *Xanthotis macleayanus* **PAGE 269**
Honeyeater, Pygmy *Toxorhamphus pygmaeum*
Ifrita, Blue-capped *Ifrita kowaldi*
Iiwi *Vestiaria coccinea* **PAGE 270**
Imperial-Pigeon, New Caledonian *Ducula goliath*
Imperial-Pigeon, Peale's *Ducula latrans*
Jacana, Comb-crested *Irediparra gallinacea* **PAGE 261**
Kagu *Rhynochetos jubatus*
Kaka, New Zealand *Nestor meridionalis*
Kakapo *Strigops habroptila*
Kea *Nestor notabilis* **PAGE 285**
Kingfisher, Blue-black *Todiramphus nigrocyaneus*
Kingfisher, Flat-billed *Todiramphus recurvirostris*
King-Parrot, Australian *Alisterus amboinensis* **PAGE 266**
Kiwi, Okarito Brown *Apteryx rowi*
Kiwi, Southern Brown *Apteryx australis* **PAGE 283**
Kookaburra, Blue-winged *Dacelo leachii* **PAGE 267**
Kookaburra, Laughing *Dacelo novaeguineae* **PAGE 262**
Kookaburra, Rufous-bellied *Dacelo gaudichaud*
Kookaburra, Shovel-billed *Clytoceyx rex*
Kookaburra, Spangled *Dacelo tyro*
Leiothrix, Red-billed *Leiothrix lutea*
Lorikeet, Rainbow *Trichoglossus haematodus*
Lory, Collared *Phigys solitarius*
Lyrebird, Albert's *Menura alberti*
Lyrebird, Superb *Menura novaehollandiae* **PAGE 268**
Mao *Gymnomyza samoensis* **PAGE 299**
Myna, Common *Acridotheres tristis*
Myzomela, Red-collared *Myzomela rosenbergii* **PAGE 258**
Nene *Branta sandvicensis*
Owlet-Nightjar, Feline *Aegotheles insignis*
Palila *Loxioides bailleui*
Parakeet, New Caledonian *Cyanoramphus saissetti*

Parotia, Lawes' *Parotia lawesii*
Parrot, Ground *Pezoporus wallicus*
Parrotbill, Maui *Psuedonestor xanthophrys*
Parrotfinch, Fiji *Erythrura pealii*
Penguin, Fiordland *Eudyptes pachyrhynchus*
Penguin, Snares *Eudyptes robustus*
Penguin, Yellow-eyed *Megadyptes antipodes* **PAGE 284**
Pigeon, Tooth-billed *Didunculus strigirostris*
Pipipi *Mohoua novaeseelandiae*
Pitohui, Hooded *Pitohui dichrous* **PAGE 292**
Plains-wanderer *Pedinomus torquatus* **PAGE 275**
Quail, Stubble *Coturnix pectoralis*
Rail, Laysan *Porzana palmeri*
Redpoll, Common *Carduelis flammea*
Rifleman *Acanthisitta chloris*
Robin, New Zealand *Petroica australis*
Rosella, Crimson *Platycercus elegans*
Saddleback *Philesturnus carunculatus*
Scrub-bird, Noisy *Atrichornis clamosus*
Scrubfowl, Orange-footed *Megapodius reinwardt*
Shama, White-rumped *Copsychus malabaricus*
Shearwater, Christmas *Puffinus nativitatis*
Shearwater, Sooty *Puffinus griseus*
Shearwater, Wedge-tailed *Puffinus pacificus*
Shining-Parrot, Masked *Prosopeia personata*
Sicklebill, Black *Epimachus fastuosus*
Sicklebill, Brown *Epimachus meyeri*
Silktail *Lamprolia victoriae*
Skylark, Eurasian *Alauda arvensis*
Stitchbird *Notiomystis cincta*
Takahe *Porphyrio mantelli*
Tern, Sooty *Onychoprion fuscatus*
Tern, White *Gygis alba*
Thrush, Song *Turdus philomelos*
Tomtit *Petroica macrocephala*
Triller, Samoan *Lalage sharpei*
Tui *Prosthemadera novaeseelandiae*
Turnstone, Ruddy *Arenaria interpres*
Warbler, Long-legged *Trichocichla rufa*
Weka *Gallirallus australis*
Whipbird, Papuan *Androphobus viridis*
Whipbird, Western *Psophodes nigrogularis*
White-eye, Japanese *Zosterops japonicus*
White-eye, Samoan *Zosterops samoensis*
Whitehead *Mohoua albicilla*
Woodswallow, Black-faced *Artamus cinereus*
Yellowhammer *Emberiza citrinella*

ACKNOWLEDGMENTS

My great hope for this book is that it opens the global birding door for good numbers of serious birders to what will surely be some of the most exciting moments of their birding lives: seeing kinds of birds for the first time that they always hoped to see or, perhaps even more compelling, seeing kinds of birds that they never imagined existed.

Several people contributed in significant ways to this book's production. I would like to acknowledge the assistance especially of David L. Pearson, for many kinds of ornithological advice and for allowing me to include in the book his brief narratives describing his international birding exploits; Jonathan Alderfer and his colleagues at National Geographic Books, for editing and designing the book, locating appropriate photographs, creating maps, and helping in a variety of other ways; my wife Cynthia Wang; my agent Russell Galen; and the many photographers who contributed their stunning images of birds and birding locations.

PHOTOGRAPHY CREDITS

Back cover: (UP LE), Glenn Bartley; (UP CTR), Glenn Bartley; (UP RT), Markus Varesuo; (LO LE), Yva Monatiuk & John Eastcott/Minden Pictures/NationalGeographicStock. com; (LO CTR), Con Foley; (LO RT), Marie Read.

1, Tim Laman; 2-3, Simon King/naturepl.com; 4, Dave Watts/naturepl.com; 6-7, Inaki Relanzon/naturepl.com; 8, Brian A. Vikander/CORBIS; 10, Glenn Bartley; 11, Glenn Bartley; 12, Marie Read; 13, Sally Mitchell/VIREO; 14, Thomas Marent/ Minden Pictures/NationalGeographicStock.com; 15, Tui De Roy/Minden Pictures/ NationalGeographicStock.com; 17, Joel Sartore; 18, Bob Krist/CORBIS; 19, Shah Nawaz Khan; 20-21, Bob Steele; 23, Ramki Sreenivasan; 24-25, Tui De Roy/Minden PIctures/NationalGeographicStock.com; 26, Francois Savigny/naturepl; 28, Michael and Patricia Fogden/NationalGeographicStock.com; 29, Roger & Liz Charlwood/WorldWildlifeImages.com; 30, Michael and Patricia Fogden/Minden Pictures/NationalGeographicStock.com; 31, Hugh Chittenden; 32, Janet Zinn; 33, Andy Trowbridge; 34, Greg and Yvonne Dean/WorldWildlifeImages.com; 37, Marie Read; 38, James Ownby; 39, Richard Webster; 40, Peter Hodum; 41, Rod Williams/ naturepl.com; 42, Bruce D'Amicis/naturepl.com; 46, Dave Watts/naturepl.com; 47, KK Hui; 48-49, Simon Norfolk; 52, James P. Blair; 53, J. Culbertson/VIREO; 54, Michael and Patricia Fogden/Minden PIctures/NationalGeographicStock.com; 55, Glenn Bartley; 56, Doug Wechsler; 57, Glenn Bartley; 58, Patricio Robles Gil/Minden Pictures/NationalGeographicStock.com; 60 (LE), Patricio Robles Gil/naturepl.com; 60 (RT), Roy Toft/NationalGeographicStock.com; 61, Glenn Bartley; 62 (LE), Andy & Gill Swash/WorldWildlifeImages.com; 62 (RT), Eladio Fernandez; 63, Glenn Bartley; 64, Glenn Bartley; 65, Doug Wechsler/VIREO; 66 (LE), Doug Wechsler/VIREO; 66 (RT), Kevin Zimmer/VIREO; 67, Manuel Grosselet/VIREO; 68, Patricio Robles Gil/ Minden Pictures/NationalGeographicStock.com; 70, Rick and Nora Bowers/VIREO; 71, Greg W. Lasley/VIREO; 72, Stanley Doctor/VIREO; 73, Patricio Robles Gil/ VIREO; 75, James Ownby; 76, Ralph Lee Hopkins/NationalGeographicStock.com; 78, Marie Read; 79, Wothe Konrad/Minden Pictures/NationalGeographicStock. com; 80, Christopher L. Wood; 81, Patricio Robles Gil/naturepl.com; 84, Gerry Ellis/Minden Pictures/NationalGeographicStock.com; 86, Glenn Bartley; 87, Kevin Schafer/VIREO; 88, Doug Wechsler/VIREO; 89, Rick and Nora Bowers/VIREO; 91, Claude Nadeau/VIREO; 92-93, Kevin Schafer/CORBIS; 96, Glenn Bartley; 98, Anne B. Keiser/NationalGeographicStock.com; 99, Kevin Schafer/VIREO; 100, Bob Steele; 102, Tui De Roy/NationalGeographicStock.com; 104 (LE), Andy & Gill Swash/WorldWildlifeImages.com; 104 (RT), Bob Steele; 105, Robert A. "Spike" Baker/VIREO; 106 (LE), J. Alonso A./VIREO; 106 (RT), Janet Zinn; 107, Glenn Bartley; 108, Glenn Bartley; 109, Glenn Bartley; 110, Doug Wechsler/VIREO; 111, Doug Wechsler/VIREO; 112, Peter Oxford/naturepl.com; 113, Glenn Bartley; 114, Theo Allofs/Getty Images; 116, Glenn Bartley/VIREO; 117, Juan Liziola; 118, Glenn Bartley; 122, Tui De Roy/Minden Pictures/NationalGeographicStock.com; 124, Ingo Arndt/Minden Pictures/NationalGeographicStock.com; 125, Mark Moffett/ Minden Pictures/NationalGeographicStock.com; 126, George Armistead/VIREO; 127, Annie Griffiths Belt/NationalGeographicStock.com; 128, Janet Zinn; 129, Tui De Roy/Minden Pictures/NationalGeographicStock.com; 130, Richard T. Nowitz/ NationalGeographicStock.com; 132, Bob Steele; 133, Roger & Liz Charlwood/ WorldWildlifeImages.com; 134, James Lowen; 135, Bob Steele; 138, Eric Dietrich/ Hedgehog House/NationalGeographicStock.com; 140, Bob Steele; 141, Paul Nicklen; 142, Bob Steele; 143, Bob Steele; 145, Brian L. Sullivan; 146-147, Jim Richardson; 150, Todd Gipstein/NationalGeographicStock.com; 151, Konrad Wothe/NationalGeographicStock.com; 152, Charlie Hamilton James/naturepl.

com; 153, Ruddie Brunye; 154, Jari Peltomäki/www.lintukuva.fi; 156, Arto Juvonen; 157 (LE), Konrad Wothe/NationalGeographicStock.com; 157 (RT), Markus Varesvuo; 158, Steve Round; 159 (LE), Steve Round; 159 (RT), Clement Francis; 160, Steve Round; 161 (LE), Markus Varesvuo; 161 (RT), Ruddie Brunye; 162, Enrique Aguirre; 164, Martin Woike/Foto Natura/Minden Pictures/NationalGeographicStock.com; 165, Jari Peltomäki/www.lintukuva.fi; 166, Markus Varesvuo; 167, Gunhild Andersen; 170, Phillippe Clement/naturepl.com; 172, Konrad Wothe/Minden Pictures/ NationalGeographicStock.com; 173, Ruddie Brunye; 174, Hanne and Jens Eriksen; 175, Markus Varesvuo; 178-179, Keren Su/CORBIS; 182, Arthur Morris/CORBIS; 183, Inaki Relanzon/naturepl.com; 184, Richard Du Toit/naturepl.com; 185, James Hager/ Robert Harding World Imagery/CORBIS; 186, Timothy Fitzharris/Minden Pictures/ NationalGeographicStock.com; 187, Suzy Eszterhas/naturepl.com; 188, Richard Du Toit/naturepl.com; 189, Francois Savigny/naturepl.com; 190, Andy & Gill Swash/ WorldWildlifeImages.com; 191 (LE), Greg & Yvonne Dean/WorldWildlifeImages. com; 191 (RT), James Ownby; 192 (LE), Johan Swanepoel/Shutterstock; 192 (RT), Andy & Gill Swash/WorldWildlifeImages.com; 193, Warwick Tarboton/VIREO; 194 (LE), Stefan Oscarsson; 194 (RT), Andy & Gill Swash/WorldWildlifeImages.com; 195, James Ownby; 196, Marco Pavan/Grand Tour/CORBIS; 199, Greg & Yvonne Dean/WorldWildlifeImages.com; 200, Doug Wechsler/VIREO; 201, Janet Zinn; 204, Nick Garbutt; 206, Nick Garbutt; 207, Nick Garbutt; 208, R.L. Pitman/VIREO; 211, Nick Garbutt; 212-213, China Photos/Getty Images; 216, Gavin Maxwell/ naturepl.com; 217, Jens Søgaard Hansen; 218, Laurent Geslin/naturepl.com; 220, Hanne & Jens Eriksen/naturepl.com; 221, Con Foley; 222, Konrad Wothe/ NationalGeographicStock.com; 224 (LE), Dhritiman Mukherjee; 224 (RT), Ramki Sreenivasan; 225, Tim Laman/VIREO; 226 (UP), Ramki Sreenivasan; 226 (LO), Con Foley; 227, Ramki Sreenivasan; 228 (UP), KK Hui; 228 (LO), Ramki Sreenivasan; 229, Ayuwat Jearwattanakanok; 230, Thierry Bornier; 232, Aflo/naturepl.com; 233, Igor Shpilenok; 234, Konrad Wothe/NationalGeographicStock.com; 238, Ramki Sreenivasan; 240, Pete Ryan/NationalGeographicStock.com; 241, Ramki Sreenivasan; 242, Challiyil Eswaramangalath Vipin; 243, Ramki Sreenivasan; 246, Klaus Nigge; 248, Nick Garbutt/naturepl.com; 249, David Pearson; 250, Klaus Nigge; 251, Roger & Liz Charlwood/WorldWildlifeImages. com; 254-255, Medford Taylor/NationalGeographicStock.com; 258, Terry S. Baltimore/VIREO; 259, Bill Hatcher/NationalGeographicStock.com; 260, Stephen L. Alvarez; 261, Marie Read; 262, Marie Read; 264 (UP), Michael Durham/Minden Pictures/NationalGeographicStock.com; 264 (LO), Bob Steele; 265, Joel Sartore/ NationalGeographicStock.com; 266, Andy & Gill Swash/WorldWildlifeImages. com; 267, Marie Read; 268 (LE), Frans Lanting/CORBIS; 268 (RT), Marie Read; 269, Marie Read; 270 (UP), George Armistead/VIREO; 270 (LO), Marie Read; 271, Tim Laman; 272, Winnie Ho; 274, Grant V. Faint/Getty Images; 275, Michael Todd; 276, Gerry Ellis/Minden Pictures/NationalGeographicStock.com; 277, Cyril Ruoso/JH Editorial/Minden Pictures/NationalGeographicStock.com; 280, Kah Kit Yoong; 283, Peter Reese/naturepl.com; 284, Peter Oxford/naturepl.com; 285, John Cancalosi/ naturepl.com; 287, Peter Reese/naturepl.com; 288, Tim Laman/naturepl.com; 290, NHPA/Bruce Beehler; 291, Tim Laman/naturepl.com; 292, W. Peckover/VIREO; 296, Diane Cook & Len Jenshel; 299, Patricio Robles Gil; 300, Kevin Schafer/VIREO; 301, Peter LaTourrette/VIREO; 303, Rolf Nussbaumer/naturepl.com.

INDEX

Bold page numbers
indicate illustrations.
Page numbers with
a "t" indicate tables.

GLOBAL BIRDING
Traveling the World in Search of Birds
LES BELETSKY

PUBLISHED BY THE NATIONAL GEOGRAPHIC SOCIETY

JOHN M. FAHEY, JR., *President and Chief Executive Officer*

GILBERT M. GROSVENOR, *Chairman of the Board*

TIM T. KELLY, *President, Global Media Group*

JOHN Q. GRIFFIN, *Executive Vice President; President, Publishing*

NINA D. HOFFMAN, *Executive Vice President; President, Book Publishing Group*

PREPARED BY THE BOOK DIVISION

BARBARA BROWNELL GROGAN, *Vice President and Editor in Chief*

MARIANNE R. KOSZORUS, *Director of Design*

CARL MEHLER, *Director of Maps*

R. GARY COLBERT, *Production Director*

JENNIFER A. THORNTON, *Managing Editor*

MEREDITH C. WILCOX, *Administrative Director, Illustrations*

STAFF FOR THIS BOOK

JONATHAN ALDERFER, *Project Editor*

SANAA AKKACH, *Art Director*

ADRIAN COAKLEY, *Illustrations Editor*

MIKE HORENSTEIN, *Production Project Manager*

MARSHALL KIKER, *Illustrations Specialist*

AL MORROW, *Design Assistant*

ALLISON GAFFNEY, *Design Intern*

PAUL HESS, *Copy Editor*

MANUFACTURING AND QUALITY MANAGEMENT

CHRISTOPHER A. LIEDEL, *Chief Financial Officer*

PHILLIP L. SCHLOSSER, *Vice President*

CHRIS BROWN, *Technical Director*

NICOLE ELLIOTT, *Manager*

RACHEL FAULISE, *Manager*

The National Geographic Society is one of the world's largest nonprofit scientific and educational organizations. Founded in 1888 to "increase and diffuse geographic knowledge," the Society works to inspire people to care about the planet. It reaches more than 325 million people worldwide each month through its official journal, *National Geographic,* and other magazines; National Geographic Channel; television documentaries; music; radio; films; books; DVDs; maps; exhibitions; school publishing programs; interactive media; and merchandise. National Geographic has funded more than 9,000 scientific research, conservation and exploration projects and supports an education program combating geographic illiteracy.

For more information, please call 1-800-NGS LINE (647-5463) or write to the following address:

National Geographic Society
1145 17th Street N.W.
Washington, D.C. 20036-4688 U.S.A.

Visit us online at www.nationalgeographic.com

For information about special discounts for bulk purchases, please contact National Geographic Books Special Sales: ngspecsales@ngs.org

For rights or permissions inquiries, please contact National Geographic Books Subsidiary Rights: ngbookrights@ngs.org

Library of Congress Cataloging-in-Publication Data
Beletsky, Les, 1956-
 Global birding : traveling the world in search of birds / Les Beletsky.
    p. cm.
 Includes bibliographical references and index.
 ISBN 978-1-4262-0640-5 (alk. paper)
 1. Bird watching. 2. Birds--Geographical distribution. I. Title.
QL677.5.B42 2010
598.072'34--dc22
                                    2010012893

Printed in China

10/RRDS/1

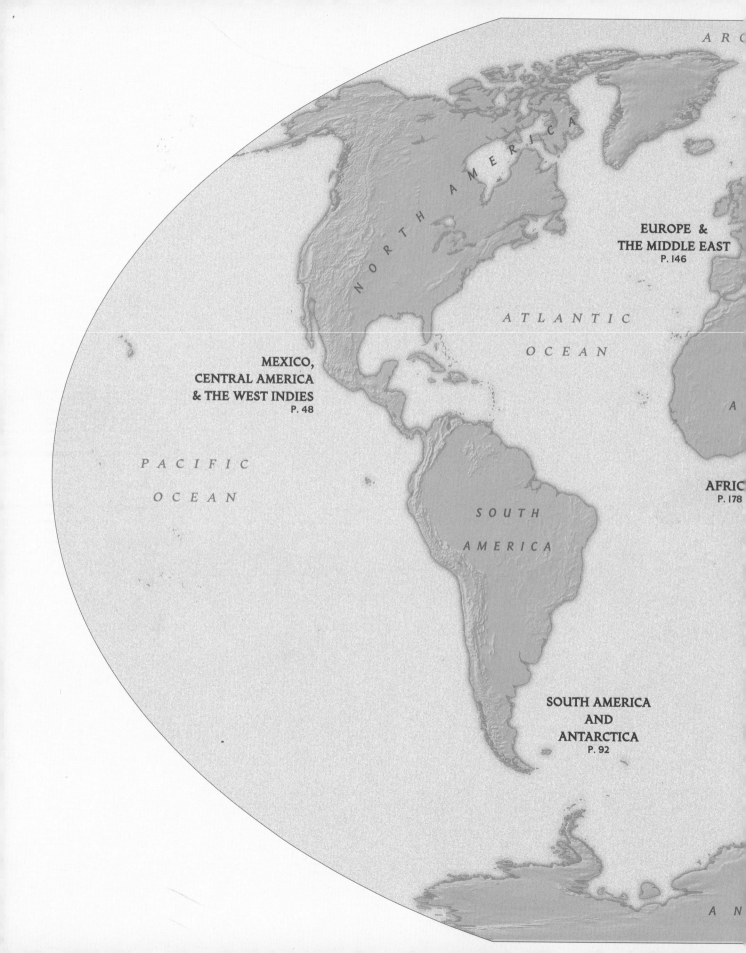

ARC

NORTH AMERICA

EUROPE &
THE MIDDLE EAST
P. 146

ATLANTIC

OCEAN

A

MEXICO,
CENTRAL AMERICA
& THE WEST INDIES
P. 48

AFRIC
P. 178

PACIFIC

OCEAN

SOUTH

AMERICA

SOUTH AMERICA
AND
ANTARCTICA
P. 92

AN